Webster's French/English Anglais/Français Dictionary

Copyright © 1997 V. Nichols
Distributed by Nichols Industries
All right reserved
Printed in the USA

Text edited by: Goodwill Vézina French
Services, LTD
Markham, Ontario - Laval Québec

Abbreviations Used In This Dictionary

n.	noun
pron.	pronoun
vb.	verb
adj.	adjective
adv.	adverb
conj.	conjunction
v.t.	transitive verb
v.r.	reciprocal verb
f.	feminine
m.	masculine

Everyday Phrases

English	French
What time is it?	Quelle heure est-it?
How are you?	Comment allez-vous?
Good day.	Bonjour.
Good night.	Bonne nuit.
Good bye.	Au revoir.
Thank you very much.	Merci beaucoup.
Please.	S'il vouss plaît
Do you speak English?	Parlez-vous anglais?
What is your name?	Comment vous appelez-vous?

Months of the Year

January	janvier
February	février
March	mars
April	avril
May	mai
June	juin
July	juillet
August	août
September	septembre
October	octobre
November	novembre
December	décembre

Days of the Week

Sunday	dimanche
Monday	lundi
Tuesday	mardi
Wednesday	mercredi
Thursday	jeudi
Friday	vendredi
Saturday	samedi

Pronunciation Guide

This pronunciation guide describes the approximate pronunciation of frequent combinations of letters and single letter of the French language.

All exceptions to established pronunciation cannot be listed in this guide. However, it does provide a fast reference to the French language.

French Letters	English Pronunciation
a,a	Between *a* in ball and *a* in calm.
â	As *a* in ball.
aî, ai	As *a* in say.
au	As *ou* in boat
b	Usually remains silent when used at The end of a word. Otherwise like the English *b*.
c	When before *e,i,y,* sounds like *s*. Otherwise as *k* in fork.
ç	Pronounced as *s*
cc	When before *e,* or *I* sounds like *x* Otherwise sounds like *k*.
ch	Pronounced as *sh* in sheep
d	Pronounced as in English.
e	Indicates previous consonant is pronounced. Normally silent when at the end of words.
é	Pronounced as *a* in late or day
è,ê	Pronounced as *e* in neck.
eau	Sounds like au.
er	Like *a* in hate (silent r)
es	Silent at end of words.
eu	Like French *e* pronounced with lips rounded. Similar to the word her.
ez	Pronounced most frequently like English *a* in lake. (Silent z)
g	Before *e, I, y* pronounced as *s* in usual. Otherwise like English *a*.
gu	Before *e, I, y* pronounced like *g* in gum.

French Letters	English Pronunciation
h	Usually silent in French
i, î	Like *I* in machine.
Ille	As in key with *y* at the end.
m, n	When single at end of syllable, before Another consonant or at the end of a word or before another consonant, indicates nasalization of previous vowel. When double, and when single between two vowel letters or at the beginning of a word, sounds like the English *m* and *n*.
o	Usually pronounced as *u* in the English word mud but rounder. Or *o* as in low.
û	Similar to *oa* in float.
oû, où, ou	Like *ou* in tour. Or *oe* in shoe.
p	Usually silent at the end of words. When between the following consonants, *m* and *t, r* and *s* and *m* and *s*, usually silent.
ph	Sounds like English *f.*
qu	Usually sounds like English *k.*
r	Sounds as a slightly rolled English *r.* Sometimes like English *z.*
s, ss	Usually sounds like *s* in say.
th	Sounds like *t* in English.
u, û	Sounds not found in English; pronounced like the *u* in rule.
v	As in English.
w	Usually like the *v* sound in English.
x	Normally sounds like *ks*, when the syllable *ex* is at the beginning of a word, followed by a vowel, *x* sounds like *gz*.
y	Usually sounds like *I* in machine, if between two vowel sounds like *y* in you.
z	Pronounced like *z* in zebra.

à, prep. at, into, to, for, with

abaisse, n.f. the undercrust of pastry

abaisser, vb. to depress, to lower, to reduce

abasourdir, v.t. to make stupid or dull

abandon, n.m. surrender, desertion

abandonné, adj. forsaken, forlorn

abandonner, vb. to desert, to leave forsake, to desert s'a., give up

abasourdir, v.t. to stun, dumbfound

abat-jour, n.m. lampshade; skylight

abattage, n.m. slaughtering of animals

abattre, v.t. to reduce, to lower

abbaye, n.f. abbey, Monastery

abbé, n.m. abbot

aboès, n.m. gathering, abscess

abdomen, n.m. abdomen

abécédaire, alphabetical

abeille, n.f. bee

aberrant, adj. straying from normal

abîmer, vb. to spoil, injure, overwhelm

abject, adj. low, abject

abjurer, vb. to give up, to renounce

aboiement, n.m. baying, barking

abolir, v.t. to abolish, to annul

abolition, n.f. abolition

abominer, v.t. to detest

abondamment, adv. fully; abundantly

abondance, n.f. plenty; great quantity

abondant, adj. plentiful; abundant

abonder de, vb. to abound

abonner, vb. s'a., subscribe to

abord, adv. d'a., at first

aborder, vb. to accost, to approach

abouler, v.t. to give

aboutir, vb. to result, to end in or at

aboyer, vb. to bark, to yelp

abréger, vb. to abbreviate, to cut down

abreuver, vb. to water animals

abréviation, n.f. abbreviation

abri, n.m. cover, shelter

abricot, n.m. apricot

abriter, vb. to shelter, to protect, to shade

abrupt, adj. steep, abrupt

absent, adj. absent, missing

absenter, vb. s'a., to leave, go away

absolution, n.f. absolution, forgiveness

absolutoire, adj. implying absolution

absorbant, adj. and n.m.

absorbable, absorbent

absorber, vb. to absorb, drink; cause to disappear

absorption, n.f. absorption

absoudre, vb. to acquit, absolve

abstenir, vb. to forgo; forbear

abstinence, n.f. sobriety, abstinence

abstraction, n.f. abstraction, abstract idea

abstrait, adj. absent-minded, abstract

abstrus, adj. obscure, difficult

absurde, adj. stupid, preposterous, silly

absurdité, n.f. foolishness, nonsense

abus, n.m. grievance, abuse

académique, adj. apporprite, proper

acajou, n.m. mahogany

accablant, adj. grievous, oppressive

accabler, vb. to overwhelm, overpower

accélération, n.f. acceleration

accélérer, vb. to hurry, quicken, to hasten

accent, n.m. stress, accent, emphasis, tone

accentuer, vb. to emphasize, accent, stress

acceptabilité, n.f. acceptability

accepter, vb. to admit, accept; agree

accès, n.m. access, approach; fit; attack

accident, n.m. crash, accident, casualty

acclamation, n.f. cheering, acclamation

accommoder, vb. to accommodate, to adapt

accompagnement, n.m. accompaniment; accompanying

accompagner, vb. to accompany, go with; to attend

accompli, adj. accomplished; performed

accomplir, vb. to perform

accomplissement, n.m. performance, achievement, accomplishment

accord, n.m. agreement, harmony; settlement; bargin

accorder, v.t. to grant; to admit

accouchée, n.f. woman who has just given birth

accoudement, n.m. act of leaning on

accoupler, v.t. to join together

accréditer, vb. to give credit

accrocher, v.t. to hook, to catch, to hitch

accroissement, n.m. addition; growth increase

accroître, v.t. to augment, to increase

accroupir, vb. **s'a.**, to crouch, squat

accueil, n.m. greeting; reception

accueillir, vb. to welcome, receive

accumuler, vb. to heap up; pile up; accumulate

accusation, n.f. indictment, charge

accusé, n.m. defendant, prisoner, accused

accuser, vb. to accuse, to charge, to blame, to indicate

acharné, adj. stubborn, intense

achat, n.m. purchasing, purchase, buying

acheminer, vb. to send towards

acheter, vb. to purchase, buy

achevaler, v.t. to straddle

achèvement, n.m. completion

achever, vb. to complete, finish, achieve; conclusion

acide, adj. and n.m. acid, sour, tart

acidité, n.f. acidity; sourness; tartness

acier, n.m. steel

acoustique, adj. acoustic

acquérir, vb. to acquire, purchase

acquêt, n.m. common property of a married couple

acquiescer à, vb. to consent, agree

acquit, n.m. discharge, release

acquittement, n.m. payment

acquitter, vb. to acquit

âcre, adj. sharp, sour, tart, pungent

acrobate, n.m.f. acrobat

acte, n.m. deed, action; **a. notarié**, deed **a. de naissance**, birth certificate

acteur, n.m. actor; actress

action, n.f. action, deed, act; work

actionnaire, n.m. shareholder

actionner, vb. to operate; to rouse up

activement, adv. busily; actively

activer, vb. to activate, to expedite

activité, n.f. activity, dispatch

actualité, n.f. current event

actuel, adj. present, actual

acupuncture, n.f. acupuncture

adage, n.m. proverb

adaptation, n.f. adaptation

adapter, vb. to adapt, fit, adjust, apply

additif, adj. additive

addition, n.f. addition, bill; adding up

additionnel, adj. additional

additionner, vb. to add, to increase

adhérent, n.m. follower

adhérer, vb. to cleave, adhere, to cling

adhésif, adj. adhesive

adieu, n.m. and interij. good bye, farewell, leave

adjacent, adj. adjacent; bordering upon

adjectif, adj. adjective

adjoindre, vb. to associate; to adjoin

adjoint, n.m. fellow-worker, assistant, associate

adjuger, vb. to grant

adjudant, n.m. warrant-officer

adjudicataire, adj. highest bidder

adjuger, v.t. to knock down

admettre, vb. to allow, admit, to let in

administrateur, n.m. manager, administrator, director

administratif, adj. administrative

administration, n.f. administration, direction, management

administrer, vb. to administer, manage, govern, direct

admirable, adj. wonderful, admirable

admirateur, n.m. praiser, admirer; adj. wondering

admiration, n.f. admiration

admirer, vb. to admire

admission, n.f. confession, admission; admittance

adolescence, n.f. adolescence

adolescent, adj. and n.m.f. youth, adolescent

adonné, adj. addicted

adoptable, adj. available to adopt

adopter, vb. to adopt; to pass; to embrace

adoption, n.f. adoption

adorable, adj. charming, delightful, adorable

adorateur, n.m. worshipper

adorer, vb. to worship, adore

adoucir, vb. to soothe

adossé, adj. with one's back against something

adresse, n.f. address; skill, ability, dexterity, cleverness

adresser, vb. to address a letter; direct, **s'a à**, to appeal

adroit, adj. clever, skillful, handy; ingenious

adulte, adj. and n.m.f. adult,

grown-up person

adultère, n.m. adultery

adverbe, n.m. adverb

adversaire, n.m.f. opponent, adversary

adverse, adj. opposite, adverse; contrary

aéré, adj. airy

aérien, adj. aerial; occuring in the air

aéroport, n.m. airport

affable, adj. courteous

affaiblir, vb. to weaken; to lessen

affaire, n.f. business, affair, lawsuit matter, concern

affairé, adj. busy

affaissement, n.m. collapse, give way

affaisser, v.r. s'a., to collapse, to subside

affamé, adj. famished, hungry

affamer, vb. to starve, famish

affecter, vb. to affect, assume, make frequent

affection, n.f. love, affection

affermir, vb. to strengthen; make firm

affété, adj. finicky, prim

affiche, n.f. poster, billboard

afficher, v.t. to publish to post up

affinité, n.f. relationship, affinity

affirmatif, adj. asserting, affirmative

affirmation, n.f. statement; assertion

affirmer, vb. to assert, state, declare testify, affirm

affliction, n.f. affliction, distress, trouble

affligé, adj. sorrowful, distress, grieved, burdened

affliger, vb. to grieve, distress, afflict, trouble

affluent, n.m. tributary

affluer, vb. to flow into, run, fall

affoler, vb. to distract, madden, drive crazy

affranchir, adj. freed, set free

affreusement, adv. terribly, dreadfully, horribly

affreux, adj. shocking, terrible, horrid

affront, n.m. affront, insult, outrage

affronter, vb. to confront, face, attack

afin, conj. so that, to, in order that

africain, adj. African

Africain, n. African

agacer, vb. to irritate, worry; excite, provoke

âge, n.m. time from birth, age,

period

âgé, adj. aged; elderly, old

agence, n.f. bureau, agency

agenouiller, v.r. s'a., to kneel down

agent, n.m. agent; a. de police, policeman

aggraver, v.t. to make worse, to aggravate

agile, adj. nimble, active

agir, v.i. to act; to produce result, to operate

agissant, adj. busy, active, effective

agitation, n.f. disturbance, commotion

agité, adj. upset, excited, restless

agiter, v.t. to shake up, to agitate, s'a., toss, flutter

agneau, n.m. lamb

agonie, n.f. agony

agrafe, n.f. clasp, fastener, clip

agrafer, v.t. to clasp, to hook

agrandir, v.t. to enlarge, to make greater

agréable, adj. likable, pleasing, enjoyable, agreeable

agréer, v.t. to accept, to allow, to approve

agrégation, n.f. aggregation, aggregate

agrément, n.m. pleasure, charm

agresseur, n.m. aggressor

agressif, adj. aggressive

agression, n.f. aggression

agricole, adj. agricultural

agriculture, n.f. agriculture

ahurir, vb. to bewilder, fluster

aide, n.f. help, aid, relief, assistance

aïeul, n.m. grandfather

aïeule, n.f. grandmother

aïeux, n.m.,pl. ancestors

aigle, n.m.f. a clever person; a genius

aiglefin, n.m. haddock

aigre, adj. tart, sour

aigrefin, n.m. adventurer, swindler

aigreur, n.f. sharpness, sourness, tartness

aigu, adj. shrill, keen, pointed, sharp, acute

aiguille, n.f. needle; index, pointer hand of watch

aiguiser, v.t. to sharpen; to point

ail, n.m. garlic

aile, n.f. brim of hat; wing

ailleurs, adv. elsewhere, somewhere

aimable, adj. pleasant, amiable, kind

aimant, adj. affectionate, loving

aimer, v.t. to love, to like, to be fond of

aine, n.f. groin

aîné, adj. elder, senior, eldest

ainsi, adv. in this or that manner, thus so

air, n.m. wind, air

aire, n.f. space, area

aise, n.f. comfort, ease, convenience

aisé, adj. well-to-do; easy, comfortable

aisselle, n.f. armpit

ajourner, v.t. to put off; to adjourn

ajouter, v.t. to add, to supply, to join

ajustage, n.m. fitting or adjusting

ajuster, v.t. to fit, to adjust, to adapt

alarme, n.f. sudden fear, alarm, uneasiness

album, n.m. scrapbook, album

alcool, n.m. alcohol

alcoolique, adj. alcoholic

alcôve, n.f. recess, alcove

alentours, n.m.,pl. surroundings, neighbourhood

alerte, adj. lively, spry, active, alert, brisk

algèbre, n.f. algebra

aligner, v.t. to line up, to align

aliment, n.m. food, nourishment

alimentation, n.f. feeding, nourishment

alimenter, v.t. to nourish, to feed; to supply

alinéa, n.m. new paragraph; indented line

allée, n.f. path, lane, aisle, alley, walk

allégation, n.f. allegation

alléger, v.t. to lighten, to alleviate, to ease, to unload

allégresse, n.f. glee, delight, gaiety

alléguer, vb. pleade, allege, advance

Allemagne, n.f. Germany

aller, v.i. to go on, to proceed, to go

alliage, n.m. mixture, alloy

alliance, n.f. union, marriage, compact, alliance

allié, adj. allied, related

allier, v.t. to combine; to mix to unite

allô, interj. hello

allocation, n.f. allowance; amount allocated

allonger, v.t. to lengthen, to prolong

allons, interj. well, come now

allouer, v.t. to allow, to allocate

allumer, vb. to light; excite

allumette, n.f. match

allure, n.f. pace, gait, behaviour, look

allusion, n.f. hint, allusion; reference

almanach, n.m. calender, almanac

alors, adv. at that time, then

alouette, n.f. lark

alphabet, n.m. alphabet

altérer, vb. to change, alter, corrupt

alternatif, adj. alternate, alternative

alterner, vb. to alternate

altitude, n.f. altitude

aluminium, n.m. aluminium

amabilité, n.f. kindness

amalgamer, v.t. to blend, to combine

amande, n.f. kernel; almond

amant, n.m. lover; sweetheart

amas, n.m. hoard, mass, pile, heap

amasser, v.t. to gather, to amass

amateur, n.m. amateur, fancier

ambassade, n.f. embassy, errand

ambassadeur, n.m ambassador

ambassadrice, n.f. ambassadress

ambigu, adj. dark, uncertain, obscure

ambitieux, adj. ambitious; pretentious

ambition, n.f. ambition

ambre, n.m. amber

ambulance, n.f. ambulance

âme, n.f. mind; soul; spirit

amélioration, n.f. improvement

améliorer, v.t. to improve, to better

aménager, v.t. to arrange, to dispose

amende, n.f. fine, forfeit, penalty

amendement, n.m. improvement

amender, vb. to improve, amend

amener, v.t. to bring, to lead

amer, adj. harsh, bitter, grievous

américain, n.m. American

Amérique, n.f. America

amertume, n.f. grief, bitterness

ameublement, n.m. furniture

ami, n.m. friend,lover, well-wisher

amical, adj. kind, friendly, amicable

amidon, n.m. starch

amiral, n.m. admiral

amitié, n.f. affection, friendship

ammoniaque, n.f. ammonia

amoindrir, vb. to reduce, decrease

amollir, vb. to soften

amortir, vb. to weaken, moderate

amour, n.m. love, passion, affection

amoureux, adj. in love, loving,

amour-propre, n.m. vanity, pride, conceit, self-respect

ample, adj. ample, spacious, large

ampleur, n.f. plenty, fullness

amplifier, vb. to increase
ampoule, n.f. blister, swelling
amputer, vb. amputate, cut off
amusement, n.m. pastime, fun entertainment
amuser, vb. to amuse, entertain. **s'a.**, have a good time, to amuse oneself
amygdale, n.f. tonsil
an, n.m. year, time, age
analogie, n.f. analogy
analogue, adj. similar, analogous
analyse, n.f. outline, analysis
analyser, v.t. to analyze
ananas, n.m. pineapple
anarchie, n.f. anarchy
anatomie, n.f. anatomy; dissection
ancêtre, n.m. ancestor, forefather
anche, n.f. reed
anchois, n.m. anchovy
ancien, adj. ancient, old, antique, former
ancre, n.f. anchor
âne, n.m. ass, donkey, stupid,
anéantir, vb. to destroy, annihilate, abolish
anecdote, n.f. anecdote
anesthésique, n.f. anaesthesia
ange, n.m. angel; a beloved person
Anglais, n.m. Englishman
anglais, adj. and n.m. English
Anglaise, n.f. Englishwoman
angle, n.m. angle, corner
Angleterre, n.f. England
angoissant, adj. in anguish
angoisse, n.f. anguish, agony, pang
anguille, n.f. eel
anguleux, adj. rugged
anicroche, n.f. hitch, impediment
animal, n.m. and adj. animal
animation, n.f. animation, life, vitality
animer, vb. to enliven, animate, excite
animosité, n.f. animosity, spite, hatred
anneau, n.m. ring, circle
année, n.f. twelve months, year
annexe, n.f. annex, appendage
annexer, vb. to annex, join, attach
annihiler, v.t. to destroy, to annihilate
anniversaire, n.m. birthday, anniversary
annonce, n.f. advertisement, announcement, notification
annoncer, vb. to advertise, announce, give notice
annotation, n.f. inventory of goods
annoter, vb. to annotate

annuaire, n.m. directory, annual
annuel, adj. yearly, annual
annulation, n.f. cancelling, annulling
annuler, v.t. to cancel, to annul
ânonner, v.t. to stammer, to mumble
anonyme, adj. anonymous
anormal, adj. abnormal, irregular
anse, n.f. handle; bay, creek
antagonisme, n.m. antagonism
antarctique, adj. antarctic
antécédent, adj. antecedent, previous, foregoing
antenne, n.f., pl. antennae
antérieur, adj. previous; front; earlier, previous
anthracite, n.m. anthracite
anticipation, n.f. encroachment, anticipation
anticiper, v.t. to anticipate, to forestall, to take up
antidote, n.m. counter-poison, antidote
antilope, n.f. antelope
antiparlementaire, n.m. suppressor
antipathie, n.f. aversion, antipathy
antiquaire, n.m. antique dealer
antique, adj. ancient, old
antiquité, n.f. antiquity, ancientness
antiseptique, adj. and n.m. antiseptic
antre, n.m. den; cavern
anxiété, n.f. worry, anxiety; uneasiness
anxieux, adj. anxious, restless, uneasy
août, n.m. August
apaiser, vb. to pacify, quiet, appease, calm, lull, still
apathie, n.f. apathy, listlessness
apercevoir, v.t. to perceive, to understand, to catch sight of
aperçu, n.m. survey, glance, summary
apéritif, n.m. appetizing
apitoyer, v.t. to move emotionally;
aplanir, vb. to even off; smooth, level
aplatir, v.t. to beat flat, flatten
aplomb, n.m. poise, boldness
apostolique, adj. apostolic
apôtre, n.m. apostle
apparaître, vb. to appear
appareil, n.m. apparatus, machinery, display
apparence, n.f. appearance, look, likelihood
apparent, adj. noticeable, apparent, visible

apparition, n.f. appearance, ghost, phantom

appartement, n.m. apartment, flat

appartenir, v.i. to belong, to pertain, to relate

appât, n.m. lure, bait, attraction

appel, n.m. call, appeal, summons

appeler, vb. to call, summon, appeal, send forth, bring

appendice, n.m. appendix, addition

appétit, n.m. desire, appetite

applaudir, vb. to applaud, clap the hands

applaudissements, n.m., pl. public praise

applicable, adj. applicable, suitable

application, n.f. applying, application

appliqué, adj. industrious, studious

appliquer, v.t. to apply, to bestow

appointements, n.m., pl. salary

apporter, vb. to bring, fetch, supply

apposer, vb. to affix, set, insert

appréciable, adj. perceptible

apprécier, vb. to value, appraise, judge

appréhension, n.f. fear, dread

apprendre, vb. to learn, study, acquire

apprenti, n.m. apprentice

apprentissage, n.m. trial, apprenticeship

apprêt, n.m. preparation, cooking food

apprêter. v.t. s'a., to prepare

apprivoiser, vb. to tame (animals)

approbation, n.f. endorsement, approval, consent

approche, n.f. advance, approach

approcher, vb. to approach, bring toward, forward, come near to

approfondir, vb. to deepen; examine completely

appropriation, n.f. appropriation, adaptation

approprier, vb. to accommodate, to clean, to adpt, to tidy

approuver, v.t. to concent, to approve, to authorize, to ratify

approvisionnement, n.m. supply, provisions

approximatif, adj. approximate

appui, n.m. prop, support, mechanical support such as handrails

appuyer vb. to support, endorse, advocate

après, prep. behind, after, in pursuit of

après-demain, n.m. day after tommorrow

après-midi, n.m.f. afternoon

à-propos, n.m. fitness, suitability

apte à , adj. suitable for, apt

aptitude, n.f. fitness, talent, ability, aptitude

aqualit, n.m. waterbed

aquarelle, n.f. painting with watercolours

aquarium, n.m. aquarium

aquatique, adj. aquatic

aqueux, adj. watery

arabe, adj. Arabic, Arabian

arachide, n.f. peanut

araignée, n.f. spider

arbitrage, n.m. arbitration

arbitraire, adj. absolute, arbitrary

arbitre, n.m.f. umpire, arbi- ter, judge, referee

arbitrer, vb. to arbitrate, settle, judge

arbre, n.m. tree

arbrisseau, n.m. shrub

arc, n.m. arch, bow

arcade, n.f. arcade, arch-shaped opening

arc-en-ciel, n.m. rainbow

arche, n.f. arch (above a bridge)

archet, n.m. bow for playing the violin

archevêque, n.m. archbishop

architecte, n.m. architect

architectural, adj. architectural

archives, n.f., pl. files, archives, family records

arctique, adj. arctic

ardemment, adv. ardently

ardent, adj. eager, fiery, ardent, burning, hot

ardeur, n.f. ardour, zeal, keenness, intense heat

ardoise, n.f. slate

arène, n.f. arena, ring

argent, n.m. silver, money, cash

argenterie, n.f. silver-plate

Argentine, n.m. Argentina

argile, n.f. potters clay, clay

argot, n.m. slang

argument, n.m. argument, evidence, proof, summary

argumenter, vb. to argue

aride, adj. dry, arid; sterile

aristocrate, n.m.f. aristocrat

arithmétique, n.f. arithmetic

arlequin, n.m. harlequin

armature, n.f. casing, gear, iron braces

arme, n.f. weapon; arm

armé, adj. equipped, armed

armée, n.f. army, forces, troops

armement, n.m. armament, arming

arme nucléaire, n.f. nuclear weapon

armer, vb. to arm; to equip or furnish with an armament

armistice, n.m. armistice

armoire, n.f. cupboard, wardrobe, closet

armure, n.f. armor; armature

aromatique, adj. aromatic, spicy, fragrant

arôme, n.m. scent, perfume, aroma

arpenter, v.t. to measure or survey land

arracher, vb. to snatch, extract

arrangement, n.m. arrangement, settlement, adjustment

arranger, vb. to settle, trim, fix, arrange

arrestation, n.f. arrest

arrêt, n.m. stop

arrêté, n.m. decree, order, decision

arrêter, vb. to stop, check, halt, arrest

arrière, adv. backward, behind

arriéré, n.m. arrear, adj. backward

arrière-garde, n.f. rearguard

arrivée, n.f. arrival

arriver, vb. to happen, arrive, come; occur

arrogance, n.f. haughtiness, arrogance

arrogant, adj. arrogant, overbearing

arroger, vb. to assume, arrogate

arrondir, vb. to round off

arroser, vb. to sprinkle, water; baste

arsenal, n.m. arsenal, naval dockyard

arsenic, n.m. arsenic

art, n.m. art; **beaux-arts**, the fine arts

artère, n.f. artery

artichaut, n.m. artichoke

article, n.m. article, item

articulation, n.f. joint

articuler, vb. to articulate, put together

artifice, n.m. artifice, trick, dodge

artificiel, adj. artificial, fictitious

artificieux, adj. artful, cunning

artillerie, n.f. artillery

artisan, n.m. artisan, craftsman

artiste, n.m. artist, performer

artistique, adj. artistic

ascenseur, n.m. elevator, lift

Asiatique, n.m.f native of Asia

Asie, n.f. Asia

asile, n.m. haven, refuge, asylum

aspect, n.m. looks, appearance, aspect

asperger, vb. to sprinkle

aspergès, n.m. holy water sprinkler

asphalte, n.m. asphalt

aspirateur, n.m. vacuum cleaner

aspiration, n.f. aspiration, longing

aspirer, vb. to aspire, inhale

assaillant, n.m. assailant, aggressor

assaillir, vb. to assail, attack

assaisonner, v.t. to season

assassin, n.m. assassin, murderer

assassinat, n.m. assassination, murder

assassiner, vb. to assassinate, murder

assaut, n.m. attack, assault

assèchement, n.m. drainage, drying up

assemblage, n.m. combination, collection

assemblée, n.f. congregation, assembly, meeting

assembler, vb. to convene, gather

assentiment, n.m. agreement, assent

asseoir, vb. to seat; place; down; establish

assertion, n.f. affirmation, assertion

asservir, vb. to enslave, reduce, master, conquer

assez, adv. enough; sufficiently

assidu, adj. diligent, industrious, attentive

assiduité, n.f. industry

assiéger, vb. to application, attention

assiette, n.f. situation, basis

assigner, vb. to assign, summon

assimiler, vb. to assimilate, compare

assis, adj. seated; established

assise, n.f. course foundation

assistance, n.f. audience, present, attendance

assister, vb. to attend, be present

association, n.f. association, partnership

assombrir, vb. s'a. to grow dark

assommer, vb. to murder, slaughter

assortiment, n.m. assortment

assortir, vb. to match, tune, pair

assoupi, dormant, dozing

assoupir, v.t. to make sleepy, drowsy

assourdir, vb. to deafen, muffle

assujettir, v.t. to compel, to subdue

assumer, vb. assume

assurance, n.f. assurance, confidence, certainty

assuré, adj. sure, assured, confident

assurer, v.t. to insure; to make firm, to steady, to fasten

assureur, n.m. insurer, underwriter

astérisque, n.m. asterisk

astre, n.m. star (celebrity)

astronaute, n.m. astronaut

astronome, n.m. astronomer

astronomie, n.f. astronomy

astucieux, adj. tricky, crafty

atelier, n.m. studio; workshop

athée, n.m.f. atheist

athlète, n.m.f. athlete

athlétique, adj. athletic

atlantique, adj. Atlantic

atlas, n.m. atlas

atmosphère, n.f. atmosphere

atome, n.m. atom

atomique, adj. atomic

atroce, adj. outrageous, atrocious

atrocité, n.f. atrocity, cruelty

attachement, n.m. attachment, affection

attacher, vb. to tie, fasten, join, attach; associate

attaque, n.f. assault, attack

attaquer, v.t. to attack, to assault

attardé, adj. late, behind

attarder, v.t. to linger, to delay

atteindre, vb. to reach, attain; strike

atteint, adj. stricken, affected, seized

atteinte, n.f. reach, stroke, blow

attelage, n.m. team, set pair

atteler, vb. to harness, hitch up

attendre, vb. to wait for, await

attendrir, vb. to soften, move, touch

attendrissement, n.m. tenderness, emotion

attentat, n.m. crime, outrage

attente, n.f. expectation, waiting

attentif, adj. thoughtful, attentive, considerate

attention, n.f. notice, heed, care

atténuer, v.t. to make thinner

atterrir, v.t. to land

attester, v.t. to attest, to witness

attirer, vb. to attract, entice, lure

attitude, n.f. attitude

attouchement, n.m. touch

attraction, n.f. attraction

attrait, n.m. charm, attraction

attraper, v.t. to catch, to take in

attrayant, adj. attractive, charming

attribuer, vb. to ascribe, attribute, assign, alot

attribut, n.m. attribute, characteristic

attrouper, v.t. to gather, to

assemble

aube, n.f. dawn

auberge, n.f. inn, tavern

aubergine, n.f. eggplant

aubergiste, n.m. landlord, innkeeper

aucun, adj. and pron. no one, none, not any; anyone

aucunement, adv. not in the least, not at all

audace, n.f. audacity, boldness, daring

audacieux, adj. daring, bold, insolent

au-dessous, prep. below

au-dessus, adv. above

audience, n.f. audience

audiovisuel, adj. audio-visual

auditoire, n.m. audience, assembly

auge, n.f. bucket, trough

auget, n.m. small trough

augmentation, n.f. increase, raise, rise

augmenter, vb. to increase, enlarge

augure, n.m sign, omen

augurer, v.t. to surmise

aujourd'hui, adv. today; nowadays

aumône, n.f. alms

aumônier, n.m. chaplain

auparavant, adv. before, previously

auprès, adv. close by, near, beside

auréole, n.f. halo

aurore, n.f. dawn, daybreak

auspice, n.m. omen, auspice

aussi, adv. too, also; so, as; likewise

austère, adj. stern, severe

austérité, n.f. austerity, severity

Australie, n.f. Australia

autant, adv. as much, as many

autel, n.m. altar

auteur, n.m. originator, author, creator

authentique, adj. genuine, authentic

auto, n.f. abbreviation for auto

autobus, n.m. bus

automatique, adj. automatic

automne, n.m. autumn, fall

automobile, n.f. automobile

autorail, n.m. rail-car

autorisation, n.f. license, authorization, permission

autoriser, vb. to authorize

autorité, n.f. authority

autoroute, n.f. speedway

auto-stop, n.m. hitch-hiking

autour, adv. around, about

autre, adj. second, another, distinct, different

autrefois, adv. formerly
autrement, adv. otherwise; else
Autriche, n.m. Austria
autrichien, adj. Austrian
autruche, n.f. ostrich
autrui, pron. someone else, others
auvent, n.m. porch roof
auxiliaire, adj. auxiliary, aiding
avachi, adj. worn out
aval, n.m. endorsement
avalaison, n.f. sudden flood
avalanche, n.f. avalanche
avalant, adj. traveling down stream
avaler, vb. to swallow, drink,
avancé, adj. forward, advanced,
early
avancement, n.m. advance;
advancement, promotion
avancer, vb. to proceed; advance,
put forward
avances, n.f., pl. advance
avant, n.m. fore, bow; adv., prep.
before
avantage, n.m. advantage, bebefit
avantageux, adj. advantageous;
profitable
avant-bras, n.m. forearm
avant-hier, n.m. day before
yesterday
avant-toit, n.m. eaves
avare, n.m.f. miser; adj. miserly,
stingy
avarice, n.f. avarice
avec, prep. with; together or along
with; at the same time as
aven, n.m. pot-hole
avenant, adj. comely, pleasing,
personable
avènement, n.m. accession,
coming, advent
avenir, n.m. future; posterity
à-venir, n.m. a summons to appear
aventure, n.f. adventure,
unexpected event
aventurer, vb. to risk, to venture
aventureux, adj. adventurous
aventurier, n.m. adnenturess,
adventurer
avenue, n.f. avenue; approach
averse, n.f. heavy shower of rain
aversion, n.f. dislike, aversion
averti, adj. informed, warned
avertir, vb. to notify, warn, inform,
let know
avertissement, n.m. warning,
notification, information
aveu, n.m. admission, confession;
consent
aveuglant, adj. dazzling
aveugle, adj. sightless, blind

aveuglement, n.m. blindness
aveuglément, adv. blindly, implicity,
rashly
aveugler, v.t. to make blind, to blind
aviateur, n.m. flier, aviator
aveulir, v.t. to render weak
aviation, n.f. air force, avi- ation
avide, adj. eager, greedy
avidement, adv. greedily
avidité, n.f. greediness; eagerness
avilir, vb. to degrade, disgrace,
depreciate
avilissant, adj. degrading
avine, adj. drunk
aviner, v.t. to fill or soak with wine
avion, n.m. airplane, aeroplane
avis, n.m. notice, opinion, advice
avir, v.t. to brown or burn the outter
side of meats or bread
aviser, vb. to notify, inform,
perceive
avocat, n.m. lawyer, advocate,
council
avoir, v.t. to have, to experience
avortement, n.m. abortion,
miscarriage
avorter vb. to miscarry, fail to
develop
avorton, n.m. abortion
avoué, n.m. attorney, lawyer
avouer, vb. to confess, admit,
avow,
avril, n.m. April
axe, n.m. axel; axis
azalée, n.f. azalea
azur, n.m. azure, blue
azuré, adj. azure, color of the sky

B

babélique, adj. gigantic
babeurre, n.m. buttermilk
babil, n.m. babble; chattering
babiller, vb. to babble, chat
bâbord, n.m. naut. port
babouin, n.m. baboon, monkey
Babylone, f. Babylon
bac, n.m. ferryboat; ferry
baccalauréat, n.m. baccalaureate
bacheller, n.m. graduate
bâcher, v.t. to cover
bacille, n.m. bacillus
bâclage, n.m. closing a port with
chains
bactéricide, adj. stopping or
destroying the growth of bacteria
bactérie, n.f. bacterium
bactériologie, n.f. bacteriology

badaud, n.m. idler, lounger

badine, n.f. wand, switch

bafouiller, v.i. to stammer; to miss (of engine)

bagages, n.m., pl. luggage, baggage

bagarre, n.f. uproar, riot, scuffle

bagatelle, n.f. trifle, trinket

bagnard, n.m. convict

baguer, v.t. to tack, to stitch, to baste

baguier, n.m. jewel box

bah, int. nonsense

baie, n.f. bay, creek; berry

baignade, n.f. bathing

baigner, v.t. to bathe

baigneur, n.m. bather

bail, n.m. lease

bâillement, n.m. yawn, yawning

bâiller, vb. to yawn, open, gape

bâillon, n.m. muzzle, gag

bain, n.m. bath

bain-marie, n.m. double boiler

baïonnette, n.f. bayonet

baisemain, n.m. kissing of the hands

baisse, n.f. decline, fall

baisser, vb. to lower, sink, let down; turn down

bal, n.m. dance, ball

balade, n.f. ramble, walk, stroll

balafre, n.f. slash, cut

balai, n.m. broom

balance, n.f. scales, balance

balancement, n.m. rocking, swinging

balancer, vb. to weigh; balance; rock; swing, sway

balayer, vb. to clear away, sweep

balancier, n.m. scales and weights maker

balcon, n.m. balcony

baleine, n.f. whale

ballade, n.f. ballad

balle, n.f. bullet, ball; bale

ballerine, n.f. ballerina

ballet, n.m. ballet

ballon, n.m. balloon; football

ballot, n.m. bundle; small pack

balourd, adj. heavy, dull

bamboche, n.f. a large puppet

bambou, n.m. bamboo

ban, n.m. ban, public order, announcement

banal, adj. trite, ordinary, common

banane, n.f. banana

banc, n.m. bench, form; pew; stand

bancaire, having to do with banking

bandage, n.m. bandage, truss; belt

bande, n.f. strip, stripe, pack, bandage; troop, gang

bander, v.t. to tie up

bandit, n.m. bandit, robber, knave

banlieue, n.f. suburbs, outskirts

banneton, n.m. basket for bread

bannière, n.f. banner, flag

bannir, vb. to exile, banish

bannissement, n.m. banishment

banque, n.f. banking, bank

banqueroute, n.f. bankruptcy, collapse, failure

banqueroutier, n.m. bankrupt

banquet, n.m. banquet, feast

banquier, n.m. banker

banquise, n.f. ice-pack

baptême, n.m. baptism, christening

baptiser, vb. to christen, baptize

Baptiste, n.m. Baptist

baptistère, n.m. baptistery

bar, n.m. bar; bass fish

baraque, n.f. booth stall, shanty, hut

baratter, vb. to churn

barbare, n.m.f. barbarian adj. barbarian, barbarous, wild

barbarie, n.f. cruelty, barbarousness, rudeness, lack of culture

barbe, n.f. beard, whiskers (of animals)

barbiche, n.f. goatee, beard only on the chin

barbier, n.m. barber

barbouiller, vb. to daub, blur

barguignage, n.m. wavering, hesitation

baril, n.m. keg, cask, small barrel

barillet, n.m. barrel or box, keg

bariolé, adj. gaudy

barioler, v.t. to variegate with colors

baroque, adj. odd, irregular, grotesque

barque, n.f. barge, boat

barrage, n.m. barrier, dam, barrage

barre, n.f. bar (of wood, metal, steel, etc.)

barreau, n.m. small bar (of wood, metal, steel, etc,)

barrer, vb. to shut out, cut off, fasten

barricade, n.f. barricade

barrière, n.f. gate; bar, railing, barrier; fence

barrique, n.f. barrel, cask

barrotin, n.m. cross-bar between beams

bascule, n.f. seesaw

base, n.f. base, basis; foundation

basique, adj. basic

basket-ball, n.m. basketball

basse-fosse, n.f. dungeon

basset, n.m. basset hound

baosln, n.m. basin, dock, pool

bataille, n.f. fight, battle

bataillon, n.m. battalion

bateau, n.m. boat

batelage, n.m. juggling

bâtiment, n.m. building, structure

bâtir, vb. to build, construct

bâton, n.m. stick, staff, cane

battant, adj. heavy down fall of rain

batte, n.f. long wooden beater; bat

battement, n.m. beating, clapping of hands, stamping of the feet

batterle, n.f. battery; row

battre, vb. to beat, strike, thrash upon

battu, adj. beaten path

baudet, n.m. ass; donkey

bauge, n.f. squirrel's nest

baume, n.m. balm; balsam

bavard, adj. talkative, gossip

bavardage, n.m. gossip, chatter

bavarder, vb. to gossip, chat(ter)

bavette, n.f. bib

bavoché, adj. smeary, uneven (print)

bavolet, n.m. trimming on the back of a hat

bazar, n.m. bazaar

bazarder, v.t. to sell at a low price

bazooka, n.m. bazooka

béat, adj. devout, blessed

béatifier, v.t. to beautify

beaucoup, adv. a lot, a great deal; much, many

beau-frère, n.m. brother-in-law

beau-père, n.m. father-in-law

beauté, n.f. beauty, elegance, neatness

beaux-arts, n.m., pl. fine arts

beaux-parents, n.m., pl. father-in-law and mother-in-law

bébé, n.m. baby

bec, n.m. beak, bill; spot; burner

bêchage, n.m. digging up

bêcher, vb. to dig

becqueter, vb. to peck

bécot, n.m. little kiss

bégalement, n.m. faltering

bégayer, vb. to stammer, lisp

bêler, vb. to bleat

Belgique, n.f. Belgium

béller, n.m. ram

belle-fille, n.f. daughter-in-law; stepdaughter

belle-mère, n.f. mother-in-law; stepmother

belliqueux, adj. martial, war-like

bénédiction, n.f. blessing, benediction

bénéfice, n.m. benefit, advantage, profit, gain

bénéficiaire, adj. receiving a benefit

bénéficier, vb. to benefit, profit

bénin, adj. good-natured, indulgent

bénir, v.t. to bless, to consecrate, to praise

béquille, n.f. crutch; support, aid, help

béquiller, v.i. to walk on crutches

berceau, n.m. cradle, bower

bercement, n.m. lulling, rocking

bercer, vb. to rock, lull to sleep

berge, n.f. steep river bank

berger, n.m. shepherd

bergère, n.f. large, deep armchair

berthon, n.m. collapsible boat

besogne, n.f. piece of work; job

besoin, n.m. need, want

bétail, n.m. cattle, livestock; animals

bête, n.f. beast, animal adj. stupid, dumb, silly

bêtement, adv. foolishly, stupidly

bêtise, n.f. nonsense, silliness

bétoire, n.m. drain hole

béton, n.m. concrete

betterave, n.f. beet

beurre, n.m. butter

bévue, n.f. blunder, boner, mistake

biais, n.m. slant; bias

bibelot, n.m. trinket, knick-knack

biberon, n.m. baby'_ bottle

Bible, n.f. Bible

bibliothèque, n.f. library; bookcase

biblique, adj. biblical

bicyclette, n.f. bicycle

bidon, n.m. can

bidonnant, adj. extremely funny

bien, n.m. good; benefit, well-being

bien, adv. well, right, fully, properly

bien-aimé, n.m.f. and adj. darling

bien-être, n.m. well-being, welfare

bienfaisant, adj. beneficient, kind, humane, charitable

bienfait, n.m. benefit, kindness; good turn

bienfaiteur, n.m. benefactor, patron

bienheureux, adj. blessed; fortunate

bientôt, adv. soon, shortly

bienveillance, n.f. benevolence, kindness, goodwill

bienveillant, adj. benevolent, kindly, friendly

bienvenu, adj. welcome

bière, n.f. beer, ale
biffer, vb. to cancel, erase, blot out
bifteck, n.m. beefsteak
bigamie, n.f. bigamy
bigot, n.m. bigotry
bijouterie, n.f. jewelry
bile, n.f. bile, spleen
billard, n.m. billiards
bille, n.f. marble
billet, n.m. ticket, note
billion, n.m. billion
biographie, n.f. biography
biologie, n.f. biology
biscotin, n.m. hard, crisp biscuit
biscuit, n.m. biscuit
bizarre, adj. queer, odd, strange, quaint
blâme, n.m. blame, reprimand
blâmer, vb. to blame, to find fault with, to criticize; to censure
blancheur, n.f. cleanliness; whiteness
blanchir, v.t. to whiten, to bleach
blanchisserie, n.f. laundry
blaser, v.t. to sicken, to cloy
blasphème, n.m. blasphemy
blasphémer, vb. to curse, to blaspheme
blatte, n.f. cockroach
blé, n.m. wheat, corn
blême, adj. pale
blessé, adj. injured, outraged
blesser, vb. to wound, hurt, injure
blessure, n.f. wound, hurt, injury
bleu, adj. blue
bloc, n.m. pad, block
blond, adj. fair, blond
bloquer, vb. to block; tighten
blouse, n.f. blouse, smock
bluff, n.m. bluff
bobine, n.f. spool, reel, bobbin
boeuf (boef), n.m. ox, beef,
Bohême, n.f. Bohemia
boire, v.t. to drink
bois, n.m. wood, forest, timber, lumber
boiserie, n.f. woodwork
boisseau, n.m. bushel
boisson, n.f. beverage, drink; drinking
boîte, n.f. box; caddy, chest
boiter, vb. to limp, halt
boiteux, adj. lame, limping, halting
bol, n.m. basin, bowl
bombardement, n.m. shelling, bombardment
bombarder, vb. to bomb, bombard
bombe, n.f. bomb, shell
bombé, adj. arched, convex
bon, adj. kind, favourable; good

bonbon, n.m. candy, bonbon, sweet
bond, n.m. jump, bound, leap
bondé, vb. to overcrowd, jam, cram, load
bondir, vb. to bound, leap, spring
bonheur, n.m. prosperity, happiness
bonhomme, n.m. good-natured
bonjour, interj. and n.m. good morning, good day, good afternoon
bonne, n.f. maid
bonnement, adv. simply, plainly
bonnet, n.m. cap, hood
bonsoir, interj. and n.m. good evening, good night
bonté, n.f. kindness, goodness
bord, n.m. edge, rim, brim, border
border, vb. to bound, edge, hem
borne, n.f. bound, limit, milestone
borner, vb. bound, limit, restrict
bosquet, n.m. clump, grove, thicket
bosse, n.f. bump, hump, bruise
bosselure, n.f. dent, embossment
bossu, adj. hunchbacked, deformed
botanique, n.f. botany
botte, n.f. boot; bunch
bottine, n.f. boot
bouche, n.f. mouth; tongue; lips
boucher, vb. stop up
boucher, n.m. butcher
boucherie, n.f. butcher's shop
bouchon, n.m. cork, plug, stopper
boucle, n.f. curl, loop, buckle
bouclier, n.m. shield, buckler
bouder, vb. to sulk, pout
boue, n.f. dirt, mud, filth
bouée, n.f. buoy
boueux, adj. dirty, muddy
bouffée, n.f. blast, buff, gust
bouffon, n.m. clown, fool, jester
bougeoir, n.m. taper stand, flat candle
bouger, v.t. to stir, to move
bougie, n.f. candle
bouillir, v.t. to boil
bouilloire, n.f. kettle
bouillon, n.m. broth
bouillonner, v.t. to bubble, to boil
bouillotte, n.f. small kettle; foot warmer
boulanger, n.m. baker
boulangerie, n.f. baking, baker's shop
boule, n.f. ball
bouleau, n.m. birch
bouledogue, n.m. bulldog
boulevard, n.m. boulevard
bouleversement, n.m. upset, overthrow, confusion

bouleverser, v.t. to upset, to overturn; to distract

bouquet, n.m. cluster, bunch, bouquet (of flowers)

bouquiniste, n.m. secondhand bookseller

bourbeux, adj. sloppy, muddy

bourdonnement, n.m. buzz, hum

bourdonner, v.t. to hum, to buzz

bourg, n.m. borough, village

bourgeois, adj. middle-class, commoner

bourgeoisie, n.f. middle class

bourgeon, n.m. bud, shoot

bourgeonner, v.t. to bud

bourre, n.f. stuffing

bourreau, n.m. executioner, hangman

bourrelet, n.m. cushion, pad

bourru, adj. gruff, moody, cross

bourse, n.f. purse; scholarship, grant exchange; fellowship

boursoufler, v.t. to bloat, to puff up

bousculer, vb. to jostle, hustle

bousiller, vb. to bungle, botch

boussole, n.f. compass; guide, direct

bout, n.m. end, tip, butt, stub

bouteille, n.f. bottle

boutique, n.f. shop; workshop

bouton, n.m. button, bud; pimple

boutonnière, n.f. buttonhole

boxe, n.f. boxing

boxeur, n.m. prize fighter, boxer

boycotter, v.t. to boycott

bracelet, n.m. bracelet

braconnier, n.m. poacher

brailler, vb. to bawl, shout

braise, n.f. coals, embers

brandir, v.t. to brandish

braquer, vb. to aim, point, level

bras, n.m. bracket, arm

brasser, v.t. to brew, to mix

brasserie, n.f. brewery

bravade, n.f. bully, bravo

brave, adj. fine, good, brave, honest, worthy

braver, vb. to face, brave, defy

bravoure, n.f. courage, bravery, gallantry

brebis, n.f. lamb, sheep, ewe

brèche, n.f. gap, breach, flaw

bref, adj. brief, short

Brésil, n.m. Brazil

brevet, n.m. certificate, warrant

bride, n.f. bridle reins, bridle

brider, v.t. to curb, to restrain

bridge, n.m. the game of bridge

brièveté, n.f. briefness

brigade, n.m. brigade; troop, gang, squad

brigadier, n.m. overseer, corporal

brigand, n.m. robber

brillant, adj. brilliant, shiny, bright, glowing, glittering

briller, vb. to shine, glisten, glare, glitter, sparkle

brindille, n.f. twig

brique, n.f. brick

briser, vb. to break, shatter, smash

britannique, adj. British

brocart, n.m. brocade

broche, n.f. spit, spindle, brooch

brochure, n.f. pamphlet, booklet, brochure

broder, v.t. to embroider, to adorn

broderie, n.f. braid, embroidery

bronzage, n.f. bronzing

bronze, n.m. bronze

broquette, n.f. carpet nail, tack

brosse, n.f. painter's brush

brouillard, n.m. fog, haze, mist

brouiller, vb. to jumble, embroil; mix, confuse

brouter, vb. to browse, graze

broyer, vb. to pound, crush, grind, pulverize

bruine, n.f. drizzle

bruit, n.m. noise, clatter; rumour; fuss, racket

brûlant, adj. hot, scorching, burning

brûler, v.t. to burn, to scorch

brume, n.f. fog, mist, haze

brumeux, adj. foggy, hazy, misty

brun, adj. brown, the color brown

brusque, adj. abrupt, curt, blunt, gruff, sudden, brusque

brut, adj. crude, gross, rough, unpolished

brutal, adj. brutal, savage, rude

brutalité, n.f. brutality

brute, n.f. brute, brutal person

bruyant, adj. loud, noisy

bûche, n.f. log; dolt

budget, n.m. budget

buffet, n.m. buffet; sideboard, refreshment table

buisson, n.m. thicket, bush, shrub

bulbe, n.m. bulb

bulle, n.f. bull; bubble; blister

bulletin, n.m. bulletin; certificate, receipt

bureau, n.m. office, bureau; department, desk

burin, n.m. chisel, graving tool

burlesque, adj. ludicrous, ridiculous

buste, n.m. head and shoulders, bust

but, n.m. aim, goal, object, purpose

butin, n.m. spoils, booty
butte, n.f. mound, hill, knoll
buvard, n.m. blotter, blotting pad

C

ca, pron. that
cabale, n.f. intrigue
cabane, n.f. cabin, hut, shed
cabaret, n.m. cabaret, tavern
cabine, n.f. cabin, berth, car
cabinet, n.m. closet; study, office; business; practice
câblage, n.m. electrical wiring
câbler, v.t. to make into cable
câblogramme, n.m. cablegram
cabosse, n.f. bump, bruise
cabot, n.m. actor
cabotage, n.m. coasting
cabri, n.m. kid
cabriole, n.f. leap
cabrouet, n.m. hand truck
cacahouète, n.f. peanut
cacao, n.m. cocoa
caché, adj. concealed, hidden
cache-cache, n.m. hide-and-seek
cache-col, n.m. scarf
cache-corset, n.m. camisole
cachemire, n.m. cashmere
cacher, v.t. to hide, to disguise, to conceal
cachet, n.m. stamp, seal
cacheter, v.t. to seal up
cachette, n.f. hiding place
cachot, n.m. prison dungeon
cacochyme, adj. decrepit
cacti, n.m. cactus
cadavre, n.m. dead body, corpse
cadeau, n.m. gift, present
cadence, n.f. cadence
cadet, adj. and s.m. cadet junior
cadran, n.m. dial
cadre, n.m. frame, framework, outline
caduc, adj. decayed, decrepit
café, n.m. coffee; café
cafetière n.f. coffeepot, percolator
cage, n.f. cage; coop; crate
cahier, n.m. notebook; memorial
caille, n.f. quail
caillot, n.m. clot of blood
caisse, n.f. crate, case, box, chest
caissier, n.m. cashier, teller
cajoler, vb. to coax
calamité, n.f. misfortune, calamity
calcium, n.m. calcium
calcul, n.m. calculation; arithmetic; counting

calculer, vb. to figure, reckon, calculate, compute
calembour, n.m. pun
calendrier, n..m. calendar, almanac
calibre, n.m. caliber
calme, adj. quiet, calm, tranquil
calmer, vb. to soothe, quiet, calm, still
calomnie, n.f. slander
calorie, n.f. calorie
camarade, n.f. comrade, mate, fellow
camaraderie, n.f. companionship, fellowship
cambrioleur, n.m. burglar
caméra n.f. camera
camoufler, vb. to camouflage
camp, n.m. camp; side
campagnard, adj. rural, rustic
campagne, n.f. country; campaign, expedition
camper, vb. to camp, pitch tents
camphre, n.m. camphor
Canada, n.m. Canada
canaille, n.f. rabble; scoundrel, mob
canal, n.m. channel, canal, stream
canapé, n.m. sofa, couch; canapé
canard, n.m. duck, drake; hoax
canari, n.m. canary
candidat, n.m. candidate, applicant
candidature, n.f. candidature
candide, adj. frank, open, candid
canevas, n.m. canvas; sail cloth
canin, adj. canine
canneberge, n.f. cranberry
cannelle, n.f. cinnamon
canon, n.m. cannon, gun
canot, n.m. boat, canoe
cantaloup, n.m. cantaloup
cantique, n.m. hymn
capable, adj. efficient, fit, able, capable
capacité, n.f. capability, capacity
capitaine, n.m. leader, captain, soldier
capital, adj. capital, main, principal
capitalisme, n.m. capitalism
caporal, n.m. corporal
capote, n.f. hood
câpre, n.f. caper
caprice, n.m. whim, fancy, humour
capricieux, adj. fickle, capricious, whimsical
capsule, n.f. capsule
captif, adj. and n.m. captive, prisoner
captiver, vb. to captivate, seduce
captivité, n.f. captivity, bondage
capture, n.f. capture, seizure
capturer, vb. to capture, to arrest

capuchon, n.m. hood

car, conj. because, for

caractère, n.m. character, type, nature, personality

caractériser, vb. to characterize; distinguish, describe

caractéristique, adj. characteristic

carafe, n.f. decanter, water bottle

caramel, n.m. caramel

carat, n.m. carat

caravane, n.f. caravan, convoy

carbone, n.m. carbon

carburateur, n.m. carburetor

carcasse, n.f. shell; carcass, skelton

cardinal, n.m. cardinal; adj. chief

caresse, n.f. caress

caresser, vb. to fondle, stroke, caress

cargaison, n.f. cargo, freight

caricature, n.f. caricature

carie, n.f. decay

carillon, n.m. chime

carnaval, n.m. carnival

carnet, n.m. notebook

carnivore, adj. carnivorous

carotte, n.f. carrot

carré, adj. square; plain

carreau, n.m. diamond; flooring, pane; title, small square

carrefour, n.m. crossroads

carrière, n.f. career; scope; quarry

carriole, n.f. light cart

carrosse, n.m. coach; carriage with four wheels

carte, n.f. chart, map, ticket

carton, n.m. cardboard; box, carton, pasteboard

cartouche, n.f. cartridge

cas, n.m. case; instance; event

case, n.f. pigeonhole; hut, shed, small house

caserne, n.f. barracks

casquette, n.f. cap

cassable, adj. breakable

casser, vb. to break, crack, shatter

casserole, n.f. cooking pan, saucepan

cassette, n.f. casket, cassette

castor, n.m. beaver

casuel, adj. casual, accidental

catalogue, n.m. catalogue

cataracte, n.f. cataract

catastrophe, n.f. disaster, catastrophe

catéchisme, n.m. catechism

catégorie, n.f. class, category

cathédrale, n.f. cathedral

catholicisme, n.m. Catholicism

catholique, adj. Catholic

cauchemar, n.m. nightmare

cause, n.f. case; cause, reason

causer, vb. to chat; cause

causerie, n.f. chat, talk. gossip

causette, n.f. chat

caution, n.f. bail, security

cavalerie, n.f. cavalry

cavalier, n.m. rider, horseman; escort

cave, n.f. cellar, cavern, cave

ceci, pron. this, this thing

cécité, n.f. blindness

cèdre, n.m. cedar

ceindre, vb. to gird, encircle

ceinture, n.f. belt, sash, girdle

cela, pron. that

célébration, n.f. celebration

célèbre, adj. celebrated; famous

célébrer, vb. to celebrate, praise

célébrité, n.f. celebrity

céleri, n.m. celery

céleste, adj. heavenly, celestial, divine

célibataire, n.m. bachelor; adj. single

cellule, n.f. cello

celtique, adj. Celtic

cendre, n.f. ashes; cinders

cendrier, n.m. ash-tray

censeur, n.m. censor, critic

censurer, v.t. to blame, to criticize

cent, adj. one hundred

centaine, n.f. hundred

centenaire, adj. hundred years old

centième, adj. hundredth

centigrade, adj. centigrade

centimètre, n.m. centimetre

central, adj. central, principal, chief, head

centraliser, vb. to centralize

centre, n.m. center, middle

cependant, adv. meanwhile

cercle, n.m. circle, ring, hoop; club

cercueil, n.m. coffin

céréale, adj. and n.f. cereal

cérémonial, adj. and n.m. ceremonial

cérémonie, n.f. ceremony, pomp

cérémonieux, adj. formal, ceremonious

cerf, n.m. stag, hart, deer

cerise, n.f. cherry

certain, adj. certain, sure, positive

certes, adv. indeed

certificat, n.m. credentials; testimonial, certificate

certifier, vb. to certify

certitude, n.f. certainty, assurance

cerveau, n.m. brain, intellect

cessation, n.f. stopping, cessation

cesser, vb. to stop, desist, cease

cession, n.f. relinquishment

chacun, pron. everybody, everyone; each; apiece

chagrin, n.m. grief, vexation, adj. fretful, gloomy

chagriner, vb. to grieve, afflict

chaîne, n.f. chain; range

chaînon, n.m. link

chair, n.f. flesh

chaire, n.f. pulpit; chair; seat

chaise, n.f. chair, seat

châle, n.m. shawl

chaleur, n.f. warmth, heat, glow, fire

chambre, n.m. room, chamber; bedroom

chameau, n.m. camel

chamois, n.m. chamois

champ, n.m. country, field

champignon, n.m. mushroom

champion, n.m. champion

championnat, n.m. championship

chance, n.f. luck, risk, fortune

chanceler, vb. to stagger, reel

chandelier, n.m. candlestick

chandelle, n.f. candle

change, n.m. exchange, barter

changeante, adj. changeable

changement, n.m. change, shift

changer, vb. to alter, shift, change

chanson, n.f. song

chant, n.m. song, chant, melody

chantage, n.m. blackmail

chanteau, n.m. remnant

chanteur, n.m. singer

chapeau, n.m. hat, bonnet; cap

chapelle, n.f. chapel

chaperon, n.m. chaperon

chapiteau, n.m. capital

chapitre, n.m. chapter; head, subject

chapon, n.m. capon

chaque, adj. every, each

char, n.m. chariot, carriage

charbon, n.m. coal

charge, n.f. load, charge; burden; attack

charger, vb. to load, burden, charge; entrust, pack

chariot, n.m. wagon; baggage cart

charisme, n.m. charisma

charitable, adj. charitable

charité, n.f. charity, alms

charlatan, n.m. charlatan

charmant, adj. delightful, lovely, charming

charme, n.m. spell, charm

charmer, vb. to charm, enchant

charnel, adj. carnal

charnu, adj. fleshy

charpente, n.f. framework

charpentier, n.m. carpenter

charretier, n.m. carter

charrette, n.f. wagon, cart

charrue, n.f. plow

charte, n.f. charter

chasse, n.f. hunting, chase, shooting

châsse, n.f. shrine

chasser, vb. to hunt, chase; drive away, pursue

chasseur, n.m. hunter; bellboy

chaste, adj. chaste

chasteté, n.f. chastity, purity

châtaigne, n.f. chestnut

château, n.m. mansion, castle, palace

châtier, vb. to punish, chastise

chatouiller, vb. to tickle

chaud, adj. hot, warm

chaudière, n.f. boiler

chauffage, n.m. warming; heating

chauffer, vb. to warm; coach; urge on

chauffeur, n.m. driver, chauffeur

chaumière, n.f. cottage

chaussée, n.f. road, pavement

chausser, vb. to wear shoes

chaussette, n.f. sock

chaussure, n.f. footwear, shoes

chauve, adj. bald, hairless

chaux, n.f. lime; limestone

chavirer, vb. to capsize

chef, n.m. leader, chief

chemin, n.m. road, way, path

chemineau, n.m. tramp

cheminée, n.f. fireplace, chimney; funnel

chemise, n.f shirt

chêne, n.m. oak

chenille, n.f. caterpillar

chèque, n.m. check

cher, adj. dear, expensive

chercher, vb. to seek, look for, search

chère, n.f. fare

chéri, adj. and n.m. beloved, darling

chérir, vb. to cherish

cheval, n.m. horse

chevaleresque, adj. chivalrous

chevalerie, n.f. chivalry

chevalet, n.m. easel; knight

chevalier, n.m. knight

cheville, n.f. ankle; peg, bolt

chèvre, n.f. goat, crab

chevron, n.m. rafter

chevrotine, n.f. buckshot

chic, adj. stylish, chic

chien, n.m. dog, hound

chiffon, n.m. rag; scrap; bit

chiffonner, vb. to crumple, rumple	**cisailles,** n.f., pl. shears
chiffre, n.m. figure; digit, calculate	**ciseau,** n.m. chisel
chiffrer, vb. to figure	**ciseaux,** n.m.,pl. scissors
Chili, n.m. Chile	**ciseler,** vb. to chisel
chimie, n.f. chemistry	**citation,** n.f. quotation, citation
chimothérapie, n.f. chemotherapy	**cité,** n.f. town, city
chimique, adj. chemical	**citer,** vb. quote, cite
chimiste, n.m.f. chemist	**citoyen,** n.m. citizen
Chine, n.f. China	**citron,** n.m. lemon
chinois, n.m. Chinese language	**citrouille,** n.f. pumpkin
chiquenaude, n.f. flick	**civil,** n.m. civilian; adj. civil
chirurgie, n.f. surgery	**civilisation,** n.f. civilization
chirurgien, n.m. surgeon	**civilisé,** adj. civilized
choc, n.m. shock, clash, collision	**civiliser,** vb. to civilize
chocolat, n.m. chocolate	**civique,** adj. civic
choeur, n.m. choir, chorus	**clair,** adj. clear, bright, light
choisir, vb. to choose, select, pick	**clairière,** n.f. glade, clearing
choix, n.m. choice, alternative	**clairon,** n.m. bugle
chômage, n.m. stoppage of work; unemployment	**clameur,** n.f. clamor, outry
choquer, vb. to shock, clash, run into, strike against, collide	**clandestin,** adj. secret
	clapoteux, adj. rough
choral, adj. choral	**claque,** n.f. slap, smack
chose, n.f. thing, matter, object	**claquement,** n.m. clapping
chou, n.m. cole, cabbage, kale	**claquer,** vb. to crack, chatter bang
chou-fleur, n.m. cauliflower	**clarifier,** vb. to clarify, purify
choyer, vb. to pamper	**clarinette,** n.f. clarinet
chrétien, adj. and n.m. Christian	**clarté,** n.f. clarity; light; brightness
chronique, adj. chronic	**classe,** n.f. order, rank; class
chuchoter, vb. to whisper	**classement,** n.m. classification
chute, n.f. fall, drop, downfall	**classer,** vb. to classify, order, grade
cible, n.f. target	**classeur,** n.m. file
cicatrice, n.f. scar, mark	**classification,** n.f. classification
cidre, n.m. cider	**classifier,** vb. to classify
ciel, n.m., pl. cieux, heaven, sky	**classique,** adj. classic, classical
cierge, n.m. wax candle, taper	**clause,** n.f. clause
cigale, n.f. locust	**clavicule,** n.f. collarbone
cigare, n.m. cigar	**clémence,** n.f. clemency, mercy
cigarette, n.f. cigarette	**clément,** adj. merciful; mild
cigogne, n.f. stork	**clerc,** n.m. clerk
cil, n.m. eyelash	**clérical,** adj. clerical
cime, n.f. top, summit	**cliché,** n.m. snapshot
ciment, n.m. cement	**client,** n.m. customer, client, patron
cimetière, n.m. churchyard, cemetery	**clientèle,** n.f. customers, practice
	clignoter, vb. to blink, wink
cinéma, n.m. cinema	**climat,** n.m. climate
cinglant, adj. lashing	**climatisation,** n.f. air conditioning
cinq, adj. and n.m. fifth, five	**climatiser,** vb. to air condition
cintre, n.m. semicircle; arch	**cloche,** n.f. bell; blister on hands and feet
circonférence, n.f. circumference	
circonstance, n.f. event, circumstance	**cloison,** n.f. partition
	cloître, n.m. cloister, convent
circuit, n.m. circuit	**clôture,** n.f. fence, enclosure
circulaire, adj. circular	**clou,** n.m. nail, stud
circulation, n.f. traffic, circulation	**clouer,** vb. to nail, tack
circuler, vb. to circulate, turn, revolve	**club,** n.m. club
	coaguler, vb. to coagulate
cire, n.f. wax, beeswax	**coalition,** n.f. coalition
cirer, vb. to polish, shine; wax	**coasser,** vb. to croak
cirque, n.m. circus	**cocaïne,** n.f. cocaine
	cochon, n.m. swine, pig

cocon, n.m. cocoon

code, n.m. code; rule; law

code postal, n.m. zip code

coeur, n.m. heart

coffre, n.m. bin; box, trunk

cogner, vb. bump, strike, run into, knock down

cohérent, adj. coherent

coiffeur, n.m. hairdresser, barber

coiffure, n.f. hair-do, style

coin, n.m. corner, wedge, angle

coïncidence, n.f. coincidence

col, n.m. collar; pass

colère, n.f. anger, temper

colimaçon, n.m. snail

colis, n.m. parcel, package

collaborateur, n.m. fellow-worker, co-worker

collaborer, vb. to work together, collaborate; work jointly

colle, n.f. glue, paste, gum

collecte, n.f. collection; collect

collectif, adj. collective

collection, n.f. collection; set

collectionneur, n.m. collector

collège, n.m. college, high school, grammar school

collègue, n.m. colleague

coller, vb. to glue, paste, stick together

collier, n.m. necklace;   collar

colline, n.f. hill

collision, n.f. collision

colombe, n.f. dove, pigeon

colon, n.m. settler, colonist, farmer, planter

colonel, n.m. colonel

colonial, adj. colonial

colonie, n.f. settlement, colony; dominion

coloniser, vb. to colonize

colonne, n.f. column, pillar

coloré, adj. colorful; coloured

colorer, v.t. to color, to dye

colossal, adj. huge, colossal, giant

colosse, n.m. giant, colossus

colporter, n.m. peddler

colporteur, n.m. peddler, hawker

combat, n.m. fight, battle

combattant, adj. and n.m. combatant

combattre, vb. to fight, combat

combien, adv. how much, how many, how long, how far

combinaison, n.f. combination

combiner, vb. to devise, combine, plan

comble, n.m. climax, top, height

combler, v.t. to heap up, to fill up

combustible, n.m. fuel; adj.

combustible

combustion, n.f. combustion, flame

comédie, n.f. comedy, players, comedians

comédien, n.m. actress, actor, comedian

comestible, adj. edible

comète, n.f. comet

comique, adj. funny, comic, comical

comité, n.m. committee, board

commandant, n.m. major, commander

commande, n.f. order; commission

commanditer, v.t. to finance

comme, adv. as, how, like, such as, nearly, almost

commémoratif, adj. memorial, commemorative

commémorer, vb. to commemorate, remember

commençant, n.m. novice,beginner

commencement, n.m. beginning, start

commencer, v.t. to begin, to start, to commence

comment, adv. how, why, wherefore

commentaire, n.m. comment, commentary, exposition

commentateur, n.m. commentator

commerçant, n.m. trader, shopkeeper, merchant

commerce, n.m. trade, commerce, trading, traffic

commettre, v.t. to commit, to appoint, to empower

commis, n.m. employee, clerk

commissaire, n.m. manager, commissioner

commission, n.f. errand, commission, charge

commodité, n.f. convenience, comfort

commun, adj. joint, common, general

communauté, n.f. community, religious community, society

communicatif, adj. open, communicative

communication, n.,f. communication

communion, n.f. communion

communiquer, vb. to communicate, in form

compagne, n.f. mate, companion

compagnie, n.f. company, fellowship

compagnon, n.m. mate, fellow, companion, comrade

comparable, adj. comparable

comparaison, n.f. comparison

comparer, v.t. to compare

compas, n.m. compass

compassion, n.f. sympathy, pity, mercy

compatible, adj. compatible, consistent

compatriote, n.m. compatriot

compensation, n.f. amends; compensation

compenser, vb. to compensate, counterbalance

compiler, vb. to compile

complaire, vb. to please

complaisance, n.f. kindness, compliance

complaisant, adj. obliging, kind, civil

complément, n.m. object; complement

complet, n.m. suit; adj. full, complete

compléter, v.t. to complete, to perfect

complexe, adj. complex, complicated

complexité, n.f. complexity

complice, n.m.f. party to, accomplice

compliqué, adj. intricate, involved, complicated

compliquer, vb. to complicate

complot, n.m. plot

composant, adj. and n.m. component

composé, adj. compound

composer, v.t. to combound, to compose, to form

compositeur, n.m. composer

composition, n.f. essay; composition

compote, n.f. stewed fruit

compréhensif, adj. comprehensive

compréhension, n.f. comprehension

comprendre, vb. to understand, realize

compresse, n.f. compress

compression, n.f. compression

comprimer, vb. to condense

compromettre, vb. to compromise

compromis, n.m. compromise

comptabilité, n.f. accounting, bookkeeping

comptable, n.m. accountant, bookkeeper

compte, n.m. account, count, score, report

compter, v.t. to reckon, to count, to

compute, calculate

comptoir, n.m. counter, bank, branch bank

comte, n.m. count

comtesse, n.f. countess

concave, adj. concave

concéder, vb. to grant, concede, allow

concentration, n.f. concentration

concentrer, vb. to condense, concentrate

concernant, prep. concerning, about, relating to

concerner, vb. to concern, regard

concert, n.m. concert, harmony

concession, n.f. grant, license, admission

concevable, adj. conceivable

concevoir, v.t. to conceive, to imagine

concierge, n.m.f. door keeper, porter

conclie, n.m. council

conciliation, n.f. conciliaton

concilier, vb. to reconcile, conciliate

concis, adj. concise, brief

concision, n.f. conciseness

concluant, adj. conclusive

conclure, vb. to complete, conclude

conclusion, n.f. end, conclusion

concombre, n.m. cucumber

concourir, vb. to concur, contribute, contend

concours, n.m. contest

concret, adj. concrete

concurrence, n.f. competition

concurrent, n.m. rival, competitor

condamnation, n.f. conviction, condemnation, sentence

condamner, vb. to convict, doom, condemn, sentence

condenser, vb. to condense

condescendance, n.f. compliance

condition, n.f. condition, rank, state

conditionnel, adj. conditional

conditionner, vb. to condition

condoléance, n.f. condolence

condominium, n.m. condominium

conducteur, n.m. conductor

conduire, vb. to lead, take, drive

condite, n.f. behavior, conduct

cône, n.m. cone

confédéré, adj. and n.m. confederate

conférence, n.f. lecture, talk

conférer, vb. to confer, grant, bestow

confesser, vb. to confess, admit, acknowledge

confesseur, n.m. confessor
confession, n.f. denomination; confession, acknowledgment
confiance, n.f. turst, belief
confiant, adj. confident
confidence, n.f. condfidence
confident, n.m. confidant
confier, vb. to confide, entrust
confiner, vb. to confine, limit
confirmation, n.f. confirmation
confirmer, vb. to confirm, strengthen
confiserie, n.f. confectionery
confisquer, vb. to confiscate
confiture, n.f. jam, jelly, preserve
conflit, n.m. conflict, collision
confondre, vb. to confuse, confound
conforme, adj. consonant, consistent
conformer, vb. to conform
conformité, n.f. accordance, likeness
confort, n.m. comfort, ease
confortable, adj. cozy, snug, comfortable
confronter, vb. to confront
confus, adj. confused, mixed, indistinct
confusion, n.f. confusion, disorder
congé, n.m. discharge; leave of absence, furlough, holiday
congélateur, n.m. freezer, refrigerator
congeler, vb. to congeal, freeze
congestion, n.f. congestion
congrès, n.m. congress, assembly
conjecture, n.f. guess, conjecture
conjonction, n.f. conjunction
conjugaison, n.f. conjugation
conjuguer, vb. to conjugate
conjuration, n.f. conspiracy, plot
conjurer, vb. to conspire, plot
connaisseur, n.m. connoisseur
connaître, v.t. to be acquainted, to know, to understand
connexion, n.f. connection
conquérir, vb. to conquer, subdue
conquête, n.f. conquest, acquisition
conscience, n.f. conscience, consciousness
conscient, adj. conscious
conscription, n.f. draft, enlistment
consécutif, adj. consecutive, following
conseiller, vb. to advise, counsel
consentement, n.m. consent, assent, approval
consentir, vb. to consent, accede

conséquence, n.f. outgrowth, result, consequence
conséquent, adj. consequent, consistent
conservateur, adj. and n.m. conservative
conservation, n.f. conservation, preservation
conserve, n.f. conserve, pickle
conserver, v.t. to conserve, to maintain, to keep
considérable, adj. considerable
considérer, vb. to consider
consigner, vb. to consign, deposit
consistance, n.f. consistency
consistant, adj. consistent
consister, vb. to consist, composed
consolateur, n.m. comforter
consolation, n.f. comfort, solace
console, n.f. bracket, console
consoler, vb. to comfort, console
consolider, vb. to consolidate, strengthen, make durable
consommateur, n.m. consumer
consommation, n.f. consumption; end consummation
consommer, vb. to consummate, complete
consomption, n.f. consumption
consonne, n.f. consonant
conspirateur, n.m. conspirator
conspiration, n.f. conspiration
conspirer, vb. to conspire
constamment, adv. continually, constantly, steadily
constance, n.f. constancy, firmness
constant, adj. constant, firm
constater, vb. to prove, verify
constellation, n.f. constellation
consternation, n.f. dismay
consterné, adj. aghast, dismayed
consterner, vb. to dismay, dishearten
constipation, n.f. constipation
constituant, adj. constituent
constituer, vb. to constitue, form, compose
constitution, n.f. constitution
constricteur, n.m. constrictor
construire, vb. to construct, build
consul, n.m. consul
consultant, adj. consulting
consulter, vb. to consult
consumer, vb. to consume, destroy
contact, n.m. touch, contact
contagieux, adj. contagious
contagion, n.f. infection
contaminer, vb. to contaminate
conte, n.m. tale, story
contemplation, n.f. contemplation

contempler, vb. to survey, observe, contemplate

contemporain, adj. contemporary

contenir, vb. to hold, restrain, contain

contenter, vb. to please, satisfy

contenu, n.m. contents; enclosure

conter, vb. to tell, relate

contester, vb. to challenge, object to, contest

contexte, n.m. context

contigu, adj. adjoining, contiguous

continent, n.m. continent, mainland

continental, adj. continental

contingent, n.m. quota, portion, share

continu, adj. continuous, uninterrupted

continuel, adj. continual, uninterrupted

continuer, vb. to carry on, keep on, go on, continue

continuité, n.f. continuity

contour, n.m. outline, contour

contourner, vb. to go round, outline

contracter, vb. to contract, bargain

contraction, n.f. contraction

contraindre, vb. to coerce, compel

contrainte, n.f. compulsion, uneasiness

contrarier, vb. to thwart, vex, annoy, oppose

contrariété, n.f. annoyance

contraste, n.m. contrast, opposition

contraster, vb. to contrast

contrat, n.m. contract, deed, agreement

contre, prep. against

contrebande, n.f. smuggling; contraband

contrée, n.f. district, province

contrefaire, vb. to forge, counterfeit

contrefort, n.m. buttress

contremaître, n.m. foreman, overseer

contribuer, vb. to contribute, pay

contribution, n.f. share, contribution

contrôle, n.m. verification

contrôler, vb. to control, check

contrôleur, n.m. checker, collector

controverse, n.f. controversy

convaincre, vb. to convince

convalescence, n.f. convalescence

convenable, adj. becoming, appropriate, suitable

convenance, n.f. convenience

convenir, vb. to suit, fit, befit, agree

convention, n.f. convention

converger, vb. to converge

conversation, n.f. conversation, talk

converser, vb. to talk, converse

conversion, n.f. change, conversion

convertir, vb. to convet, transform

convexe, adj. convex

conviction, n.f. conviction

convive, n.f. guest, companion

convoi, n.m. convoy, funeral procession

convoiter, vb. to covet

convoitise, n.f. covetousness; lust

convoquer, vb. to summon, call

convulsion, n.f. convulsion

copie, n.f. copy, transcript

copier, vb. to copy, imitate

copieux, adj. copious, plentiful

coq, n.m. rooster

coquille, n.f. shell

cor, n.m. horn; corn

corail, n.m., pl. **coraux,** coral

corbeau, n.m. raven, crow

corbeille, n.f. wide, flat basket

corde, n.f. rope, string, cord

cordial, adj. harty, cordial

cordon, n.m. rope, cord

cordonnier, n.m. shoemaker

Corée, n.f. Korea

corne, n.f. horn

corneille, n.f. crow

cornemuse, n.f. bagpipe

cornichon, n.m. gherkin

corporation, n.f. corporation

corporel, adj. bodily

corps, n.m. body, matter, substance

corpulent, adj. burly, stout

correction, n.f. correction, correctness

corrélation, n.f. correlation

correspondance, n.f. connection; similarity

correspondant, n.m. correspondent adj. similar, corresponding

correspondre, vb. to correspond

corriger, vb. to mend, reclaim, correct

corroborer, vb. to strengthen, corroborate

corroder, vb. to corrode

corrompre, vb. to bribe, corrupt

corrompu, adj. corrupt, bribed

corruption, n.f. bribery, graft, corruption

corsage, n.m. bodice

corset, n.m. corset

cortège, n.m. procession

cosmétique, adj. and n.m. cosmetic

cosmopolite, adj. and n.m.f. cosmopolitan

costume, n.m. attire, dress, uniform

cote, n.f. quota, proportion, share

côte, n.f. rib; slope

côté n.f. side, part

côtelette, n.f. chop, cutlet

coton, n.m. cotton

cou, n.m. neck

couche, n.f. layer, bed; diaper

coucher, vb. to put to bed, lay down

couchette, n.f. bunk, berth, small bed

coucou, n.m. cuckoo

coude, n.m. elbow, bend, angle

coudoyer, v.t. to jostle, to elbow

coudre, vb. to sew, stitch

couler, vb. to flow, sink, run

couleur, n.f. hue, color, dye, paint

couloir, n.m. corridor, passage, lobby

coup, n.m. blow, stroke, hit, bump, knock, cast

coupable, adj. guilty, to blame, at fault

couper, v.t. to cut, to dock

couple, n.f. couple, pair

coupon, n.m. remnant; coupon

coupure, n.f. cut, clipping

cour, n.f. courtyard; courtship

courage, n.m. bravery, pluck courage

courageux, adj. brave

couramment, adv. fluently, readily

courant, adj. current, stream, course

courbe, n.f. curve, sweep, bent

courber, vb. to bend, curve

courbure, n.f. curvature, curve

coureur, n.m. runner, racer

courir, vb. to run, hasten

couronne, n.f. crown, wreath

couronner, vb. to crown, honor

courrier, n.m. mail, messenger

courroie, n.f. strap; driving belt

courroux, n.m. wrath, anger

cours, n.m. course, current flow

course, n.f. running, race, course

court, adj. short, brief, concise

courtepointe, n.f. quilt

courtier, n.m. broker, agent

courtisan, n.m. courtier

courtois, adj. courteous, polite

courtoisie, n.f. courtesy, politeness

cousin, n.m. cousin

coussin, n.m. cushion, hassock

coussinet, n.m. bearing

coût, n.m. cost, charge

couteau, n.m. knife

coutellerie, n.f. cutlery, cutler's business

coûter, vb. to cost

coûteux, adj. expensive, costly

coutume, n.f. custom

couture, n.f. seam **haute couture,** high fashion

couturière, n.f. dressmaker

couvée, n.f. brood

couvent, n.m. covent, monastery

couver, vb. to brood, hatch; smolder

couvercle, n.m. lid, cover

couvert, adj. covered

couverture, n.f. blanket, cover

couvrir, vb. to cove, wrap

crabe, n.m. crab

crachat, n.m. spit, expectoration

craie, n.f. chalk

crainte, n.f. fear, dread, awe

craintif, adj. fearful, apprehensive

crampe, n.f. cramp

crampon, n.m. cramp, crampiron

crâne, n.m. skull, cranium

crapaud, n.m. toad

craquement, n.m. crack, creaking

craquer, v.t. to crack, to creak

cratère, n.m. crater

cravater, v.t. to put on a necktie

crayon, n.m. pencil

créance, n.f. belief, trust, confidence

créancière, n.m. creditor

création, n.f. creation; the universe

créature, n.f. creature

crédit, n.m. credit, trust

credo, n.m. creed, belief

crédule, adj. credulous

créer, vb. to create, make, produce

crème, n.f. cream, custard

crêpe, n.f. pancake

crête, n.f. ridge, crest

crétin, n.m. dunce, idiot

cretonne, n.f. cretonne

creuser, vb. to dig, scoop out, hollow

creux, adj. hollow; deep; empty

crevasse, v.t. to split, to chap

crever, vb. to burst; die, split, crack

crevette, n.f. shrimp

crible, n.m. sieve

crier, vb. to yell, shout, scream

crime, n.m. crime

criminel, adj. criminal, unlawful

crise, n.f. crisis, conjuncture

cristal, n.m. crystal, glass

critiquer, vb. to criticize

crochet, n.m. bracket, hook

crochu, adj. hooked, crooked

crocodile, n.m. crocodile

croire, vb. to believe, hold true

croisade, n.f. crusade
croisé, n.m. crusader
croiser, vb. to cross, lay across
croiseur, n.m. cruiser
croisière, n.f. cruise
croissance, n.f. growth, increase
croissant, n.m. crescent
croître, vb. to grow, increase
croix, n.f. cross
croquant, adj. crisp, crackling
croquet, n.m. croquet game, biscuit
crotale, n.m. rattlesnake
crouler, vb. to fall apart, give way
croup, n.m. croup
croupir, vb. to wallow, lie stagnant
croûte, n.f. crust; pie crust
croûton, n.m. crusty end
croyable, adj. believeable
croyance, n.f. belief, creed
croyant, n.m. believer
cru, n.m. growth
cruauté, n.f. cruelty, inhumanity
cruche, n.f. pitcher, jar, jug
crucifier, vb. to crucify
crucifix, n.m. crucifix
cruel, adj. cruel, merciless
Cuba, n.m. Cuba
cube, n.m. cube; adj. cubic
cueillir, vb. to pick, gather
cuir, n.m. leather, hide
cuirassé, n.m. battleship
cuire, vb. to cook; sting, smart
cuisine, n.f. kitchen, cooking
cuisinier, n.m. cook
cuisse, n.f. thigh; quarter
cuivre, n.m. copper
cul-de-sac, n.m. blind alley
culotte, n.f. breeches, shorts
culpabilité, n.f. guilt
culte, n.m. worship; cult
culture, n.f. cultivation; farming
cure, n.f. cure, healing
curieux, adj. curious; inquisitive
curiosité, n.f. curiosity
cursif, adj. cursive
cuticule, n.f. cuticle
cuve, n.f. vat, tub
cuvette, n.f. wash basin
cuvier, n.m. washtub
cycle, n.m. cycle of events
cycliste, n.m.f. cyclist
cyclone, n.m. cyclone
cylindre, n.m. cylinder
cymbale, n.f. cymbal
cynique, n.m. cynic; adj. cynical
cynisme, n.m. cynicism
cyprès, n.m. cypress
czar, n.m. czar

D

dactylographe, n.m. typist
daim, n.m. buck, deer
daine, n.f. doe
dais, n.m. canopy
dame, n.f. lady
danger, n.m. danger, risk, hazard
dangereux, adj. dangerous
dans, prep. in, into, within;
  according to
danse, n.f. dance; dancing
danser, v.t. to dance
danseur, n.m. dancer
dard, n.m. dart; sting
date, n.f. date
dater, vb. to date
datte, n.f. date
davantage, adv. more, any further,
  any more, any longer
débarquer, vb. to land, disembark
débarrasser, vb. to rid, free
débat, n.m. debate, dispute, contest
débattre, vb. to canvass; debate,
  argue
débit, n.m. retail; output, sale
  market
débiter, v.t. to sell, to supply, to
  retail
déblayer, vb. to clear away
débordé, adj. overflowing river
déboucher, vb. to flow into
débourser, vb. to disburse, lay out
débris, n.m., pl. wreck, debris
début, n.m. beginning, first
  appearance, debut
débuter, vb. to make one's first
  appearance, set out
décadence, n.f. decay, decadence,
  downfall
décaféiné, adj. decaffeinated
décédé, n.m. deceased
décembre, n.m. December
décence, n.f. decency
décent, adj. decen; modest
déception, n.f. disappointment,
  deceit
décerner, vb. to award, bestow,
  confer
décès, n.m. death, death, demise
décevoir, vb. to disappoint;
  deceive, mislead
décharge, n.f. unlading; unloading;
  discharge; outlet
décharger, vb. to unload,
  discharge, empty
décharné, adj. gaunt, lean,
  emaciated
déchausser, vb. to take off shoes
déchets n.m., pl. waste, loss
déchiffrer, vb. to decipher, unravel,
  penetrate

déchirer, vb. to tear, rend, lacerate

déchirure, n.f. tear, rent

décidé, n.m. decide, resolve, determined

décider, vb. to prevail upon, decide, settle

décimal, adj. decimal

décisif, adj. decisive

décision, n.f. decision, determination

déclamer, vb. to recite, declaim

déclaration, n.f. statement, announcement

déclarer, vb. to state, proclaim

déclin, n.m. ebb; decline, decay

décliner, vb. to decline, refuse

décolorant, adj. bleaching

décolorer, vb. to bleach, fade

décomposer, vb. to spoil, decompose, split up

déconcerter, vb. to disconcert, put out

décongestionner, v.t. to relieve congestion

décontracté, adj. relaxed

décoratif, adj. decorative, ornmental

décoration, n.f. decoration, trimming, embellishment

découper, vb. to carve meat, cut up

découragé, adj. despondent

découragement, n.m. discouragement

décourager, vb. to dishearten

découverte, n.f. discovery, detection

découvreur, n.m. discoverer

découvrir, vb. to detect, discover

décrépit, adj. decrepit, worn out

décret, n.m. decree, enactment, order

décréter, vb. to enact, order, decree

décrire, vb. to desccribe, depict

dédaigneux, adj. scornful, disdainful

dédain, n.m. scorn, disdain, disregard

dedans, n.m. inside, within, in

dédicace, n.f. dedication

dédier, vb. to dedicate, consecrate

déduction, n.f. deduction, allowance

déduire, vb. to infer, deduce, deduct

défaire, vb. to undo; ob scure, eclipse

défaite, n.f. defeat, undone

défaut, n.m. flaw, failure, absence

défectueux, adj. faulty, defective, imperfect

défendeur, n.m. defendant; respondent

défendre, vb. to forbid, protect, shelter

défense, n.f. prohibition, plea, protection, defense

défenseur, n.m. adovcate, defender, supporter

défensif, adj. defensive

déférer, vb. to defer

défi, n.m. challenge, defiance

défiance, n.f. mistrust, distrust

déficit, n.m. deficit, deficiency

défier, vb. to challenge, defy, confront

défigurer, vb. to deface, disfigure

défiler, vb. to march off, defile

défini, adj. definite, determined

définir, vb. to define, determine

définitif, adj. final, definitive, ultimate

définition, n.f. definition

défraîchir, v.t. to tarnish, to take away the gloss, freshness or brilliancy

défricher, vb. to reclaim, clear

défunt, n.m. and adj. deceased

dégagé, adj. breezy; unconstrained

dégât, n.m. damage, havoc

dégénérer, vb. to degenerate, decline

dégoût, n.m. distaste, disgust, dislike

dégoûtant, adj. foul, disgusting

dégoûter, vb. to disgust

dégoutter, vb. to drip, trickle

dégradation, n.f. degradation

dégrader, vb. to degrade, deface, damage

degré, n.m. degree, step, stair, grade

déguisement, n.m. disguise

déguiser, vb. to disguise

dehors, adv. outside, out, without

déifier, vb. to defy

déjà , adv. already, previously, before

déjeuner, n.m. and vb. lunch, luncheon

déjouer, vb. to baffle, frustrate

delà , adv. beyond; on the other side

délabrement, n.m. decay

délabrer, vb. to ruin, wreck

délai, n.m. delay; reprieve

délaissement, n.m. helplessness

délaisser, vb. to forsake, adandon

délassement, n.m. relaxation

délasser, vb. to refresh, relax

délateur, n.m. informer

délayé, adj. watery

délectable, adj. delicious, delightful

délectation, n.f. enjoyment, delight

délecter, vb. to delight

délégation, n.f. delegation

délégué, n.m. delegate

déléguer, vb. to delegate, deputy

délétère, adj. harmful; offensive

délibératif, adj. deliberative

délibéré, adj. deliberate, decided

délicat, adj. dainty, delicate, exquisite

délicatesse, n.f. delicacy, weakness

délice, n.f., pl. delight, pleasure

délicieux, adj. delicious

délié, adj. slender; keen

délier, vb. to untie, release

délinquant, n.m. delinquent, offender

délirant, adj. delirious, frantic, ecstatic

délirer, vb. to rave, wander

délit, n.m. offense, crime

délivrance, n.f. rescue, deliverance

délivrer, vb. to rescue, set free, deliver

déloger, vb. to dislodge, remove

déloyal, adj. disloyal, false

déloyauté, n.f. disloyalty

déluge, n.m. deluge, flood

déluré, adj. clever, cute, sharp

demain, adv. tomorrow

demande, n.f. application, request, inquiry, question

demander, vb. to ask, beg, request

demandeur, n.m. plaintiff, applicant

démangeaison, n.f. itch

démanger, v.t. to itch, to long

démanteler, vb. to dismantle

démarcation, n.f. demarcation

démarche, n.f. walk, bearing; proceeding

démarrage, n.m. start

démarrer, vb. to start off, cast off

démarreur, n.m. self-starter

démasquer, vb. to unmask; expose, reveal, show up

démembrer, vb. to dismember

déménagement, n.m. removing furniture

déménager, vb. to remove furniture

démence, n.f. insanity, madness

démener, vb. to struggle, strive hard

dément, adj. insane, mad person

démenti, n.m. denial; disappointment

démentir, vb. to contradict

démesuré, adj. immense,

excessive, enormous

demeure, n.f. abode, home, dwelling

demeurer, vb. to dwell, lodge

demi, n.m. and adj. half

demi-cercle, n.m. semicircle

demi-dieu, n.m. demigod

demi-frère, n.m. stepbrother, half-brother

demi-heure, n.f. half an hour

démilitariser, vb. to demilitarize

demi-place, n.f. half fare; half price

demi-saison, n.f. spring or autumn

demi-soeur, n.f. stepsister, halfsister

démission, n.f. resignation

démobilisation, n.f. demobilization

démobiliser, vb. to demobilize

démocrate, adj. democratic

démocratie, n.f. democracy

démocratique, adj. democratic

démodé, adj. old fashioned

demoiselle, n.f. young lady

démolir, vb. to demolish, pull down

démolition, n.f. demolition

démon, n.m. demon

démonétiser, vb. to demonetize

démonstration, n.f. demonstration; exhibition

démonter, v.t. to dismount as from a horse

démontrable, adj. demonstrable

démontrer, vb. to demonstrate

démoralisation, n.f. demoralization

démouler, vb. to remove, from a mold

démuni, adj. short of, lacking

dénationaliser, vb. to denationalize

dénaturer, vb. to denature

dénégation, n.f. denial

dénivelé, adj. not level

dénombrement, n.m. census, count of persons

dénombrer, vb. to count, number

dénommer, vb. to name; designate

dénoncer, vb. to report, denounce

dénonciaton, n.f. denunciation; information

dénoter, vb. to denote

dénouer, vb. to untie, loosen

dense, adj. dense., close

densité, n.f. density, thickness

dent, n.f. tooth

dentale, adj. dental

denté, adj. cogged

dentelle, n.f. lace

dentiste, n.m. dentist

dénuder, vb. to strip, denude

dénué, adj. destitute, bare

dénuement, n.m. deprivation

dénuer, vb. to strip

dépareillé, adj. odd, unmatched

départ, n.m. departure, start

département, n.m. department

départir, vb. to distribute

dépasser, vb. to outrun, go beyond

dépêche, n.f. dispatch

dépêcher, vb. to dispatch, do quickly

dépendant, adj. dependent

dépendre, vb. to take down

dépens, n.m., pl. expenses, costs

dépense, n.f. expenditure, expense

dépenser, vb. to spend, consume

dépérir, vb. to waste away; decline

dépecer, vb. to dismember

déplacement, n.m. displacement

déplacer, vb. to displace, move, shift

déplaire, vb. to displease, offend

déplaisant, adj. displeasing

déplanter, vb. to transplant

déplier, vb. to unfold

déploiement, n.m. deployment, unfolding

déplorable, adj. wretched, deplorable

déplorer, vb. to deplore, lament

déployer, vb. to deploy, unfold, unroll

déplumer, vb. to pluck feathers from

déportation, n.f. transportation

déportements, n.m., pl. misconduct

déporter, vb. to deport

déposant, n.m. depositor

déposer, vb. to deposit, set down

dépositaire, n.m. trustee; agent

déposséder, vb. to oust; dispossess

dépôt, n.m. deposit, depot

dépouille, n.f. hide, skin, pelt

dépourvu, adj. devoid; needy

dépoussiérer, n.m. vacuum cleaner

dépravation, n.f. depravity

dépraver, vb. to deprave, corrupt

dépréciation, n.f depreciation

déprécier, vb. to depreciate, cheapen

déprédation, n.f. depredation

dépression, n.f. depression

déprimer, vb. to depress, press down

déraciner, vb. to uproot, eradicate

déraison, n.f. unreason

déraisonnable, adj. unreasonable

derechef, adv. once again

dérégler, vb. to upset, disorder

dérider, vb. to smooth; cheer up

dérive, n.f. drift

dériver, vb. to derive; drift

dernier, adj. last, latter

dernièrement, adv. lately

dérober, vb. to rob, steal

dérouler, vb. to unroll, unfold

déroute, n.f. rout

dérouter, vb. to mislead; confuse

derrière, prep. behind

derviche, n.m. dervish

dès, prep. since, from

désabuser, vb. to disabuse

désaccord, n.m. disagreement

désaccoutumer, vb. to break a habit

désagréable, adj. nasty, distasteful

désaligné, adj. out of alignment

désaltérer, vb. to quench one's thirst

désappointement, n.m. disappointment

désappointer, vb. to deceive

désapprobation, n.f. disapproval

désapprouver, vb. to disapprove

désarmement, n.m. disarmament

désarmer, vb. to disarm

désarroi, n.m. disorder

désastre, n.m. disaster

désastreux, adj. disastrous

désavantage, n.m. disadvantage

désaveu, n.m. denial

désavouer, vb. to disown

descendance, n.f. descent

descendant, n.m offspring, descendant; adj. downward

descendre, vb. to go down, come down, descend

descente, n.f. raid; descent

descriptif, adj. descriptive

description, n.f. description

désembarquer, vb. to disembark

désenchanter, vb. to disenchant

désenivrer, vb. to sober up

désert, n.m. wilderness, desert

déserteur, n.m. deserter

désespéré, adj. hopeless, forlorn, desperate

désespérer, vb. to despair, despond

désespoir, n.m. desperation, despair

déshabiller, vb. to undress

déshériter, vb. to disinherit

déshonnête, adj. improper, indecent

déshonneur, n.m. disgrace, dishonor

déshonorant, adj. dishonorable

déshonorer, vb. to disgrace, dishonor

déshydrater, vb. to dehydrate

désignation, n.f. nomination

désigner, vb. to nominate; point out
désillusion, n.f. disillusion
désinfectant, n.m. disinfectant
désinfecter, vb. to disinfect, fumigate
désinfection, n.f. disinfection
désintégration, n.f. disintegration
désintégrer, vb. to disintegrate
désintéressé, adj. unselfish, impartial
désintéressement, n.m. unselfishness
désir, n.m. desire, wish
désirable, adj. desirable
désirer, vb. to desire, wish
désireux, adj. desirous, anxious
désistement, n.m. withdrawal
désobéir à, vb. to disobey
désobéissance, n.f. disobedience
désobéissant, adj. disobedient
désoeuvré, adj. idle, unoccupied
désolation, n.f. desolation
désoler, vb. to desolate, afflict
désordonné, adj. disorderly
désordonner, vb. to upset, confuse
désordre, n.m. disorder, confusion
désorganiser, vb. to disorganize
dessécher, vb. to dry out, parch; drain
dessein, n.m. plan, intent
desserrer, vb. to loosen, relax
dessert, n.m. dessert
dessin, n.m. design, sketch, draft
dessinateur, n.m. designer
dessiner, vb. to draw, design
dessus, n.m. top
destin, n.m. fate, destiny
destination, n.f. destination
destinée, n.f. destiny
destiner, vb. to destine, intend
destituer, vb. to dismiss, discharge
destructif, adj. destructive
destruction, n.f. destruction
désuet, adj. obsolete, out-of-date
désuétude, n.f. disuse
désunir, vb. to disconnect
détaché, adj. loose, detached
détachement, n.m. detachment
détacher, vb. to detach, untie
détail, n.m. item, particular, detail
détective, n.m. detective
détenir, vb. to detain, keep back
détente, n.f. trigger
détention, n.f. custody, withholding
détermination, n.f. determination
déterminer, vb. to determine, fix
détestable, adj. detestable, hateful
détester, vb. to loathe, detest, hate
détonation, n.f. detonation
détonner, vb. to make out of tune

détour, n.m. turn; detour
détourner, vb. to turn away; avert
détresse, n.f. trouble, distress
détriment, n.m. detriment, injury
détruire, vb. to destroy, demolish
dette, n.f. debt, obligation
deuil, n.m. mourning, grief
deux, adj. and n.m. two, both
deuxième, adj. second
deux-points, n.m. colon
dévaliser, vb. to rob, strip
dévaliseur, n.m. robber, theif
dévastation, n. devastation, havoc
dévaster, vb. to devastate
déveine, n.f. bad luck
développement, n.m. development, growth
développer, vb. to develop
devenir, vb. to become, grow
déverser, vb. to divert
dévêtir, vb. to undress, disrobe
déviation, n.f. deviation, diversion
dévider, vb. to unwind
dévier, vb. to turn away, turn aside
deviner, vb. to guess, foretell
devinette, n.f. puzzle, riddle
devis, n.m. estimate, specification
devise, n.f. motto, device
dévisser, vb. to unscrew
dévoiler, vb. to disclose, reveal, unveil
devoir, n.m. duty
dévorer, vb. to devour, destroy
dévot, adj. devout, devoted
dévotion, n.f. devotion
dévoué, adj. devoted
dévouement, n.m. devotion
dévouer, vb. to dedicate, devote
dextérité, n.f. dexterity
diabétique, adj. and n. diabetic
diable, n.m. devil
diablerie, n.f. mischief
diacre, n.m. deacon
diadème, n.m. diadem, coronet
diagnostiquer, vb. to diagnose
diagonal, adj. diagonal
diagramme, n.m. diagram
dialectal, adj. dialect
dialogue, n.m. dialogue
dialoguer, vb. to talk together, converse
diamant, n.m. diamond
diamètre, n.m. diameter
diaphragme, n.m. diaphragm, midriff
diarrhée, n.f. diarrhea
diatribe, n.f. diatribe, bitter
dictateur, n.m. dictator
dictature, n.f. dictatorship
dictée, n.f. act of dictation

dicter, vb. to dictate
diction, n.f. diction, style
dictionnaire, n.m. dictionary
diction, n.m. proverb, common saying
didactique, adj. didactic
dièse, adj. and n.m. sharp
diète, n.f. diet
diététique, adj. dietetical
dieu, n.m. God
diffamant, adj. libellous
diffamation, n.f. defamation
diffamer, vb. to defame
différence, n.f. difference, unlike
différencier, vb. to differentiate
différend, n.m. difference, dispute, quarrel
différent, adj. different, unlike
différer, vb. to differ, put off
difficile, adj. arduous, hard; difficult
difficilement, adv. with difficulty
difficulté, n.f. trouble; difficulty
difforme, adj. deformed
difformité, n.f. deformity, malformation
diffus, adj. diffuse
diffusion, n.f. spread
digérer, vb. to digest, ponder, discuss
digestible, adj. digestible
digestif, adj. and n.m. digestive
digital, adj. digital
digne, adj. worthy, dignified
dignitaire, n.m. dignitary
dignité, n.f. dignity, nobility
digression, n.f. digression
digue, n.f. dike, dam, embankment
dilapidation, n.f waste
dilater, vb. to expand, dilate
dilemme, n.m. dilemma
dilettante, n.m. amateur
diligence, n.f. diligence, dispatch
diluer, vb. to dilute
dilution, n.f. dilution
dimanche, n.m. Sunday, Sabbath
dimension, n.f. dimension
diminuer, vb. to lessen, decrease, diminish
diminution, n.f. decrease, reduction
dindon, n.m. turkey
dîner, n.m. dinner; vb. to dine
dîneur, n.m. diner
diphtérie, n.f. diphtheria
diplomate, n.m. diplomate
diplomatie, n.f. diplomacy
diplomatique, adj. diplomatic
diplôme, n.m. diploma
dipsomanie, n.f. dipsomania
dire, vb. to say, tell
direct, adj. direct, immediate

directement, adv. directly
directeur, n.m. manager, director
direction, n.f. management, leadership
dirigeant, adj. ruling, directing
diriger, vb. to manage, boss, direct
discernable, adj. barely visible
discernement, n.m. judgment
discerner, vb. to discern, distinguish
disciple, n.m. follower, disciple
disciplinaire, adj. disciplinary
discipline, n.f. discipline
discipliner, vb. to discipline
disco, adj. disco
discontinuer, vb. to discontinue
discordance, n.f. discord
discorde, n.f. discord, disagreement
discourir, vb. to speak one's view
discours, n.m. speech, oration, talk, discourse
discourtois, adj. discourteous
discrédit, n.m. disrepute, discredit
discréditer, vb. to disparage
discret, adj. discreet
discrétion, n.f. discretion
disculper, vb. to exonerate
discursif, adj. discursive
discussion, n.f. argument, discussion
discutable, adj. debatable
discuter, vb. to argue, debate, discuss
disette, n.f. famine, want, poverty
diseur, n.m. talker
disgrâce, n.f disgrace
disjoindre, vb. to sever, disjoint
dislocation, n.f. dislocation
disparaître, vb. to disappear, vanish
disparate, adj. unlike, dissimilar
disparition, n.f. disappearance
dispendieux, adj. expensive, costly
dispensaire, n.m. dispensary
dispense, n.f. military exemption
dispenser, vb. to dispense, bestow
disperser, vb. to scatter, disperse
dispersion, n.f. dispersal
disponible, adj. available; unoccupied
dispos, adj. fit and well
disposer, vb. to dispose, settle
dispositif, n.m. device, appliance
disposition, n.f. arrangement
dispute, n.f. fight, quarrel, dispute
disputer, vb. to dispute, argue
disqualifier, vb. to disqualify
disque, n.m. disk, record
dissemblable, adj. unlike,

dissimilar

dissension, n.f. dissension, discord

dissentiment, n.m. dissent, disagreement

disséquer, vb. to dissect

dissertation, n.f. essay, composition

dissimulation, n.f. pretense

dissimuler, vb. to dissemble, pretend

dissipation, n.f. dissipation

dissiper, vb. to dispel, waste

dissolu, adj. dissolute

dissolution, n.f. dissolution

dissoudre, vb. to dissolve, break up

dissuader, vb. to dissuade

distance, n.f. distance

distancer, vb. to outdistance, outrun

distant, adj. distant, remote

distinct, adj. distinct

distinctif, adj. distinctive

distinction, n.f. distinction

distingué, adj. distinguished

distinguer, vb. to discriminate

distraction, n.f. distraction, pastime

distraire, vb. to distract, amuse

distrait, adj. absentminded

distribuer, vb. to give out, deal out, distribute

distributeur, n.m. distributor

distribution, n.f. distribution; delivery; cast

district, n.m. district; region

dit, adj. called, spoken, said

divaguer, vb. to ramble, go astray

divan, n.m. davenport, couch

divergence, n.f. divergence

diverger, vb. to diverge

divers, adj. various

diversion, n.f. diversion; change

diversité, n.f. diversity, difference

divertir, vb. to divert, entertain

divertissement, n.m. diversion

dividende, n.m. dividend

divin, adj. divine, godlike

divinateur, n.m. soothsayer

divinité, n.f. divinity

diviser, vb. to part, divide

divisible, adj. divisible

division, n.f. division, partition

divorce, n.m. divorce, separation

divorcer, vb. to divorce

divulguer, vb. to divulge, reveal

dix, adj. and n.m. ten

dix-huit, adj. and n.m. eighteenth

dixième, adj. and n.m. tenth

dix-neuf, adj and n.m. nineteen

dix-sept, adj and n.m. seventeen

dizaine, n.f. group of ten

docile, adj. docile, submissive

docilité, n.f. docility

docte, adj. learned, wise

docteur, n.m. doctor, scholar

doctorat, n.m. doctorate, doctor's degree

doctrine, n.f. doctrine

document, n.m. document, certificate

documenter, vb. to document

dodu, adj. plumb

dogmatique, adj. dogmatic

dogme, n.m. dogma

dogue, n.m. watchdog

doigt, n.m. finger

doit, n.m. debit

dollar, n.m. dollar

domaine, n.m. domain, property, estate

dôme, n.m. dome, canopy

domestique, n.m.f. servant; adj. domestic

domicile, n.m. residence

dominant, adj. dominant

domination, n.f. sway, domination

dominer, vb. to rule, dominate

domino, n.m. domino

dommage, n.m. injury, damage

dompter, vb. to tame, subdue

don, n.m. gift, donation

donateur, n.m. donor, giver

donation, n.f. donation

donc, conj. therefore, then, hence

donne, n.f. deal cards

donner, vb. to give, bestow, make present

donneur, n.m. giver, donor

dont, pron. whose, of whom, of which

dorénavant, adv. to hereafter

dorloter, vb. to coddle, pamper, fondle

dormant, adj. dormant, asleep, stagnant

dormir, vb. to sleep

dos, n.m. back, rear, ridge

dose, n.f. dose, quantity

doser, vb. to decide the amount

dossier, n.m. record

dot, n.f. dowry, marriage, portion

doter, vb. to endow, give

douane, n.f. customs, custom house

douanier, n.m. customs officer

double, adj. and n.m. double

doubler, vb. to double, double up

doublure, n.f. lining; understudy

doucement, adv. gently, softly

doucereux, adj. sugary, sweetish

douceur, n.f. sweetness, gentleness
douche, n.f. shower, bath; douche
douer, vb. to endow, bestow upon
douille, n.f. socket
douleur, n.f. pain, sorrow, grief
douloureux, adj. painful, sore, grievous
doute, n.m. doubt, uncertainty
douter, vb. to doubt, question
douteux, adj. doubtful, questionable
douve, n.f. ditch, trench
douzaine, n.f. dozen
douze, adj. and n.m. twelve
douzième, adj. and n.m. twelfth
doyen, n.m. dean
dragon, n.m. dragon; dragoon
draguer, vb. to dredge, sweep
drainage, n.m. drainage
drainer, vb. to drain
dramatique, adj. dramatic
drame, n.m. drama
drap, n.m. sheet, cloth
drapeau, n.f. flag, streamer
draper, vb. to drape, cover
drêche, n.f. draff
drelin, n.m. tinkle, jingle
dressage, n.m. raising, training of animals; pitching a tent
dresser, v.t. to set up, to mount, to raise
dribble, n.m. dribble
drogue, n.f. drug, dope
droit, n.m. right; law, straight
droite, n.f. right
drôle, adj. funny; strange, curious
drome, n.f. main beam
duc, n.m. duke, horned owl
duchesse, n.f. duchess
ductile, adj. ductile
dûment, adv. duly, properly
dune, n.f. dune, sandhill
duo, n.m. duet
duperie, n.f. trickery, dupery, trickery
duplicité, n.f. duplicity
dur, adj. hard, tough, merciless
durabilité, n.f. durability
durable, adj. lasting, durable, solid
durant, prep. during
durcir, vb. to harden
durcissement, n.m. hardening
durée, n.f. duration
durement, adv. hard, harshly
durer, vb. to last, continue
dureté, n.f. hardness, toughness
dynamique, adj. dynamic
dynamite, n.f. dynamite
dynamo, n.f. dynamo

dynastie, n.f. dynasty
dynastique, adj. dynstic
dyslexie, n.f. dyslexia

E

eau, n.f. water
eau-de-vie, n.f. brandy
ébahissement, n.m. amazement
ébarber, vb. to trim, clip
ébauche, n.f. outline, rough draft
ébène, n.m. ebony
éblouir, vb. to dazzle, amaze
ébouriffer, vb. to ruffle
ébranler, vb. to shake
écaille, n.f. scale
écart, n.m. separation
écarté, adj. isolated; lonely
écartement, n.m. gap, separation
écarter, vb. to set aside
échange, n.m. exchange
échangeable, adj. exchangeable
échanger, vb. to exchange
échappement, n.m. exhaust
échapper, vb. to escape
écharde, n.f. splinter
écharpe, n.f. scarf, sling
échasse, n.f. stilt
échauder, vb. to scald
échauffer, vb. to heat up, warm
échéance, n.f. maturity
échecs, n.m., pl. chess
échelle, n.f. ladder, scale
échelon, n.m. step; rung
échine, n.f. spine
écho, n.m. echo
échoir, vb. to fall due, expire
échouer, vb. to fail
éclabousser, vb. to splash
éclair, n.m. flash, lightning
éclairage, n.m. lighting
éclaircie, n.f. clearing
éclaircir, vb. to clear up, clarify
éclairer, vb. to enlighten, light
éclaireur, n.m. boy scout
éclat, n.m. chip, splinter, burst
éclatant, adj. loud; bursting
éclipse, n.f eclipse
éclore, vb. to blossom
écluse, n.f. lock
école, n.f. school, college
écolier, n.m. schoolboy, student
écologie, n.f. ecology
économe, adj. economical, saving
économie, n.f. economy, thrift
économique, adj. economical
économiser, vb. to economize, save

économiste, n.m. economist
écoper, vb. to bail out
écorce, n.f. bark, rind
écorcher, v.t. to skin, to peel
écorchure, n.f. graze, scratch
Écosse, n.f. Scotland
écot, n.m. share
écouter, vb. to hear, listen to
écouteur, n.m. listener, ear phone
écran, n.m. screen
écraser, vb. to crush
écrémer, vb. to skim
écrier, vb. s'é., to exclaim
écrin, n.m. case, casket
écrire, vb. to write; machine à é., typewriter
écrit, adj. written
écriteau, n.m. notice
écriture, n.f. writing
écrou, n.m. nut
écru, adj. natural
écu, n.m. shield
écuelle, n.f. bowl
écume, n.f. lather, foam
écureuil, n.m. squirrel
écurie, n.f. stable
écuyer, n.m. squire
édenté, adj. toothless
édifice, n.m. building
édifier, vb. to build, construct
édit, n.m. edict
éditeur, n.m. publisher
édition, n.f. edition
éditorial, adj. editorial
éducateur, n.m. educator, teacher
éducation, n.f. education
éduquer, vb. to educate, bring up
effacer, vb. to erase, rub out
effectif, adj. actual
effectuer, vb. to effect
efféminé, adj. woman like
effet, n.m. effect
efficace, adj. effective
efficacité, n.f. effectiveness
effigie, n.f. effigy
effleurer, vb. to graze
effondrement, n.m. collapse
efforcer, vb. s'e., to endeavor, try hard
effort, n.m. endeavor, exertion, effort
effrayant, adj. fearful, frightful
effrayer, vb. to frighten, startle
effréné, adj. unrestrained
effroi, n.m. fright, terror
effronté, adj. brazen
effusion, n.f. shedding
égal, adj. even, equal
également, adv. equally
égaler, vb. to equal

égaliser, vb. to equalize
égalité, n.f. evenness
égard, n.m. regard, esteem
égaré, adj. astray
égarer, vb. to mislay, bewilder
égayer, vb. to cheer up
église, n.f. church
égoïste, adj. selfish
égorger, vb. to kill
égout, n.m. sewer, drain
égoutter, v.t. to drain
égratignure, n.f. scratch
Égypte, n.m. Egypt
éhonté, adj. brazen
élaboration, n.f. working out
élaborer, vb. to draft, elaborate
élan, n.m. zest, run
élargir, vb. to widen, increase
élasticité, n.f. elasticity
élastique, adj. and n.m. elastic
électif, adj. elective
élection, n.f. election
électricien, n.m. electrician
électricité, n.f. electricit
élégance, n.f. elegance
élégant, adj. elegant, stylish
élément, n.m. element
élémentaire, adj. elementary
éléphant, n.m. elephant
élevage, n.m. breeding
élévation, n.f. lifting
élève, n.m.f. pupil
élevé, adj. lofty
élever, vb. to raise, lift up
éleveur, n.m. breeder
éligibilité, n.f. eligibility
éligible, adj. eligible
élimination, n.f. elimination
éliminer, vb. to eliminate
élite, n.f. pick, choice
elle, pron. f. she, her; pl., they
elle-même, pron. herself
éloge, n.m. praise
éloigné, adj. remote, distant
éloignement, n.m. distance
éloigner, vb. to remove
élu, adj. chosen
éluder, vb. to elude
emballer, vb. to pack
embarcation, n.f. small craft
embargo, n.m. embargo
embarquer, vb. to embark
embarras, n.m. awkward, difficulty
embarrassant, adj. embarassing
embaumer, vb. to perfume
embellir, vb. to beautify
embêter, vb. to annoy, bore
emblème, n.m. emblem
embolie, n.f. embolism
embouchure, n.f. mouth

embranchement, n.m. junction
embrasser, vb. to embrace, kiss
embrayage, n.m. clutch
embrouillement, n.m. tangle
embrouiller, vb. to entangle, confuse
embrun, n.m. spray
embuscade, n.f. ambush
émeraude, n.f. emerald
émerger, vb. to emerge
émerveiller, vb. to astonish
émettre, vb. to emit, transmit
émeute, n.f. riot, disturbance
émietter, vb. to crumble
émigrant, n.m. emigrant
émigration, n.f. emigration
émigrer, vb. to emigrate
éminemment, adv. in a high degree
éminence, n.f. eminince
éminent, adj. high
émission, n.f. issue, circulation
emmagasiner, vb. to store, warehouse
emmener, vb. to take away
émotif, adj. emotional
émotion, n.f. feeling, emotion
émotionnable, adj. emotional
émotionner, vb. to thrill
émoussé, adj. blunt
émouvant, adj. moving, affecting
émouvoir, vb. to move
empêcher, vb. to stop, hinder
empêtrer, vb. to entangle
emphase, n.f. emphasis
emphatique, adj. emphatic
empléter, vb. to trespass
empire, n.m. empire, nation
emplette, n.f. purchase
emploi, n.m. employment
employé, n.m. employee, clerk
employer, vb. to employ, use
employeur, n.m. employer
empoisonné, adj. poisoned
empoisonner, vb. to poison
emporter, vb. to take away
empreinte, n.f. print, stamp
empressement, n.m. eagerness
emprise, n.f. expropriation
emprisonnement, n.m. imprisonment
emprunt, n.m. loan, borrowing
emprunter, vb. to borrow from
ému, adj. touched, stirred
émule, n.m.f. rival, competitor
encadrer, vb. to frame
en-cas, n.m. reserve
enceinte, adj. f. pregnant
encens, n.m. incense
enchaîner, vb. chain; detain
enchantement, n.m. enchantment

enchanter, vb. to charm, enchant
enchère, n.f. bid
enclore, vb. to fence in, enclose
enclume, n.f. anvil
encoche, n.f. notch
encoller, vb. to paste, glue
encombrant, adj. cumbersome
encombrement, n.m. congestion
encombrer, vb. to clutter, jam
encore, adv. still, yet, again
encourageant, adj. encouraging
encouragement, n.m. encouragement
encourager, vb. to urge, promote
encourir, vb. to incur
encre, n.f. ink
encyclopédie, n.f. encyclopedia
endolorir, vb. to make painful, tender
endommager, vb. to damage, injure
endormi, adj. asleep
endossement, n.m. endorsement
endroit, n.m. place
enduire, vb. to smear, daub
endurance, n.f. endurance
endurant, adj. patient
endurcir, vb. to harden, toughen
endurcissement, n.m. hardening
énergie, n.f. energy
énergique, adj. energetic
énervé, adj. nervous
enfant, n.m.f. child, baby
enfantement, n.m. childbirth
enfanter, vb. to give birth to
enfantillage, n.m. childishness
enfantin, adj. childdish
enfariner, vb. to coat with flour
enfermer, vb. to shut in
enfiévrer, vb. to excite, inspire
enfin, adv. finally, at last
enflammer, vb. to inflame
enfler, vb. to swell, puff up
enflure, n.f. swelling
enfoncer, vb. to sink, push in
enfouir, vb. to bury
enfreindre, vb. to violate
enfumer, vb. to fill with smoke
engageant, adj. charming
engagement, n.m. pledge, engagement
engager, vb. to engage
engendrer, vb. to beget
engin, n.m. engine, motor
englober, vb. to include, unite
engloutir, vb. to devour, swallow
engorgement, n.m. choking
engouement, n.m. congestion
engouffrer, vb. to engulf
engourdir, vb. to dull

engrais, n.m. fertilizer, manure
engraisser, vb. to fatten
engrenage, n.m. gear
enhardir, vb. to make bolder
énigme, n.f. riddle
enivrant, adj. intoxicating
enivrement, n.m. intoxication
enivrer, vb. to intoxicate. s'e., get drunk
enjambé, n.f. stride
enjeu, n.m. stake
enjoindre, vb. to enjoin; call upon
enjoliver, vb. to beautify
enjoué, adj. playful
enjouement, n.m. playfulness
enlacer, vb. to entwine; embrace
enlèvement, n.m. removal, abduction
enlever, vb. to abduct, take away
enneigé, adj. snow-covered
ennemi, adj. and n.m. enemy
ennoblir, vb. to exalt; ennoble
ennui, n.m. nuisance, bother
ennuyer, vb. to bore, annoy
ennuyeux, adj. boring, dull
énoncer, vb. to express, state
énonciation, n.f. enunciation
énorme, adj. enormous
énormité, n.f. enormity
enquérir, vb. to inquire
enquête, n.f. inquiry
enraciner, vb. to root
enragé, adj. rabid, mad
enrageant, adj. maddening
enregistrement, n.m. registration
enregistrer, vb. to record, list
enrichir, vb. to enrich
enrober, vb. to coat, envelop
enrôlement, n.m. enlistment
enrôler, vb. to enlist, enroll
enroué, adj. hoarse, husky
enrouement, n.m. hoarseness
enseigne, n.f. sign, ensign
enseignement, n.m. teaching
enseigner, vb. to teach
ensemble, n.m. set, whole, mass
ensevelir, vb. to bury, swallow up
ensoleillé, adj. sunny
ensommeillé, adj. sleepy
ensuite, adv. then; next
ensuivre, vb. to s'e., to ensue
entacher, vb. to taint, besmirch
entamer, vb. to begin
entendement, n.m. understanding
entendre, vb. to hear, understand
entendu, adj. understood, agreed
enténébré, adj. gloomy
entente, n.f. understanding
entêté, adj. perverse
entêtement, n.m. stubbornness

entêter, vb. s'e., to insist
enthousiasme, n.m. enthusiasm
enthousiaste, n.m.f. enthusiast
entichement, n.m. infatuation
entier, adj. whole, entire
entonnoir, n.m. funnel
entorse, n.f. sprain
entourage, n.m. circle of friends, acquaintances
entourer, vb. to surround
entournure, n.f. armhole
entrain, n.m. zest
entraîner, vb. to draw, along, entail
entraîneur, n.m. coach, trainer
entrant, adj. incoming
entraver, vb. to clog, shackle
entre, prep. among, between
entre-clos, adj. ajar
entre-deux, n.m. interval
entrée, n.f. admission, entry
entregent, n.m. tact; spirit
entrelacer, vb. to interlace
entremetteur, n.m. intermediary
entreposer, vb. to store, warehouse
entrepôt, n.m. warehouse
entreprenant, adj. enterprising
entreprendre, vb. to undertake
entrepreneur, n.m. contractor
entreprise, n.f. undertaking
entrer, vb. to enter, come in, go in
entretenir, vb. to entertain
entretien, n.m. maintenance
entrevoir, vb. to glimpse
énumérer, vb. to enumerate, count
envahir, vb. to invade
envahissement, n.m. invasion
enveloppe, n.f. envelop, wrapper
envers, n.m. wrong side
enviable, adj. enviable
envie, n.f. desire, envy
envier, vb. to envy
envieux, adj. envious, jealous
environ, prep. and adv. about
environner, vb. to surround
envisager, vb. to consider, look at
envol, n.m. shipment, parcel
envoler, vb. s'envoler, to fly away
envoyé, n.m. envoy
envoyer, v.t. to send, to forward
enzyme, n.f. enzyme
épais, adj. thick, dense
épaisseur, n.f. thickness
épaissir, vb. to thicken
épancher, v.t. to pour out
épanouir, vb. to cause to bloom
épargne, n.f. savings, economy
épargner, vb. to save, spare
éparpiller, vb. to scatter
épars, adj. scattered, sparse

épatement, n.m. amazement

épater, vb. to amaze

épaule, n.f. shoulder

épée, n.f. sword

épeler, vb. to spell

épellation, n.f. spelling

éperdu, adj. distracted, aghast

éperlan, n.m. smelt

éperon, n.m. spur

épervier, n.m. hawk

épeuré, adj. frightened, scared

épice, n.f. spice

épicé, adj. spicy

épicerie, n.f. grocery

épicier, n.m. grocer

épidémie, n.f. epidemic

épilepsie, n.f. epilepsy

épilogue, n.m. epilogue

épinards, n.m., pl. spinach

épine, n.f. spine, thorn

épinet, n.f. spinet

épineux, adj. thorny

épiscopal, adj. Episcopal

épisode, n.m. episode

épitaphe, n.f. epitaph

épitomé, n.m. abridgment

épître, n.f. epistle

éplore, adj. tearful

épointé, adj. dull, blunted

éponge, n.f. sponge

épopee, n.f. epic

épouse, n.f. wife, spouse

épouser, vb. to marry

épouvantable, adj. terrible

épouvante, n.f. fright

époux, n.m. husband, spouce

étreindre, vb. to squeeze

éprendre, vb. s'é., to fall in love

épreuve, n.f. trial, test, proof

éprouver, vb. to experience

éprouvette, n.f. test tube

épulser, vb. to exhaust

épuration, n.f. purification

épurer, vb. to purify, clarify

équateur, n.m. equator

équation, n.f. equation

équestre, adj. equestrian

équilibre, n.m. poise, balance

équipage, n.m. crew

équipe, n.f. crew, gang, shift

équipement, n.m. equipment

équiper, vb. to equip

équitable, adj. fair, just

équité, n.f. equity, fairness

équivalent, adj. and n.m. equivalent

équivaloir, vb. to equal in value

équivoque, adj. uncertain

érable, n.m. maple

éraflure, n.m. scratch; graze

érailler, vb. to unravel

ère, n.f. era

érection, n.f. construction

éreintant, adj. exhausting

éreinter, vb. to exhaust

ériger, vb. to erect, raise

éroder, vb. to erode

érosif, adj. erosive

érosion, n.f. erosion

érotique, adj. erotic

errant, adj. wandering

erratique, adj. erratic

errer, vb. to wander; err

erreur, n.f. mistake, error

erroné, adj. erroneous

éructation, n.f. belch

érudit, adj. learned, scholarly

éruption, n.f. rash, eruption

escabeau, n.m. step stool

escalader, vb. to scale; escalate

escalier, n.m. stairs, staircase

escalope, n.f. cutlet

escapade, n.f. prank

escarcelle, n.f. wallet

escargot, n.m. snail

escarole, n.f. endive

escarpé, adj. abrupt

escarre, n.f. scab

esclavage, n.m. slavery

esclave, n.m.f. slave

escompte, n.m. discount

escorte, n.f. escort

escouade, n.f. squad

escrime, n.f. fencing

escrimer, vb. to fight

escroc, n.m. swindler

escroquer, vb. to swindle

comestible, adj. edible

espace, n.m. space, room

espacé, adj. far apart

espacer, vb. to space out

espadon, n.m. swordfish

Espagne, n.f. Spain

espèce, n.f. species, kind

espérance, n.f. hope

espérer, v.t. to hope

espiègle, adj. mischievous

espièglerie, n.f. mischief

espion, n.m. spy

espionnage, n.m. spying

espionner, vb. to spy on

esplanade, n.f. parade

espoir, n.m. hope

esprit, n.m. spirit, mind, wit

esquimau, adj. Eskimo

esquinter, vb. to exhaust, tireout

esquisse, n.f. sketch

esquiver, vb. to avoid

essai, n.m. testing, attempt

essaim, n.m. swarm

essayer, vb. to try; assay

essence, n.f. gasoline; essence
essentiel, adj. essential
solitude, n.m. solitude
essieu, n.m. axle
essor, n.m. flight
essorer, vb. to dry, wring out
essuie-glace, n.m. windshield wiper
essuyer, vb. to wipe
estacade, n.f. stockade
estafette, n.m. courier
estagnon, n.m. oil drum
estaminet, n.m. bar, tavern
estampe, n.f. engraving, print
estampille, n.f. trademark, mark
estimable, adj. estimable
estimateur, n.m. appraiser
estimatif, adj. estimated
estimation, n.f. estimate
estime, n.f. esteem; estimation
estimer, vb. to value, rate
estivant, n.m. summer tourist
estiver, v.t. to spend the summer
estoc, n.m. tree trunk
estomac, n.m. stomach
estourbir, vb. to kill
estrade, n.f. platform; stage
estropié, n.m. cripple
esturgeon, n.m. surgeon
et, conj and
étable, n.f. barn
établi, n.m. worktable
établir, vb. to settle, establish
établissement, n.m. establishment
étage, n.m. floor, story
étagère, n.f. whatnot shelf
étain, n.m. tin; pewter
étal, n.m. butcher shop
étalage, n.m. display
étaler, vb. to display, spread
étalon, n.m. stallion
étampe, n.f. stamp; die; punch
étanche, adj. water tight
étancher, vb. to stop
étang, n.m. pond, pool
étape, n.m. stage, station
États-Unis, n.m., pl. United States
été, n.m. summer
éteindre, vb. to extinguish
éteint, adj. extinct
étendage, n.m. clotheslines
étendard, n.m. standard
étendre, vb. to spread, reach,
  expand
étendu, adj. extensive, wide
étendue, n.f. extent, reach
éternel, adj. everlasting
éterniser, vb. to perpetuate
éternuement, n.m. sneeze
éternuer, vb. to sneeze
éthéré, adj. ethereal

Éthiopie, n.f. Ethiopia
éthique, n.f. ethics
étinceler, vb. to sparkle
étincelle, n.f. spark, sparkle
étiqueter, vb. to label
étiquette, n.f. tag; etiquette
étirer, vb. to stretch out
étoffe, n.f. material, cloth
étoffer, vb. to stuff
étoile, n.f. star
étonnement, n.m. astonishment
étonner, vb. to astonish
étouffer, vb. to smother
étourdir, vb. to daze, stun
étourdissement, n.m. dizziness
étrange, adj. strange
étranger, n. and adj. alien
étrangler, vb. to strangle
étrave, n.f. stem, bow
étrécir, vb. to shrink
étreindre, vb. to clasp
étreinte, n.f. hug, embrace
étrier, n.m. stirrup
étroit, adj. narrow
étude, n.f. study
étudiant, n.m. student
étudier, vb. to study
étuve, n.f. steam room
eucalyptus, n.m. eucalyptus
Europe, n.f. Europe
eux, pron. m. them
évacuation, n.f. evacuation
évacuer, vb. to evacuate
évader, vb. s'e., to escape
évaluateur, n.m. appraiser
évaluation, n.f. appraisal
évangéliste, n.m. evangelist
évangile, n.m. gospel
évanouir, vb. s'e., to faint
évaporation, n.f. evaporation
évaporer, vb. to evaporate
évasif, adj. evasive
évasion, n.f. escape
éveil, n.m. alertness
éveillé, adj. sprightly
éveilleur, n.m. awakener
événement, n.m. event
éventail, n.m. fan
éventrer, vb. to disembowel
éventualité, n.f. eventually
éventuel, adj. possible
éventuellement, adv. possibly
évêque, n.m. bishop
évidemment, n.m. scooping out
évident, adj. obvious
évider, vb. to scoop out
évier, n.m. sink
évincer, vb. to eject
évitable, adj. avoidable
éviter, vb. to avoid

évocation, n.f. raising up	**exiger,** vb. to require, demand
évoquer, vb. to evoke	**exil,** n.m. exile
exactitude, n.f. precision	**exilé,** adj. exiled
exagération, n.f. exaggeration	**exiler,** vb. to banish
exagérér, adj. excessive	**existant,** adj. existent
exaltant, adj. exciting	**existence,** n.f. existence
exaltation, n.f. exaltation	**exister,** vb. to exist
exalter, vb. to exalt	**exode,** n.m. exodus
examiner, vb. to examine	**exorbitant,** adj. exorbitant
exaspérer, vb. to aggravate	**exorciser,** vb. to exorcize
excavation, n.f. excavation	**exotique,** adj. exotic; foreign
excaver, vb. to excavate	**expansif,** adj. expansive
excédent, n.m. excess	**expansion,** n.f. expansion
excéder, vb. to exceed	**expatrier,** v.t. to exile
excellence, n.f. excellence	**expédier,** vb. to disptach
excellent, adj. excellent	**expédition,** n.f. expedition,
exceller, vb. to excel	shipment
excentrique, adj. eccentric	**expérience,** n.f. experence
excepté, prep. except	**expérimental,** adj. experimental
exception, n.f. exception	**expérimentation,** n.f.
exceptionnel, adj. exceptional	experimentation
excès, n.m. excess	**expérimenté,** adj. experienced
excessif, adj. extreme	**expert,** adj. and n.m. expert
exciser, vb. to excise, cut out	**expiration,** n.f. expiration
excitable, adj. excitable	**expirer,** v.t. to breathe out
excitant, adj. exciting	**explicite,** adj. clear
exciter, vb. to excite	**expliquer,** vb. to explain
exclamatif, adj. exclamative	**exploit,** n.m. feat, exploit
exclamation, n.f. exclamation	**explorateur,** n.m. explorer
exclamer, vb. to exclaim	**exploratoire,** adj. exploratory
exclure, vb. to exclude	**exploration,** n.f. exploration
exclusif, adj. exclusive	**explorer,** vb. to explore
exclusion, n.f. exclusion	**explosible,** adj. explosive
excorier, vb. to excoriate	**explosif,** adj. and n.m. explosive
excréter, vb. to excrete	**explosion,** n.f. blast, explosion
excrétion, n.f. excretion	**exportation,** n.f. exportation
excuse, n.f. plea	**exporter,** vb. to export
excuser, vb. to excuse, pardon	**exposé,** n.m. account, statement
exécuter, vb. to enforce	**exposer,** vb. to expound, expose
exécuteur, n.m. executor	**exposition,** n.f. exposition,
exécutif, adj. and n.m. executive	exposure, show, display
exécution, n.f. enforcement	**exprès,** n.m. special delivery
exemplaire, n.m. copy	**expressif,** adj. expressive
exemple, n.m. example	**expression,** n.f. expression
exempt, adj. exempt	**exprimable,** adj. expressible
exempt de droits, adj. duty free	**exprimer,** vb. to express
exempter, vb. to exempt	**expulser,** vb. to expel
exemption, n.f. exemption	**expulsion,** n.f. expulsion
exerçant, adj. practicing	**exquis,** adj. exquisite
exercer, vb. to exercise, drill	**exsuder,** vb. to exude
exercise, n.m. practice, drill	**extase,** n.f. ecstasy
exhalation, n.f. exhalation	**extatique,** adj. ecstatic
exhaler, vb. to exhale	**extensif,** adj. extensive
exhaussions, n.f. exhaust	**extension,** n.f. extension
exhiber, vb. to present; exhibit	**extérieurement,** adv. externally
exhibition, n.f. exhibition	**exterminer,** vb. to exterminate
exhortation, n.f. exhortation	**externe,** adj. external
exhorter, vb. tc encourage	**extincteur,** n.m. fire extinguisher
exhumer, vb. to exhume	**extorsion,** n.f. extortion
exigence, n.f. unreasonable	**extraction,** n.m. descent

extraire, vb. to extract
extrait, n.m. abstract
extraordinaire, adj. extraordinary
extravagant, adj. extravagant
extrême, adj. and n.m. extreme
extrémiste, n.m. extremist
exultation, n.f. exultation
exulter, vb. to exult

F

fable, n.f. fable
fabliau, n.m. fabliau
fabricant, n.m. manufacturer
fabricateur, n.m. forger
fabrication, n.f. make
fabrique, n.f. factory
fabriquer, vb. to manufacture
fabuleux, adj. fabulous
fabuliste, n.m. fabulist
facette, n.f. facet
fâcher, vb. to anger, offend
fâcherie, n.f. disagreement
fâcheux, adj. troublesome
facial, adj. facial
facile, adj. easy
facilité, n.f. readiness
façon, n.f. manner, way
façonner, vb. to shape, fashion
fac-similé, n.m. facsimile
facteur, n.m. factor, element
factice, adj. artificial
factieux, adj. quarrelsome
faction, n.f. faction, party
factionnaire, n.m. sentry
facture, n.f. invoice, bill
facturer, vb. to bill
faculté, n.f. faculty
fadaise, n.f. nonsense
fade, adj. insipid
fagot, n.m. bundle
faible, adj. weak, faint, feeble
faiblement, adv. weakly
faiblir, vb. to weaken
faillite, bankrupt.
faim, n.f. hunger
fainéant, n.m. loafer
faire, vb. to make do
faisan, n.m. pheasant
falloir, vb. to be necessary
falsificateur, n. forger m.
falsifier, vb. to falsify
fameux, adj. famous
familiariser, vb. to familiarize
familiarité, n.f. familiarity
familier, adj. familiar
familièrement, adv. familiarly
famille, n.f. household

famine, n.f. famine
fanatique, adj. and n.m. fanatic
fanatisme, n.m. fanaticism
faner, vb. to fade
fanfare, n.f. fanfare
fanfaronnade, n.f. boast
fange, n.f. filth; vice
fantaisie, n.f. fancy, fantasy
fantasque, adj. fantastic
fantoche, n.m. puppet
fantôme, n.m. phantom, ghost
faon, n.m. fawn
farce, n.f. stuffing; farce
farcir, vb. to stuff
fard, n.m. makeup for the face
fardeau, n.m. burden
farinacé, adj. farinaceous
farine, n.f. meal, flour
farniente, n.m. idleness
farouche, adj. sullen
fascinant, adj. fascinating
fascination, n.f. fascination
fastidieux, adj. dull
fatal, adj. mortal, fatal
fatalisme, n.m. fatalism
fataliste, n.m.f. fatalist
fatiguer, v.t. to tire
fatuité, n.f. smugness
faubourg, n.m. suburb
faubourien, adj. suburban
faucher, vb. to mow
faucheur, n.m. mower
faucille, n.f. sickle
faucon, n.m. hawk
fauconneau, n.m. young hawk
fauconnerie, n.f. falconry
faufil, n.m. basting
faufiler, vb. to baste
faune, n.f. wildlife
faussaire, n. forger; liar
faussement, adv. falsely
fausser, vb. to warp, distort
fausset, n.m. spigot, faucet
fausseté, n.f. falseness
faute, n.f. fault, mistake
fauteuil, n.m. armchair
fautif, adv. wrong
fauve, adj. wild beast
faux, n.m. falsehood; adj. false
faux-filet, n.m. sirloin
favorable, adj. favorable
favorablement, adv. favorably
favori, n.m. whisker
favoriser, vb. to favor
favoritisme, n.m. favoritism
féal, adj. faithful
fécond, adj. fertile
féconder, vb. to fertilize
fécondité, n.f. fertility
féculent, adj. starchy

fédéral, adj. federal
fédération, n.f. confederacy
fédérer, vb. to federate
fée, n.f. fairy
féerie, n.f. fairyland
féerique, adj. fairylike
feindre, vb. to feign, pretend
fêle, vb. to crack
félicitation, n.f. congratulation
félicité, n.f. bliss, happiness
féliciter (de), vb. to congratulate
félin, adj. feline
félon, adj. disloyal
femelle, adj. and n.f. female
féminin, adj. female, feminine
femme, n.f. woman, wife
fendille, n.f. crack
fendoir, n.m. cleaver
fendre, vb. to split, rip
fenêtre, n.f. window
fenil, n.m. hayloft
fente, n.f. crack, rip, split
féodalité, n.f. feudalism
fer, n.m. iron
fermail, n.m. clasp
ferme, n.f. farm
ferme, adj. steady, fast
fermeté, n.f. firmness
fermier, n.m. farmer
féroce, adj. fierce
férocité, n.f. fierceness
fertile, adj. fertile
fertilisant, adj. fertilizable
fertilisation, n.f. fertilization
fertiliser, vb. to fertilize
fertilité, n.f. fertility
férule, n.f. cane, rod
fervemment, adv. fervently
fervent, adj. fervent
ferveur, n.f. fervor
fesse, n.f. buttock
fessée, n.f. spanking
fesser, vb. to spank
festin, n.m. feast
feston, n.m. feston
fête, n.f. party, feast
fétiche, n.m. fetish
feuillage, n.m. foilage
feuille, n.f. sheet, foil
feutre, n.m. felt
fève, n.f bean
février, n.m. February
fiacre, n.m. cab
fiançailles, n.f., pl. engagement
fiancé, n.m. fiancé
fiancer, vb. to betroth
fiasco, n.m. fiasco
fibre, n.f. fiber
ficelle, n.f. string, twine
fiche, n.f. piece of paper

fichu, adv. ruined
fictif, adj. fictitious
fiction, n.f. fiction
fidèle, adj. faithful
fief, n.m. feud
fiel, n.m. gall
fiente, n.f. dung
fier, vb. se f., to trust
fièvre, n.f. fever
figue, n.f. fig
figuratif, adj. figurative
figure, n.f. face, figure
fil, n.m. thread, string
filament, n.m. filament
file, n.f. file
filet, n.m. net
filin, n.m. rope
fille, n.f. daughter
film, n.m. film
filou, n.m. thief
fils, n.m. son
filtration, n.f. filtrtion
filtre, n.m. filter
filtrer, vb. to filter
fin, n.f. end; adj. fine; sharp
final, adj. final
finalité, n.f. finality
finance, n.f. finance
financer, vb. to finance
finir, vb. to finish
Finlande, n.f. Finland
Finnois, n.m. Finn
firmament, n.m. firmament
firme, n.f. company
fiscal, adj. fiscal
fixer, vb. to fix, secure, settle
fixité, n.f. fixity
flacon, n.m. bottle
flageller, vb. to flog
flagrant, adj. flagrant
flair, n.m. flair
flairer, vb. to smell
flambant, adj. flaming
flambeau, n.m. torch
flambée, n.f. blaze
flamber, vb. to blaze
flamboyant, adj. flamboyant
flamboyer, vb. to flare
flamme, n.f. flame
flanc, n.m. side, flank
flaque, n.f. puddle
flasque, adj. flabby
flatter, vb. to flatter
flatterie, n.f. flattery
flatteur, n.m. flatterer
fléau, n.m. scourge, plague
flèche, n.f. arrow
fléchir, vb. to bend
flétrir, vb. to wilt, wither
fleur, n.f. flower, blossom

fleuret, n.m. foil
fleuri, adj. flowery
fleurir, vb. to flower, blossom
fleuriste, n.m. florist
fleuve, n.m. river
flexibilité, n.f. flexibility
flexible, adj. flexible
flirt, n.m. flirtation
flirter, vb. to flirt
flocon, n.m. flake
flot, n.m. wave. à flot, afloat
flottant, adj. floating
flotte, n.f. fleet
flottement, n.m. wavering
flotteur, n.m. fishing boat
flou, adj. hazy, indistinct
fluctuation, n.f. fluctuation
fluide, adj. and n.m. fluid
flûte, n.f. flute
flûté, adj. soft; flute-like
flux, n.m. flow, flux
fluxion, n.f. inflammation
foi, n.f. faith; trust
foie, n.m. liver
foin, n.m. hay
foire, n.f. fair
fois, n.f. time
foison, n.f. abundance, plenty
foisonner, vb. to abound
folâtre, adj. frisky
folâtrer, vb. to frolic
folichon, adj. playful
folie, n.f. madness, folly
folklore, n.m. folklore
follement, adv. foolishly
follet, adj. merry, playful
foncé, adj. dark
fonction, n.f. function
fonctionnaire, n.m. official, civil
  servant
fonctionner, vb. to function, work
fond, n.m. bottom, ground
fondamental, adj. basic,
  fundamental
fondateur, n.m. founder
fondation, n.f. foundation,
  establishment
fondé, adj. authentic
fondement, n.m. foundation
fonder, vb. to find, establish
fonderie, n.f. foundry
fondre, vb. to melt, fuse
fondrière, n.f. bog
fonds, n.m. fund
fongus, n.m. fungus
fontaine, n.f. fountain
fonte, n.f. melting
fonts, n.m.,pl. font
football, n.m. football
footing, n.m. walking

forain, n.m. peddler
forcément, adv. of necessity
forcené, adj. frantic
forcir, vb. to thrive
forer, vb. to bore, drill
forestier, n.m. forest ranger
foret, n.m. drill
forêt, n.f. forest
foreuse, n.f. machine drill
forfait, n.m. forfeit; contract
forfanterie, n.f. bragging
forge, n.f. forge
forgeron, n.m. blacksmith
forgeur, n.m. forger; inventor
formaliser, vb. to offend
formaliste, adj. formal; precise
formalité, n.f. ceremony
formation, n.f. formation
forme, n.f. shape, form
formel, adj. formal
former, vb. to form shape
formidable, adj. formidable
formule, n.f. formula, form
formuler, vb. to formulate, draw up
fort, n.m. fort; adj. strong
forteresse, n.f. fortress
fortifiant, adj. strengthening
fortification, n.f. fortification
fortifier, vb. to strengthen
fortuit, adj. accidental
fortune, n.f. fortune
fortuné, adj. luck, fortunate
fosse, n.f. pit
fossé, n.m. ditch; dike
fossette, n.f. dimple
fossile, n.m. fossil
foudroyant, adj. terrifying
foudroyer, vb. to crush, blast
fouet, n.m. whip lash
fougère, n.f. fern
fougue, n.f. dash
fougueux, adj. impetuous, hot
fouille, n.f. excavation
fouiller, vb. to ransack
fouillis, n.m. litter, mess
fouir, vb. to dig, burrow
foulard, n.m. scarf
foule, n.f. crowd, mob
fouler, vb. to trample
foulure, n.f. sprain, wrench
four, n.m. oven
fourbir, vb. to polish, furbish
fourche, n.f. fork
fourgon, n.m. wagon
fourmi, n.f. ant
fourmillement, n.m. swarming
fourmiller, vb. to mill
fourneau, n.m. stove, furnace
fournée, n.f. batch
fourniment, n.m. equipment

fournir, vb. to furnish
fournisseur, n.m. tradesman
fourrage, n.m. fodder, forage
fourrager, vb. to forage
fourreau, n.m. sheath
fourrer, vb. to thrust in
fourreur, n.m. furrier
fourrure, n.f. fur
fourvoyer, vb. to mislead
foyer, n.m. focus, hearth
frac, n.m. dress coat
fracas, n.m. noise, bustle
fraction, n.f. fraction
fracture, n.f. fracture
fracturer, vb. to break, fracture
fragile, adj. brittle, delicate, frail, fragile
fragilité, n.f. fragility
fragment, n.m. fragment
fragmenter, vb. to divide up
fraîcheur, n.f. freshness
frais, n.m., pl. expenses, cost
fraise, n.f. strawberry; ruffle
framboise, n.f. rasberry
Francais, n.m. Frenchman
français, adj. and n.m. French
Française, n.m. Frenchwoman
France, n.f. France
franchement, adv. frankly
franchir, vb. to clear, cross
franchise, n.f. frankness
franc-parler, n.m. frankness
franc-tireur, n.m. sniper; freelancer
frange, n.f. fringe
frapper, vb. to strike, hit
frasque, n.f. prank
fraternel, adj. brotherly
fraternité, n.f. brotherhood
fraude, n.f. fraud
frauder, vb. to defraud
fraudeur, n.m. smuggler
frauduleux, adj. fraudulent
frayer, vb. to open up
frayeur, n.f. fright
fredaine, n.f. prank
frein, n.m. brake, check
freiner, vb. to brake, restrain
frelater, vb. to adulterate
frêle, adj. frail
frelon, n.m. hornet
frémir, vb. to tremble, quiver
frémissement, n.m. thrill
frêne, n.m. ash tree
frénésie, n.f. frenzy
frénétique, adj. frantic
fréquemment, adv. often
fréquence, n.f. frequency
fréquent, adj. frequent
frère, n.m. brother
fret, n.m. freight

frétillant, adj. lively
frétiller, vb. to quiver
fretin, n.m. young fish
frette, n.f. iron hoop
friand, adj. dainty; fond of
fricoter, vb. to cook, stew
friction, n.f. friction
frictionner, vb. to chafe
frigo, n.m. frozen meat
frigorifier, vb. to refrigerate
frileux, adj. chilly
frime, n.f. pretense, sham
fringant, adj. lively, frisky
friper, vb. to crush, rumple
fripier, n.m. second-hand
fripouille, n.f. rascal
frire, vb. to fry
friser, vb. to curl
frisoir, n.m. hair curler
frisson, n.m. shudder, shiver
frissonner, vb. to shudder, shiver
frites, n.f., pl. potato chips
friture, n.f. frying
frivole, adj. frivolous
frivolité, n.f. frivolity
froc, n.m. (monk_) frock
froid, n.m. cold, coldness
froideur, n.f. coldness
froissement, n.m. crumpling
froisser, v.t. to crumble
frôler, vb. to graze
fromage, n.m. cheese
froment, n.m. wheat
froncement, n.m. puckering, contraction
froncer, vb. to pucker
frondaison, n.f. foilage
fronde, n.f. sling
frondeur, n.m. slinger; censurer
front, n.m. forehead
frontière, n.f. boundary, border, frontier
frottement, n.m. rubbing
frotteur, n.m. rubber
fructueux, adj. fruitful
frugal, adj. frugal
frugalité, n.f. frugality
fruit, n.m. fruit
fugace, adj. fleeting
fugitif, adj. fugitive
fuir, vb. to flee; shun; leak
fuite, n.f. escape, flight; leak
fumée, adj. smoked
fumer, vb. to smoke
fumeux, adj. smoky
fumier, n.m. dung, manure
funérailles, n.f., pl. funeral
funeste, adj. disastrous, fatal
fureur, n.f. fury, rage
furieux, adj. furious

furtif, adj. sly
fuseau, n.m. spindle
fusée, n.f. rocket
fuser, vb. to melt, spread
fusil, n.m. rifle
fusion, n.f. merger
futé, adj. cunning, crafty
futile, adj. futile
futur, n.m. and adj. future
futurologie, n.f. futurology
fuyant, adj. passing, fugitive
fuyard, n.m. fugitive

G

gâchette, n.f. tumbler
gâcheux, adj. sloppy
gage, n.m. pledge, wage
gageure, n.f. bet, wager
gagnage, n.m. pastureland
gagnant, n.m. winner
gagner, vb. gain, win
gai, adj. cheeful, merry
galeté, n.f. mirth, cheer, merriment
gaillard, adj. hearty, sound
gain, n.m. gain, profit
gaine, n.f. girdle
galant, n.m. beau; adj. gallant
galanterie, n.f. compliment
galbe, n.m. outline, contour
galère, n.f. galley
galerie, n.f. gallery
galet, n.m. boulder
gallon, n.m. gallon
galon, n.m. braid
galop, n.m. gallop
gambader, vb. frolic, skip
gamin, n.m. urchin, youngster
gamme, n.f. scale
gant, n.m. glove
garage, n.m. garage
garagiste, n.m. garage keeper
garant, n.m. sponsor
garantie, n.f. pledge
garantir, vb. guarantee, pledge
garçon, n.m. boy; waiter; bachelor
garde, n.f. watch, guard
garde-boue, n.m. fender
garde-manger, n.m. pantry
garder, vb. guard, keep
gardeur, n.m. keeper
gardien, n.m. guard, watchman
garer, vb. garage, park
gargarisme, n.m. gargle
garni, adj. garnished
garnir, vb. trim, garnish
garniture, n.f. furniture
gars, n.m. chap

gaspillage, n.m. waste
gaspiller, vb. squander, waste
gâteau, n.m. cake
gâter, vb. to spoil
gâterie, n.f. excessive indulgence
gâteux, adj. senile
gaucherie, n.f. clumsiness
gaufre, n.f. waffle
gaule, n.f. pole, switch
gausser, vb. se g. de, to mock
gaz, n.m. gas
gaze, n.f. gauze
gazeux, adj. gaseous
gazon, n.m. turf, lawn
géant, n.m. giant
geindre, vb. whine
gelé, adj. frozen
gelée, n.f. jelly, frost
geler, vb. to freeze
gémir, vb. to wail, moan
gémissement, n.m. groan, moan
gênant, adj. troublesome
gencive, n.f. gum
gendarme, n.m. policeman
gendarmerie, n.f. police force
gendre, n.m. son-in-law
gêne, n.f. uneasiness
gêné, adj. uneasy, embarrassed
généalogie, n.f. pedigree
gêner, vb. to hinder, bother
général, n.m. and adj. general
généraliser, vb. to generalize
généralité, n.f. generality
génération, n.f. generation
généreusement, adv. generously
généreux, adj. generous, liberal
générosité, n.f. generosity
génie, n.m. genius
genièvre, n.m. gin
genou, n.m. knee
genre, n.m. gender
gens, n.m.f., pl. persons, folk
gentilhomme, n.m. nobleman
gentillesse, n.f. gracefulness
géographie, n.f. geography
géographique, adj. geographical
géométrie, n.f. geometry
géométrique, adj. geometrical
gérant, n.m. manager, director
gerçure, n.f. chap
gérer, vb. to manage
germe, n.f. germ
germer, vb. to sprout
gésir, vb. to lie
geste, n.m. gesture
gestion, n.f. management
gibier, n.m. game
giboulée, n.f. hailstorm
gicler, vb. to spurt
gifler, vb. to slap

gigantesque, adj. great, huge
gigue, n.f. jig
gingembre, n.m. ginger
giron, n.m. lap
gitane, n.m.f. gypsy
givre, n.m. frost
glaçage, n.m. frosting
glace, n.f. ice, ice cream
glacer, vb. to freeze
glacial, adj. icy
glacier, n.m. glacier
glacière, n.f. icebox
glacis, n.m. slope
glaise, n.f. clay
gland, n.m. acorn
glande, n.f. gland
glaner, vb. to glean
glapir, vb. to screech
glas, n.m. knell
glissade, n.f. slip
glissant, adj. slippery
glisser, vb. to slide, slip
global, n.m. globe
gloire, n.f. glory
glorieux, adj. glorious
glorifier, vb. to glorify
glose, n.f. criticism; gloss
glossaire, n.m. glossary
glousser, vb. to cluck
gluant, adj. sticky
gobelet, n.m. goblet
gober, vb. to swallow
goéland, n.m. seagull
golfe, n.m. gulf
gomme, n.f. gum; eraser
gommeux, adj. gummy
gond, n.m. hinge
gonfler, vb. to inflate; swell
gonfleur, n.m. tire, pump
gorge, n.f. throat; gorge
gorger, vb. to cram, stuff
gosier, n.m. throat
gothique, adj. Gothic
goudron, n.m. tar
gouffre, n.m. gulf, abyss
goulu, adj. gluttonous
gourde, n.f. flask, bottle
gourmand, n.m. glutton; adj. greedy
gourmander, vb. to scold
gourmandise, n.f. greediness
gourmer, vb. to curb
gousse, n.f. pod, shell
goût, n.m. taste, relish
goûter, n.m. snack; vb. taste
goutte, n.f. drop; gout
goutteux, adj. gouty
gouttière, n.f. gutter
gouvernail, n.m. rudder, helm
gouvernement, n.m. government

gouverner, vb. to rule, govern
grabuge, n.m. squabble
grâce, n.f. grace
gracier, vb. to pardon
gracieux, adj. graceful, gracious
grade, n.m. grade, rank
gradin n.m. tier, step
graduel, adj. gradual
graduer, vb. to graduate
grain, n.m. grain, berry
graine, n.f. berry, seed
graissage, n.m. greasing
graisse, n.f. grease, fate
graisser, vb. to grease
grammaire, n.f. grammar
gramme, n.m. gram
grand, adj. great, tall
grandement, adv. grandly, greatly
grandeur, n.f. height, size
grandiose, adj. grand
grandir, vb. to grow
grand-mère, n.f. grandmother
grand-père, n.m. grandfather
grange, n.f. barn
granit, n.m. granite
graphique, n.m. chart
grappe, n.f. bunch, cluster
gras, adj. stout, fat
grassement, adj. plentifully
grasset, adj. plump
grassouillet, adj. plump
gratification, n.f. bonus
gratifier, vb. to bestow
gratitude, n.f. gratitude
gratte-ciel, n.m. skyscraper
gratter, vb. to scrape, scratch
gratuit, adj. free
grave, adj. grave
graveleux, adj. gritty
graver, vb. to engrave
graveur, n.m. engraver
gravier, n.m. gravel
gravir, vb. to climb
gravité, n.f. gravity
graviter, vb. to gravitate
gravure, n.f. engraving
gré, n.m. pleasure
grec, adj. Greek
grec, n.m. Greek language
gréement, n.m. rig
gréer, vb. to rig
greffier, n.m. clerk, recorder
grêle, adj. thin, slight
grêlon, n.m. hailstone
grelotter, vb. to shiver
grenier, n.m. attic, loft
grenouille, n.f. frog
grève, n.f. strike
gréviste, n. striker
gribouiller, vb. to scribble

grief, n.m. grievance
grièvement, adv. seriousness
griffe, n.f. claw, clutch
griffer, vb. to seize; scratch
griffonner, vb. to scribble
grignoter, vb. to nibble
gril, n.m. grill
grillade, n.f. broiling
grille, n.f. grate, gate
griller, vb. to broil roast, toast
grillon, n.m. cricket
grimace, n.f. grimace
grimacer, vb. to make faces
grimer, vb. to make up
grimper, vb. to climb
grincer, vb. to creak, grate, grind
grincheux, adj. ill-tempered
gringalet, n.m. weak
gris, adj. gray; drab; drunk
griser, vb. to get drunk, tipsy
grive, n.f. thrush
grogner, vb. to snarl, grumble
gros m., grosse f. adj. gross, overly large
groseille, n.f. currant
grosseur, n.f. size, thickness
grossier, adj. coarse, gross
grossièreté, n.f. coarseness
grossir, vb. to magnify, grow
grotesque, adj. grotesque
grouiller, vb. to stir, swarm
groupe, n.m. party; cluster
groupement, n.m. grouping
grouper, vb. to group
grue, n.f. crane
guêpe, n.f. wasp
guère, adv. hardly
guérir, vb. to heal
guérison, n.f. cure; recovery
guérite, n.f. cabin
guerre, n.f. war
guerrier, adj. warlike
guet, n.m. watch
guetter, vb. to watch for
gueule, n.f. mouth
gueulement, n.m. howl
gueuler, v.t. to seize
gueuser, v.t. to beg
gueux, n.m. tramp
gui, n.m. mistletoe
guide, n.m. guide book
guider, vb. to guide
guindé, adj. strained, stiff
guingan, n.m. gingham
guipons, n.m. mop
guirlande, n.f. garland
guise, n.f. way, manner
guitare, n.f. guitar
guitoune, n.f. dug-out
gumène, n.f. cable

gustation, n.f. tasting
gymnase, n.m. gymnasium

H

habile, adj. skillful, clever, smart
habileté, n.f. craft, ability
habillement, n.m. cloths
habiller, vb. to dress
habitant, n.m. inhabitant
habitation, n.f. dwelling
habiter, vb. to inhabit, live
habitude, n.f. habit, practice
habituel, adj. usual
hache, n.f. ax
hacher, vb. to mince, chop
hachette, n.f. hatchet
hachis, n.m. hash, minced
hale, n.f. hedge
haine, n.f. hatred
haineux, adj. hating
haïr, vb. to hate
haïssable, adj. hateful
hâle, n.m. tan, sunburn
haleine, n.f. breath
haler, vb. to haul, tow
hâler, vb. to tan
haleter, vb. to pant, gasp
halle, n.f. market
halte, n.f. halt
hamac, n.m. hammock
hameau, n.m. hamlet
hameçon, n.m. hook
hampe, n.f. handle
hanche, n.f. hip
hangar, n.m. shed
hanter, vb. to haunt
harcèlement, n.m. harrassment
harceler, vb. to worry, bother
hardes, n.f., pl. togs
hardi, adj. bold
hardiesse, n.f. boldness
hareng, n.m. herring
hargneux, adj. cross, snarling
harmonie, n.f. harmony
harmoniser, vb. to harmonize
harnacher, vb. to harness
harpe, n.f. harp
hasard, n.m. chance
hasarder, vb. to venture
hasardeux, adj. hazardous, unsafe
hâte, n.f. hurry, haste
hâter, vb. to hasten, hurry
hâtif, adj. early, hasty
haussement, n.m. raising, shrug
haut, n.m. top; adj. high, loud
hautain, adj. haughty, proud
hautbois, n.m. oboe

hauteur, n.f. height
hauturier, adj. sea-going
hâve, adj. gaunt
hebdomadaire, adj. weekly
héberger, vb. to shelter
hébété, adj. bewildered
hébreu, n.m. Hebrew language
héler, vb. to call, hail
hélice, n.f. propeller
hélicoptère, n.m. helicopter
hémisphère, n.m. hemisphere
hémorragie, n.f. hemorrhage
hennir, vb. to neigh
héraut, n.m. herald
herbage, n.m. pasture
herbe, n.f. herb; marijuana
herbeux, adj. grassy
héréditaire, adj. hereditary
hérisser, vb. to bristle
héritage, n.m. inheritance
hériter, vb. to inherit
héritier, n.m. heir
hernie, n.f. hernia
héroïne, n.f. heroine
héroïque, adj. heroic
héroïsme, n.m. heroism
héros, n.m. hero
hésitation, n.f. hesitation
hésiter, vb. to hesitate, waver
hétérosexuel, adj. heterosexual
hêtre, n.m. beech
heure, n.f. hour; time
heureusement, adv. happily, luckily
heureux, adj. glad, happy; lucky
heurter, vb. to collide with
heurtoir, n.m. door knocker
hibou, n.m. owl
hideux, adj. hideous
hier, adv. yesterday
hilare, adj. hilarious
hilarité, n.f. hilarity
Hindou, n.m. Hindu
hippodrome, n.m. race course
hippopotame, n.m. hippopotamus
hirondelle, n.f. swallow
hispanique, adj. Hispanic
hisser, vb. to hoist
histoire, n.f. history, story
historien, n.m. historian
historique, adj. historic
hiver, n.m. winter
hocher, vb. to nod, shake
hochet, n.m. rattle
hoirie, n.f. inheritance
hollandais, adj. and n.m. Dutch
Hollande, n.f. Holland
holocauste, n.m. holocaust
hologramme, n.m. hologram
holographie, n.f. holography
homard, n.m. lobster

hommage, n.m. homage
hommasse, adj. mannish
homme, n.m. man
homogène, adj. of the same kind,
homosexuel, adj. homosexual
Hongrie, n.f. Hungary
honnête, adj. honest
honnêteté, n.f. honesty, fairness
honorable, adj. honorable
honoraires, n.m., pl. fee
honorer, vb. to honor
honteux, adj. ashamed, shameful
hôpital, n.m. hospital
hoquet, n.m. hiccup
horizon, n.m. horizon
horizontal, adj. horizontal
horloge, n.f. clock
horloger, n.m. watchmaker
hormis, prep. except
horreur, n.f. horror
horrifier, vb. to horrify
horrifique, adj. hair-raising
horripiler, vb. to annoy
hors-bord, n.m. outboard
hors de, prep. out of, outside
horticole, adj. horticultural
hospice, n.m. refuge
hospitalier, adj. hospitable
hospitaliser, vb. to hospitalize
hospitalité, n.f. hospitality
hostie, n.f. host
hostile, adj. hostile
hostilité, n.f. hostility
hôte, n.m. host; guest
hôtel, n.m. hotel; mansion
hôtelière, n.m. innkeeper
hôtesse, n.f. hostess
hôtesse de l'air, n.f. stewardess
houblon, n.m. hop
houe, n.f. hoe
houille, n.f. coal
houillère, n.f. coal mine
houle, n.f. surge
houleux, adj. stormy, rough
houppe, n.f. tuft
hourra, n.m. cheer
housse, n.f. covering
houx, n.m. holly
hublot, n.m. porthole
huer, vb. to shout
hulle, n.f. oil
huissier, n.m. usher
huit, adj. and n.m. eight
huître, n.f. oyster
humain, adj. human, humane
humanité, n.f. humanity
humble, adj. lowly, humble
humecter, vb. to moisten
humer, vb. to suck up, sniff up
humeur, n.f. humor; mood, temper

humide, adj. humid
humiliation, n.f. humiliation
humilité, n.f. humility
humoristique, adj. humorous
humour, n.m. humor
huppe, n.f. tuft, crest
hurlement, n.m. noise, howling
hurler, vb. to howl, roar, yell
hutte, n.f. shed
hybride, adj. and n.m. hybrid
hydrogène, n.m. hydrogen
hyène, n.f. hyena
hygiénique, adj. hygenic
hymne, n.m. hymn; n.f. church
  hymn
hypnotiser, vb. to hypnotize
hypothèque, n.f. mortgage
hypothèse, n.f. hypothesis
hystérie, n.f. hysteria
hystérique, adj. hysterical

I

ici, adv. here
ictère, n.m. jaundice
idéal, adj. and n.m. ideal
idéalisme, n.m. idealism
idéaliste, n.m.f. idealist
identificaton, n.f. identification
idiot, adj. and n.m. idiotic
idolâtrer, vb. to idolize
idole, n.f. idol
ignare, adj. ignorant
ignoble, adj. vile, mean
ignorant, adj. ignorant
il, pron. he, it
île, n.f. island
illégal, adj. illegal
illimité, adj. boundless
illustrer, vb. to illustrate
image, n.f. picture
imaginaire, adj. imaginary
imagination, n.f. imagination
imaginer, vb. to imagine
imbiber, vb. to steep
imitation, n.f. copy, imitation
imiter, vb. to imitate, copy
immédiat, adj. immediate
immense, adj. immense, huge
imminent, adj. imminent
immiscer, vb. to interfere
immixtion, n.f. mixing
immobile, adj. motionless
immoral, adj. immoral
immortaliser, vb. to immortalize
immunité, n.f. immunity
impair, adj. odd
imparfait, adj. and n.m. imperfect

impartial, adj. impartial
impassible, adj. impassive
impatience, n.f. impatience
impatienter, vb. to provoke
impeccable, adj. faultless
impératrice, n.f. empress
impérial, adj. imperial
impérialisme, n.m. imperialism
imperméabiliser, vb. to waterproof
impitoyable, adj. merciless
impliquer, vb. to imply, involve
implorer, vb. to implore
impoli, adj. impolite, rude
impolitesse, n.f. discourtesy
importance, n.f. importance
importer, vb. to matter; import
importun, adj. bothersome
importuner, vb. to pester
imposable, adj. taxable
impossible, adj. impossible
imposteur, n.m. fraud, impostor
imposture, n.f. deception
impôt, n.m. tax, tariff
impotent, adj. weak, infirm
imprégner, vb. to impregnate
impression, n.f. print
impressionnable, adj. sensitive
impressionner, vb. to affect
imprimeur, n.m. printer
improbité, n.f. dishonesty
improductif, adj. unproductive
impropre, adv. unfit, improrper
impuissance, n.f. impotence
impuissant, adj. impotent, helpless
impulsif, adj. impulsive
impur, adj. impure, foul
impureté, n.f. impurity
inaccoutumé, adj. unusual
inachevé, adj. unfinished
inadvertance, n.f. oversight
inanimé, adj. lifeless
inanité, n.f. uselessness,
  emptiness
inattendu, adj. unexpected
inaugurer, vb. to inaugurate
inavouable, adj. shameful
incalculable, adj. countless
incapable, adj. unable
incarcérer, vb. to imprison
incertain, adj. uncertain
incertitude, n.f. suspense
inceste, n.m. incest
incident, n.m. incident
incision, n.f. incision
inclinaison, n.f. slope
incliner, vb. to slant, nod, bow
inclure, vb. to include, enclose
incolore, adj. colorless
incommode, adj. uncomfortable
incomplet, adj. unfinished

Inconduite, n.f. misconduct
Inconnu, adj. unknown
Inconsidéré, adj. thoughtless
Inconvénient, n.m. inconvenience
Incorrect, adj. incorrect
Incriminer, vb. to accuse
Incroyable, adj. incredible
Incroyant, n.m. unbeliever
Inculper, vb. to charge, accuse
Incurable, adj. incurable
Incurie, n.f. carelessness, neglect
Inde, n.f. India
Indécis, adj. doubtful, dim
Indépendance, n.f. independence
Indépendant, adj. independent
Index, n.m. forefinger; index
Indien, n.m. Indian
Indifférence, n.f. indifference
Indigène, n.m.f. native
Indigne, adj. worthless, unworthy
Indigner, vb. to anger
Indiquer, vb. to indicate
Indirect, adj. indirect
Individuel, adj. individual
Industrie, n.f. industry
Industriel, adj. industrial
Inébranlable, adj. immovable, firm
Inédit, adj. unpublished
Inepte, adj. stupid, inept
Inépuisable, n.f. inexhaustible
Inestimable, adj. inestimable
Inévitable, adj. inevitable
Infâme, adj. infamous
Infanterie, n.f. infantry
Infécond, adj. barren, sterile
Infect, adj. rotten, infected
Infecter, vb. to infect
Infection, n.f. infection
Inférieur, adj. and n.m. inferior
Infernal, adj. infernal
Infester, vb. to infest
Infidèle, adj. unfaithful
Infime, adj. mean
Infirme, adj. and n.m.f. invalid
Infirmer, vb. to invalidate, weaken
Infirmière, n.f. nurse
Infirmité, n.f. infirmity
Inflammation, n.f. inflammation
Inflation, n.f. inflation
Infliger, vb. to inflict
Influence, n.f. influence
Influent, adj. influential
Informatique, n.f. computer science
Informatiser, vb. to computerize
Informe, adj. shapeless
Infraction, n.f. breach
Ingambe, adj. nimble
Ingénieur, n.m. engineer
Ingénieux, adj. ingenious
Ingéniosité, n.f. ingenuity

Ingénu, adj. naive, ingenuous
Ingrat, adj. ungrateful
Inguérissable, adj. incurable
Inhabile, adj. incapable
Inhiber, vb. to inhibit
Inhumain, adj. cruel, inhuman
Inique, adj. unfair
Initial, adj. initial
Injecter, vb. to inject
Injection, n.f. injection
Injures, n.f., pl. abuse
Injurier, vb. to abuse, insult
Injurieux, adj. insulting, abusive
Injuste, adj. unfair
Injustice, n.f. injustice
Innocence, n.f. innocence
Innocent, adj. innocent
Innocenter, vb. to declare, innocent
Innombrable, adj. countless
Inodore, adj. odorless
Inoffensif, adj. harmless, innocuous
Inondation, n.f. flood
Inonder, vb. to flood
Inopiné, adj. unexpected
Inoubliable, adj. unforgettable
Inquiet, adj. restless, uneasy
Inquiétude, n.f. misgiving, worry
Insalubre, adj. unhealthy
Inscrire, vb. to inscribe; enter
Insecte, n.m. bug, insect
Insensé, adj. mad
Inséparable, adj. inseparable
Insérer, vb. to insert
Insignifiant, adj. insignificant
Insinuer, vb. to hint
Insipide, adj. tasteless
Insolation, n.f. sunstroke
Insolite, adj. unusual
Insondable, adj. bottomless
Inspecter, vb. to examine, survey
Inspecteur, n.m. inspector
Inspection, n.f. inspection
Inspirer, vb. to inspire
Instinct, n.m. instinct
Instituer, vb. to institute
Instructeur, n.m. teacher
Instructif, adj. instructive
Instruction, n.f. education, instruction
Instruire, vb. to instruct, educate
Instrument, n.m. instrument
Insuccès, n.m. failure
Insuffisance, n.f. deficiency
Intègre, n.f. upright
Intellect, n.m. intellect
Intelligence, n.f. intelligence
Intelligent, adj. intelligent
Intendance, n.f. administration
Intendant, n.m. director
Intense, adj. intense

Intensif, adj. intensive
Intensité, n.f. intensity
Intention, n.f. intention
Intercepter, vb. to intercept
Interdire, vb. to forbid
Intéressant, adj. interesting
Intérêt, n.m. interest
Intérieur, adj. and n.m. interior
Interloquer, vb. to embarass
International, adj. international
Interne, adj. internal
Interpellation, n.f. questioning
Interpeller, vb. to ask
Interrogateur, n.m. examiner
Interrogation, n.f. interrogation
Interroger, vb. to question
Interruption, n.f. intermission, break
Intervenir, vb. to interfere
Intervention, n.f. interference
Intervertir, vb. to transpose
Interview, n.m. or f. interview
Intestin, n.m. bowels
Intimation, n.f. notification
Intime, adj. intimate
Intimer, vb. to notify
Intimité, n.f. intimacy
Intituler, vb. to entitle
Intolérance, n.f. intolerance
Intoxication, n.f. poisoning
Intoxiquer, vb. to poison
Intrépide, adj. fearless
Intrigue, n.f. plot, intrigue
Intriguer, vb. to intrigue; puzzle
Introduction, n.f. introduction
Introduire, vb. to introdue, insert
Intrus, n.m. intruder
Intrusion, n.f. trespass
Inusité, adj. unusual
Inutile, adj. needless
Invalide, n.m.f. invalid; adj. disabled
Invalider, vb. to invalidate
Invasion, n.f. invasion
Invectiver, vb. to abuse, revile
Inventaire, n.m. inventory
Inventer, vb. to invent
Inventeur, n.m. inventor
Investigation, n.f. investigation, inquiry
Investir, vb. to invest
Invisible, adj. invisible
Invitation, n.f. invitation
Invité, n.m. guest
Inviter, vb. to invite, ask
Involontaire, adj. involuntary
Iode, n.m. iodine
Irak, n.m. Iraq
Iran, n.m. Iran
Iris, n.m. iris
Irisé, adj. iridescent

Irlandais, adj. Irish
Ironie, n.f. irony
Irréfléchi, adj. thoughtless, rash
Irrégulier, adj. irregular
Irrespectueux, adj. disrespectful
Irrigation, n.f. irrigation
Islam, n.m. Islam
Isoler, vb. to isolate
Israël, n.m. Israel
Issue, n.f. issue, outlet, outcome
Italie, n.f. Italy
Italique, n.m. italics; adj. italic
Itinéraire, n.m. route, itinerary
Ivoire, n.m. ivory
Ivre, adj. intoxicated, drunk
Ivrogne, n.m. drunkard
Ivrognerie, n.f. drunkenness

J

Jaboter, n.m. chattering
Jacasser, vb. to chatter
Jacasse, n.f. magpie
Jacent, adj. vacant
Jacinthe, n.f. hyacinth
Jack, n.m. telephone jack
Jacquet, n.m. backgammon
Jactance, n.f. boasting
Jacter, vb. to speak
Jade, n.m. jade
Jadis, adv. formerly
Jaguar, n.m. jaguar
Jaillir, vb. to gush, spurt, spout
Jaillissement, n.m. gush, spurt
Jais, n.m. jet
Jale, n.f. large bowl
Jalonner, vb. to mark out
Jalouser, vb. to envy
Jalousie, n.f. jealousy, envy; venetian blind
Jaloux, adj. jealous
Jamais, adv. never, ever
Jambe, n.f. leg
Jambon, n.m. ham
Jambonneau, n.m. ham knuckle
Jante, n.f. rim
Janvier, n.m. January
Japon, n.m. Japan
Japonais, n.m. Japanese person
Jappement, n.m. yelping
Japper, vb. to yelp
Jaquette, n.f. jacket
Jardin, n.m. garden
Jardinage, n.m. gardening
Jardinier, n.m. gardener
Jarre, n.f. jar
Jarretière, n.f. garter
Jaser, vb. to chatter

Jaserie, n.f. chattering

Jatte, n.f. bowl

Jaunâtre, adj. yellowish

Jaune, adj. yellow; n.m. yolk of an egg

Jaunisse, n.f. jaundice

Javelliser, vb. to sterilize water

Jazz, n.m. jazz

Je, pron. I

Jeep, n.f. jeep

Jetée, n.f. pier

Jersey, n.m. jersey

Jésus, m. Jesus

Jeter, vb. to throw

Jeton, n.m. token

Jeu, n.m. game, play; mettre en j., stake

Jeudi, n.m. Thursday

Jeun, adv. fasting

Jeune, adj. youthful, young

Jeûne, n.m. fast, abstinence

Jeunesse, n.f. youth

Jeunet, adj. very young

Jeûneur, n.m. faster

Ji, adv. yes

Joaillier, n.m. jeweller

Jobard, n.m. fool

Jockey, n.m. jockey

Jocrisse, n.m. ninny

Joie, n.f. joy

Joignant, prep. adjoining

Joindre, vb. to join

Joint, n.m. joint, seam

Jointé, adj. jointed

Jointolement, n.m. grouting

Jointoyer, vb. to grout

Jointure, n.f. joint of the body

Joli, adj. preety, pleasing

Joliment, adv. prettily; awfully

Jonc, n.m. rush

Jonchée, n.f. strewing

Joncher, vb. to scatter, strew

Jonction, n.f. joining, junction

Jongler, vb. to juggle

Jongleur, n.m. juggler

Joue, n.f. cheek

Jouer, vb. to play, frolic

Jouet, n.m. toy

Joueur, n.m. player

Joug, n.m. yoke, bondage

Jouissance, n.f. enjoyment

Jouisseur, n.m. pleasure seeker

Jour, n.m. day, daylight

Journal, n.m. newspaper, diary

Journalier, adj. daily

Journalisme, n.m. journalism

Journaliste, n.m. journalist

Journée, n.f. day

Joute, n.f. joust

Joyau, n.m. jewel

Joyeux, adj. joyful, cheerful

Jubilant, adj. jubilant

Jubilé, n.m. golden wedding anniversary, jubilee

Jubiler, vb. to exult

Jucher, vb. to roost, perch

Juchoir, n.m. roosting place

Judaïque, adj. Jewish

Judaïsme, n.m. Judaism

Judiciare, adj. judicial, legal

Judicleusement, adv. discreetly

Judicieux, adj. wise, judicious

Juge, n.m. judge, magistrate, umpire

Jugé, adj. judged

Jugement, n.m. judgment, reason, view

Juger, vb. to judge

Jugulaire, adj. jugular

Juif, adj. Jewish

Juillet, n.m. July

Juin, n.m. June

Julep, n.m. julep

Jumeau, adj. and n. twin

Jumelage, n.m. matching

Jumeler, vb. to couple, join

Jumelles, n.f., pl. opera glasses

Jument, n.f. mare

Jungle, n.f. jungle

Jupe, n.f. skirt

Jupe-culotte, n.f. split skirt

Jupiter, n.m. Juipter

Jupon, n.m. petticoat

Juré, adj. sworn

Jurement, n.m. swearing, oath

Jurer, vb. to swear

Juridiction, n.f. jurisdiction

Juridique, adj. judicial

Jurisconsulte, n.m. lawyer

Juriste, n.m. jurist

Juron, n.m. oath

Jury, n.m. jury

Jus, n.m. gravy, juice

Jusant, n.m. ebb-tide

Jusque, prep. up to

Juste, adj. just, right, fair; adv. just

Justement, adv. precisely, exactly

Justice, n.f. justice, integrity

Justicier, v.t. to punish

Justifiant, adj. justifying

Justification, n.f. justification

Justifier, vb. to justify

Jute, n.m. jute

Juter, v.t. to be juicy

Juteux, adv. juicy

Juvénile, adj. juvenile, youthful

Juxtaposer, v.t. to place side by side

kakatoès, n.m. cockatoo
kaki, adj. khaki (the color)
kaléidoscope, n.m. kaleidoscope
kangourous, n.m. kangaroo
kaolin, n.m. porcelain clay
karaté, n.m. karate
kascher, adj. kosher
kayac, n.m. flat canoe
képi, n.m. cap
kermesse, n.f. fair
kérosène, n.m. kerosene
ketchup, n.m. ketchup
kidnapper, v.t. to kidnap
kif, n.m. marijuana
kif-kif, adj. exactly alike
kilo, n.m. kilogramme
kilométrage, n.m. mileage
kilomètre, n.m. kilometer
kilowatt-heure, n.m. kilowatt hour
kimono, n.m. kimono
kinkajou, n.m. honey-bear
klosque, n.m. newstand
kiwi, n.m. kiwi
klaxon, n.m. horn
klaxonner, v.t. to hoot
knock-out, n.m. knock out
kola, n.m. kola
kommandantur, n.f. military
  commad headquarters
korrigan, n.m. elf, goblin
krach, n.m. financial crash
kraft, n.m. wrapping paper
krak, n.m. medieval castle
kyrielle, n.f. litany
kyste, n.m. cyst

L

la, pron. her
là, adv. there
labeur, n.m. labor
laboratoire, n.m laboratory
laborieux, adj. industrious
labour, n.m. plowing
labourer, vb. to plow
labyrinthe, n.m. maze
lac, n.m. lake
lacérer, vb. to lacerate; tear up
lacet, n.m. shoelace; winding
lâche, n.m.f. coward; adj. cowardly
lâchement, adv. loosely,
  shamefully
lâcher, vb. to loose, let go
lâcheté, n.f. cowardice
lacis, n.m. network
lacté, adj. milky
lacune, n.f. blank, gap
ladre, adj. mean, stingy

lagune, n.f. lagoon
laid, adj. ugly
laideron, n.m. ugly person
laideur, n.f. ugliness
laine, n.f wool
laineux, adj. wooly; downy
laïque, n.m. layman
laisse, n.f. leash
laisser, vb. to leave, let
laisser-aller, n.m. freedom
laissez-passer, n.m. pass, leave
lait, n.m. milk
laiterie, n.f. dairy
laiteux, adj. milky
laitier, n.m. milkman
laiton, n.m. brass
laitue, n.f. lettuce
lambeau, n.m. rag
lambin, adj. slow, dawdling
lame, n.f. blade
lamentable, adj. grievous
lamentation, n.f. lamentation;
  lament
lamenter, vb. to mourn, lamont
laminer, vb. to laminate
lamper, vb. to gulp
lampiste, n.m. lamplighter,
  lampmaker
lance, n.f. lance
lancer, vb. to hurl; launch
lanceur, n.m. pitcher
lande, n.f. wasteland, moor
langage, n.m. language
langue, n.f. tongue, language
languette, n.f. small tongue
langueur, n.f. languor
languissant, adj. languid
lanière, n.f. strap, lash
lanterne, n.f. lantern
lapider, vb. to abuse
lapin, n.m. rabbit
laps, n.m. lapse of time
lapsus, n.m. slip
laquais, n.m. footman, lackey
laque, n.f. shellac; hairspray
larcin, n.m. larceny, theft
lard, n.m. bacon, fat
larder, vb. to lard; pierce
large, adj. wide
largeur, n.f. width
larguer, vb. to loosen, let go
larme, n.f. tear
larmoyer, vb. to whimper, weep
larron, n.m. thief, robber
las, adj. weary
lascif, adj. lewd, wanton
laser, n.m. laser
lasser, vb. to weary
latéral, adj. lateral
Latin, n.m. Latin person

latin, n.m. Latin language
latte, n.f. lath
laurier, n.m. bay
lavabo, n.m. lavatory
lavande, n.f. lavender
lavandière, n.f. laundress
lavement, n.m. enema
laver, vb. to wash
laxatif, n.m. laxative
lécher, vb. to lick
leçon, n.f. lesson
lecteur, n.m. reader
lecture, n.f. reading
légal, adj. lawful, legal
légaliser, vb. to legalize
légalité, n.f. legality
légation, n.f. legation
légendaire, adj. legendary
légende, n.f. inscription
léger, adj. light
légèreté, n.f. lightness
légion, n.f. legion
législateur, n.m. legislator
législatif, adj. legislative
législation, n.f. legislation
légitime, adj. lawful, legitimate
léguer, vb. to bequeath
légume, n.m. vegetable
lent, adj. slow
lenteur, n.f. slowness
lèpre, n.f. leprosy
lequel, pron. who, which
les, pron. them
lesbien, adj. Lesbian
lesbienne, n.f. Lesbian
léser, vb. to wrong, hurt
lésine, n.f. stinginess
lésion, n.f. wrong
lessive, n.f. laundry
lest, n.m. ballast
leste, adj. nimble, clever
lettre, n.f. letter
lettré, adj. lettered
leurre, n.m. trap, lure
leurrer, vb. to lure
levain, n.m. yeast, leaven
lever, vb. to raise
levier, n.m. lever
lèvre, n.f. lip
lévrier, n.m. greyhound
lexique, n.m. lizard
liaison, n.f. connection, linkage
liant, adj. supple; affable
liasse, n.f. file, bundle
libelle, n.m. libel
libéral, adj. liberal
libérateur, n.m. rescuer, deliverer
libérer, vb. to free, liberate
liberté, n.f. liberty, freedom
libraire, n.m. bookseller

librairie, n.f. bookstore
libre, adj. free, at large, at liberty
licence, n.f. license, leave
licite, adj. lawful
licorne, n.f. unicorn
lie, n.f. dregs
liège, n.m. cork
lien, n.m. bond, link, tie
lierre, n.m. ivy
lieu, n.m. place, position
lieu-commun, n.m. commonplace
lieue, n.f. league
lieutenant, n.m. lieutenant
lièvre, n.m. hare
ligne, n.f. line
lignée, n.f. offspring
ligoter, vb. to bind up
ligue, n.f. league, confederacy
liguer, vb. to unite in a league
lilas, n.m. lilac
limaçon, n.m. snail
lime, n.f. file; lime fruit
limier, n.m. bloodhound
limitation, n.f. limitation
limitation des naissances, n.f.
  birth control, contraception
limite, n.f. border, limit
limiter, vb. to limit, confine
limon, n.m. mud, slime
limonade, n.f. lemonade
limoneux, adj. muddy; slimy
limpide, adj. clear, limpid
lin, n.m. flax
linceul, n.m. shroud
linge, n.m. linen, wash
lingerie, n.f. linen goods, underwear
linteau, n.m. lintel
lion, n.m. lion
lippu, adj. thick-lipped
liqueur, n.m. liquid, liqueur
liquidation, n.f. liquidation
liquide, adj. and n.m. liquid, fluid
liquider, vb. to liquidate, settle
liquoreux, adj. sweet
lire, vb. to read
lis, n.m. lily
liseré, n.m. border, piping
liseur, n.m. reader
liseuse, n.f. bookmark
lisible, adj. legible, readable
lisière, n.f. edge
lisse, adj. smooth, sleek
liste, n.f. list, roll
lit, n.m. bed
litanie, n.f. litany
litée n.f. litter of animals
literie, n.f. bedding
litière, n.f. litter
litige, n.m. litigation
litre, n.m. liter

littéral, adj. literal
littérature, n.f. literature
livide, adj. livid
livre, n.f. pound
livre, n.m. book
livrer, vb. to deliver
local, adj. local, give up
localiser, v.t. to localized
localité, n.f. locality
locataire, n.m.f. tenant
loch, n.m. log
locomotive, n.f. locomotive
locuste, n.f. locust; shrimp
loge, n.f. box
logement, n.m. lodging
loger, vb. to lodge
logis, n.m. dwelling, house
loi, n.f. law
loin, adv. away, far, at a distance
lointain, adj. distant
loisible, adj. optional, allowable
loisir, n.m. leisure, spare time
Londres, n.m. London
longe, n.f. leash; loin of veal
longer, vb. to go along
longeron, n.m. beam, girder
longitude, n.f. longitude
longtemps, adv. long, long while
longueur, n.f. length
lopin, n.m. plot, small piece
loquace, adj. talkative
loque, n.f. morsel, rag
loquet, n.m. latch; clasp
loqueteux, adj. tattered
lorgner, vb. to glance at
lorgnon, n.m. eye glasses
loriot, n.m. oriole
lors, adv. then
lorsque, conj. when; at the time
losange, n.m. diamond shaped
lot, n.m. lot, prize, portion
loterie, n.f. raffle, lottery
lotion, n.f. lotion
lotir, vb. to divide, apportion
louage, n.m. hiring
louange, n.f. praise
louche, adj. shady, suspicious
loucher, vb. to squint
louer, vb. to priase; rent, hire
loueur, n.m. hirer
loup, n.m. wolf
louper, vb. to spoil, botch
lourd, adj. heavy
lourdaud, n.m. clod; lubber
lourdeur, n.f. dullness, heaviness
loyal, adj. loyal, fair, honest
loyauté, n.f. loyalty, honesty
loyer, n.m. rent, hire
lubrifier, vb. to lubricate
lucide, adj. lucid, clear

lucidité, n.f. clearness
luciole, n.f. firefly
lueur, n.f. gleam, glimmer
lugubre, adj. dismal, doleful
lui, pron. he; to him, to her
lui-même, pron. itself, himself
luire, vb. to gleam, shine
luisant, adj. shiny, glitter
lumière, n.f. light; daylight
lumineux, adj. luminous
lunaire, adj. lunar
lunatique, adj. whimsical
lundi, n.m. Monday
lune, n.f. moon
lunetier, n.m. optician
lunettes, n.f., pl. glasses
lustré, n.m. glossy
lustrer, vb. to polish, gloss
luth, n.m. lute
lutiner, vb. to tease
lutte, n.f. strife, contest, struggle
lutter, vb. to struggle, contend
luxe, n.m. luxury
luxueux, adj. luxurious
luxure, n.f. lust
lycée, n.m. high school
lycéen, n.m. high-school student
lynche, vb. to lynch
lyre, n.f. lyre
lyrique, adj. lyric
lyrisme, n.m. lyric poetry

M

M. (abbr. for Monsieur) n.m. Mr.
macabre, adj. macabre, ghastly
macédoine, n.f. salad, mixture
macérer, vb. to macerate, soak
mâché, vb. to chew
machin, n.m. thing, gadget
machinal, adj. mechanical
machination, n.f. plot, scheme
machine, n.f. machine
machiner, vb. to plot, contrive
machiniste, n.m. machinist
mâchoire, n.f. jaw
mâchonner, vb. to munch, mumble
maçon, n.m. mason
maculer, vb. to spot, blot
madame, n.f. madam, Mrs.
madeleine, n.f. light cake
mademoiselle, n.f. Miss
madone, n.f. Madonna
mafflu, adj. chubby cheeked
magasin, n.m. store, warehouse
mages, n.m., pl. wise men
magicien, n.m. magician
magie, n.f. magic

magique, adj. magical
magistrat, n.m. magistrate
magnanime, adj. magnanimous
magnat, n.m. magnate
magnétique, adj. magnetic
magnificence, n.f. magnificence
magnifique, adj. magnificent
mahométan, adj. Mohammedan
mai, n.m. May
maigre, adj. lean, meager
maigrir, vb. to lose weight
maille, n.f. stitch; mesh
maillot, n.m. shorts; T-shirt
main, n.f. hand paw, claw
main-d'oeuvre, n.f. man power
maint, adj. many
maintien, n.m. maintenance
mais, n.m. why; but
maison, n.f. home, premises
maître, n.m. ruler, master
maîtrise, n.f. control; mastery
maîtriser, v.t. to master
majoration, n.f. over estimate
majorité, n.f. majority
malabare, n.m. burly, big
malade, adj. ill, sick, poorly
maladie, n.f. illness, sickness
maladif, adj. sickly, ailing
maladresse, n.f. awkwardness
malaise, n.m. uneasiness
malaxage, n.m. kneading of dough
mâle, adj. male
maléfice, adj. hurtful
malfaçon, n.f. bad work
malheur, n.m. unhappiness
malin, adj. malicious
malitorne, adj. awkward
mallette, n.f. small case
malotru, n.m. uncouth person
malpropre, adj. untidy
mamelon, n.m. nipple
mammouth, n.m. mammoth
manager, n.m. manager
maraude, n.f. marauding
manche, n.f. sleeve
manchette, n.f. ruffle, cuff
mandant, n.m. employer
mandat, n.m. authority
maous, adj. big; strong
mappemonde, n.f. map of the
  world
maquereau, n.m. pander
marbre, n.m. marble
marchand, n.m. merchant
marchander, vb. to bargain, haggle
marchandise, n.f. merchandise
marche, n.f. march, step, walk
marché, n.m. market, bargain
marchepied, n.m. running-board
marcher, vb. to walk, step, march,

marcheur, n.m. pedestrian
mardi, n.m. Tuesday
mare, n.f. pool, pond
marécage, n.m. bog, marsh
marécageux, adj. marshy
maréchal, n.m. marshal
marée, n.f. tide, flood
margarine, n.f. margarine
marge, n.f. margin
margelle, n.f. edge, brink
marguerite, n.f. daisy
mari, n.m. husband
mariage, n.m. marriage, wedlock
marié, n.m. bridegroom
mariée, n.f. married; n.f. bride
marier, vb. to marry
marijuana, n.f. marijuana
marin, n.m. sailor; adj. marine
marinade, n.f. mixture for pickling
marine, n.f. navy
mariner, vb. to pickle
marionnette, n.f. puppet
maritime, adj. marine
marmite, n.f. pot
marmiter, vb. to blast with gunfire
marmot, n.m. urchin, brat
marmotter, vb. to mumble
marotte, n.f. fad
marque, n.f. brand, mark
marquer, vb. to mark
marqueur, n.m. marker,
  scorekeeper
marquis, n.m. marquis
marraine, n.f. godmother, sponsor
marron, n.m. chestnut; brown
marronnier, n.m. chestnut tree
mars, n.m. March
marteau, n.m. hammer
marteler, vb. to hammer
martial, adj. warlike
martre, n.f. marten
martyr, n.m. martyr
mascarade, n.f. masquerade
mascotte, n.f. mascot
masculin, adj. masculin
masque, n.m. mask
masquer, vb. to mask
massacre, n.m. slaughter
massage, n.m. massage
masse, n.f. mass
masser, vb. to mass; massage
massif, adj. solid, massive
massue, n.f. club
mastiquer, vb. to chew
mat, adj. dull
mât, n.m. mast
matelas, n.m. mattress
matelot, n.m. sailor
matérialiser, vb. to materialize
matériaux, n.m., pl. materials

matériel, adj. material, real
maternel, adj. native; maternal
maternité, n.f. maternity
mathématique, adj. mathematical
mathématiques, n.f., pl.
  mathematics
matière, n.f. matter
matin, n.m. morning
matinal, adj. early
matinée, n.f. morning
matineux, adj. rising early
matois, adj. sly
matraque, n.f. heavy club
matrice, n.f. womb
matricule, n.f. registration
matriculer, vb. to enroll
matrimonial, adj. marital
maturité, n.f. maturity
maudire, vb. to curse
maudit, adj. miserable
maugréer, vb. to curse, grumble
maussade, adj. sullen, cross
mauvais, adj. bad
maxime, n.f. maxim
maximum, n.m. maximum
me, pron. me, myself
méandre, n.m. winding
mécanicien, n.m. mechanic,
  engineer
mécanique, adj. mechanical
mécaniser, vb. to mechanize
mécanisme, n.m. mechanism,
  machinery
mécano, n.m. mechanic
méchamment, adv. maliciously
méchanceté, n.f. wickedness,
  malice
méchant, adj. wicked, malicious
mèche, n.f. lock; wick, fuse
mécompte, n.m. disappointment
méconnaissable, adj.
  unrecognizable
méconnaître, vb. to fail to
  recognize
mécontent, adj. discontented
mécontentement, n.m. discontent
mécontenter, vb. to dissatisfy
mécréant, n.m. unbeliever
médaille, n.f. medal
médaillon, n.m. locket
médecin, n.m. physician
médecine, n.f. medicine
médiation, n.f. mediation
médical, adj. medical
médicinal, adj. medicinal
médiéval, adj. medieval
médiocre, adj. mediocre
médiocrité, n.f. mediocrity
médire, vb. to slander, defame
médisance, n.f. slander

méditation, n.f. meditation
méditerranée, adj. Mediterranean
médium, n.m. modium
méduse, n.f. jellyfish
méduser, vb. to stupefy
méfait, n.m. misdeed
méfiance, n.f. distrust
méfiant, adj. distrustful
méfier, vb. se m. de, to distrust
meilleur, adj. better, best
mélancolie, n.f. melancholy
mélange, n.m. mixture
mélasse, n.f. molasses
mêlée, n.f. struggle
mélèze, n.m. larch
melliflue, adj. sweet
mélodie, n.f. melody
mélodieux, adj. melodious
mélodique, adj. melodic
mélodrame, n.m. melodrama
melon, n.m. melon
membrane, n.f. membrane
membre, n.m. member, limb
membrure, n.f. frame, limbs
mémento, n.m. notebook
mémoire, n.f. memory, memoir
mémorable, adj. memorable
mémorandum, n.m. memorandum
mémorial, n.m. memorial
menaçant, adj. threatening
menace, n.f. threat
menacer, vb. to threaten
ménage, n.m. household
ménagement, n.m. discretion
ménagère, n.f. housewife
ménagerie, n.f. menagerie
mendiant, n.m. beggar
mendicité, n.f. begging
mendier, vb. to beg
menées, n.m., pl. schemes
mener, vb. to lead
ménestrel, n.m. minstrel
ménétrier, n.m. country fiddler
meneur, n.m. leader, ring-leader
méningite, n.m. meningitis
menottes, n.f., pl. handcuffs
mensonge, n.m. falsehood, lie
mensonger, adj. false, deceptive
mensuel, adj. monthly
mesurable, adj. measurable
mental, adj. mental
mentalité, n.f. mentality
menterie, n.f. lie
menteur, n.m. liar
menthe, n.f. mint
mention, n.f. mention
mentionner, vb. to mention
mentir, vb. to lie
menton, n.m. chin
menu, n.m. menu

menuet, n.m. minuet
menuiserie, n.f. woodwork
menuisier, n.m. carpenter
méprendre, vb. se m., to be mistaken
mépris, n.m. contempt, scorn
méprisable, adj. mean, contemptible
méprisant, adj. contemptuous
méprise, n.f. mistake, misunderstanding
mépriser, vb. to scorn, despise
mer, n.f. sea; mal de m., seasickness
mercanti, n.m. profiteer
mercantile, adj. mercantile
mercerie, n.f. haberdashery
merci, n.m. thanks
mercredi, n.m. Wednesday
mercure, n.m. mercury
mère, n.f. mother
méridien, n.m. meridian
méridional, adj. southern
meringue, n.f. meringue
mérite, n.m. merit, desert
mériter, vb. to merit, deserve
méritoire, adj. meritorious
merle, n.m. blackbird
merveille, n.f. marvel
merveilleux, adj. marvelous, wonderful
mésalliance, n.f. misalliance
mésaventure, n.f. mishap, accident
mesdames, pl. of madame
mesdemoiselles, pl. of mademoiselle
mésestime, n.f. low opinion
mésintelligence, n.f. discord
mesquin, adj. shabby, stingy
mesquinerie, n.f. meanness
message, n.m. message
messager, n.m. messenger
messe, n.f. Mass
Messie, n.m. Messiah
messieurs, pl. of monsieur
mesurage, n.m. measurement
mesure, n.f. measure
mesuré, adj. measured, cautious
mesurer, vb. to measure
métairie, n.f. small farm
métal, n.m. metal
métallique, adj. metalic
métamorphose, n.f. transformation
métaphore, n.f. metaphore
métayer, n.m. small farmer
météore, n.m. meteor
métèque, n.m. alien
méthode, n.f. method
méticuleux, adj. meticulous
métier, n.m. loom; craft, trade

métis, adj. hybrid
métrage, n.m. measurement
mètre, n.m. meter
métrique, adj. metric
métro, n.m. subway
métropole, n.f. metropolis; native land
métropolitain, adj. metropolitan
mets, n.m. food, dish
mettable, adj. wearable
mettre, vb. to set, put, place
meuble, n.m. furniture
meubler, vb. to outfit
meule, n.f. stack
meunier, n.m. miller
meurtre, n.m. murder
meurtrier, n.m. murderer
meurtrière, n.f. murderess
meurtrir, vb. to bruise
meute, n.f. mob
Mexicain, n.m. Mexican
mexicain, adj. Mexican
Mexique, n.m. Mexico
mezzanine, n.f. mezzanine
mi, adj. mid, half
miaou, n.m. mew
miauler, vb. to mew
mica, n.m. mica
miche, n.f. loaf of bread
micro, n.m. microphone
microbe, n.m. microbe
midi, n.m. noon; south
midinette, n.f. young sales- woman, business woman
mie, n.f. crumb
miel, n.m. honey
mielleux, adj. honeyed, sweet
miette, n.f. crumb
mièvre, adj. affected
mignard, adj. dainty, mincing
mignon adj. delicate, dainty; n.m.f. darling
migraine, n.f. headache
migration, n.f. migration
mijoter, vb. to simmer, cook slowly
mil, num. thousand
milice, n.f. militia
milieu, n.m. middle, center
militaire, adj. military
militant, adj. militant
militarisme, n.m. militarism
militer, vb. to militate
mille, n.m. mile; adj. and n.m. thousand
millionnaire, adj. and n.m.f. millionaire
mime, n.m. mime, mimic
minauder, vb. to simper
mince, adj. slender, thin, slight
minceur, n.f. slimness

miner, vb. to wear away; weaken
mineral, n.m. ore
minéral, adj. and n.m. mineral
mineur, n.m. miner; adj. and n.m. minor
miniature, n.f. miniature
minier, adj. of mines
minime, adj. very small
minimum, n.m. minimum
ministère, n.m. ministry, department
ministériel, adj. ministerial
ministre, n.m. minister
minorité, n.f. minority
minuit, n.m. midnight
minuscule, adj. minute
minute, n.f. minute
minutie, n.f. trifle
mioche, n.m.f. urchin
miracle, n.m. miracle
miraculeux, adj. miraculous
mirage, n.m. mirage
mirer, vb. to aim at
mirifique, adj. wonderful
miroir, n.m. mirror
miroiter, vb. to glisten
miser, vb. to bid
misère, n.f. misery
miséreux, adj. miserable
miséricorde, n.f. mercy
miséricordieux, adj. merciful
missel, n.m. missal
mission, n.f. mission
missive, n.f. missive
mitaine, n.f. mitten
mite, n.f. moth
miteux, adj. shabby
mitiger, vb. to moderate
mitoyen adj. jointly owned
mitrailleuse, n.f. machine gun
mixte, adj. mixed, joint
Mme (abbr. for Madame) n.f. Mrs.
mobile, adj. movable
mobilier, adj. movable
mobilisation, n.f. mobilization
mobiliser, vb. to mobilize
mobilité, n.f. mobility, insta bility
mode, n.f. fashion mode, moode
modéliste, n.m.f. dress designer
modérateur, n.m. moderator
modération, n.f. moderation
modéré, adj. moderate
modérer, vb. to check, moderate
moderne, adj. modern
moderniser, vb. to modernize
modernité, n.f. modernity
modeste, adj. modest
modestie, n.f. modesty
modicité, n.f. small quantity
modification, n.f. alteration

modifier, vb. to modify, qualify
modique, adj. moderate, unimportant
modiste, n.f. milliner
modulation, n.f. modulation
moduler, vb. to modulate
moelle, n.f. marrow
moelleux, adj. mellow, soft
moeurs, n.f., pl. manners, custom
moi, n.m. ego
moignon, n.m. stump
moindre, adj. lesser, less, least
moine, n.m. monk
moineau, n.m. sparrow
moins, adv. less, least
mois, n.m. month
moisi, adj. moldy
moisir, vb. to mold
moisissure, n.f. mold
moisson, n.f. harvest, crop
moissonner, vb. to reap, harvest
moissonneur, n.m. harvest
moite, adj. moist
moiteur, n.f. dampness
môle, n.m. pier
molécule, n.f. molecule
molester, vb. to molest
mollasse, adj. flabby, soft
mollesse, n.f. softness, weakness
molletière, n.f. legging
molleton, n.m. heavy flannel
mollir, vb. to soften, slacken
mollusque, n.m. mollusc
moment, n.m. moment
momentané, adj. momentary
monarchiste, n.m. monarchist
monarque, n.m. monarch
monastère, n.m. monastery
monastique, adj. monastic
monceau, n.m. pile
mondain, adj. worldly
monde, n.m. world, people
mondial, adj. world-wide
monétaire, adj. monetary
moniteur, n.m. monitor
monnaie, n.f. money, change
monnayer, vb. to mint
monologue, n.m. monologue
monoplan, n.m. monoplane
monopole, n.m. monopoly
monopoliser, vb. to monopolize
monstre, n.m. monster
monstrueux, adj. monstrous
mont, n.m. hill, mountain
montage, n.m. carrying up
montagnard, n.m. mountaineer
montagne, n.f. mountain
montagneux, adj. mountainous
montant, n.m. amount
mont-de-plété, n.m. pawnshop

monté, adj. mouned, supplied
montée, n.f. ascent, rise, climb
monter, vb. to go up, climb, rise
montre, n.f. watch; display
montrer, vb. to show
montreur, n.m. showman
montueux, adj. hilly
monture, n.f. mount
monument, n.m. monument
monumental, adj. monumental
moquer, vb. se m. de, to make fun of, mock, laugh at
moquerie, n.f. mockery, ridicule
moqueur, adj. mocking
moral, adj. ethical, moral
morale, n.f. morals, morality, morale
moraliser, vb. to moralize
moraliste, n.m.f. moralist
moralité, n.f. morals, morality
morbide, adj. morbid
morceau, n.m. piece, bit, morsel
morceler, vb. to cut up
mordant, adj. pointed
mordiller, vb. to nibble
mordre, vb. to bite
morfondre, vb. to chill
morgue, n.f. morgue
moribond, adj. dying
morne, adj. bleak, dismal, dreary
morose, adj. morose
morosité, n.f. moroseness
morphine, n.f. morphine
morphinomane, n. drug addict
morphologie, n.f. morphology
mors, n.m. horse's bit
morse, n.m. walrus
morsure, n.f. bite
mort, n.m. dummy, dead man; n.f. death. adj. dead
mortaise, n.f. mortise
mortalité, n.f. mortality
mort-bois, n.m. undergrowth
morte-eau, n.f. neap tide
mortel, adj. deadly; mortal
morte-saison, n.f. off season
mortier, n.m. mortar
mortifier, vb. to mortify
mort-né, adj. still-born
mortuaire, adj. mortuary
morue, n.f. cod
morutier, n.m. cod fisher
mosaïque, n.f. mosaic
Moscou, n.m. Moscow
mosquée, n.f. mosque
mot, n.m. word; cue, remark, sentence
motel, n.m. motel
moteur, n.m. motor
motif, n.m. motive

motion, n.f. motion
motiver, vb. to motivate, justify
motocyclette, n.f. motorcycle
motocycliste, n.m. motorcyclist
motte, n.f. clod
mou, adj. soft, mellow
mouchard, n.m. spy
moucharder, vb. to spy
mouche, n.f. fly
moucher, vb. to blow the nose
moucheron, n.m. gnat
moucheté, adj. spotted
moucheture, n.f. spot
mouchoir, n.m. handkerchief
moudre, vb. to grind
moue, n.f. pout, wry face
mouette, n.f. gull
moufette, n.f. skunk
moufle, n.f. mitten
mouillage, n.m. wetting
mouillé, adj. wet
mouiller, vb. to soak
moulage, n.m. cast from a mold
moule, n.m. mold
mouler, vb. to mold
mouleur, n.m. molder
moulin, n.m. mill
moulure, n.f. molding
mourant, adj. dying
mourir, vb. to die
mousquetaire, n.m. musketeer
mousse, n.f. moss; foam, lather
mousseline, n.f. muslin
mousser, vb. to foam, froth
mousseux, adj. foaming
mousson, n.m. monsoon
moustache, n.f. mustache, whisker
moustiquaire, n.f. mosquito net
moustique, n.m. mosquito
moutarde, n.f. mustard
mouton, n.m. sheep
moutonner, vb. to curl; make wooly
mouture, n.f. grinding
mouvant, adj. moving, shifting
mouvement, n.m. movement, stir
mouvoir, vb. to move
moyennant, prep. by means of
moyenne, n.f. average
Moyen Orient, n.m. Middle East
muabilité, n.f. changeability
mue, n.f. molting; changing
muet, muette f. adj. dumb, mute
mufle, n.m. cad
mugir, vb. to roar, bellow
mugissement, n.m. bellowing, roaring
muguet, n.m. lily of the valley
mulâtre, n.m. and adj. mulatto
mulet, n.m. mule
muletier, n.m. muleteer

mulot, n.m. field mouse
multiple, adj. multiple, manifold
multiplication, n.f. multiplication
multiplicité, n.f. multiplicity
multiplier, vb. to multiply
multitude, n.f. multitude
municipal, adj. municipal
municipalité, n.f. municipality
munificence, n.f. liberality
munificent, adj. very generous
munir, vb. to provide, supply
munitionner, vb. to supply, provision
mur, n.m. wall
mûr, adj. ripe, mature, mellow
muraille, n.f. high wall, thick
mural, adj. mural
mûrier, n.m. mulberry tree
mûrir, vb. to ripen, mature, bring completeness
murmure, n.m. murmur; grumbling, muttering
murmurer, vb. to murmur, whisper
musarder, vb. to dawdle, waste time
muscade, n.f. nutmeg
muscle, n.m. muscle
musculaire, adj. muscular
musculeux, adj. muscular, brawny
muse, n.f. muse
museau, n.m. muzzle, snout, nose
musée, n.m. museum, art gallery
museler, vb. to gag; muzzle
muselière, n.f. muzzle
muser, vb. to trifle, dawdle
musical, adj. musical
musique, n.f. music, band, musicians
mutabilité, n.f. mutability
mutation, n.f. replacement
mutilation, n.f. mutilation
mutiler, vb. to mutilate, mangle
mutinerie, n.f. mutiny, unruliness
mutisme, n.m. muteness
mutuel, adj. mutual
myope, adj. near-sighted
myopie, n.f. near-sightedness
myosotis, n.m. forget-me-not
myriade, n.f. myriad
myrrhe, n.f. myrrh
mystère, n.m. mystery
mystérieux, adj. mysterious, weird
mysticisme, n.m. mysticism
mystification, n.f. hoax
mystifier, vb. to mystic, mystify
mythe, n.m. myth, fable
mythique, adj. mythical
mythologie, n.f. mythology

N

nabot, n.m. dwarf
nacre, n.f. mother-of-pearl
nacré, adj. pearly
nage, n.f. act of swimming
nageoire, n.f. fin
nager, vb. to swim
nageur, n.m. swimmer
naguère, adv. a short time ago
nain, adj. and n.m. dwarf
naissance, n.f. birth
naissant, adj. newborn
nantir, vb. to give as security
nantissement, n.m. guarantee
naphte, n.m. naphtha
nappe, n.f. tablecloth
narcisse, n.m. daffodil
narcotique, n.m. narcotic
narguer, vb. to defy, flout
narine, n.f. nostril
narrateur, n.m. storyteller
narration, n.f. narrative
narrer, vb. to narrate, relate
nasal, adj. nasal
naseau, n.m. nostril
nasse, n.f. fish trap
natal, adj. native
natation, n.f. swimming
natif, n.m. and adj. native
nation, n.f. nation
national, adj. national
nationalité, n.f. nationality
nativité, n.f. nativity
naturaliser, vb. to naturalize
naturalisme, n.m. naturalism
naturaliste, n.m. naturalist
nature, n.f. nature
naturel, n.m. nature; adj. natural
naufrage, n.m. shipwreck
nauséabond, adj. offensive
nausée, n.f. nausea
nautique, adj. nautical
naval, adj. naval
navet, n.m. turnip
navette spatiale, n.f. space shuttle
navigable, adj. navigable; seaworthy, airworthy
navigateur, n.m. seaman, navigator
navigation, n.f. seafaring, navigation
naviguer, vb. to sail, navigate
navire, n.m. ship
navrant, adj. distressing, causing grief
navrer, vb. to wound, grieve
né, adj. born
néanmoins, adv. yet, nevertheless
nébuleux, adj. worried; cloudy
nécessaire, adj. requisite, necessary
nécessité, n.f. necessity

nécessiter, vb. to make necessary
nécessiteux, adj. needy
nécrologe, n.m. obituary
nef, n.f. nave
néfaste, adj. ill-omened, unlucky
négatif, adj. negative
négation, n.f. negative word
négative, n.f. negative argument
négligé, adj. neglected, sloppy; n.m. state of undress
négligeable, adj. negligible
négligence, n.f. neglect
négligent, adj. negligent
négliger, vb. to overlook, neglect
négoce, n.m. commerce, trace
négociable, adj. negotiable
négociant, n.m. merchant
négociation, n.f. negotiation
négocier, vb. to negotiate
nègre, adj. and n.m. Black
négresse, n.f. Black
neige, n.f. snow
neiger, adj. snow
neigeux, adj. snowy
néon, n.m. neon
nerf, n.m. nerve
nerveux, adj. nervous
nervosité, n.f. nervousness
netteté, n.f. neatness, clearness
nettoyer, vb. to cleanse, scour
neuf, adj. and n.m. nine
neuf, m. **neuve** f. adj. brandnew
neutraliser, vb. to counteract
neutralité, n.f. neutrality
neutre, adj. and n.m. neutral
neveu, n.m. nephew
névrite, n.f. neuritis
névrose, n.f. neurosis
névrosé, adj. and n.m. neurotic
nez, n.m. nose
niais, adj. foolish
niaiserie, n.f. silliness, trifle
nichée, n.f. brood
nicher, vb. **se n.,** to nestle
nickel, n.m. nickel
nid, n.m. nest
nièce, n.f. niece
nielle, n.f. wheat blight
nier, vb. to deny
nigaud, n.m. fool, simpleton
nimbe, n.m. halo
nippes, n.f., pl. old clothes
nitrate, n.m. nitrate
niveau, n.m. level; **au n. de,** level with
niveler, vb. to make level
nivellement, n.m. surveying
noblesse, n.f. nobility
noce, n.f. wedding; **faire la noce,** revel

nocif, adj. harmful
noctambule, n.m. sleep-walker, prowler
nocturne, adj. nocturnal
Noël, n.m. Christmas carol
noeud, n.m. knot
noir, adj. and n.m. black
noircir, vb. to blacken
noix, n.f. nut, walnut
nolis, n.m. freight
nom, n.m. name; noun
nombrer, vb. to number
nombreux, adj. numerous, manifold
nomination, n.f. appointment
nommément, adv. namely, particularly
non, adv. no. **non plus,** neither
nonchalant, adj. nonchalant
nonne, n.f. nun
nonobstant, prep. in spite of
nonpareil, adj. unequaled
non-sens, n.m. nonsense
nord, n.m. north
normal, adj. normal
norme, n.f. norm
Norvège, n.f. Norway
Norvégien, n.m. Norwegian person
nostalgie, n.f. nostalgia
notabilitié, n.f. notability
notable, n.m. notable; remarkable
notaire, n.m. lawyer, notary
notamment, adv. particularly
notation, n.f. notation
note, n.f. note, bill
noter, vb. to note
notice, n.f. notice, review
notification, n.f. notification
notifier, vb. to notify
notion, n.f. notion
notoire, adj. notorious
nôtre, pron. **le n.,** ours
nouer, vb. to tie
noueux, adj. knotty
nouilles, n.f., pl. noodles
nourrir, vb. to feed, nourish
nourriture, n.f. food, nourishment
nous, pron. we, us, ourselves
nouveauté, n.f. novelty
nouvel an, n.m. new year
nouvelle, n.f. news
novembre, n.m. November
novice, n.m.f. novice
noviciat, n.m. novitiate
noyade, n.f. drowning
noyau, n.m. kernel, nucleus
noyer, vb. to drown
noyer, n.m. walnut tree
nu, adj. naked, bare
nuage, n.m. cloud; gloom
nuageux, adj. cloudy

nuance, n.m. shade, degree
nucléaire, adj. nuclear
nudité, n.f. bareness
nuire, vb. to injur, harm
nuisible, adj. hurtful
nuit, n.f. night
nul, adj. no, none; void
numéro, n.m. number
nu-pieds, adv. barefoot
nuptial, adj. bridal
nuque, n.f. nape
nutritif, adj. nutritious
nutrition, n.f. nutrition
nylon, n.m. nylon
nymphe, n.f. nymph
nymphéa, n.m. white water lily

O

oasis, n.f. oasis
obéir à, vb. to obey
obéissance, n.f. obedience
obéissant, adj. obedient
obérer, vb. to burden with debt
obèse, adj. obese
obésité, n.f. obesity
objecter, vb. to object
objectif, adj. and n.m. objective
objection, n.f. objection
objet, n.m. object
obligation, n.f. obligation
obligatoire, adj. mandatory
obliger, vb. to oblige, accmmodate
oblique, adj. slanting; devious
oblitérer, vb. to obliterate
oblong, adj. oblong
obscène, adj. filthy, obscene
obscénité, n.f. obscenity
obscur, adj. obscure, dark, dim
obscurcir, vb. to darken, obscure
obscurément, adv. obscurely
obscurité, n.f. dimness, obscurity
obséder, vb. to harass, huant
obsèques, n.f., pl. funeral
observance, n.f. observance
observateur, n.m. observer
observation, n.f. observation
observer, vb. to observe, watch
obsession, n.f. obsession
obstacle, n.m. obstacle bar
obstétrical, adj. obstetrical
obstination, n.f. subborness
obstiné, adj. stubborn, obstinate
obstiner, vb. s'o., to persist
obstruction, n.f. obstruction
obstruer, vb. to stop up, obstruct
obtempérer, vb. to obey
obtenir, vb. to obtain, get

obtention, n.f. obtaining
obtus, adj. dull, stupid
obus, n.m. shell
obusier, n.m. howitzer
occasion, n.f. chance, opportunity bargain
occasionnel, adj. occasional
occasionner, vb. to cause, bring about
occident, n.m. west
occidental, adj. western, westerly
occulte, adj. occult
occupant, n.m. tenant, occupant, occupier
occupation, n.f. pursuit, business
occupé, adj. busy
occuper, vb. to occupy, busy; to take up
occurrence, n.f. occurrence; event
océan, n.m. ocean
océanique, adj. oceanic
ocre, n.f. ochre
octave, n.f. octave
octobre, n.m. October
ode, n.f. ode
odeur, n.f. smell, scent, perfume
odorant, adj. sweet-smelling; fragrant
odorat, n.m. sense of smell
oeillade, n.f. quick look, wink
oeillère, n.f. eyetooth
oeillet, n.m. carnation
oeuf, n.m. egg; ovum
oeuvre, n.f. work, labour
offensant, adj offensive
offense, n.f. offense
offenser, vb. to offend
offenseur, n.m. offender
offensif, adj. offensive
office, n.m. office, pantry; service
officiant, n.m. person who officiates
officiel, adj. official
officier, n.m. officer, mate; vb. officiate
officieux, adj. officious; semi official
offrande, n.f. offering
offre, n.f. offer
offrir, vb. to offer, present
offusquer, vb. to shadow, obscure, irritate
ogre, n.m. ogre
oie, n.f. goose
oindre, vb. to anoint
oiseau, n.m. bird
oiselet, n.m. small bird
oiseux, adj. useless, idle, empty
oisif, adj. idle, unoccupied
oisillon, n.m. young bird
oléagineux, adj. oily
olive, n.f. olive

olivier, n.m. olive tree
olympique, adj. Olympic
ombilical, adj. umbilical
ombrage, n.m. shade
ombragé, adj. shady
ombrager, vb. to shade
ombrageux, adj. doubtful,
  suspicious
ombre, n.f. shade, shadow
ombreux, adj. shady
omelette, n.f. omelet
omettre, vb. to omit
omission, n.f. omission
omnibus, n.m. bus
omnipotent, adj. omnipotent
omoplate, n.f. shoulder blade
on, pron. one
once, n.f. ounce
oncle, n.m. uncle
onde, n.f. wave, billow
ondé, adj. wavy; streaked
ondoyer, vb. to wave
ondulation, n.f. wave
onduler, vb. to wave
onéreu, adj. burdensome
ongle, n.m. finger nail
onglée, n.f. numb feeling
onguent, n.m. ointment, salve
onze, adj. and n.m. eleven
onzième, adj. and n.m.f. eleventh
opale, n.f. opal
opaque, adj. opaque
opéra, n.m. opera
opérateur, n.m. operator
opération, n.f. operation, working
opératoire, adj. opertive
opéré, adj. (med.) operated; n.
  patient
opérer, vb. to operate
opérette, n.f. operetta
opiner, vb. to hold or express an
  opinion
opiniâtre, adj. stubborn
opiniâtreté, n.f. subbornness
opinion, n.f. opinion
opium, n.m. opium
opportun, adj. timely
opportunité, n.f. timeliness
opposé, adj. opposite, averse
opposer, vb. to oppose; s'o. à ,
  oppose, resist
opposition, n.f. opposition
oppresseur, n.m. oppressor
oppressif, adj. oppressive
oppression, n.f. oppression
opprimer, vb. to oppress, crush
opprobre, n.m. disgrace, infamy
opter, vb. to decide, select
opticien, n.m. optician
optimiste, adj. optimistic; n.m.f.

optimist
option, n.f. option, choice
optique, adj. optic
opulence, n.f. opulence, riches
opuscule, n.m. small work
or, n.m. gold; old ornament
oracle, n.m. oracle
orage, n.m. storm
orageusement, adv. turbulently
orageux, adj. stormy
oraison, n.f. oration, prayer
oral, adj. oral
orange, n.f. orange
oranger, n.m. orange tree
orateur, n.m. speaker, spokesman
orbe, n.m. orb, sphere
orbite, n.m. orbit, socket (eye)
orchestre, n.m. band, orchestra
orchestrer, vb. to orchestrate
orchidée, n.f. orchid
ordinaire, adj. and n.m. ordinary
ordinal, adj. and n.m ordinal
ordinateur, n.m. computer
ordonnance, n.f. prescription,
  decree
ordonné, adj. tidy, orderly
ordonner, vb. to bid, order, ordain
ordre, n.m. command, order,
  mandate
ordure, n.f. refuse, filth, garbage
ordurier, adj. foul
oreille, n.f. ear
oreiller, n.m. pillow
oreillons, n.m., pl. mumps
orfèvrerie, n.f. gold or silver jewelry
organdi, n.m. organdy
organe, n.m. organ
organique, adj. organic
organisateur, n.m. organizer;
  adj. organizing
organisation, n.f. organization,
  arrangement
organiser, vb. to organize
organisme, n.m. organism
organiste, n.m.f. organist
orge, n.f. barley
orgie, n.f. orgy
orgue, n.m. organ
orgueil, n.m. pride
orgueilleux, adj. proud, haughty
Orient, n.m. Orient, East
Oriental, n.m. Oriental
oriental, adj. Oriental, eastern
orienter, vb. to orient
orifice, n.m. orifice, hole
originaire, adj. original, native
originairement, adv. originally
original, n.m. queer person; adj.
  original
originalement, adv. originally;

unusually
originalité, n.f. originality
origine, n.f. origin, source
originel, adj. original
oripeau, n.m. tinsel
orme, n.m. elm
orné, adj. ornate
ornement, n.m. trimming, ornament, adornment
ornemental, adj. ornamental
ornementation, n.f. ornamentation
orner, vb. to adorn, trim, ornament
ornière, n.f. rut, track
ornithologie, n.f. ornithology
orphelin, n.m. orphan
orphelinat, n.m. orphanage
orphéon, n.m. choral group
orteil, n.m. toe
orthodoxe, adj. orthodox
orthodoxie, n.f. orthodoxy
orthographier, vb. to spell correctly
ortie, n.f. nettle
os, n.m. bone
oscillant, adj. oscillating
oscillation, n.f. sway
osciller, vb. to fluctuate, oscillate
osé, adj. attempted, bold
oser, vb. to dare, to venture
osier, n.m. willow
ossature, n.f. bony structure, skeleton
ossements, n.m., pl. human remains
osseux, adj. bony
ossifier, vb. to ossify
otage, n.m. hostage; pledge
ôter, vb. to take off, take away
ou, conj. or, either, else
où, adv. where; whither
ouater, vb. to pad
oubli, n.m. forgetfulness, oblivion
oublier, vb. to forget
oublieux, adj. forgetful
ouest, n.m. west
oui, adv. yes
ouï-dire, n.m. gossip, hearsay
ouïe, n.f. gill
ouïr, vb. to hear
ouragan, n.m. hurricane
ourler, vb. to hem
outil, n.m. implement, tool
outilleur, vb. to supply with tools
outrage, n.m. outrage, injury
outrageant, adj. outrageous
outrager, vb. to outrage
outrance, n.f. degree, extreme
outre, adv. and prep. beyond; en o., besides, furthermore
outrecuidant, adj. excessively
outre-mer, adv. overseas

outrer, vb. to overdo, irritate
ouvert, adj. open
ouverture, n.f. gap, opening; overture
ouvrable, adj. work, workable
ouvrage, n.m. work
ouvrer, vb. to work
ouvrier, n.m. workman, worker, hand, workwoman
ouvrir, vb. to open, unlock
ouvroir, n.m. work room or shop
ovaire, n.m. ovary
ovale, adj. and n.m. oval, egg-shaped
ovation, n.f. ovation
oxygène, n.m. oxygen

p

pacage, n.m. pasture land
pacificateur, adj. pacifying; n.m. peacemaker
pacification, n.f. peace-making
pacifier, vb. to pacify, soothe
pacifique, adj. peaceful, peaceable
pacifisme, n.m. pacifism
pacotille, n.f. small wares
pagayer, vb. to paddle
pagayeur, n.m. paddler
pagination, n.f. pagination
paginer, vb. to number pages
pagode, n.f. pagoda
paiement, n.m. payment
païen, adj. and n.m. pagan, heathen
paillard, adj. lewd, indecent
paillasse, n.f. mattress of straw
paillasson, n.m. door mat
paille, n.f. straw; flaw
paillette, n.f. defect; spangle
pain, n.m. bread, cake, loaf
pair, n.m. peer; adj. even, equal
paire, n.f. pair, brace, couple
paisible, adj. peaceful, peaceable
paître, vb. to graze, feed
paix, n.f. peace, quiet, calm
palabre, n.m. palaver
palais, n.m. palate; palace
palan, n.m. gear for hoisting
pale, n.f. stake, blade
pâle, adj. pale, ghastly
palefrenier, n.m. groom
palet, n.m. quoit
paletot, n.m. overcoat
pâleur, n.f. paleness
palier, n.m. stair landing
pâlir, vb. to grow pale or dim
palissade, n.f. paling, fence
pâlissant, adj. becoming pale

palme, n.f. palm, palm tree
palper, vb. to touch, feel
palpitant, adj. fluttering, palpitating
palpiter, vb. to flutter, palpitate
paludéen, adj. marshy
pâmer, vb. se p., to faint, swoon
pamphlet, n.m. pamphlet, booklet
pamphlétaire, n.m. pamphleteer
pamplemousse, n.m. grapefruit
pan, n.m. side, piece, flap
panacée, n.f. panacea
panache, n.m. plume, tuft
panais, n.m. parsnip
pandit, n.m. pundit
pané, adj. dotted with bread crumbs
panier, n.m. basket, hamper
panique, n.f. and adj. panic
panne, n.f. fat, lard; accident
panneau, n.m. panel
panse, n.f. paunch, cud
pansement, n.m. dressing
panser, vb. to groom; dress
pantalon, n.m. trousers
panteler, vb. to pant, gasp
panthère, n.f. panther
pantomime, n.f. pantomime
pantoufle, n.f. slipper
paon, n.m. peacock
papal, adj. papal
papauté, n.f. papcy
pape, n.m. pope
paperasse, n.f. waste paper; official documents
paperassier, adj. petty, scribbling
papeterie, n.f. stationery
papetier, n.m. stationer
papier, n.m. paper
papier à notes, n.m. notepaper
papier à tapisser, n.m. wallpaper
papillon, n.m. butterfly
papillonner, vb. to trifle, flutter
pâque, n.f. Passover
paquebot, n.m. small liner
pâquerette, n.f. daisy
Pâques, n.m. Easter
paquet, n.m. package, parcel, deck as in cards
par, prep. by; through
parabole, n.f. parable
parachute, n.m. parachute
parade, n.f. procession, parade
parader, vb. to show off
paradis, n.m. paradise
paradoxal, adj. paradoxical
paradoxe, n.m. paradox
paraffine, n.f. paraffin
parage, n.m. ancestry, descent
paragraphe, n.m. paragraph
paraître, vb. to appear, seem

parallèle, adj. and n.m.f. parallel
paralyser, vb. to paralyze
paralysie, n.f. paralysis
paralytique, adj. and n.m.f. paralytic
paramètre, n.m. parameter
parangon, n.m. model, type
parapluie, n.m. umbrella
parasite, n.m. parasite
paratonnerre, n.m. lightning rod
paravent, n.m. screen
parc, n.m. park; pen
parcelle, n.f. part, installment
parce que, conj. because
parcheminé, n.m. parchment like
parcimonie, n.f. parsimony
parcourir, vb. to run through
parcours, n.m. course, journey
pardessus, n.m. overcoat
pardon, n.m. pardon, forgiveness; interj. sorry
pardonner, vb. to forgive, pardon
pardonneur, n.m. pardoner
pare-boue, n.m. mudguard
pare-chocs, n.m. bumper
pareil, adj. like
parent, n.m. relative; pl. parents
parenté, n.f. relationship
parenthèse, n.f. parenthesis
parer, vb. to attire, deck out
paresse, n.f. sloth, idleness
paresser, vb. to laze, waste time
paresseux, adj. lazy, idel
parfaire, vb. to complete, finish up
parfait, adj. perfect, faultless
parfois, adv. sometimes, occasionally
parfum, n.m. perfume, odour
parfumer, vb. to perfume
parfumerie, n.f. perfumery
pari, n.m. bet, wager
parité, n.f. equality, parity
parjure, n.m. perjury
parjurer, vb. se p., to commit perjury
parlement, n.m. parliament
parlementaire, adj. parliamentary
parlementer, vb. to parley
parler, vb. to talk, speak
parleur, n.m. one who speaks
parloir, n.m. parlor
parmi, prep. among
parodie, n.f. parody
parodier, vb. to parody, imitate
paroisse, n.f. parish
parole, n.f. speech, word
paroxysme, n.m. fit of violence
parquer, vb. to park, enclose
parquet, n.m. floor
parrain, n.m. godfather

parsemer, vb. to spread, strew
part, n.f. share, part
partage, n.m. partition, share, sharing
partager, vb. to share, divide
partance, n.f. going, sailing
partant, n.m. one who leaves
partenaire, n.m.f. partner
parti, n.m. party
partial, adj. partial
partialité, n.f. bias, partiality
participant, adj. and n.m. participant
participation, n.f. participation, share
participer à, vb. to partake of
particularité, n.f. peculiarity
particule, n.f. particle
particulier, adj. particular, special
partie, n.f. part, party
partiel, adj. partial
partir, vb. to depart, leave, sail
partisan, n.m. follower
partitif, adj. partitive
partition, n.f. score
partout, adv. everywhere
parure, n.f. ornament
parvenir, vb. to reach
parvenu, n.m. upstart
pas, n.m. step, pace
passable, adj. fair
passage, n.m. aisle, alley
passager, n.m. passenger; adj. passing, fugitive
passant, n.m. passer-by
passavant, n.m. permit
passe, n.f. pass, permit; channel
passé, adj. and n.m. past
passe-partout, n.m. passport, skeleton
passeport, n.m. passport
passer, vb. to go by; pass; spend; strain; se p. de, go without
passereau, n.m. sparrow
passerelle, n.f. bridge
passe-temps, n.m. pastime
passible, adj. capable of feeling
passif, adj. and n.m. passive
passion, n.f. passion
passionné, adj. passionate
passionnel, adj. due to passion
passionner, vb. to interest, excite se p., be eager or excited over
passoire, n.f. device for straining
pastel, n.f. device for straining
pastèque, n.f. watermelon
pasteur, n.m. pastor
pasteuriser, vb. to pasteurize
pastille, n.f. cough drop, lozenge

pastoral, adj. pastoral
pataud, adj. awkward
patauger, vb. to flounder
pâte, n.f. paste, dough, batter
patenôtre, n.f. Lord'_ prayer
patent, adj. patent, evident
patente, n.f. license
paterne, adj. paternal
paternel, adj. paternal
paternité, n.f. fatherhood
pâteux, adj. pasty, thick
pathétique, adj. pathetic
pathologie, n.f. pathology
patience, n.f. patience
patient, adj. and n.m. patient
patin, n.m. skate
patineur, n.m. skater
pâtir, vb. to suffer
pâtisserie, n.f. pastry
patois, n.m. dialect, gibberish
pâtre, n.m. shepherd
patriarche, n.m. patriarch
patricien, adj. and n.m. patrician
patrie, n.f. native country, homeland
patrimoine, n.m. patrimony
patriote, n.m.f. patriot
patriotique, adj. patriotic
patriotisme, n.m. patriotism
patron, n.m. employer; boss; pattern
patronat, n.m. management
patronner, vb. to patronize, provide for
patrouille, n.f. patrol
patte, n.f. paw, leg, flap
pâturage, n.m. pasture
pâture, n.f. fodder, pasture
paume, n.f. palm
paupière, n.f. eyelid
pause, n.f. pause
pauvre, adj. poor
pauvreté, n.f. poverty
pavaner, vb. se p., to strut, swagger
pavé, n.m. pavement
paver, vb. to pave
pavillon, n.m. pavilion
pavot, n.m. poppy
paye, n.f. payment, salary
payement, n.m. payment
payer, vb. to pay, settle
payeur, n.m. payer
pays, n.m. country
paysage, n.m. scenery, landscape
paysan, n.m. peasant
péage, n.m. toll
pêche, n.m. angling, fishing
péché, n.m. sin
pécher, vb. to sin
pêcher, vb. to fish; n.m. peach tree

pêcherie, n.f. fishing place
pécheur, m. **pécheresse** f. n. sinner; adj. sinful
pêcheur, n.m. fisherman
pécule, n.f. savings
pécuniaire, adj. pecuniary
pédagogie, n.f. pedagogy
pédale, n.f. pedal
pédanterie, n.f. pedantry
pédestre, adj. pedestrian
pédiatre, n.m. pediatrician
pédicure, n.m. chiropodist
peigne, n.m. comb
peigner, v.t. to comb
peignoir, n.m. dressing-gown
peindre, vb. to paint, portray, depict
peine, n.f. pain, penalty
peiner, vb. to labor; grieve
peintre, n.m. painter
peinture, n.f. paint, painting
pelage, n.m. coat
pelé, adj. bald, uncovered
peler, vb. to peel, pare
pèlerin, n.m. pilgrim
pèlerinage, n.m. pilgrimage
pèlerine, n.f. pilgrim
pélican, n.m. pelican
pelle, n.f. shovel
pelletier, n.m. furrier
pellicule, n.f. film
pelote, n.f. ball, pellet
peloton, n.m. ball; group of soldiers
pelure, n.f. peel
pénal, adj. penal
pénalité, n.f. penalty
penaud, adj. awkwardly embarrassed or bashful
penchant, n.m. bent, tendency, liking
pencher, vb. to tilt, lean, droop
pendant, prep. during, pending
pendiller, vb. to dangle
pendre, vb. to hang
pendule, n.m. clock; pendulum
pénétrable, adj. penetrable
pénétrant, adj. keen
pénétration, n.f. penetration
pénétrer, vb. to penetrate, pervade
pénible, adj. painful
péninsule, n.f. peninsula
pénitence, n.f. penance
pénitencier, n.m. penitentiary
pénitent, adj. and n.m. penitent
penne, n.f. feather
pénombre, n.f. gloom, shadow
pensée, n.f. thought; pansy
penser, vb. to think of
penseur, n.m. thinker
pensif, adj. thoughtful, pensive

pension, n.f. board, pension
pensionnat, n.m. boarding school
pente, n.f. slant, slope
pépier, vb. to chirp
pépin, n.m. pip, kernel
pépinière, n.f. nursery
pépite, n.f. nugget
perçant, adj. sharp
percepteur, n.m. tax collector
perception, n.f. perception
percer, vb. to pierce, bore
percevoir, vb. to collect, perceive
perche, n.f. perch, pole
percher, vb. **se p.**, to perch
perchoir, n.m. perch
perclus, adj. crippled, lame
percussion, n.f. percussion
percuter, vb. to strike, hit
perdition, n.f. perdition
perdre, vb. to waste; lose
perdrix, n.f. partridge
père, n.m. father
péremptoire, adj. peremptory
perfection, n.f. perfection
perfectionnement, n.m. improvement, finishing
perfectionner, vb. to finish, perfect
perfide, adj. treacherous
perfidie, n.f. treachery
perforation, n.f. perforation
perforer, vb. to drill
péricliter, vb. to shake, be in danger
péril, n.m. danger, peril
périlleux, adj. perilous, dangerous
périmètre, n.m. perimeter
période, n.f. period, term, stage
périodique, adj. periodic
péripétie, n.f. shift of luck
périr, vb. to perish
périscope, n.m. periscope
périssable, adj. perishable
perle, n.f. pearl, bead
perlé, adj. pearly, perfect
permanence, n.f. permanence
permanent, adj. permanent
perméable, adj. permeable
permettre, vb. to permit, allow
permis, n.m. permit, license
permission, n.f. permission
permuter, vb. to change, exchange
perpétrer, vb. to commit
perpétuel, adj. perpetual
perplexe, adj. perplexed, undecided
perplexité, n.f. perplexity
perron, n.m. flight of steps
perroquet, n.m. parrot
perruque, n.f. wig
perse, adj. Persian
persécuter, vb. to persecute

persécution, n.f. persecution

persévérance, n.f. perseverance

persévérant, adj. persevering, resolute

persévérer, vb. to persevere

persienne, n.f. blind, shutter

persifler, vb. to ridicule

persil, n.m. parsley

persistance, n.f. persistence

persistant, adj. persistent

persister, vb. to persist

personnage, n.m. character

personnalité, n.f. personality

personne, n.f. person; pron. nobody

personnel, n.m. personnel; adj. personal

personnifier, vb. to personify

perspective, n.f. perspective, prospect

perspicace, adj. discerning

perspicacité, n.f. insight

persuader, vb. to persuade, convince

persuasif, adj. persuasive

perte, n.f. loss, waste

pertinent, adj. relevant, pertinent

perturbateur, n.m. agitator, disturber

pervers, adj. perverse, contrary

pervertir, vb. to pervert

pesant, adj. ponderous, heavy

pesanteur, n.f. weight, dullness

peser, vb. to weigh

pessimisme, n.m. pessimism

peste, n.f. pestilence; nuisance

pestilence, n.f. pestilence, nuisance

pétale, n.m. petal

pétiller, vb. to twinkle, crackle

petit, adj. petty, little, small; n.m. cub

petite-fille, n.f. granddaughter

petitesse, n.f. smallness, petitness

petit-fils, n.m. grandson

pétition, n.f. petition

pétitionner, vb. to request, ask

petits-enfants, n.m., pl. grandchildren

pétrifiant, adj. petrifying

pétrir, vb. to mold, knead

pétrole, n.m. kerosene, petroleum

peu, n.m. few; little

peuplade, n.f. clan, tribe

peuple, adj. gross

peuplier, n.m. poplar

peur, n.f. fear

peureux, adj. shy, timid

peut-être, adv. maybe, perhaps

phare, n.m. beacon, lighthouse

pharmacie, n.f. drug store, pharmacy

pharmacien, n.m. druggist

phase, n.f. phase

phénix, n.m. pheonix; superior person

phénoménal, adj. phenomenal

phénomène, n.m. phenomenon; freak

philatélie, n.f. stamp-collecting

philosophe, n.m. philosopher

philosophie, n.f. philosophy

phobie, n.f. phobia

phonétique, adj. and n.f. phonetic, phonetics

phonographe, n.m. phonograph

phoque, n.m. seal

photocopie, n.f. photocopy

photographe, n.m. photographer

photographie, n.f. photograph, photography

phrase, n.f. sentence

phtisie, n.f. consumption

physique, n.f. physics; adj. physical

piailler, vb. to peep, squeal

pic, n.m. peak

picoter, vb. to prick, peck

pièce, n.f. piece, coin, patch

pied, n.m. foot

piège, n.m. snare, trap

pierre, n.f. stone

pierreries, n.f., pl. gems, jewelry

pierrot, n.m. clown in pantomime

piéton, n.m. pedestrian

pieu, n.m. stake, pile

pieuvre, n.f. octopus

pile, n.f. stack; battery

piler, vb. to crush, blast

pillage, n.m. plundering

piller, vb. to plunder

pilotage, n.m. piloting

piloter, vb. to pilot, lead

pilule, n.f. pill

piment, n.m. allspice

pin, n.m. pine

pinceau, n.m. paint-brush

pincer, vb. to pinch, nip

piocher, vb. to dig

pion, n.m. pawn, peon

pionnier, n.m. pioneer

pipe, n.f. pipe

piquant, adj. sharp

pique, n.m. spade

pique-nique, n.m. picnic

piquer, vb. to pick, sting

piquet, n.m. picket, peg, stake

pirate, n.m. pirate

piraterie, n.f. piracy

pirouette, n.f. pirouette, shift

pis, adv. worse, worst

piscine, n.f. pool

piste, n.f. track
pistolet, n.m. pistol
pistonner, vb. to help, push
piteux, adj. pitiful
pitié, n.f. pity, mercy
pitre, n.m. clown
pittoresque, adj. picturesque
pivoine, n.f. peony
pivoter, vb. to turn, pivot, revolve
pizza, n.f. pizza
place, n.f. place, room
placement, n.m. investment, placing
placer, vb. to invest, place
placide, adj. placid
placidité, n.f. placidity
plafond, n.m. ceiling
plagier, n.m. one who plagiarizes
plagiat, n.m. plagiarism
plagier, vb. to plagiarize
plaid, n.m. plaid
plaideur, n.m. pleader
plaie, n.f. wound, sore
plaignant, n.m. plaintiff
plaindre, vb. to pity; se p., complain
plainte, n.f. complaint
plaintif, adj. mournful
plaire, vb. to please
plaisance, n.f. pleasure, ease
plaisanter, vb. to joke
plaisir, n.m. pleasure
plan, n.m. plan; plane, schedule
planche, n.f. board, plank, shelf
plancher, n.m. floor
planer, vb. to glide; hover
planeur, n.m. glider
plantation, n.f. plantation
planter, v.t. to plant
planteur, n.m. planter
plaque, n.f. plate, slab
plaquer, vb. to plate, abandon
plastique, adj. plastic
plastronner, vb. to strut jauntily
plat-bord, n.m. gunwale
plateau, n.m. plateau, tray
plate-bande, n.f. flower bed
plate-forme, n.f. platform
platine, n.f. plate; n.m. platinum
platitude, n.f. flatness
plâtras, n.m. rubbish, rubble
plâtre, n.m. plaster
plausible, adj. plausible
plébéien, adj. ignoble
plein, adj. full, crowded
plénier, adj. complete, plenary
plénitude, n.f. fullness
pleurer, vb. to cry, weep, lament, mourn
pleurésie, n.f. pleurisy

pleurnicher, vb. to complain, whine
pleurs, n.m., pl. tears, weeping
pleutre, n.m. cad, coward
pleuvoir, vb. to rain
pliable, adj. pliable
pliant, n.m. folding chair
plier, vb. to fold, bend
plisser, vb. to pleat
plomb, n.m. lead
plomberie, n.f. plumbing
plongeon, n.m. plunge
plonger, vb. to plunge, dive, dip
ployer, vb. to incline, bend
pluie, n.f. rain
plumage, n.m. feathers
plume, n.f. pen, feather
plumeau, n.m. feather duster
plumet, n.m. plume
plumier, n.m. pen or pencil case
pluriel, adj. and n.m. plural
plusieurs, adj. and pron. several
plutôt, adv. rather
pneumonie, n.f. pneumonia
pochade, n.f. hasty, sketch
poche, n.f. pocket
pocheter, vb. to pocket
pochette, n.f. handkerchief
pochoir, n.m. stencil
poêle, n.m. stove
poésie, n.f. poem, poetry
poète, n.f. poet
poétique, adj. poetic
poids, n.m. weight
poignard, n.m. dagger
poignarder, vb. to stab
poigne, n.f. grip, power
poignée, n.f. handful; handle
poignet, n.m. wrist; cuff
poil, n.m. hair
poinçon, n.m. punch
poing, n.m. fist
point, n.m. point, dot, period
pointage, n.m. pointing
pointe, vb. to point, aim
pointillage, n.m. dotting
pointiller, vb. to dot; tease
pointilleux, adj. fussy, precise
pointu, adj. pointed
pointure, n.f. size
poireau, n.m. leek
poirier, n.m. pear tree
pois, n.m. pea
poison, n.m. poison
poisson, n.m. fish
poitrinaire, adj. and n.m. consumptive
poitrine, n.f. chest
poivre, n.m. pepper
poix, n.f. pitch
polaire, adj. polar

pôle, n.m. pole
polémique, n.f. argument
police, n.f. police
policer, vb. to refine
polichinelle, n.m. Punch puppet
polir, vb. to polish
polisseur, n.m. polisher
polisson, n.m. scamp; adj. running wild
politesse, n.f. good manners
politicien, n.m. politician
politique, n.f. policy, politics; adj. politic, political
polka, n.f. polka
pollen, n.m. pollen
polluer, vb. to pollute
Pologne, n.f. Poland
Polonais, n.m. Pole
polonais, adj. and n.m. Polish
polygone, n.m. polygon
pommade, n.f. pomade, salve
pomme, n.f. apple
pommette, n.f. cheekbone
pommier, n.m. apple tree
pomper, vb. to pump
pompeux, adj. pompous
pompier, n.m. fireman
ponctualité, n.f. punctuality
ponctuation, n.f. punctuation
ponctuel, adj. punctual
ponctuer, vb. to punctuate
poney, n.m. pony
pont, n.m. bridge; deck
ponton, n.m. pontoon
popeline, n.f. poplin
populaire, adj. popular
populariser, vb. to popularize
popularité, n.f. popularity
population, n.f. population
porc, n.m. pig, pork
porcelaine, n.f. china
porche, n.m. porch
pore, n.m. pore
poreux, adj. porous
port, n.m. harbor; carrying; postage
portable, adj. wearable
portail, n.m. portal
portatif, adj. portable
portée, n.f. range, scope, reach
portefaix, n.m. porter
portefeuille, n.m. case, portfolio
portement, n.m. carrying
porte-monnaie, n.m. purse
porter, vb. to carry, bear; wear
porteur, n.m. porter, bearer
portion, n.f. portion, share
portique, n.m. portico, porch
portrait, n.m. portrait
Portugal, n.m. Portugal
pose, n.f. pose, attitude

posé, n.f. set, poised
poseur, n.m. person or thing that places or applies; affected person
positif, adj. and n.m. positive
position, n.f. stand, place, position
possesseur, n.m. possessor
possessif, adj. and n.m. possessive
possession, n.f. possession
possibilité, n.f. possibility
postal, adj. postal
postérieur, adj. rear, posterior
postiche, adj. fales, unnecessary
postulat, n.m. applicant
postuler, vb. to apply for
posture, n.f. posture
pot, n.m. pot, pitcher, jar
potage, n.m. soup
potager, adj. vegetable
poteau, n.m. post
potée, n.f. potful
potence, n.f. gallows
potentiel, adj. and n.m. potential
poterie, n.f. pottery
potier, n.m. potter
potion, n.f. potion, draught
potiron, n.m. pumpkin
pou, n.m. louse
pouding, n.m. pudding
poudre, n.f. powder
poulailler, n.m. hen-house
poulain, n.m. colt
poule, n.f. hen, chicken
poulie, n.f. pulley
poulpe, n.m. octopus
pouls, n.m. pulse
poumon, n.m. lung
poupée, n.f. doll
poupin, adj. smart, chic
pourboire, n.m. tip, gratuity
pourceau, n.m. hog
pour-cent, n.m. percent
pourcentage, n.m. percentage
pourchasser, vb. to pursue
pourparler, n.m. discussion, parley
pourpoint, n.m. doublet
pourpre, adj. purple
pourquoi, adv. why
pourri, adj. rotten
pourriture, n.f. rot
poursuite, n.f. pursuit
poursuivre, vb. to sue, prosecute
pourtant, adv. however
pourvu que, conj. provided that
pousse, n.f. shoot, sprouting
poussée, n.f. push
pousser, vb. to push, urge, drive; grow
poussière, n.f. dust

poussiéreux, adj. dusty
poutre, n.f. beam
prairie, n.f. meadow
praticable, adj. practicable
praticien, n.m. practitioner
pratique, n.f. practice, exercise;
  adj. practical
pratiquer, vb. to practice, exercise
pré, n.m. meadow
préalable, adj. preliminary
préavis, n.m. advance notice
précédent, n.m. precedent
précéder, vb. to precede
précepte, n.m. precept
précepteur, n.m. tutor
prêche, n.m. sermon; the
  Protestant religion
prêcher, vb. to preach
précieux, adj. precious, valuable
préciosité, n.f. preciosity
précipitation, n.f. hurry
précipité, adj. hasty
précis, adj. precise, exact, accurate
précisément, adv. precisely,
  definitely **préciser,** vb. to state
précision, n.f. accuracy, precision
précoce, adj. precocious
précompter, vb. to deduct in
  advance
préconiser, vb. to extol, praise
prédicateur, n.m. preacher
prédiction, n.f. prediction
prédominant, adj. predominant
préface, n.f. preface
préférence, n.f. preference
préfet, n.m. perfect
préfixe, n.m. prefix
prégnante, adj. pregnant
préhistorique, adj. prehistoric
préjudice, n.m. injury
préjugé, n.m. prejudice
préjuger, vb. to prejudge
préliminaire, adj. preliminary
prélude, n.m. prelude
prématuré, adj. premature
premier, adj. first, foremost; early
prémisse, n.f. premise
prémunir, vb. to take precautions
prendre, vb. to take
prénom, n.m. given name
préoccupation, n.f. care, worry
préoccuper, vb. to worry
prépaiement, n.m. prepayment
préparatifs, n.m., pl. preparation
préparation, n.f. preparation
préparer, vb. to prepare
préposé, n.m. one in charge
préposition, n.f. preposition
prérogative, n.f. pregrogative
près, adv. near

présage, n.m. omen
prescription, n.f. prescription
prescrire, vb. to prescribe
préséance, n.f. precedence
présence, n.f. presence,
  attendance
présent, adj. and n.m. present
présentable, adj. presentable
présentation, n.f. presentation,
  introduction
présentement, adv. now, at present
présenter, vb. to present, introduce
préservatif, adj. and n.m.
  preservative
préservation, n.f. preservation
préserver, vb. to preserve
présidence, n.f. presidency
président, n.m. president
présidentiel, adj. presidential
présider, vb. to preside
présomptif, adj. apparent,
  presumed
présomptueux, adj. presumptuous
presque, adv. almost, nearly
pressage, n.m. pressing
pressant, adj. urgent, pressing
presse, n.f. press, crowd
pressentir, vb. to foresee
presser, vb. to press; urge; hurry
pression, n.f. pressure
pressoir, n.m. or device for
  squeezing
pressurer, vb. to squeeze
preste, adj. exterous, nimble
prestesse, n.f. vivacity, nimbleness
prestige, n.m. prestige, illusion
présumer, vb. to presume
présupposer, vb. to presuppose
prêt, n.m. loan; adj. ready
prétendant, n.m. claimant
prétendre, vb. to claim
prêter, vb. to lend
prêteur, n.m. lender
prétexte, n.m. pretext
prêtre, n.m. priest
preuve, n.f. proof
prévaloir, vb. to prevail
prévenant, adj. prepossessing
prévenir, vb. to prevent; warn
prévention, n.f. prevention; bias
prévenu, adj. partial, biased
prévision, n.f. forecast, expectation
prévoir, vb. to foresee
prévoyance, n.f. foresight
prévoyant, adj. farseeing, prudent
prière, n.f. prayer
prieur, n.m. prior
prieuré, n.m. priory
primaire, adj. primary
primer, vb. to outdo, excel

primeur, n.f. freshness, earliness
primitif, adj. original
princesse, n.f. princess
principal, adj. chief, main, principal
principe, n.m. principle
printemps, n.m. spring
priorité, n.f. priority
prisable, adj. estimable
prise, n.f. grasp, hold, grip
prisée, n.f. appraisal
priser, v.t. to use snuff
priseur, n.m. auctioneer, appraiser
prison, n.f. jail, prison
prisonnier, n.m. prisoner
privé, adj. private
privilège, n.m. privilege, license
 privilégier, vb. to license
probabilité, n.f. chances,
 probability
probable, adj. likely, probable
problème, n.m. problem
procédé, n.m. procedure, process
procéder, vb. to proceed
procédure, n.f. proceeding
procès, n.m. trial, lawsuit, action
processif, adj. litigious
procession, n.f. procession
processionnel, adj. processional
prochain, n.m. neighbor; adj. next
prochainement, adv. soon
proche, adj. near, close
proclamation, n.f. proclamation
proclamer, vb. to proclaim
procréation, n.f. procreation
procurer, vb. to procure, get
procureur, n.m. attorney
prodigalement, adv. prodigally
prodigalité, n.f. extravagance
prodige, n.m. prodigy
prodigieux, adj. wondrous
prodigue, adj. extravagant, lavish
prodiguer, vb. to lavish
producteur, n.m. producer
productif, adj. productive
production, n.f. production
productivité, n.f. productivity
produire, vb. to breed, produce,
 yield
produit, n.m. product, commodity
proéminence, n.f. prominence
proéminent, adj. prominent,
 standing out
profane, adj. profane
profaner, vb. to misuse, profane
proférer, vb. to say, utter
professeur, n.m. professor, teacher
profession, n.f. profession
professionnel, adj. professional
professoral, adj. professorial
professorat, n.m. professorship

profil, n.m. profile
profiler, vb. to show a profile of
profit, n.m. profit
profitable, adj. profitable
profiter, vb. to profit
profiteur, n.m. profiteer
profond, adj. deep, in-dept,
 profound
profondeur, n.f. depth
profus, adj. profuse
profusion, n.f. profusion, excess
progéniture, n.f. offspring
programme, n.m. program
progrès, n.m. progress, advance
progresser, vb. to progress
progressif, adj. progressive
progressiste, n.m. progressive
prohiber, vb. to prohibit
proie, n.f. prey
projecteur, n.m. projector
projectile, n.m. missile
projection, n.f. projection
projeter, vb. to project, plan
prolétariat, n.m. proletariat
prolifique, adj. prolific
prolixe, adj. prolix, wordy
prologue, n.m. prologue
promenade, n.f. excursion; ride;
 walk
promeneur, n.m. walker
promesse, n.f. promise
promettre, vb. to promise
promoteur, n.m. promoter
promotion, n.f. promotion
prompt, adj. prompt
promptitude, n.f. quickness
pronom, n.m. pronoun
prononcer, vb. to pronounce;
 deliver
prononciation, n.f. pronunciation
propager, vb. to propagate
propension, n.f. propensity,
 inclination
prophétie, n.f. prophecy
prophétiser, vb. to prophesy
propice, adj. favorable
proportion, n.f. proportion
proportionner, vb. to keep in
 proportion
propos, n.m. subject
proposable, adj. suitable,
 appropriate
proposer, vb. to propose; move
proposition, n.f. proposal
propre, adj. proper; clean
propulser, vb. to push, propel
propulseur, n.m. propeller
proroger, vb. to postpone, extend
 time limit
proscrire, vb. to outlaw, proscribe

prose, n.f. prose
prosodie, n.f. prosody
prospecteur, n.m. prospector
prospère, adj. prosperous
prospérer, vb. to flourish, prosper
prospérité, n.f. prosperity
prosterner, vb. to prostrate
prostituée, n.f. prostitute
prostitution, n.f. prostitution
protecteur, n.m. protector; patron; adj. protective
protection, n.f. protection
protectorat, n.m. protectorate
protéger, vb. to protect, patronize
protéine, n.f. protein
protestant, adj. and n.m. Protestant
protestantisme, n.m. Protestantism
protestation, n.f. protest
protester, vb. to protest
protocole, n.m. protocol
protubérance, n.f. protuberance
proue, n.f. prow, front
prouesse, n.f. prowess
prouver, vb. to prove
provenance, n.f. product; place of origin
provenir, vb. to come from
proverbe, n.m. proverb, saying
proverbial, adj. proverbial
providence, n.f. providence
province, n.f. province
provincial, adj. and n.m. provincial
provincialisme, n.m. provincialism
provision, n.f. store, supply, provision
provisoire, adj. temporary
provocateur, n.m. person who provokes action
provocation, n.f. provocation
provoquer, vb. to provoke
proximité, n.f. proximity, closeness
prudence, n.f. caution, prudence
prudent, adj. cautious, prudent
pruderie, n.f. prudishness
prune, n.f. plum
pruneau, n.m. prune
Prussien, n.m. Prussian
psaume, n.m. palm
psautier, n.m. psalm book
psychiatre, n.m. psychiatrist
psychique, adj. psychic
psychologie, n.f. psychology
psychologue, n.m. psychologist
psychose, n.f. psychosis
puant, adj. shameful
puberté, n.f. puberty
publication, n.f. publication
publiciste, n.m. publicist
publicité, n.f. publicity
publier, vb. to publish, issue

puce, n.f. flea
pucelle, n.f. virgin, young girl
pudeur, n.m. modesty
pudique, adj. modest
puer, vb. to have an offensive odor
puéril, adj. childish
pugiliste, m. boxer
puis, adv. then
puisatier, n.m. well-digger
puisque, conj. since, as
puissamment, adv. very, powerfully
puissant, adj. powerful, mighty
pulpe, n.f. pulp
pulsar, n.m. pulsar
pulsation, n.f. beating
pulvérisateur, n.m. spray, vaporizer
pulvériser, vb. to spray, pulverize
punir, vb. to punish
punitif, adj. punitive
punition, n.f. punishment
pupitre, n.m. desk; music stand, reading stand
pur, adj. pure
purée, n.f. mash
purement, adv. purely
pureté, n.f. purity
purge, n.f. cleansing
purification, n.f. purification
purifier, vb. to purify, cleanse
puritain, adj. and n.m. Puritan
pustule, n.f. pimple
putois, n.m. skunk, polecate
pyjama, n.m. pajamas
pyramidal, adj. overwhelming
pyramide, n.f. pyramid

Q

quadragénaire, adj. forty years of age
quadrangle, n.m. quadrangle
quadrangulaire, adj. quadrangular
quadrillé, adj. check, ruled off
quadrillage, n.m. arrangement or pattern in squares
quadrupède, n.m. and adj. quadruped
quadruple, n.m. and adj. four fold, quadruple
quai, n.m. pier, dock, wharf
qualifiable, adj. qualifiable
qualificatif, adj. qualifying
qualification, n.f. qualication
qualifié, adj. qualified
qualifier, v.t. to qualify
qualité, n.f. quality, nature, grade,

property

quand, adv. when, whenever

quant, prep. as to, as for

quant-à-soi, n.m. dignity, reserve

quantité, n.f. amount, quantity

quantième, n.m. which

quarantaine, n.f. quarantine

quarante, adj. and n.m. forty

quart, n.m. fourth, quarter

quartier, n.m. district, quarter

quartz, n.m. quartz

quasar, n.m. quasar

quasi, adv. nearly; n.m. thick end of a loin of meat

quasi-contrat, n.m. implied contract

quasi-délit, n.m. injury that is caused involuntarily

quasiment, adv. nearly, almost

quaterne, n.m. four winning numbers

quatorze, adj. and n.m. fourteen; fourteenth

quatre, adj. and n.m. four, fourth

quatre-vingt-dix, adj. and n.m. ninety

quatrième, adj. and n.m. fourth

quatuor, n.m. quartet

quayage, n.m. wharfage

que, pron. whom, which, that; conj. that, than

quel, adj. which; what; of what kind

quelconque, adj. some, any

quelquefois, adv. sometimes

quelqu'un, pron. m. someone, somebody, anybody

quelque, adj. a few

quelques-uns, pron. m. a few

quelqu'un, pron. somebody, someone

quenotte, n.f. tooth of young children

querelle, n.f. quarrel, quarreling

quereller, vb. to quarrel with; scold

querelleur, n.m. quarreler; adj. inclined to quarrel

quérir, v.t. to fetch

qu'est-ce que, pron. what?

question, n.f. question, issue, matter

questionnaire, n.m. book or paper with a list of questions

questionner, v.t. to question, to interrogate

questionneur, n.m. questioner; adj. inquisitive

quête, n.f. quest, seeking; collection

quêter, vb. to seek, go in quest of something, look for

queue, n.f. tail; line

faire la q., stand in line

queue-d'aronde, n.f. dovetail

queue-de-cheval, n.f. horse tail

qui, rel. pron. who, whom; which

quiconque, pron. whoever, whomsoever, whichever

quignon, n.m. large piece of bread

quille, n.f. keel

quincaillerie, n.f. hardware

quinine, n.f. quinine

quinquagénaire, adj. fifty years old

quintal, n.m. unit of weight 100 kilograms

quintuple, adj. quintuple

quinze, adj. and n.m. fifteen

quinzième, adj. and n.m. fifteenth

quiproquo, n.m. blunder, mistake

quittance, n.f. receipt

quitte, adj. free, quit, released

quitter, vb. to quit, leave

quoi, pron. and interj. what

quoique, conj. though

quote-part, n.f. quota, part portion

quotidien, adj. daily

quotité, n.f. share; amount

R

rabais, n.m. abatement, reduction

rabaisser, vb. to lessen, lower

rabattre, vb. to put down, suppress

rabbin, n.m. rabbi

rabot, n.m. plane

raboter, vb. to plane, perfect

raboteux, adj. knotty, rugged

raccommodage, n.m. fixing, mending

raccommoder, vb. to mend, repair

raccorder, vb. to join, bring together

raccourcir, vb. to shorten, curtail

raccourcissement, n.m. shortening

raccrocher, vb. to hook up; recover

race, n.f. race, stock, breed

rachat, n.m. redemption

racheter, vb. to redeem, to buy back

racine, n.f. root

radage, n.m. action of scraping

racler, vb. to scrape

raconter, vb. to narrate, tell, recount

radar, n.m. radar

radeau, n.m. raft

radiant, adj. radiant

radical, adj. and n.m. radical

radier, vb. to radiate; erase

radieux, adj. beaming, glorious, radiant

radio, n.f. radio; wireless
radiodiffuser, vb. to broadcast
radiogramme, n.m. radiogram
radiographie, n.f. radiography
radis, n.m. radish
radium, n.m. radium
radoter, vb. to babble, drivel
radoucir, vb. to quiet, soften, appease
rafale, n.f. blast, gust, squall
raffinement, n.m. refinement
raffiner, vb. to refine
raffinerie, n.f. refinery
rafistoler, vb. to patch, mend
rafler, vb. to carry off
rafraîchir, vb. to refresh
rafraîchissement, n.m. refreshment
rage, n.f. rage, fury
rager, vb. to rage, be angry
rageur, n.m. irritable person
ragoûtant, adj. pleasing, tasty
ragréer, vb. to refinish, renovate
raid, n.m. raid
raide, adj. stiff; taut; steep
raideur, n.f. stiffness
raifort, n.m. horseradish
rail, n.m. rail
railler, vb. to make fun of
raillerie, n.f. jesting
railleur, n.m. jester, scoffer
rais, n.m. ray, spoke
raisin, n.m. grapes; r. sec, raisin
raison, n.f. reason, judgment
raisonnable, adj. reasonable
raisonnement, n.m. reason, argument
raisonner, vb. to reason
rajeunir, vb. to rejuvenate
ralentir, vb. to slow down, slacken
rallier, vb. to rally
rallonger, vb. to make an addition to
ramage, n.m. flower pattern; babble
ramassé, adj. thick-set, dumpy
ramasser, vb. topick up
ramasseur, n.m. collector
rame, n.f. oar
rameau, n.m. branch
ramener, vb. to bring, take back
restaurateur, vb. to restorer
ramer, vb. to row
rameur, n.m. rower
ramilles, n.f. twig
ramollir, vb. to soften, weaken
rampe, n.f. banister; ramp
ramper, vb. to crawl, creep
rance, adj. and n.m. rancid
rançon, n.f. ransom
rancune, n.f. grudge, spite
rancunier, adj. rancorous, bitter

rang, n.m. row; rank
rangée, n.f. file, row
ranger, vb. to rank, array
rapace, adj. predatory, greedy
râpe, n.f. file, rasp
râper, vb. to grate
rapide, n.m. rapid; adj. rapid, fast, quick
rapidité, n.f. rapidity
raplécer, v.t. to patch
rapin, n.m. pupil, art student
rapiner, vb. to plunder, rob
rappel, n.m. reminder, recall, repeal
rappeler, vb. to recall, remind
rapport, n.m. report; relation, productiveness
rapporter, vb. to bring back; report, correspond
rapporteur, n.m. reporter, tattletale
rapprochement, n.m. bringing close
rapprocher, vb. to bring together; se r. de, approximate
rapt, n.m. rape, kidnapping
raquette, n.f. racket
rare, adj. scarce, rare
raréfier, vb. to rarefy
rarement, adv. seldom, rarely
rareté, n.f. rarity, scarcity
ras, adj. smooth-shaven, open
raser, vb. to shave
rasoir, n.m. razor
rassasier, vb. to cloy, sate
rassemblement, n.m. rally
rassembler, vb. to gather, congregate, muster
rasseoir, v.t. to seat again, to replace, to calm
rasséréner, vb. to clear up, as in weather
rassis, adj. stale
rassurer, vb. to reasure, comfort
rat, n.m. rat
ratatiner, vb. to shrivel, shrink
rate, n.f. spleen
râteau, n.m. rake
râtelier, n.m. rack
rater, vb. to miss
ratière, n.f. rat trap
ratifier, vb. to ratify
ration, n.f. ration
rationnel, adj. rational
rationnement, n.m. rationing
rationner, vb. to ration
ratissoire, n.f. scraper, rake
rattacher, vb. to fasten
rattraper, vb. to overtake
raturer, vb. to erase, blot out
rauque, adj. horse, raucous
ravage, n.m. havoc

ravager, vb. to lay waste

ravauder, vb. to mend, patch

ravigoter, vb. to enliven, refresh

ravir, vb. to ravish; delight

ravissant, adj. ravishing, charming, ravenous

ravissement, n.m. rapture

ravisseur, n.m. ravisher, robber

raviver, vb. to revive

rayer, vb. to streak; cross out

rayon, n.m. ray, beam; shelf; r. X, X-ray

rayonne, n.f. rayon

rayonnement, n.m. radiation, radiance

rayonner, vb. to radiate, beam

rayure, n.f. streak, blemish

réabonnement, n.m. renewal of subscription

réabonner, vb. to renew, resubscribe

réagir, vb. to react

réalisable, adj. realizable

réalisation, n.f. attainment

réaliser, vb. to realize; se r., materialize

réaliste, n.m.f. realist; adj. realist

réalité, n.f. reality

réassurer, vb. to reinsure

rébarbatif, adj. forbidding

rebattre, vb. to repeat, beat again

rebattu, adj. trite

rebelle, n.m.f. rebel; adj. rebel, rebelious

rebeller, vb. se r., to rebel

rébellion, n.f. rebellion, revolt

rebondi, adj. plump

rebondir, vb. to bounce

rebord, n.m. border, edge

rebuffade, n.f. rebuff, rebuke

rebut, n.m. trash, junk, rubbish

rebuter, vb. to rebuke, discard, reject

receler, vb. to accept stolen goods, hide

récemment, adv. recently

recensement, n.m. census

recenser, vb. to make a census

récent, adj. recent

réceptacle, n.m. receptacle

récepteur, n.m. receiver

réceptif, adj. receptive

réception, n.f. reception, receipt

recette, n.f. recipe, receipt; pl. returns

receveur, n.m. conductor; receiver

recevoir, vb. to receive, get; entertain

réchapper, vb. to escape, get out

réchaud, n.m. food warmer, chafing dish

réchauffer, vb. to warm again, excite

recherche, n.f. inquiry research; quest

rechercher, vb. to investigate

rechute, n.f. relapse

récif, n.m. reef

récipient, n.m. container

réciproque, adj. mutual

récit, n.m. account

réciter, vb. to recite, tell

réclamation, n.f. complaint

réclame, n.f. advertisement

réclamer, vb. to claim, demand

reclus, adj. withdrawn, secluded

réclusion, n.f. solitary confinement

recoin, n.m. recess, corner

récolte, n.f. crop, harvest

récolter, vb. to harvest, gather

recommandable, adj. advisable

recommandation, n.f. recommendation

recommander, vb. to reccomend; register letter

recommencer, vb. to start again

récompense, n.f. reward

récompenser, vb. to reward

réconcilier, vb. to reconcile

reconduire, vb. to accompany, show out, dismiss

reconnaissance, n.f. recognition; gratitude

reconnaissant, adj. grateful

reconnaître, vb. to recognize, admit, acknowledge

reconstituer, vb. to rebuild, restore

recourir, vb. to resort to

recours, n.m. resort, recourse

recouvrer, vb. to recover, retrieve

recouvrir, vb. to recover, cover completely

récréation, n.f. amusement

récréer, vb. to entertain

recrue, n.f. recruit

recruter, vb. to recruit

rectangle, n.m. rectangle

recteur, n.m. rector

rectifier, vb. to rectify, correct

reçu, n.m. receipt; adj receive

recueil, n.m. collection, compilation

recueillir, vb. to gather, collect, glean

recul, n.m. kick, recoil

reculade, n.f. backing, retreat

reculer, vb. to recoil, draw back

récuser, vb. to challenge, reject

recycler, vb. to recycle

rédacteur, n.m. editor

rédaction, n.f. editorial staff

reddition, n.f. surrendering
rédemption, n.f. redemption
rédiger, vb. to draw up
redingote, n.m. frock-coat
redire, vb. to repeat, reveal
redoutable, adj. alarming, redoubtable
redouter, vb. to dread
redresser, vb. to straighten
réduction, n.f. cut, decrease
réduire, vb. to reduce
réduit, n.m. retreat, hovel
réel, adj. real, actual
réfection, n.f. reconstruction; refreshments
réfectoire, n.m. dining room
référence, n.m. reference
référer, vb. to refer
refermer, vb. to close up or again
réfléchir, vb. to ponder, consider
reflet, n.m. reflection
refléter, vb. to reflect
réflexe, adj. and n.m. reflex
réflexion, n.f. thought, reflection, consideration
refluer, vb. to return to source, ebb
reflux, n.m. ebb
refondre, vb. to improve, cast gain; remodel
réformateur, adj. reforming; n.m. crusader, reformer
réforme, n.f. reform, reformation
réformer, vb. to reform
refoulement, n.m. forcing back, retreat
refouler, vb. to dirve back, repel
réfractaire, adj. refractory
réfrigérant, n.m. refrigerator
réfrigérer, vb. to put under refrigeration
refroidir, vb. chill, cool
refroidissement, n.m. cooling, refrigeration, chill
refuge, n.m. refuge
réfugier, vb. **se r.,** to take refuge
refus, n.m. refusal, denial
refuser, vb. to refuse, withhold, deny
réfutation, n.f. rebuttal
réfuter, vb. to disprove, refute
regagner, vb. to regain, recover
regain, n.m. regrowth, renewal
régal, n.m. feast, repast
régaler, vb. to entertain, treat
regard, n.m. look
regarder, vb. to look at; concern
régence, n.f. regency
régénérer, vb. to regenerate
régent, adj. and n.m. regent
régenter, vb. to direct, dominate

régime, n.m. diet; government; direction
régiment, n.m. regiment
région, n.f. area, region
régional, adj. regional
régir, vb. to rule
régisseur, n.m. manager
registre, n.m. register, record
règle, n.f. rule; ruler
règlement, n.m. settlement; regulation
réglementaire, adj. according to regulations
régler, vb. to regulate; rule; settle
régner, vb. to reign
régression, n.f. regression
regret, n.m. regret
regrettable, adj. regrettable
regretter, vb. to regret
régulariser, vb. to regularize
régularité, n.f. regularity
régulateur, n.m. regulator
régulier, adj. regular
rehabiliter, vb. to rehabilitate
rehausser, vb. to enhance
rein, n.m. kidney
reine, n.f. queen
rejet, n.m. rejection
rejeter, vb. to reject
rejeton, n.m. plant shoot
rejoindre, vb. to overtake, rejoin
réjouissance, n.f. festivity
relâche, adj. loose
relâcher, vb. to relax, slacken
relais, n.m. relay
relater, vb. to relate
relatif, adj. relative
relation, n.f. connection, relation
relaxation, n.f. release, relaxation
relayer, vb. to relay
relèvement, n.m. bearing
relever, vb. to relieve; lift; point out
relief, n.m. relief; **mettre en r.,** emphasize
relier, vb. to bind; link
relieur, n.f. binding
religieuse, n.f. nun
religieux, adj. religious
religion, n.f. religion
reliquaire, n.m. receptacle for relic
reluire, vb. to shine, glisten
remanier, vb. to redo, modify
remarquable, adj. noticeable; remarkable
remarque, n.f. remark
remarquer, vb. to remark; notice
rembarrer, vb. to put in one_ place
remboursement, n.m. refund
remède, n.m. remedy, cure
remédiable, adj. remediable

remédier à, vb. to remedy

remerciement, n.m. thanks

remettre, vb. to put back; restore; remit; pardon; deliver

remise, n.f. discount; delivery

rémission, n.f. remission

remontrance, n.f. remonstrance

remontrer, vb. to show anew, point out error

remorquer, vb. to tow

remorqueur, n.m. tug boat

rémouleur, n.m. sharpener, grinder

remous, n.m. eddy

remplaçant, n.m. substitute

remplacer, vb. to replace, substitute

rempli, n.m. tuck, hitch

remplier, vb. to take a tuck in

remplir, vb. to fill; carry out; crowd

remporter, vb. to take away

remuer, vb. to stir **se r.**, bustle

renaissance, n.f. rebirth, revival

renard, n.m. fox; sly person

rencontre, n.f. meeting

rencontrer, vb. to meet; come across

rendement, n.m. output

rendez-vous, n.m. date, appointment

rendre, vb. to give back; repay; surrender. **se r. compte de**, realize

rêne, n.f. rein

rené, adj. born again

renégat, adj. and n.m. renegade

renfermer, vb. to enclose

renfler, vb. to swell, inflate

renforcer, vb. to reinforce

renfort, n.m. reinforcement, aid

renfrogner, vb. **se r.** to scowl, frown

renne, n.m. reindeer

renom, n.m. renown, repute

renommée, n.f. fame, renown, reputation

renoncer à, vb. to renounce, forego

renonciation, n.f. renunciation

renouvellement, n.m. renewing, retying

renouveau, n.m. springtime, spring

renouveler, vb. to renew, renovate

renouvellement, n.m. renewal

renseignements, n.m., pl. information

renseigner, vb. to inform. **se renseigner**, inquire

rente, n.f. income; interest; annuity

rentrée, n.f. return

rentrer, vb. to go back, go home

renversant, adj. over whelming

renverse, adj. thrown down; reverse

renvoi, n.m. dismissal; return

renvoyer, vb. to dismiss, send back

repaître, vb. to feed, feast

répandre, vb. to diffuse, spill, scatter

répandu, adj. prevalent, widespread

réapparaître, vb. to reappear

réparateur, n.m. restorer, repairer

réparation, n.f. repair, amends

réparer, vb. to repair

repartie, n.f. reply, quick retort

repartir, vb. to leave again; retort

repas, n.m. meal

repasser, vb. to press; pass; look over

repentir, n.m. repentance; vb. **se r.**, repent

répercussion, n.f. repercussion

répercuter, vb. to reverberate, echo

repère, n.m. guiding mark

répertoire, n.m. list, repertory

répéter, vb. to repeat, rehearse

répétition, n.f. repetition

répit, n.m. respite

replacer, vb. to replace

replier, vb. to fold again or up

réplique, n.f. rejoinder; cue

répliquer, vb. to rejoin

répondant, n.m. respondent, bail

répondre, vb. to answer, reply; **r. de**, vouch for

réponse, n.f. answer reply

report, n.m. in bookkeeping, the amount brought forward

reportage, n.m. reporting

reporter, n.m. reporter; vb. take back

repos, n.m. rest

reposer, vb. to rest, repose

repousser, vb. to push back, repel; spurn

repoussoir, n.m. foil

répréhensible, adj. objectionable

répréhension, n.f. reprehension, censure

reprendre, vb. to take back, resume

représailles, n.f., pl. retaliation

représentatif, n.m. representative

représentation, n.f. representation, performance

représenter, adj. represent

répressif, adj. repressive

répression, n.f. repression

réprimande, n.f. reproof, rebuke, reprimand

réprimander, vb. to chide, reprove, reprimand

réprimer, vb. to quell

reprise, n.f. recovery; turn
repriser, vb. to darn
réprobation, n.f. reprobation
reproche, n.m. reproach
reprocher, vb. to reproach
reproduction, n.f. reproduction
reproduire, vb. to reproduce
réprouver, vb. to censure
reptile, n.m. reptile
républicain, adj. and n.m. replubican
république, n.f. republic
répudier, vb. to repudiate
répugnance, n.f. repuganance
répulsion, n.f. repulsion
réputation, n.f. reputation
réputer, vb. to consider, esteem
requête, n.f. request, plea
requin, n.m. shark
requis, adj. required, necessary
réquisition, n.f. requisition
rescousse, n.f. rescue
réseau, n.m. network
réserve, n.f. reserve, reservation; qualification
réserver, vb. to reserve
réserviste, n.f. reservist
réservoir, n.m. tank, reservoir
résidant, adj. resident
résidence, n.f. residence, dwelling
résider, vb. to reside
résidu, n.m. residue
résignation, n.f. resignation
résigner, vb. to resign
résiliation, n.f. cancelling
résine, n.f. resin
résister, vb. to resist
résolu, adj. resolute
résonnance, n.f. resonnance
résonnant, adj. resonant
résonner, vb. to resound
résoudre, vb. to solve, resolve
respect, n.m. respect
respecter, vb. to respect
respectif, adj. respective
respectueux, adj. respectful
respiration, n.f. breathing
respirer, vb. to breathe
responsabilité, n.f. responsibility
responsable, adj. responsible; liable
ressaisir, vb. to regain possession
ressemblance, n.f. likeness
ressembler, vb. to resemble
ressentir, vb. to feel, resent, show
resserrer, vb. to tighten, compress
ressort, n.m. elasticity
ressortir, vb. to stand out
ressource, n.f. resort, resource
restaurant, n.m. restaurant

restaurateur, n.m. restorer
restauration, n.f. restoration
restaurer, vb. to restore
reste, n.m. remainder, rest
rester, vb. to remain, stay
restituer, vb. to give back, restore
restreindre, vb. to restrict
restrictif, adj. restrictive
restriction, n.f. restriction
résultant, n.m. outcome, result
résulter, vb. to result
résumé, n.m. summing up
résumer, vb. to sum up
rétablir, vb. to restore
rétablissement, n.m. recovery
retard, n.m. delay, retard
retenir, vb. to retain; keep; hold back; detain
rétentif, adj. retentive
retentir, vb. to resound; ring
réticence, n.f. silence, reticence
retirer, vb. to withdraw
retoucheuse, n.f. retoucher
retour, n.m. return; de r., back
retourner, vb. to go back, invert; se r., turn around
retrait, n.m. contraction, retraction
retraite, n.f. retreat; privacy
retrancher, vb. to cut off, curtail
rétrécir, vb. to shrink, contract
rétribution, n.f. salary, recompense
retrousser, vb. to turn up
retrouver, vb. to find; recover
réunion, n.f. meeting, convention, reunion
réunir, vb. to unite; se r., assemble
réussir, vb. to succeed
réussite, n.f. successful outcome
revanche, n.f. revenge; en r., in return
rêve, n.m. dream
réveil, n.m. awaking; revival
réveiller, vb. to wake up, arouse
révélateur, adj. revealing; n.m. revelaer
révélation, n.f. revelation
révéler, vb. to disclose, reveal
revenant, n.m. ghost, specter
revendeur, n.m. retailer
revendiquer, vb. to claim
revenir, vb. to come back, return
revenu, n.m. income, revenue
rêver, vb. to dream
respectueusement, adv. reverently
révérence, n.f. reverence; curtsy, bow
révérer, vb. to revere
rêverie, n.f. dreaming, reverie
revers, n.m. reverse, wrong side

rêveur, n.m. dreamer; adj. pensive

réviser, vb. to revise

réviseur, n.m. reviser, inspector

révision, n.f. revision, review

revivre, vb. to revive, to come to life

révocation, n.f. revocation, annulment

révolte, n.f. revolt

révolution, n.f. revolution, turn

révolutionnaire, adj. and n.m. revolutionary

révoquer, vb. to revoke

revue, n.f. review, magazine

rez-de-chaussée, n.m. ground floor

rhétorique, n.f. rhetoric

rhinocéros, n.m. rhinoceros

rhubarbe, n.f. rhubarb

rhum, n.m. rum

rhumatisme, n.m. rheumatism

rhume, n.m. cold

riche, adj. wealthy

richesse, n.f. wealth

ricocher, vb. to spring back

rictus, n.m. grin

ride, n.f. wrinkle, ripple

rideau, n.m. curtain

rider, vb. to ripple, wrinkle

ridicule, n.m. ridicule; adj. ridiculous

ridiculiser, vb. to ridicule

rien, pron. nothing

rieur, n.m. laugher

rigide, adj. rigid

rigidité, n.f. rigidity

rigole, n.f. ditch, gutter

rigoureux, adj. rigorous

rigueur, n.f. rigor

rime, n.f. rhyme

rimer, vb. to rhyme

rince-doigts, n.m. ringer bowl

rincer, vb. to rinse

ripaille, n.f. feasting, revelry

riposte, n.f. retort

rire, n.m. laugh, laughter; vb. laugh

ris, n.m. laugh; sweetbread

risée, n.f. laugh, mocking

risible, adj. laughable

risque, n.m. risk

risquer, vb. to risk

risque-tout, n.m. daredevil

rissoler, vb. to brown food

rite, n.m. rite

rituel, adj. ritual

rivage, n.m. shore, bank

rival, adj. and n.m. rival

rivaliser, vb. to compete, rival

rivalité, n.f. rivalry

rive, n.f. bank

river, vb. to clinch

rivet, n.m. rivet

rivière, n.f. river, stream

rixe, n.f. brawl

riz, n.m. rice

rizerie, n.f. rice field

robe, n.f. dress, frock, robe

robinet, n.m. faucet, tap

robuste, adj. robust, hardy, strong

roc, n.m. rock

rocailleux, adj. rock, rough

rocher, n.m. rock

rocheux, adj. rocky

rock, adj. rock music

rôder, vb. to prowl

rôdeur, n.m. prowler

rogner, vb. to pare, trim down

rognon, n.m. kidney

rogue, adj. arrogant

roi, n.m. king

rôle, n.m. role, part, list

Romain, n.m. Roman

romain, adj. Roman

roman, n.m. novel

romance, n.f. ballad

romancier, n.m. novelist

romanesque, adj. romantic

roman-feuilleton, n.m. serial

romanichel, n.m. gypsy

rompre, vb. to break

rond, n.m. round; circle; adj. round

rondeur, n.f. roundness

ronflement, n.m. snoring, roar

ronfler, vb. to snore

ronger, vb. to gnaw; fret

rongeur, adj. and n.m. rodent

rosaire, n.m. rosary

rose, n.f. rose; adj. pink

roseau, n.m. reed

rosée, n.f. dew

rosier, n.m. rosebush

rossignol, n.m. nighingale

rotatoire, adj. rotary

roter, vb. to belch

rôti, n.m. roast

rôtir, vb. to roast

rotondité, n.f. rotundity

rotule, n.f. kneecap

roturier, adj. commonplace

roublardise, n.f. cunningness

roue, n.f. wheel

rouge-gorge, n.m. robin redbreast

rougeole, n.f. measles

rougeur, n.f. flush, blush

rougir, vb. to blush

rouille, n.f. rust

rouiller, vb. to rust

rouir, vb. to soak

rouleau, n.m. roll, roller, scroll

roulement, n.m. rolling, winding

rouler, vb. to roll, wind

roulette, n.f. little wheel, caster

roulis, n.m. roll
Roumanie, n.f. Rumania
rousseur, n.f. redness;
 tache de r., freckle
roussir, vb. to scorch
route, n.f. road, way, course
routine, n.f. routine
routinier, v.t. to accustom; to teach
 by routine
royal, adj. royal, regal, kinglike,
 kingly
royaliste, adj. and n.m.f. royalist
royaume, n.m. kingdom
royauté, n.f. royalty
ruban, n.m. ribbon, tape; band
rubescent, adj. reddish
rubis, n.m. ruby
ruche, n.f. hive
rude, adj. gruff, harsh; rugged,
 rough, uneven
rudesse, n.f. harshness, roughness,
 coarseness
rudiments, n.m. rudiment, element,
 primer
rudimentaire, adj. rudimentary
rudoyer, vb. to bully
rue, n.f. street, road
ruée, n.f. rush; onslaught
ruelle, n.f. lane, alley
ruer, vb. se r.,to rush
rugir, vb. to roar, bellow
rugissement, n.m. roar
rugosité, n.f. rugosity, roughness
rugueux, adj. harsh, rugged
ruine, n.f. ruin, decay, decline,
 overthrow
ruiner, vb. to ruin, lay waste,
 destroy
ruisseau, n.m. brook, creek, gutter
ruisseler, vb. to stream, flow
rumeur, n.f. noise, rumor
ruminant, adj. and n.m. ruminant
rupin, adj. rich, smart
rupture, n.f. break, rupture
rural, adj. rural
ruse, n.f. trick; cunning, trick, guile
Russe, n.m.f. Russian person
russe, n.m. Russian language;
 adj. Russian
Russie, n.f. Russia
rustique, adj. rustic
rustre, adj. and n.m. boor, boorish
rythme, n.m. rhythm
rythmique, adj. rhythmical

S

sabbat, n.m. Sabbath

sable, n.m. sand
sabler, vb. to sand; quaff
sablier, n.m. sandbox, hourglass,
 sandman
sablonneux, adj. sandy
sablonnière, n.f. sand pit
sabord, n.m. porthole
sabot, n.m. wooden shoe
sabotage, n.m. sabotage
saboteur, n.m. awkward bungler
sabre, n.m. saber
sac, n.m. sack, bag; **s. à main,**
 pocketbook
saccade, n.f. jerk
saccager, vb. to ransack, plunder
sacerdoce, n.m. priesthood
sachet, n.m. sachet
sacre, n.m. coronation
sacré, adj. sacred, holy
sacrement, n.m. sacrament
sacrer, vb. to consecrate; curse
sacrifice, n.m. sacrifice
sacrifier, vb. to sacrifice
sacristain, n.m. sexton
sadisme, n.m. sadism
sagace, adj. shrewd
sage, n.m. sage; adj. wise, good
sage-femme, n.f. midwife
sagesse, n.f. wisdom
saignée, n.f. bleeding
saigner, vb. to bleed
saillant, adj. prominent, pro-
 jecting
saillie, n.f. projection
saillir, vb. to protrude
sain, adj. health, sound
saindoux, n.m. lard
saint, n.m. saint; adj. holy
Saint-Esprit, n.m. Holy Ghost
sainteté, n.f. holiness
saisie, n.f. seizure
saisir, vb. to grasp, snatch, grab
saisissement, n.m. chill, seizure
saison, n.f. season
salade, n.f. salad
saladier, n.m. dish, salad bowl
salaire, n.m. wages, earnings, pay
salarié, adj. salaried; n.m.f.
 person earning a salary
sale, adj. dirty
saler, vb. to salt
saleté, n.f. dirt
salin, adj. salt, salty
salir, vb. to get dirty
salive, n.f. saliva
salle, n.f. large room, hall,
 hospital ward; **s. de. classe,**
 classroom
salon, n.m. parlor
salubre, adj. healthful

salubrité, n.f. healthfulness
saluer, vb. to greet, salute
salut, n.m. bow, salute; salvation
salutaire, adj. wholesome, beneficial
salutation, n.f. greeting
salve, n.f. salute
samedi, n.m. Saturday
sanctifier, vb. to hallow
sanction, n.f. sanction
sanctionner, vb. to sanction
sanctuaire, n.m. sanctuary
sandale, n.f. sandal
sang, n.m. blood
sang-froid, n.m. calmness, composure
sanglant, adj. bloody
sangler, vb. to strap, fasten
sanglier, n.m. wild boar
sanglot, n.m. sob
sangloter, vb. to sob
sangsue, n.f. leech
sanguinaire, adj. bloodthirsty
sanitaire, adj. sanitary
sans, prep. without, out of
sans-souci, adj. carefree, careless
santé, n.f. health
saper, vb. to sap, weaken
saphir, n.m. sapphire
sapin, n.m. fir
sarcasme, n.m. sarcasm
sarcastique, adj. sarcastic
sarcler, vb. to weed, root out
sardine, n.f. sardine
sardonique, adj. sardonic
satanique, adj. satanic
satellite, n.m. satellite
satin, n.m. satin
satire, n.f. satire
satiriser, vb. to satirize
satisfaction, n.f. satisfaction
satisfaire, vb. to satisfy
satisfaisant, adj. satisfactory
saturer, vb. to saturate
sauce, n.f. sauce, **s. piquante,** catsup
saucisse, n.f. sausage
sauf, prep. but; adj. safe
sauge, n.f. sage
saugrenu, adj. preposterous
saule, n.f. willow
saumon, n.m. salmon
saumure, n.f. brine
saut, n.m. spring, jump
saute, n.f. wind shift
sauter, vb. to spring, jump, leap,
sauterelle, n.f. grasshopper
sautiller, vb. to hop
sauvage, n.m.f. savage; adj. savage

sauvegarde, n.f. safeguard
sauve-qui-peut, n.m. stampede
sauver, vb. to save; **se s.,** run away
sauvetage, n.m. salvage
sauveur, n.m. savior, Saviour
savane, n.f. prairie
savant, n.m. scholar; adj. learned
saveur, n.f. flavor, zest
savoir, vb. to now, be aware, have knowledge; n.m. knowledge
savoir-faire, n.m. pose, ability
savon, n.m. soap
savonner, vb. to soap, lather
savourer, vb. to relish
savoureux, adj. tasty
scabreux, adj. rough, harsh
scalper, vb. to scalp
scandale, n.m. scandal
scandaleux, adj. scandalous
scandaliser, vb. to shock
scander, vb. to scan
Scandinave, n.m.f. Scandinavian
Scandinavie, n.f. Scandinavia
scarabée, n.m. beetle
scarlatine, n.f. scarlet fever
sceau, n.m. seal
scélérate, n.m. vilain, criminal, knave, ruffian
sceller, vb. to seal
scène, n.f. scene, stage
scénique, adj. scenic
scepticisme, n.m. skepticism
sceptre, n.m. scepter
shampooing, n.m. shampoo
schisme, n.m. schism
scie, n.f. saw
science, n.f. science
science-fiction, n.f. science fiction
scientifique, adj. scientific
scier, vb. to saw
scinder, vb. to divide
scintiller, vb. to twinkle
scission, n.f. cutting
scolaire, adj. scholastic. **système s.,** school system
scolastique, adj. scholastic
scrupule, n.m. scruple
scrupuleux, adj. scrupulous
scruter, vb. to scan, scrutinize
scrutin, n.m. ballot, poll
sculpter, vb. to carve
sculpteur, n.f. sculptor
sculpture, n.f. sculpture
se, pron. himself, herself, each other, oneself, themselves
séance, n.f. sitting, session; meeting
séant, adj. sitting, proper
seau, n.m. pail, bucket
sec m., sèche f. adj. dry

sécession, n.f. secession

sécher, vb. to dry

sécheresse, n.f. dryness, drought

second, n.f. second

secondaire, adj. secondary

seconde, n.f. second

seconder, vb. to support, help

secouer, vb. to shake, rouse

secourir, vb. to relieve, help

secours, n.m. help, relief;
  premiers soins, first aid

secousse, n.f. jar, shock

secret, adj. and n.m. secret

secrétaire, n.m.f. secretary

sécréter, vb. to secrete

sectaire, adj. sectarian

secte, n.f. sect

secteur, n.m. district, sector

section, n.f. section

sectionner, vb. to cut into sections

séculier, adj. lay

sécurité, n.f. safety

sédatif, adj. and n.m. sedative

sédentaire, adj. stationary

sédition, n.f. seditiion

séduction, n.f. seduction

séduire, vb. to seduce, attract,
  allure

séduisant, adj. attractive

segment, n.m. segment

ségrégation, n.f. segregation

seigle, n.m. rye

seigneur, n.m. lord, peer

seigneurie, n.f. lordship

sein, n.m. bosom, breast

seize, adj. and n.m. sixteen

seizième, adj. and n.m. sixteenth

séjour, n.m. stay

sel, n.m. salt

sélection, n.f. selection

selle, n.f. saddle

seller, vb. to saddle

selon, prep. according to

seltz, n.m. eau de s., soda water

semailles, n.f., pl. sowing

semaine, n.f. weekly pay

semblable, adj. similar, alike

semblant, n.m. show; appearance

sembler, vb. to seem, appear

semelle, n.f. sole

semence, n.f. seed

semer, vb. to sow

semestre, n.m. semester

semeur, n.m. sower

sémillance, n.f. briskness

semoncer, vb. to lecture

sénat, n.m. senate

sénateur, n.m. senator

sénile, adj. senile

sénilité, n.f. senility

sens, n.m. meaning, direction;
  sense

sensation, n.f. sensation, feeling

sensationnel, adj. sensational

sensé, adj. sensible

sensibilité, n.f. sensitivity

sensible, adj. sensible, sensitive

sensitif, adj. sensitive

sensuel, adj. sensual

sentence, n.f. sentence

sentencieux, adj. sententious

senteur, n.f. smell

sentier, n.m. path

sentiment, n.m. feeling

sentimental, adj. sentimental

sentinelle, n.f. sentry

sentir, vb. to feel; smell

séparable, adj. separable

séparation, n.f. separation, parting

séparé, adj. separate

séparer, vb. to separate, segregate

septembre, n.m. September

septième, adj and n.m. seventh

septique, adj. septic

séquestrer, vb. to withdraw,
  remove

serein, adj. serene, placid

sérénade, n.f. serenade

sérénité, n.f. serenity

sergent, n.m. sergeant

série, n.f. series

sérieux, adj. serious, sober, grave;
  n.m. gravity

serin, n.m. canary

seringue, n.f. syringe

serment, n.m. oath

sermon, n.m. sermon

sermonner, vb. to lecture, preach

serpent, n.m. serpent, snake

serpenter, vb. to wind, wander

serre, n.f. greenhouse; claw

serré, adj. tight

serre-joint, n.m. clamp

serrer, vb. to tighten, squeeze,
  press, crowd, shake hands

serrure, n.f. lock

sérum, n.m. serum

servant, adj. serving; n.m. server

servante, n.f. maid

serviable, adj. helpful

service, n.m. service, favor

serviette, n.f. napkin; towel

servile, adj. menial

servir, vb. to serve

sevrage, n.m. weaning

serviteur, n.m. attendant, servant

servitude, n.f. slavery

session, n.f. session

seuil, n.m. threshold

seul, adj. alone, only, single

seulement, adv. only, solely
sève, n.f. sap
sévère, adj. severe, stern
sévérité, n.f. severity, rigor
sévir, vb. to punish, rage
sevrer, vb. to wean, withhold
sexe, n.m. sex
sexisme, n.m. sexism
sexiste, adj. sexist
sexuel, adj. sexual
seyant, adj. becoming
shoot, n.m. shot
short, n.m. shorts
shrapnel, n.m. shrapnel
shunt, n.m. shunt
si, conj. if whether, supposing
sicaire, n.m. hired assassin
siècle, n.m. century
siège, n.m. seat; siege
siéger, vb. to sit, convene, reside
sien, pron. le sien, la sienne,
  hers, his, its
sieste, n.f. siesta
siffler, vb. to whistle, hiss
sifflement, n.f. hissing, whistling
sifflet, n.m. whistle
signal, n.m. signal
signalement, n.m. description,
  details
signaler, vb. to point out
signature, n.f. signature
signe, n.m. sign
signer, vb. to sign; se s., cross
  oneself
significatif, adj. significant,
  meaningful
signification, n.f. significance,
  meaning
signifier, vb. to signify, mean
silence, n.m. silence
silencieux, adj. noiseless, silent
silex, n.m. fling
silhouette, n.f. outline, profile
sillage, n.m. wake, course
sillon, n.m. furrow made with a
  plough
sillonner, vb. to plow
simagrée, n.f. pretence
similaire, adj. similar
simple, adj. plain, simple, mere
simplicité, n.f. simplicity
simplifier, vb. to simplify
simulation, n.f. simulation
simuler, vb. to pretend
simultané, adj. simultaneous
sincère, adj. candid, sincerity
singe, n.m. imitator
singularité, n.f. singularity; peculiar
singulier, adj. and n.m. singular;
  peculiar, strange

sinistre, n.m. disaster; adj. sinister
sinon, conj. otherwise
sinueux, adj. winding, sinuous
sirène, n.f. siren
sirop, n.m. syrup
siroter, vb. to sip
site, n.m. site
sitôt, adv. as soon as
situation, n.f. situation, office,
  position, location,
situer, vb. to situate, locate
six, adj. and n.m. six
sixième, adj. and n.m. sixth
ski, n.m. ski
smoking, n.m. dinner jacket, tux
sobre, adj. temperate, sober
sobriété, n.f. moderation,
  temperance
sobriquet, n.m. nickname
sociable, adj. sociable
social, adj. social
socialisme, n.m. socialism
socialiste, adj. and n.m.f. socialiste
société, n.f. society; company
sociologie, n.f. sociology
sociologiste, n.m. sociologist
soeur, n.f. sister
soie, n.f. silk goods
soif, n.f. thirst; avoir s., be thirsty
soigné, adj. trim; mal s., sloppy
soigner, vb. to tend, take care of,
  look after
soir, n.m. evening; ce s., tonight;
  hier s., last night; le s., at night
soirée, n.f. evening
soixantaine, adj. and n.m. about
  sixty
soixante-dix, adj. and n.m. seventy
sol, n.m. earth, soil, ground
solaire, adj. solar
soldat, n.m. soldier
solde, n.m. balance
sole, n.f. sole
soleil, n.m. sun, shunshine
solennel, adj. solemn
solenniser, vb. to solemnize
solennité, n.f. solemnity
solidariser, vb. se s., to join
  together, unite
solidarité, n.f. joint responsibility
solide, adj. and n.m. solid
solidifier, vb. to solidify
solidité, n.f. solidity
soliloque, n.m. soliloquy
soliste, n.m. solosit
solitaire, adj. lonely, lonesome
solitude, n.f. solitude
solliciter, vb. to solicit, ask, apply
sollicitude, n.f. solicitude

soluble, adj. soluble

solution, n.f. solution

solvable, adj. solvent

sombre, adj. dark, somber, dim, gloomy

sombrer, vb. to sink

sommaire, n.m. summary

sommation, n.f. appeal, summons

somme, n.f. amount, sum; n.m. lap

sommeil, n.m. sleep

sommeiller, vb. to doze, slumber

sommer, vb. to summon

sommet, n.m. top, peak, summit

somnolence, n.f. drowsiness

somnolent, adj. drowsy, sleepy

somptueux, adj. lavish, sumptuous

son, n.m. sound, ring; bran; adj. his, hers, its

sonder, vb. to fathom; probe

songe, n.m. dream

songer à , vb. to think of, dream

songeur, adj. dreamy, thoughtful; n.m. dreamer

sonner, vb. to ring, sound, strike

sonnerie, n.f. ringing

sonnette, n.f. bell

sonore, adj. sonorous

sophiste, n.m. sophist

soprano, n.m. soprano

sorcier, n.m. wizard

sorcière, n.f. witch

sordide, adj. sordid

sort, n.m. lot

sorte, n.f. sort, kind

sortie, n.f. exit, way yout

sortilège, n.m. sorcery

sottise, n.f. foolishness

sou, n.m. cent; sans le sou, penniless

soubassement, n.m. basement

soubresaut, n.m. bound, jerk

souche, n.f. stub, stump

souci, n.m. care, worry, concern

soucieux, adj. anxious

soucoupe, n.f. saucer

soudain, adj. sudden

soudaineté, n.f suddenness

soude, n.f. soda

souder, vb. to solder, fuse

souffle, n.m. breath

souffler, vb. to blow

soufflet, n.m. bellows; blow, slap

souffleter, vb. to slap one_ face

souffrir, vb. to suffer, bear

soufre, n.m. sulphur

souhait, n.m. wish

souhaiter, vb. to wish for

souiller, vb. to soil, defile

souillure, n.f. stain, dirt

soulager, vb. to relieve, alleviate

soûler, vb. to fill with food and drink

soulever, vb. to lift, raise, arouse

soulier, n.m. shoe

souligner, vb. to underline

soumettre, vb. to submit, subdue

soumis, adj. obedient, submissive

soumission, n.f. submission

soupape, n.f. valve

soupçon, n.m. suspicion

soupçonner, vb. to suspect

soupçonneux, adj. suspicious

soupe, n.f. soup

souper, n.m. supper

soupir, n.m. sigh

soupirer, vb. to sigh

souple, adj. flexible

souplesse, n.f. suppleness, pliability

source, n.f. source; spring

sourcil, n.m. eyebrow

sourciller, vb. to frown

sourcilleux, adj. haughty, disdainful

sourd, adj. deaf

sourd-muet, n.m. deaf mute

souricière, n.f. mouse trap

sourire, n.m. and vb. smile

souris, n.f. mouse

sournois, adj. sly

sous, prep. under

souscription, n.f. subscription

souscrire, vb. to subscribe

sous-estimer, vb. to underestimate

sous-louer, vb. to sublet

sous-marin, n.m. submarine

soussigné, adj. undersigned

sous-sol, n.m. basement

sous-titre, n.m. subtitle

soustraction, n.f. subraction

soustraire, vb. to subtract

soutane, n.f. cassock

soute, n.f. storeroom

soutenir, vb. to support, uphold, back up, maintain; claim

soutenu, adj. steady

souterrain, adj. underground

soutien, n.m. support

soutien-gorge, n.m. brassiere

souvenance, n.f. recall, recollection

souvenir, n.m. remberance, memory

souvent, adv. often

souverain, n.m. ruler, sovereign

souveraineté, n.f. sovereignty

soyeux, adj. silky

spacieux, adj. spacious

spasme, n.m. spasm

spatule, n.f. spatula

spécial, adj. special

spécialiser, vb. to specialize
spécialiste, n.m.f. specialist
spécialité, n.f. specialty
spécifier, vb. to specify
spécifique, adj. specific
spécimen, n.m. specimen
spectacle, n.m. sight, show
spectaculaire, adj. spectacular
spectateur, n.m. spectator
spectre, n.m. ghost; spectrum
spéculation, n.f. speculation
spéculer, vb. to speculate
sphère, n.f. sphrer
spinal, adj. spinal
spiral, adj. spiral
spirale, n.f. spiral
spirite, n.m.f. spiritualist
spiritisme, n.m. spiritualism
spirituel, adj. spiritual; witty
splendeur, n.f. splendor
splendide, adj. splendid
spontané, adj. spontaneous
spontanéité, n.f. spontaneity
sporadique, adj. sporadic
sport, n.m. sport
sportif, adj. of sport
squelette, n.m. skeleton
stabiliser, vb. to stabilize
stabilité, n.f. stability
stable, adj. stable, steady
stage, n.m. priod of probation
stagnant, adj. stagnant
stalle, n.f. stall
stance, n.f. stanza
station, n.f. stand, stop
stationnaire, adj. stationary
stationner, vb. to park
statique, adj. static
statistique, n.f. statistics
statue, n.f. statue
statuer, vb. to decree, decide
stature, n.f. stature
statut, n.m. statute
sténographe, n.m.f. stenographer
sténographie, n.f. stenography
stéréophonique, adj. sterophonic
stérile, adj. barren
stériliser, vb. to sterilize
stéthoscope, n.m. stethoscope
stigmatiser, vb. to mark, stigmatize
stimulant, n.m. stimulus
stimuler, vb. to stimulate
stipuler, vb. to stipulate
stoïque, adj. and n.m.f. stole
store, n. m. window shade, blind
stratagème, n.m. stratagem
stratégie, n.f. strategy
stratégique, adj. strategic
strict, adj. severe, strict

strier, vb. to mark, streak, make grooves
structure, n.f. structure
stuc, n.m. stucco
studieux, adj. studious
stupéfait, adj. astounded
stupéfiant, n.m. dope, narcotic
stupéfier, vb. to astound
stupeur, n.f. amazement
stupide, adj. stupid
stupidité, n.f. stupidity
style, n.m. style
styler, vb. to rain, teach
subdiviser, vb. to subdivide
subir, vb. to undergo
subit, adj. sudden
subjectif, adj. subjective
subjonctif, adj. and n.m. subjunctive
subjuguer, vb. to subdue, overcome
sublime, adj. sublime, exalted
submerger, vb. to submerge, flood
subordonné, adj. and n.m. subordinate
subreptice, adj. surrepitious
subséquent, adj. subsequent
subside, n.m. subsidy
subsister, vb. to subsist, live
substance, n.f. substance
substantiel, adj. substantial
substantif, n.m. noun
substituer, vb. to substitute
substitution, n.f. substitution
subtil, adj. subtle
subtilité, n.f. subtlety
subvention, n.f. grant, subsidy
subventionner, vb. to subsidize
subversif, adj. subverversive
suc, n.m. juice
succéder à , vb. to succeed, follow
succès, n.m. success; hit
successeur, n.m. successor
successif, adj. successive
succession, n.f. succession
succion, n.f. suction
succursale, n.f. branch office
sucer, vb. to suck
sucre, n.m. sugar
sud, n.m. south
sudation, n.f. sweating
sud-est, n.m. southeast
sud-ouest, n.m. southwest
Suède, n.f. Sweden
Suédois, n.m. Swede
suédois, adj. and n.m. Swedish
suer, vb. to sweat
sueur, n.m. sweat
suffire, vb. to suffice
suffisance, n.f. adequacy, conceit

suffisant, adj. sufficient, adequate
suffixe, n.m. suffix
suffoquer, vb. to suffocate
suffrage, n.m. suffrage
suggérer, vb. to suggest
suggestion, n.f. suggestion
suicide, n.m. suicide
suicider, vb. se s., to kill oneself
suif, n.m. tallow
suinter, vb. to seep
Suisse, n.m. Swiss; n.f.
  Switzerland
suisse, adj. Swiss
suite, n.f. sequence; retinue
suivant, n.m. follower; adj. next,
  following, subsequent
suivre, vb. to follow; attend; **faire
  s.,** forward
sujet, n.m. subject; topic; adj.
  subject; **s. à ,** liable to
sujétion, n.f. subjection, slavery
superbe, adj. superb, magnificent
superficie, n.f. surface
superficiel, adj. superficial, shallow
superflu, adj. superfluous
supérieur, adj. and n.m. higher,
  superior
supériorité, n.f. superiority
superlatif, adj. and n.m. superlative
superstar, n.m. superstar
superstitieux, adj. superstitious
superstition, n.f. superstition
suppléant, adj. and n.m. assistant, substitute
suppléer, vb. to substitute
supplément, n.m. supplement
supplémentaire, adj. extra;
heures supplémentaires, overtime
supplice, n.m. punishment, torture
supplier, vb. to beseech, supplicate
support, n.m. support, stand
supporter, vb. to support, bear,
  stand, endure
supposer, vb. to suppose, assume
supposition, n.f. assumption,
  supposition
suppôt, n.m. implement, tool, agent
suppression, n.f. suppression
supprimer, vb. to suppress, put
  down, take out
supputation, n.f. computation
supputer, vb. to compute
suprématie, n.f. supremacy
suprême, adj. supreme
sur, prep. on, upon. over
sûr, adj. safe, sure, secure
surabonder, vb. to be very
  abundant
suranné, adj. out-of-date
surcroît, n.m. addition

surdité, n.f. deafness
suret, adj. sour
sûreté, n.f. safety, security,
  reliability
surface, n.f. surface, area
surgélateur, n.m. deep freeze
surgir, vb. to spring up, arise
surintendant, n.m. superintendent
sur-le-champ, adv. immediately, at
  once
surmener, vb. to overwork
surmonter, vb. to overcome,
  surmount
surnaturel, adj. and n.m. super-
  natural
surnom, n.m. nickname
surpasser, vb. to surpass
surplomber, vb. to overhang
surplus, n.m. surplus, excess
surprendre, vb. to surprise
surprise, n.f. surprise
sursaut, n.m. start
sursauter, vb. to give a start
sursis, n.m. delay, putting off
surveillance, n.f. supervision,
  watch
surveillant, n.m. superintendent
surveiller, vb. to supervise
survenir, vb. to happen
survie, n.f. survival
survivance, n.f. survival
survivre, vb. to survive
susceptible, adj. liable
suspect, adj. suspicious
suspecter, vb. to suspect
suspendre, vb. to suspend, sling
suspension, n.f. suspension
suspicion, n.f. suspicion
sustenter, vb. to sustain, bulwark,
  support, maintain
svelte, adj. slender, slim
sycomore, n.m. Sycamore
syllabaire, n.m. spelling book
syllabe, n.f. syllable
sylvicole, adj. living in the woods
sylviculture, n.f. forestry
symbole, n.m. symbol, sign,
  emblem, creed
symboliser, vb. to symbolize
symétrie, n.f. symmetry
sympathie, n.f. sympathy; **avoir
  de la s. pour,** like
sympathique, adj. likeable
sympathisant, n.m. fellow traveler
sympathiser, vb. to sympathize
symphonie, n.f. symphony
symptôme, n.m. symptom
syndrome, n.m. syndrome
synonyme, n.m. synonym
synthèse, n.f. synthesis

synthétique, adj. synthetic
systématique, adj. systematic
système, n.m. system

T

tabac, n.m. tobacco
table, n.f. table
tableau, n.m. picture
tabler, vb. to count, on depend
tablette, n.f. tablet
tablier, n.m. apron
tabou, n.m. taboo
tabouret, n.m. stool
tache, n.f. spot, blot, smear
tâche, n.f. task; assignment
tacher, vb. to spot, stain, blot
tâcher, vb. to try
tacite, adj. silent
tact, n.m. tact
tacticien, n.m. tactician
tactique, adj. of tactics; n.f. tactics
taffetas, n.m. taffeta
taie, n.f. pillowcase
taillade, n.f. slash
taille, n.f. waist, figure, size
tailler, vb. to trim, cut
tailleur, n.m. tailor
taire, vb. to keep quiet
talent, n.m. ability, talent
talon, n.m. heel
talus, n.m. slope
tambour, n.m. drum
tambourin, n.m. tambourine
tamis, n.m. sieve
tampon, n.m. plug, pad
tamponner, vb. to plug; run
  together
tan, n.m. tan leather
tandis que, conj. whereas, while
tangible, adj. tangible
tant, adv. so many, so much; t.
  que, as long as
tante, n.f. aunt
tantième, n.m. part, percentage
tantôt, adv. presently, soon
tapage, n.m. din
tapageur, adj. rowdy
taper, vb. to pat, tap; type
tapis, n.m. carpet, rug
tapisserie, n.f. tapestry
tapissier, n.m. upholsterer
taquiner, vb. to tease
taquinerie, n.f. teasing
tard, adv. late
tarder, vb. to delay
tardif, adj. slow, tardy, late
tarif, n.m. scale of charges

tartan, n.m. plaid
tarte, n.f. pie
tartre, n.m. tartar
tas, n.m. heap, pile
tasse, n.f. cup
tasser, vb. to pack, fill up
tâter, vb. to feel
taupe, n.f. mole
taureau, n.m. bull
taux, n.m. rate
taverne, n.f. tavern
taxe, n.f. tax
taxer, vb. to tax, assess
taxi, n.m. cab, taxi
te, pron. you, yourself
technicien, n.m. technician
technique, n.f. technique; adj.
  technical
technologie, n.f. technology
teindre, vb. to dye
teint, n.m. complexion
teinte, n.f. tint, shade
teinter, vb. to tint, stain
teinturier, n.m. dry-cleaner
tel, adj. such
télégramme, n.m. telegram
télégraphe, n.m. telegraph
télégraphie, n.f. telegraphy
télégraphier, vb. to telegraph
téléphone, n.m. telephone
téléphoner, vb. to telephone
télescope, n.m. telescope
télescoper, vb. to crash
télévision, n.f. television
tellement, adv. so much
téméraire, adj. rash
témoignage, n.m. testimony
témoigner, vb. to testify
témoin, n.m. witness
tempe, n.f. temple
tempérament, n.m. temperament
tempérant, adj. temperate
température, n.f. temperature
tempéré, adj. temperate
température, n.f. temperature
tempérer, vb. to moderate, calm
tempête, n.f. storm, tempest
tempétueux, adj. tempestuous
temple, n.m. temple
temporaire, adj. temporary
temporiser, vb. to temporize, evade
temps, n.m. time, weather
tenace, adj. tenacious
ténacité, n.f. tenacity
tenailles, n.f., pl. tongs
tendance, n.f. tendency, trend
tendre, adj. tender, fond, loving; vb.
  tend, extend
tendresse, n.f. fondness,
  tenderness

tendu, adj. tense; uptight

ténèbres, n.f. pl. gloom, darkness

ténébreux, adj. dismal

teneur, n.m. t. de livres,
  bookkeeper

tenir, vb. to hold

tennis, n.m. tennis

ténor, n.m. tenor

tension, n.f. strin; stress

tentacule, n.m. tentacle

tentative, adj. tentative

tentative, n.f. attempt

tente, n.f. tent; awning

tenter, vb. to tempt, try, attract

tenture, n.f. wallcovering

tenue, n.f. rig; conduct, manners

ténuité, n.f. tenuity, unimportance

térébenthine, n.f. turpentine

terme, n.m. term, period; end

terminaison, n.f. ending

terminer, vb. to end

terminologie, n.f. terminology

terne, adj. drab, dull, dim, dingy

ternir, vb. to tarnish, dull

terrain, n.m. grounds

terrasse, n.f. terrace

terrasser, vb. to conquer, heap up,
  embank; knock down

terre, n.f. ground, earth, land

terrestre, adj. earthly

terreur, n.f. terror, fright, fear

terrible, adj. terrible, awful

terrifier, vb. to terrify

territoire, n.m. territory

terroir, n.m. soil

terroriser, vb. to terrorize

tertre, n.m. mound

tesson, n.m. broken piece,
  fragment

testament, n.m. testament, will

tête, n.f. head

téter, vb. to suck

teton, n.m. breast

texte, n.m. text

textile, adj. textile

thé, n.m. tea

théâtral, adj. theatrical

théâtre, n.m. theater

thélère, n.f. teapot

thème, n.m. theme

théologie, n.f. theology

théorie, n.f. theory

théorique, adj. theoretical

thermomètre, n.m. thermometer

thésauriser, vb. to hoard

thèse, n.f. thesis

thym, n.m. thyme

ticket, n.m. ticket, check, coupon

tiède, adj. lukewarm

tiédir, vb. to make or become cool

tien, pron. le tien, la tienne, yours

tiers, n.m. third

tige, n.f. stem, stalk

tigre, n.m. tiger

tilleul, n.m. linden, limetree

timbre, n.m. stamp; t-poste,
  postage stamp

timbrer, vb. to stamp

timide, adj. timid, shy, bashful

timidité, n.f. timidity

tintamarre, n.m. racket

tinter, vb. to ring, knell, tinkle

tirailleur, n.m. sharpshooter

tire, n.m. yank, pull

tirer, vb. to draw, pull; shoot

tiret, n.m. blank

tiroir, n.m. drawer

tisane, n.f. drink

tisser, vb. to weave

tisserand, n.m. weaver

tissu, n.m. web; cloth, fabric

titre, n.m. title, right

toast (-t), n.m. toast

toile, n.f. web; canvas; linen

toilette, n.f. toilet; dressing,
  dress

toison, n.f. fleece

toit, n.m. roof

toiture, n.f. roofing

tolérance, n.f. tolerance

tolérer, vb. to tolerate, bear

tomate, n.f. tomato

tombe, n.f. grave

tombeau, n.m. tomb

tombée, n.f. fall, decline

tomber, vb. to fall; laisser t., drop

ton, n.m. tone, pitch

tondeuse, n.f. lawn mower

tondre, vb. to mow; shear

tonne, n.f. ton; barrel

tonneau, n.m. cask, barrel

tonner, vb. to thunder

topaze, n.f. topaz

torche, n.f. torch

tordre, vb. to twist, wrench, wring

torpille, n.f. torpedo

torrent, n.m. torrent

torride, adj. torrid

torse, n.m. torso

tort, n.m. wrong

tortiller, vb. to twist, wiggle

tordu, adj. crooked

tortue, n.f. turtle, tortoise

torture, n.f. torture

torturer, vb. to torture

tôt, adv. early, soon

totalisateur, n.m. adding machine

totaliser, vb. to total, add up

totalité, n.f. entirety

touchant, prep. concerning

touche, n.f. key
touffe, n.f. tuft, bunch
touffu, adj. bushy
toujours, adv. always, ever, yet
tour, n.m. turn; trick; stroll;
  faire le t de, go around
tourbe, n.f. rabble
tourbillon, n.m. whirl; t. d'eau,
  whirlpool
tourbillonner, vb. to whirl
tourelle, n.f. turret
touriste, n.m.f. tourist
tourment, n.m. torment
tourmenter, vb. to torment
tourne-disques, n.m. record player
tournée, n.f. round
tourner, vb. to turn, revolve
tournesol, n.m. sunflower
tournevis, n.m. screwdriver
tournoi, n.m. tournament
tournure, n.f. figure
tousser, vb. to cough
toutefois, adv. however
tout-puissant, adj. almighty
toux, n.f. cough
toxique, adj. toxic
tracasser, vb. to worry
trace, n.f. trace, track, footprint
tracer, vb. to outline, trace
tracteur, n.m. tractor
tradition, n.f. tradition
traditionnel, adj. traditional
traducteur, n.m. translator
traduction, n.f. translation
traduire, vb. to translate
trafic, n.m. traffic
tragédie, n.f. tragedy
tragique, adj. tragic
trahir, vb. to betray
trahison, n.f. treason
train, n.m. train
traînard, n.m. dawdler
traîne, n.f. train of a dress
traîneau, n.m. sled sleigh
traîner, vb. to drag, haul
traire, vb. to milk
trait, n.m. feature; draft; shot
traité, n.m. treaty
traitement, n.m. treatment
traiter, vb. to treat, deal
traître, n.m. traitor
traîtrise, n.f. treachery
trajet, n.m. crossing
trame, n.f. plan, plot
tramer, vb. to devise
tramway, n.m. streetcar
tranchant, adj. sharp, crisp
tranche, n.f. slice
tranchée, n.f. trench
trancher, vb. to cut

tranquille, adj. quiet
tranquilliser, vb. to make tranquil
tranquillité, n.f. quiet, stillness
transaction, n.f. transaction
transe, n.f. fright, fear
transférer, vb. to transfer
transformer, vb. to transform
transfuser, vb. to transfuse
transfusion, n.f. transfusion
transition, n.f. transition
transitoire, adj. transitory
transmettre, vb. to transmit, convey
transparent, adj. transparent
transpiration, n.f. perspiration
transpirer, vb. to perspire
transplanter, vb. to transplant
transport, n.m. transfer, transport,
  transportation; ecstasy
transporter, vb. to transport,
  transfer, convey
transposer, vb. to transpose
transsexuel, adj. transsexual
travail, n.m. work, job, labor
travailler, vb. to work
travailleur, n.m. worker, laborer;
  adj. industrious
travée, n.f. span
travers, n.m. breadth; à t., across,
  through; de t., awry
traversée, n.f. crossing
traverser, vb. to cross
traversin, n.m. bolster
travestir, vb. to disguise
trébucher, vb. to stumble, trip
treillis, n.m. denim
treize, adj. and n.m. thirteen
tremblement, n.m. trembling
trembler, vb. to tremble, quake,
  shake
trembloter, vb. to quiver
trémousser, vb. to flutter
trempe, n.f. temper, cast
tremper, vb. to soak, drench,
  temper
trente, adj. and n.m. thirty
trépasser, vb. to die
trépied, n.m. tripod, trivet
très, adv. very
trésor, n.m. treasure, treasury
trésorier, n.m. treasurer
tressaillement, n.m. thrill; start
tressaillir, vb. to thrill; start
tresse, n.f. braid
tresser, vb. to braid
tréteau, n.m. trestle
trêve, n.f. truce
triangle, n.m. triangle
tribade, n.f. Lesbian
tribu, n.f. tribe
tribulation, n.f. tribulation

tribut, n.m. tribute
tributaire, adj. tributary
tricher, vb. to cheat
tricherie, n.f. cheating
tricoter, vb. to knit
trier, vb. to sort
trimestre, n.m. term
trimestriel, adj. quarterly
triomphant, adj. triumphant
triomphe, n.m. triumph
triompher, vb. to triumph
triple, adj. and n.m. triple
triste, adj. sad
tristesse, n.f. sadness
trivial, adj. trivial
trivialité, n.f. triviality
troc, n.m. barter
trois, adj. and n.m. three
troisième, adj. third
trompe, n.f. horn
tromperie, n.f. deceit
trompette, n.f. trumpet
trompeur, adj. deceitful
tronc, n.m. trunk
trône, n.m. throne
trop, adv. too much; too
trophée, n.m. trophy
tropical, adj. tropical
tropique, n.m. tropic
troquer, vb. to barter, trade
trot, n.m. trot
trotter, vb. to trot
trottiner, vb. to trot, jog
trottoir, n.m. sidewalk
trou, n.m. hole
trouble, n.m. disturbance, riot
troublé, adj. anxious, worried
troubler, vb. to perturb
trouer, vb. to pierce
troupe, n.f. troop
troupeau, n.m. herd, flock. drove
troupier, n.m. soldier
trousseau, n.m. outfit
trousser, vb. to turn up
trouvaille, n.f. discovery; finding
trouver, vb. to find, discover
truc, n.m. trick; thing
truelle, n.f. trowel
truite, n.f. trout
truquer, vb. to fake
trust, n.m. trust
tu, pron., you
tuant, adj. exhausting, tiresome, killing
tub, n.m. tub
tuba, n.m. tuba
tube, n.m. tube, pipe
tuberculeux, adj. tuberculous
tuberculose, n.f. tuberculosis
tubulaire, adj. tubular

tuer, vb. to slay; kill, slaughter
tuerie, n.f. slaughter, massacre
tueur, n.m. slayer, thug, killer
tulle, n.f. tile
tulipe, n.f. tulip
tuméfier, vb. to make swollen
tumeur, n.f. tumor
tumulte, n.m. turmoil, uproar, confusion
tunnel, n.m. tunnel
turbin, n.m. work
turbine, n.f. turbine
turbulence, n.f. tubulence
turc, adj. Turkish
turlutaine, n.f. a sentence or word that a person likes to repeat
turne, n.f. dirty, unorderly house
tunique, n.f. tunic
tunnel, n.f. tunnel
turc, m., **turque** f. adj. Turkish language
turnep, n.m. field turnip
Turquie, n.f. Turkey
turquin, adj. dark, deep blue
tutelle, n.f. protection
tuteur, n.m. guardian; trustee, protector
tutu, n.m. short ballet skirt
tuyau, n.f. pipe; hose; tube
tympan, n.m. eardrum
type, n.m. model, type, pattern; sample
typhus, n.m. typhus
typique, adj. typical, symbolical
tyran, n.m. tyrant
tyrannie, n.f. tyranny
tyranniser, vb. to tyrannize; oppress
tzigane, n. gypsy

U

ulcère, n.m. ulcer
ultérieur, adj. ulterior, further
ultime, adj. ultimate
unanime, adj. unanimous
unanimité, n.f. unanimity
unifier, vb. to unify
uniforme, adj. uniform
union, n.f. union
unique, adj. unique
unir, vb. to unite
unisexuel, adj. unisex
unisson, n.m. unison
unité, n.f. unit, unity
univers, n.m. universe
universel, adj. universal
université, n.f. university, college

urbain, adj. urban
urgence, n.f. urgency
urgent, adj. urgent, pressing
urticaire, n.m. hives
usage, n.m. use; custom
usager, adj. for daily use
user, vb. to make use of, wear out
usine, n.f. factory
ustensile, n.m. utensil
usuel, adj. usual
usure, n.f. wear and tear
utile, adj. helpful, useful
utilisation, n.f. use
utopie, n.f. utopia

V

vacance, n. vacancy
vacant, adj. vacant
vacarme, n.m. uproar, racket
vaccin, n.m. vaccine
vacciner, vb. to vaccinate, immunize
vache, n.f. cow; cow hide
vaciller, vb. to waver, flicker
vacuité, n.f. emptiness, vacuity
vagabond, adj. vagrant
vagabonder, vb. to roam, tramp
vague, n.f. wave; adj. vague
vaguer, vb. to wander
vaillant, adj. brave, gallant
vain, adj. idle, futile
vaincre, vb. to defeat
vainqueur, n.m. victor
vaisseau, n.m. ship
vaisselle, n.f. dishes
valeur, n.f. value, worth
valeureux, adj. brave, valorous
valide, adj. valid
valise, n.f. suitcase
vallée, n.f. valley
vallon, n.m. valley, vale
valoir, vb. to be worth
valse, n.f. waltz
vandale, n.m.f. vandal
vanille, n.f. vanilla
vanité, n.f. conceit, vanity
vaniteux, adj. vain
vantard, adj. boastful
vapeur, n.m. steamship
vaporisateur, n.f. vaporizer, spray
variation, n.f. variation, change
varicelle, n.f. chicken-pox
varier, vb. to vary
variété, n.f. variety
variole, n.f. smallpox
vase, n.m. vase, vessel
vasectomie, n.f. vasectomy

vaseux, adj. slimy
vassal, n.f. vassal
vaste, adj. vast, spacious
veau, n.m. calf
végéter, vb. to vegetate
véhicule, n.m. vehicle
veille, n.f. eve, day before
veiller, vb. to watch over, sit up
veine, n.f. vein; luck
velours, n.m. velvet
velouté, adj. like velvet
velu, adj. hairy
vendange, n.f. vintage
vendeur, n.m. clerk, salesman
vendre, vb. to sell, sell out
vendredi, n.m. Friday
vénéneux, adj. poisonous
vénérer, vb. to venerate
vengeance, n.f. revenge, vengeance
venger, vb. to avenge
venimeux, adj. venomous
venin, n.m. venom
venir, vb. to come
vent, n.m. wind
vente, n.f. sale
venteux, adj. windy
ventilateur, n.m. fan, ventilator
ventiler, vb. to ventilate
ventre, n.m. belly, stomach
venue, n.f. advent, arrival
vêpres, n.f., pl. vespers
ver, n.m. worm
véracité, n.f. veracity
véranda, n.f. porch
verbe, n.m. verb
verbeux, adj. wordy, verbose
verdeur, n.f. sharpness, vigor
verdict, n.m. verdictston, n.m. coat
vêtement, n.m. garment; pl. clothes
vétéran, n.m. veteran
vétérinaire, n.m. veterinary
vêtir, vb. to clothe
veto, n.m. veto
veuf, n.m. widower
veuve, n.f. widow
vexation, n.f. vexation
vexer, vb. to vex
viaduc, n.m. viaduct
viande, n.f. meat
vibrant, adj. vibrant, vibrating
vibration, n.f. vibration
vibrer, vb. to vibrate
vicaire, n.m. vicar
vice, n.m. vice, defect
vice-roi, n.m. viceroy
vicieux, adj. vicious; wrong
victime, n.f. victim
victoire, n.f. victory
victorieux, adj. victorious

vidange, n.f. emptying, drain
vide, n.m. emptiness, vacuum, blank; adj. empty, void, vacant
vidéodisque, n.m. videodisc
vider, vb. to empty, drain
vie, n.f. life; livelihood
vieil, adj. old
vieillard, n.m. old man
vieille, n.f. old woman
vieillesse, n.f. old age
vieillir, vb. to age
vierge, n.f. virgin; virginal
vieux, adj. old
vif m., **vive** f. adj. lively, quick brisk, full of life
vigie, n.f. lookout
vigilance, n.f. vigilance
vigilant, adj. watchful
vigoureux, adj. vigorous
vigueur, n.f. vigor, force
vil, adj. vile
vilain, adj. ugly, wicked
village, n.m. village
ville, n.f. city, town
vin, n.m. wine
vinaigre, n.m. vinegar
vindicatif, adj. vindictive
violateur, n.m. violator
violation, n.f. violation
violemment, adj. violently
violence, n.f. violence
violent, adj. violent
violer, vb. to violate
violet, adj. purple, violet
violette, n.f. violet
violon, n.m. violin
vipère, n.f. viper
virgule, n.f. comma
viril, adj. manly
virilité, n.f. manhood
virtuel, adj. virtual
virtuose, n.m.f. virtuoso
virus, n.m. virus
vis, n.f. screw
visa, n.m. visa
visage, n.m. face
vis-à-vis, adv. opposite, across from; facing
viser, vb. to aim at
visibilité, n.f. visibility
visible, adj. visible
visière, n.f. visor; keenness
vision, n.f. vision
visite, n.f. call, visit
visiter, vb. to visit
visiteur, n.m. visitor
visqueux, adj. viscous, sticky
visser, vb. to screw
visuel, adj. visual
vital, adj. vital

vitalité, n.f. vitality
vitamine, n.f. vitamin
vite, adv. quick, fast, swift
vitesse, n.f. speed, rate; gear
vitrail, n.m. stained-glass window
vitre, n.f. window, pane
vitrine, n.f. display case
vivacité, n.f. vivacity
vivant, adj. alive
vivement, adv. quickly, vividly
vivre, vb. to live
vocabulaire, n.m. vocabulary
vocal, adj. vocal
vocation, n.f. vocation
voeu, n.m. vow
vogue, n.f. bogue
voici, vb. to here is, behold
voie, n.f. track, road
voilà , vb. to there is; behold
voile, n.m. veil; sail
voiler, vb. to veil, hide
voilure, n.f. sails
voir, vb. to see. **faire** v., show
voirie, n.m. dump
voisin, n.m. neighbor; adj. nearby
voisinage, n.m. neighborhood
voisiner, vb. to act like a neighbor
voiture, n.f. car, carriage
voix, n.f. voice
vol, n.m. flight; robbery; ripoff
volage, adj. fickle
volaille, n.f. fowl, poultry
volatil, adj. volatile
volcan, n.m. volcano
volcanique, adj. volcanic
volée, n.f. flight, covey; herd
voler, vb. to fly; steal, rip off
volet, n.m. shutter, blind
voleur, n.m. thief, robber
vol frété, n.m. charter flight
volontaire, n.m. volunteer
volonté, n.f. will
volontiers, adv. gladly, willingly
voltigement, n.m. flutter
voltiger, vb. to flutter; hover
volubilité, n.f. volubility
volume, n.m. volume
volumineux, adj. bulky
volupté, n.f. pleasure
vomir, vb. to vomit
vorace, adj. voracious
votant, n.m. voter
votre, adj. yours
vouer, vb. to vow, dedicate
vouloir, vb. to want, wish, require
vous, pron. you, yourself
voûte, n.f. vault
voûter, vb. to arch
voyage, n.m. journey, trip
voyager, vb. to travel

voyageur, n.m. traveler, passenger
voyelle, n.f. vowel
vrai, adj. true, real
vraisemblance, n.f. probability
vue, n.f. view, sight
vulgaire, adj. vulgar, coarse, rude
vulgarité, n.f. vulgarity

X

xérès, n.m. sherry (wine)
xylophone, n.m. xylophone

Y

y, adv. here, there, within
yacht, n.m. yachtnerable
yaourt, n.m. yogurt
iodler, vb. to yodel
yucca, n.m. yucca

Z

zèbre, n.m. zebra
zèle, n.m. zeal, warmth, ardour
zélé, adj. zealous
zénith, n.m. zenith
zéro, n.m. zero
zézayer, vb. to lisp
zibeline, n.f. sable
zigzaguer, vb. to zigzag
zodiaque, n.m. zodiac
zona, n.m. shingles
zone, n.f. area, zone
zoo, n.m. zoo
zoologiste, n. zoologist
zieuter, v.t. to look at

Anglais/Français

English/French

a, art. un, m., une f.
aardvark, n. oryctérope m.
abacus, n. abaque m.
abandon, vb. abandonner
abandon, n. abandon m.
abandoned, adj. abandonné
abate, vb. diminuer
abatement, n. diminution f.
abbey, n. abbaye
abbreviate, vb. abréger
abbreviation, n. abréviation f.
abdicate, vb. abdiquer
abdomen, n. abdomen m.
abdominal, adj. abdominal
abduct, vb. enlever
abductor, n. ravisseur m.
abettor, n. aide m. complice m.
abeyance, n. suspension f.
abide, vb. (tolerate) supporter;
  (remain) demeurer; (a. by the
  law) respecter la loi
ability, n. talent m.
abject, adj. abject
able, adj. capable; (to be able)
  pouvoir
able-bodied, adj. fort, robuste
ably, adv. compétence
aboard, adv. à bord
abode, n. demeure f.
abolish, vb. abolir
abolishment, n. abolition m.
abominate, vb. abominer
abomination, n. abomination f.
abortion, n. avortement m.
abortive, adj. abortif, manqué
abound, vb. abonder (de or en)
about, adv. (approximately) à
  peu près; autour
above, adv. au-dessus; prep.
  au-dessus de; plus de
abrasive, adj. abrasif m.
abreast, adv. de front
abroad, adv. à l'étranger
abrupt, adj. (hasty) brusque
abscess, n. abcès m.
absence, n. absence f.
absent, adj. absent
absolute, adj. absolu
absolutely, adv. absolument
absolution, n. absolution f.
absolve, vb. absoudre
absorb, vb. absorber
absorbed, adj. absorbé
absorbent, adj. absorbant m.
absorbing, adj. absorbant
absorption, n. absorption
abstinence, n. abstinence f.
abstract, adj. abstrait
absurd, adj. absurde
abundance, n. abondance f.

abundant, adj. abondant
abuse, n. abus m.
abusive, adj. (insulting) injurieux
abut, vb. aboutir (à)
abyss, n. abîme m.
academic, adj. académique
academy, n. académie f.
accede, vb. consentir
accelerate, vb. accélérer
accelerator, n. accélérateur m.
accent, n. accent m.
accept, vb. accepter
acceptance, n. acceptation f.
access, n. accès, abord m.
accessory, n. accessoire m.
accident, n. accident m.
accidental, adj. accidentel
acclaim, vb. acclamer
acclamation, n. acclamation f.
acclimate, vb. acclimater
accomodate, vb. (lodge) loger;
  (oblige) obliger
accompany, vb. accompagner
accomplish, vb. accomplir
accomplished, adj. accompli,
  achevé
accord, n. accord, rapport m.
accordance, n. accord m.
accordingly, adv. en conséquence
account, n. compte m.
accountant, n. comptable m.
accounting, n. comptabilité f.
accretion, n. accroissement m.
accumulate, v.t. accumuler
accumulation, n. entassement m.
accumulative, adj. (chose) qui
  s'accumule
accuracy, n. précision f.
accurate, adj. précis
accusative, n. and adj. accusatif m.
accuse, v.t. accuser
accustom, v.t. accoutumer
ace, n. as m.
acetate, n. acétate m.
acetylene, n. acétylène m.
ache, n. douleur f.
achieve, vb. exécuter
achievement, n. accomplissement
  m.
acid, adj. acide m.
acidity, n. acidité f.
acknowledge, vb. reconnaître
acne, n. acné f.
acorn, n. gland m.
acquaint, vb. informer (de)
acquaintance, n. connaissance f.
acquainted, adj. connu, familier
  (avec)
acquiesce(in), vb. acquiescer (à)
acquire, vb. acquérir

acquit, vb. acquitter
acre, n. arpten m., acre f.
acrid, adj. âcre
acrobat, n. acrobate
across, prep. à travers
act, n. acte m. vb. jouer
acting, n. jeu m.
action, n. action f.
active, adj. actif, agile, alerte
activity, n. activité f.
actor, n. acteur m.
actress, n. actrice f.
actual, adj. réel
actually, adv. réellement, en effet
actuate, vb. mettre en action, animer
acupuncture, n. acuponcture f.
acutely, adv. vivement
acuteness, n. finesse f.
adapt, v.t. adapter
adaptable, adj. adaptable
adaptability, n. faculté d'adaptation f.
adaptation, n. adaptation f.
adapter, n. qui adapte
add, v.t ajouter; additionner
adder, v. vipère f.
addict, n. personne adonnée à f.
addition, n. addition f.
additional, adj. additionnel
address, n. adresse m.
adenoid, adj. and n. adénoïde f.
adept, adj. habile adepte
adequacy, n. suffisance f.
adequate, adj. suffisant
adhere, vb. adhérer
adherent, n. adhérent m.
adhesion, n. adhésion f.
adieu, n. and adv. adieu
adjective, n. adjectif m.
adjoin, vb. adjoindre
adjourn, vb. ajourner
adjunct, n. and adj. adjoint, accessoire m.
adjust, vb. ajuster, arranger, régler
adjuster, n. ajusteur m.
adjustment, n. ajustement accommodement m.
administer, vb. administrer
administration, n. administration f.
administrative, adj. administratif
administrator, n. administrateur m.
admirable, adj. admirable
admiral, n. amiral m.
admiration, n. admiration f.
admire, vb. admirer
admirer, n. admirateur m.
admiringly, adv. avec admiration
admission, n. (entrance) entrée f.

admit, vb. laisser entrer
admittance, n. accès m.
admonish, vb. réprimander
adolescence, n. adolescence f.
adolescent, adj. and n. adolescent m., adolescente f.
adopt, vb. adopter
adoption, n. adoption f.
adorable, adj. adorable
adoration, n. adoration f.
adore, vb. adorer
adorn, vb. orner
adult, adj. and n. adulte m.f.
adulterer, n. adultère m.
adulteress, n. femme adultère f.
adultery, n. adultère m.
advance, v.t. avancer, faire
advanced, adj. avancé
advancement, n. avancement m.
advantage, n. avantage m.
advantageous, adj. avantageux
advent, n. venue f.; (eccles.) Avent m.
adventure, n. aventure f.
adventurer, n. aventurier m.
adventurous, adj. aventureux
adverb, n. adverbe m.
adverse, adj. adverse
advert, vb. faire allusion (à)
advertise, vb. annoncer
advertisement, n. annoncer
advertising, n. publicité f.
advice, n. conseil m.
advise, vb. conseiller
advocate, n. avocat m.
aerate, vb. aérer
aeration, n. aération f.
aerial, adj. aérien
aerie, n. aire f.
aesthetic, adj. esthétique
afar, adv. loin, de loin
affair, n. affaire f.
affect, vb. toucher, intéresser
affected, adj. maniéré
affecting, adj. touchant, émouvant
affection, n. affection f.
affiance, vb. fiancer
affidavit, n. déclaration par écrit sous serment attestation f.
affiliate, vb. affilier
affinity, n. affinité f.
affirm, vb. affirmer
affirmation, n. affirmation f.
affix, vb. apposer
afflict, vb. affliger (de)
affliction, n. affliction f.
affluence, n. affluence, opulence f.
affluent, adj. affluent, opulent
afford, vb. donner, fournir
affront, n. affront m.

afloat, adv. à flot

afraid, adj. effrayé pris de peur

Africa, n. l' Afrique f.

after, prep. après; sur, à la suite de

afternoon, n. après-midi m.f.

afterward, adv. ensuite

again, adv. encore

against, prep. contre

age, n. âge m.

ageless, adj. toujours jeune

agency, n. agence f.

agenda, n. ordre du jour, agenda m.

agent, n. agent m.

aggravate, vb. aggraver

aggravation, n. aggravation f., agacement m.

aggregate, adj. global

aggression, n. agression f.

aggressive, adj. agressif

aggressor, n. agresseur m.

aghast, adj. consterné

agitate, vb. agiter, exciter

agitator, n. agitateur m.

ago, adv. passé, il y a

agonized, v.t torturer

agony, n. angoisse, agonie f.

agree, vb. être d'accord

agreeable, adj. agréable

agreeably, adv. agréablement

agreement, n. accord m.

agriculture, n. agriculture f.

ahead, adv. and interj. en avant

aid, n. aide, assistance f.

AIDS, n. (acronym) - acquired immune deficiency syndrome - le SIDA (syndrome d'immuno-déficience acquise)

ail, vb. être souffrant

ailment, n. indisposition f.

aim, n. point de mire, but m.

air, n. air, vent m., brise f.

airbag, n. sac à air m.

airborne, adj. aéroporté

air-condition, vb. climatiser

air-conditioning, n. climatisation f.

aircraft, n. avion, les avions, m., pl.

air gun, n. fusil à vent

airliner, n. avion m.

air mail, n. poste aérienne f.

airplane, n. avion m.

air pollution, n. pollution de l'air f.

airport, n. aéroport m.

air pressure, n. pression d'air f.

airsickness, n. mal de l'air

airtight, adj. imperméable à l'air

airy, adj. ouvert à l'air; aéré

aisle, n. bas-côté m.

ajar, adv. entrouvert

akin, adj. allié (à). parent (de)

alarm, n. alarme, alerte f.

albino, n. albinos m.

album, n album m.

alcohol, n. alcool m.

alcoholic, adj. alcoolique

alert, adj. alerte

algebra, n. algèbre f.

alibi, n. alibi m.

alien, adj. étranger

align, vb. aligner

alike, adj. semblable; adv. également

alive, adj. vivant, envie

alkali, n. alcali m.

alkaline, adj. alcalin

all, adj. tout m. sg , toute f. sg., tous m., pl toutes f., pl; adv. and pron. tout; surtout; tout d'un coup

allay, vb. apaiser

allegation, n. allégation f.

allege, vb. alléguer

allegiance, n. fidélité f.

allergy, n. allergie f.

alleviate, vb. soulager

alley, n. ruelle f.

alliance, n. alliance f.

allied, adj. allié

alligator, n. alligator m.

allocate, vb. assigner

allot, vb. répartir

allotment, n. partage m.

allow, vb. permettre; admettre

allowance, n. allocation, ration

alloy, n. alliage m.

allure, vb. séduire

allusion, n. allusion f.

ally n. allié m.

alamanc, n. almanach m.

almond, n. amande f.

aloft, adv. en haut, en l'air

alone, adj. seul, solitaire

along, adv. le long de

aloud, adv. à haute voix

alphabet, n. alphabet m.

alphabetical, adj. alphabétique

Alps, n. les Alpes f., pl.

already, adv. déjà

also, adv. aussi

altar, n. autel m.

alter, vb. changer

alteration, n. modification f.

alternate, vb. alterner, faire alternativement

alternative, n. alternative f.

although, conj. bien que

altitude, n. altitude f.

altogether, adv. tout à fait

alum, n. alun m.

aluminium, n. aluminium m.

always, adv. toujours
amalgam, n. amalgame m.
amass, vb. amasser
amateur, n. amateur m.
amaze, vb. étonner
amazement, n. stupeur f.
amazing, adj. étonnant
ambassador, n. ambassadeur m.
amber, n. ambre m.
ambidextrous, adj. ambidextre
ambition, n. ambition f.
ambitious, adj. ambitieux
ambulance, n. ambulance f.
ambulatory, adj. ambulatoire
ambush, n. embuscade f.
amend, vb. amender
amenity, n. aménité f., agrément m.
America, n. l'Amérique f.
American, adj. américain, n.;
  Américain m.
amethyst, n. améthyste f.
amid, prep. au milieu de
amiss, adv. mal, en mauvaise part
amity, n. amitié f.
ammonia, n. ammoniaque f.
amnesty, n. amnistie f.
among, prep. parmi, entre
amount, n. somme, (quantity)
  quantité f.
ampere, n. ampère m.
amphibious, adj. amphibie
amphitheatre, n. amphithéâtre m.
ample, adj. ample
amplify, vb. amplifier
amputate, n. amputer
amputee, n. amputé m.
amuse, vb. amuser
an, art. un m., une f.
analysis, n. analyse f.
analyst, n. analyste m.
analyze, vb. analyser
anatomy, n. anatomie f.
ancestor, n. ancêtres m., pl.
ancestral, adj. d'ancêtres,
  héréditaire
ancestry, n. ancêtres m., pl.
anchor, vb. ancre f.
anchorage, n. mouillage, ancrage
  m.
anchovy, n. anchois m.
ancient, adj. ancien m.
and, conj. et
anecdote, n. anecdote f.
anemia, n. anémie f.
anesthetist, n. anesthésiste m.
anew, adv. de nouveau
angel, n. ange m.
anger, n. colère f.
angle, n. angle m.
angry, adj. fâché

anguish, n. angoisse f.
animal, n. and adj. animal m.
animate, vb. animer
animation, n. animation f.
animosity, n. animosité f.
anise, n. anis m.
ankle, n. cheville f.
annals, n., pl. annales f., pl.
annex, n. dépendance f.
annexation, n. annexation f.
annihilate, vb. anéantir
anniversary, n. anniversaire m.
annotate, vb. annoter
annotation, n. annotation f.
announce, vb. annoncer
announcement, n. annonce f.
announcer, n. annonciateur
annoy, vb. (vex) contrarie
annoyance, n. contrariété f.
annual, adj. annuel
annuity, n. annuité f.
annul, vb. annuler
anoint, vb. oindre
anonymous, adj. anonyme
another, adj. and pron. un autre m.,
  une autre f.
answer, vb. répondre; n. réponse f.
ant, n. fourmi f.
antagonize, vb. éveiller
  l'antagonisme
antarctic, adj. antarctique m.
antelope, n. antilope f.
antenna, n. antenne f.
anterior, adj. antérieur
anthem, n. hymne m.
anthrax, n. anthrax m.
antic, n. bouffonnerie f.
anticipate, vb. anticiper; prévoir
anticipation, n. anticipation f.
antidote, n. antidote m.
antinomy, n. antinomie f.
antipathy, n. antipathie f.
antique, n. antique m.; (antique
  dealer) antiquaire m.
antiquity, n. antiquité f.
antiseptic, adj. and n. antiseptique
  m.
antisocial, adj. antisocial
antler, n. andouiller m.
anvil, n. enclume f.
anxiety, n. anxiété f.
anxious, adj. inquiet m.
any, adj. du, de la
anybody, pron. (somebody)
  quelqu'un
anyhow, adv. de toute façon
anyone, pron. quelqu'un, chacun,
  quique ce soit
anything, pron. quelque chose m.
anywhere, adv. n'importe où

apart, adv. à part

apartheld, n. ségrégation f.

apartment, n. logement m.

apathy, n. apathie f.

ape, n. singe m.

apex, n. sommet m.

aplece, adv. chacun

apologize, vb. s'excuser, faire des excuses

apology, n. excuses f., pl.

apostle, n. apôtre m.

appal, vb. épouvanter

apparatus, n. appareil m.

apparel, n. habillement, vêtement m.

apparent, adj. apparent

appeal, n. appel m.; vb. en appeler (de)

appear, vb. apparaître

appearance, n. apparition f.

appease, vb. apaiser, pacifier

appeaser, n. personne qui apaise

appendage, n. accessoire m.

appendectomy, n. appendéctomie f.

appendicltis, n. appendicite f.

appendix, n. appendice m.

appetite, n. appétit m.

appetizer, n. apéritif m.

applaud, vb. applaudir

applause, n. applaudissements m., pl.

apple, n. pomme f.

applesauce, n. compote de pommes f.

appliance, n. appareil m.

applicant, n. postulant m.

application, n. demande f.

applied, adj. appliqué

apply, vb. appliquer (à), s'appliquer

appoint, vb. nommer; désigner

appointment, n. nomination f.

apposition, n. apposition f.

appraisal, n. évaluation f.

appraise, n. expert m.

appreciable, adj. appréciable

appreciate, vb. apprécier, estimer

appreciation, n. appréciation f.

apprehend, vb. saisir, arrêter

apprehension, n. arrestation f.

apprehensive, adj. intelligent

approach, n. approche f.

approbation, n. approbation f.

approval, n. approbation f.

approve, vb. approuver

approximate, adj. approximatif

approximately, adv. approximativement, à peu près

apricot, n. abricot m.

April, n. avril m.

apron, n. tablier m.

apt, adj. sujet, enclin, porté (à)

aptitude, n. aptitude f.

aquarium, n. aquarium m.

aquatic, adj. aquatique

aqueduct, n. aqueduc m.

aqueous, adj. aqueux

Arab, n. Arabe m.f. adj. arabe

Arabic, adj. and n. arabe m.

arbiter, n. arbitre m.

arbitrary, adj. arbitraire

arbitrate, vb. arbitrer

arbitration, n. arbitrage m.

arbitrator, n. arbitre m.

arbor, n. arbre m.

arc, n. arc m.

arcade, n. arçade f

arch, n. arc m.; (of bridge) arche f. adj. espiègle

arohbishop, n. archevêque m.

archduke, n. archiduc m.

archer, n. archer m.

archery, n. tir à l'arc m.

architect, n. architecte m.

architecture, n. architecture f.

archives, n. archives f., pl.

archway, n. voûte f., passage (sous une voûte) m.

arctic, adj. arctique

ardor, n. ardeur f.

area, n. aire; région, surface f.

area code, n. indicatif interurbain m.

arena, n. arène f.

argue, vb. argumenter

argument, n. argument m.; (dispute) discussion f.

arid, adj. aride

arise, vb. s'élever; provenir de

aristocracy, n. aristocratie f.

aristocrat, n. aristocrate m.f.

arithmetic, n. arithmétique f.

ark, n. arche f.

arm, n. bras m.; arme f. vb. armer

arm-chair, n. fauteuil m.

armed forces, n. forces armées f., pl.

armful, n. brassée f.

armhole, n. emmanchure f.

armistice, n. armistice m.

armor, n. armure f.

armpit, n. aisselle f.

arms, n. armes f., pl.

army, n. armée f.

aroma, n. arôme m.

aromatic, adj. aromatique

around, adv. autour; prep. autour de

arouse, vb. soulever; réveiller

arraign, vb. accuser, poursuivre en justice

arrange, vb. arranger, régler
arrangement, n. arrangement m.
array, vb. ranger
arrest, n. arrestation f.; arrêts m., pl.
arrival, n. arrivée f.
arrive, vb. arriver
arrogant, adj. arrogant
arrogate, vb. attribuer injustement
arrow, n. flèche f.
arrowhead, n. pointe de flèche f.
arsenal, n. arsenal m.
arsenic, n. arsenic m.
arson, n. crime d'incendie m.
art, n. art m.; beaux arts
arterial, adj. artériel
artery, n. artère f.
artful, adj. artificieux; adroit
arthritis, n. arthrite f.
article, n. article m.
artillery, n. artillerie f.
artist, n. artiste m.
artistic, adj. artistique
artistry, n. habileté f.
as, adv. comme; aussi...que;
  conj. de façon à; pendant que
asbestos, n. asbeste m.
ascend, vb. monter
ascendancy, n. ascendant m.
ascendant, adj. ascendant,
  supérieur
ascertain, vb. s'assurer
ascetic, n. ascétique m.
ascribe, vb. attribuer
ash, n. cendre f.; (tree) frêne m.
ashamed, adj. honteux, confus
ashore, adv. à terre; débarquer
Asia, n. l'Asie f.
Asian, n. Asiatique m.f.; adj.
  asiatique
aside, adv. de côte
ask, vb. demander à; inviter
askance, adv. de travers,
  obliquement
asleep, adj. endormi
asparagus, n. asperges f., pl.
aspect, n. aspect m.
asphalt, n. asphalte m.
asphyxiate, vb. asphyxier
aspirant, n. aspirant m., candidat
  m.
aspiration, n. aspiration f.
aspirator, n. aspirateur m.
aspire, vb. aspirer
ass, n. âne m., ânesse f.
assail, vb. assaillir
assailant, n. assaillant m.
assassin, n. assassin m.
assassination, n. assassinat m.
assault, n. assaut m.
assay, n. essai m., vérifica-

tion, épreuve f. vb. essayer
assemblage, n. assemblage m.
assemble, vb. assembler
assembly, n. assemblée f.
assert, vb. affirmer
assess, vb. évaluer, fixer
assets, n., pl. actif m.
assign, vb. assigner
assignable, adj. assignable,
  transférable
assignation, n. assignation f.,
  rendezvous m.
assignment, n. attribution,
  assignation
assistance, n. aide f.
assistant, n. qui aide, auxiliaire
associate, vb. associe
association, n. association f.
assort, vb. assortir
assorted, adj. assorti
assortment, n. assortiment, m.
assume, vb. prendre sur soi
assuming, adj. prétentieux,
  arrogant
assumption, n. supposition f.
assurance, n. assurance f.
assure, vb. assurer
aster, n. aster m.
asterisk, n. astérisque m.
astern, adv. à l'arrière, sur l'arrière
asteroid, n. astéroïde m.
asthma, n. asthme m.
astonish, vb. étonner
astonishment, n. étonnement m.
astound, vb. étonner, ébahir
astride, adv. à califourchon
astringent, n. and adj. astringent m.
astrology, n. astrologie f.
astronaut, n. astronaute m.
astronomy, n. astronomie f.
at, prep. à; en, dans; contre
atheist, n. athée
athlete, n. athlète m.
athletic, adj. athlétique
Atlantic, adj. atlantique
atlas, n. atlas m.
atomsphere, n. atmosphère f.
atom, n. atome m.
atomic, adj. atomique
atomic bomb, n. bombe atomique
  f.
atonement, n. expiation f.
atrocity, n. atrocité f.
atrophy, n. atrophie f.
attach, vb. attacher
attaché, n. attaché m.
attachment, n. attachement
attack, n. attaque f.
attain, vb. atteindre
attainment, n. acquisition f.

attempt, n. tentative f.
attend, vb. soigner; servir; assister
attendance, n. service m.; présence f.
attention, n. attention f.
attentive, adj. attentif
attest, vb. attester
attic, n. grenier m.
attire, n. costume m.
attitude, n. attitude f.
attorney, n. avoué m.
attract, vb. attirer
attraction, n. attraction f.
attractive, adj. attrayant
attribute, n. attribut m.
attune, vb. accorder
auction, n. enchère
auctioneer, n. commissaire-priseur m.
audacity, n. audace f.
audible, adj. intelligible
audience, n. auditoire m.
audit, vb. vérifier (des comptes); n. vérfication des comptes
audition, n. audition f.
auditor, n. vérificateur m.
auditorium, n. salle f.
auditory, adj. auditif
August, n. août m.
aunt, n. tante f.
Australia, n. l'Australie f.
authentic, adj. authentique
authenticity, n. authenticité f.
author, n. auteur m.
authority, n. autorité f.
authorization, n. autorisation f.
authorize, vb. autoriser
auto, n. auto f.
autobiography, n. autobiographie f.
autogrpah, n. autographe m.; vb. autographier
automatic, adj. automatique
automatically, adv. automatiquement
automobile, n. automobile f.
autopsy, n. autopsie f.
autumn, n. automne m.
auxiliary, adj. auxiliaire m.
avail, vb. servir
available, adj. disponible
avenge, vb. venger
avenue, n. avenue f.
average, n. moyenne f. adj. moyen
averse, adj. opposé
aversion, n. aversion f.
avert, vb. détourner
aviation, n. aviation f.
aviator, n. aviateur m.
avid, adj. avide
avoid, vb. éviter

avow, vb. avouer
await, vb. attendre
awake, vb. éveill
award,, n. prix m.; sentence f.; vb. dècerner
away, adv. loin; absent
awful, adj. terrible
awhile, adv. pendant quelque temps
awkward, adj. gauche; embarrassant
awning, n. tente f.
axe, n. hache f.
axis, n. axe m.
axle, n. arbre, essieu
azure, n. azur m.

B

babble, vb. babiller
babe, n. enfant m.f.
baboon, n. babouin m.
baby, n. bébé m.
bachelor, n. célibataire m.
back n. dos m.; vb. reculer; adv. en arrière
backbone, n. épine dorsale f.
background, n. fond m.
backhand, adj. donné avec le revers de la main
backward, adv. en arrière
backwardness, n. état arriéré m.
backwater, n. eau stagnante f.
bacon, n. lard m.
bacterium n. bactérie f.
bad, adj. mauvais; méchant
baffle, vb. déconcerter
bag, n. sac m.; (suitcase) valise f.
baggage, n. bagage m.
bagpipe, n. cornemuse f.
ball, n. caution f. vb. vider
bailiff, n. huissier m.
bait, n. appât m.
bake, vb. faire cuire au four
baker, n. boulanger m.
bakery, n. boulangerie f.
baking, n. cuisson f.
balance, n. équilibre, solde m.; balance f. vb. balancer, peser
balcony, n. balcon m.
baldness, n. calvitie f.
bale, n. balle f.
balk, vb. frustrer
ball, n. balle f., boule f., bal m.
ballad, n. romance f.; ballade f.
ballast, n. lest m.
ball bearing, n. roulements à billes m.
ballerina, n. ballerine f.

ballet, n. ballet m.
balloon, n. ballon m.
ballot, n. scrutin m.
balm, n. baume m.
balmy, adj. embaumé
balsam, n. baume m.
balustrade, n. balustrade f.
bamboo, n. bambou m.
ban, interdire
banal, adj. banal
banana, n. banane f.
band, n. bande f.
bandage, n. bandeau m.
bandanna, n. foulard m.
bandbox, n. carton m.
bandit, n. bandit m.
bandsman, n. musicien m.
bandstand, n. kiosque á musique m.
baneful, adj. pernicieux
bang, vb. frapper violemment; n. coup m.
banish, vb. bannir
banishment, n. bannissement m.
banister, n. rampe, f.
bank, n. rivage m.
bankbook, n. livret de banque m.
banker, n. banquier m.
banking, n. banque f.
bank note, n. billet de banque m.
bankrupt, adj. failli, en faillite m.
bankruptcy, n. faillie f.
banner, n. bannière f.
banquet, n. banquet m.
banter, n. badinage m.; vb. badiner, railler
baptism, n. baptême m.
baptismal, adj. baptismal
Baptist, n. Baptiste m.
baptistery, n. baptistère m.
baptize, vb. baptiser
bar, n. bar, barreau m.
barb, n. barbillon m.
barbarism, n. barbarie f., (gramm.) barbarisme m.
barber, n. coiffeur m.
barbiturate, n. barbiturique m.
bare, adj. nu; vb. découvrir
bareback, adv. à dos nu
barefoot, adv. nu-pieds
barely, adv. à peine
bareness, n. nudité f.
bargain, n. marché m.
bargain, vb. marchander
barge, n. chaland m.
bark, n. (tree) écorce f.; (dog) aboiement m.; vb. (dog) aboyer
barley, n. orge f.
barn, n. (grain) grange f.; (live-stock) étable f.

barnacle, n. (shellfish) anatife m.; (goose) bernache f.
barometer, n. baromètre m.
barometric, adj. barométrique
baron, n. baron m.
baroness, n. baronne f.
baronial, adj. baronnial, sei-gneurial
baroque, adj. baroque m.
barrack, n. caserne f.
barrel, n. baril m.
barren, adj. stérile
barrenness, n. stérilité f.
barricade, n. barricade f.
barrier, n. barrière f.
barter, n. troc m.
base, n. base f.; adj. bas m.
baseball, n. base-ball m.
basement, n. sous-sol m.
bashful, adj. timide
bashfully, adv. timidement
bashfulness, n. timidité f.
basic, adj. fondamental
basin, n. cuvette f., bassin m.
basis, n. base f.
bask, vb. se chauffer
basket, n. panier m., corbeille f.
bass, n. basse f; (fish) bar m.
bassinet, n. bercelonnette f.
bassoon, n. basson m.
bastard, n. bâtard m.
baste, vb. arroser; (sewing) faufiler
bat, n. (animal) chauve-souris f.; (baseball) batte f.
batch, n. fournée f.
bate, vb. rabattre
bath, n. bain m.
bathe, vb. se baigner
bather, n. baigneur m.
baton, n. bâton m.
battalion, n. bataillon m.
batter, n. (cooking) pâte f.
battery, n. batterie
battle, n. bataille f.
battle, vb. lutter
battlefield, n. champ de bataille m.
battleship, n. cuirassé m.
bawl, vb. brailler
bayonet, n. baïonnette f.
bazaar, n. bazar m.
be, vb. être
beach, n. plage f.
beacon, n. phare m.
bead, n. perle f.
beak, n. bec m.
beaker, n. gobelet m., coupe f.
beam, n. putre f., rayon m.; vb. rayonner
beaming, adj. rayonnant
bean, n. haricot m.

bear, n. ours m.; vb. porter, supporter, enfanter
beard, n. barbe f.
bearer, n. porteur m.
bearing, n. maintien, coussinet, relèvement m.
beast, n. bête f.
beat, vb. battre; n. battement m.
beaten, adj. battu
beatify, vb. béatifier
beating, n. battement m., rossée f.
beau, n. galant m.
beautiful, adj. beau m.
beaver, n. castor m.
because, conj. parce que
beckon, vb. faire signe (à)
become, vb. devenir
becoming, adj. convenable
bed, n. lit m.
bedclothes, n. les draps et couvertures f., pl.
bedridden, adj. alité
bedroom, n. chambre à coucher f.
bedside, n. bord du lit m.
bedspread, n. dessus de lit m.
bedstead, n. bois de lit m.
bedtime, n. l'heure du coucher
bee, n. abeille f.
beef, n. boeuf m.
beehive, n. ruche f
beer, n. bière f.
beeswax, n. cire jaune f.
beet, n. betterave f.
beetle, n. scarabée m.
befit, vb. convenir à
befitting, adj. convenable
before, adv. en avant, avant; prep. devant, avant
beforehand, adv. d'avance
befriend, vb. seconder, aider
beg, vb. mendier, prier
beggar, n. mendiant m.
begin, vb. commencer
beginner, n. commençant m.
beginning, n. commencement m.
beguile, vb. tromper, séduire
behalf, n. de la part de, en faveur de
behave, vb. se conduire
behavior, n. conduite f.
behind, n. derrière m.
behold, vb. voir; interj. voici
beige, adj. beige m.
being, n. être m.
belated, adj. attardé
belch, vb. éructer
belfry, n. clocher, beffroi m.
Belgian, n. Belge m.f.; adj. beige
Belgium, n. Belgique f.
belief, n. croyance, confiance f.

believable, adj. croyable
believe, vb. croire
believer, n. croyant m.
bell, n. cloche, clochette f.
bellboy, n. chasseur m.
bellow, vb. mugir
bellows, n., pl. soufflet m.
belly, n. ventre m.
belongings, n., pl. effets m., pl.
beloved, adj. and n. chéri m.
below, prep. en aval, au-dessous de
belt, n. ceinture f.
bench, n. banc m.
bend, vb. plier, courber tourner
beneath, prep. sous, au-dessous
benediction, n. bénédiction f.
benefactor, n. bienfaiteur m.
beneficent, adj. bienfaisant
beneficial, adj. salutaire
beneficiary, n. bénéficiaire m.
benefit, n. bienfait, profit m.
benevolent, adj. bienveillant
benign, adj. bénin m. bénigne f.
bent, n. penchant m
bequeath, vb. léguer
bequest, n. legs m.
bereave, vb. priver (de)
bereavement, n. privation f., perte f., deuil m.
berry, n. baie f.
beseech, vb. supplier, implorer
beside, prep. à côté de
besides, adv. en outre
besiege, vb. assiéger
best, adj. le meilleur; adv. le mieux
bestial, adj. bestial
bestir, vb. remuer
bestow, vb. accorder
bet, n. pari m.; vb. parier
betray, vb. trahir
betroth, vb. fiancer
betrothal, n. fiançailles f.,pl.
better, adj. en biseau; vb. biaiser
beverage, n. boisson f.
bewilder, vb. égarer
bewildering, adj. déroutant
bewilderment, n. égarement m.
bewitch, vb. ensorceler
beyond, adv. au delà; prep. au delà de
biannual, adj. semestriel
bias, n. biais m.
bib, n. bavette f.
Bible, n. Bible f.
biblical, adj. biblique
bibliography, n. bibliographie f.
biceps, n. biceps m.
bicker, vb. se quereller, se chamailler

bicycle, n. bicyclette f.
bicyclist, n. cycliste m.
bid, n. enchère f., appel m.; vb. ordonner, inviter
bidder, n. enchérisseur m.
bide, vb. demeurer, attendre
bier, n. corbillard m., civière f.
bifocal, adj. bifocal
big, adj. grand
bigamy, n. bigamie f.
bigot, n. bigot m.
bigotry, n. bigoterie f.
bilateral, adj. bilatéral
bile, n. bile f.
bilingual, adj. bilingue
bilious, adj. bilieux
bill, n. addition, note f., billet m.
billet, n. (mil.) billet de logement m.
billiard, adj. de billard
billion, n. billion m.
billow, n. grande vague, lame f.
bi-monthly, adj. bimensuel
bin, n. coffre m.
bind, vb. lier; (books) relier
bindery, n. atelier de reliure m.
binding, n. (book) reliure f.; adj. obligatoire
binocular, adj. binoculaire
biochemistry, n. biochimie f.
biography, n. biographie f
biological, adj. biologique
biology, n. biologie f.
biped, n. bipède m.
bird, n. oiseau m.
birth, n. naissance f.
birth control, n. limitation des naissances f.
birthday, n. anniversaire m.
birthplace, n. lieu de naissance m.
birth rate, n. natalité f.
birthright, n. droit d'aînesse m.
biscuit, n. biscuit; petit four m.
bishop, n. évêque m.
bison, n. bison m.
bitch, n. chienne f.
bite, n. morsure f.; vb. mordre
biting, adj. mordant, piquant
bitterly, adv. amèrement, avec amertume
bitterness, n. amertume f.
bivouac, n. bivouac m.
biweekly, adj. and adv. (de) tous les quinze jours
black, adj. noir
blackberry, n. mûre
blackboard, n. tableau noir m.
blackmail, n. chantage m.
black-market, n. marché noir m.
blackout, n. évanouissement m.
blacksmith, n. forgeron m.

bladder, n. vessie f.
blade, n. lame f., brin m.
blame, n. blâme m.; vb. blâmer
blameless, adj. innocent, sans tache
blanch, vb. blanchir; pâlir
bland, adj. doux, aimable
blank, n. blanc m., vide m; adj. blanc m., blance f., vide
blanket, n. couverture f.
blast, n. (wind) rafale f.; (mine) explosion f.
blaze, n. flambée f.; vb. flamber
blazing, adj. enflammé, flamboyant
bleach, vb. blanchir
bleak, adj. morne
bleakness, n. froideur f.
bleed, vb. saigner
blemish, n. défaut m.
blend, n. mélange m.; vb. mêler
blended, adj. mélangé
bless, vb. bénir
blessed, adj. béni, saint
blessing, n. bénédiction f.
blight, vb. flétrir, détruire, nieller, brouir;
blind, n. store m.; adj. aveugle
blindness, n. cécité f.
blink, vb. clignoter
bliss, n. béatitude f.
blissful, adj. bienheureux
blissfully, adv. heureusement
blister, n. ampoule f.
blithe, adj. gai, joyeux
blizzard, n. tempête de neige f.
bloat, vb. boursoufle
block, n. bloc m.; vb. bloquer
blockade, n. blocus m.
blond, adj. and n. blond m.
blood, n. sang m.
bloodhound, n. limier m.
bloodless, adj. exsangue
bloodshed, n. effusion de sang f.
bloodshot, adj. injecté de sang
bloody, adj. sanglant
bloom, n. fleur f.; vb. fleurir
blooming, n. floraison f.; adj. fleurissant
blossom, n. fleur f.
blot, n. tache f.; vb. tacher
blotch, n. tache f.
blotchy, adj. tacheté
blouse, n. blouse f.
blow, n. coup m.; vb. souffler
blue, adj. bleu
blueprint, n. dessin négatif m.
bluff, n. bluff m.
blunder, n. bévue f.
blunt, adj. émoussé; brusque
bluntly, adv. brusquement

bluntness, n. brusquerie f.
blur, vb. barbouiller
blush, n. rougeur f.; vb. rougir
boar, n. sanglier m.
board, n. planche, pension f.
boast, vb. se vanter
boaster, n. vantard m.
boastful, adj. vantard m.
boat, n. bateau m.
boathouse, n. garage (à beaux) m.
bob, vb. (hair) couper court
bode, vb. présager
bodice, n. corsage m.
bodily, adj. corporel
body, n. corps m.
boil, vb. bouillir; intr., faire
 bouillir; n. furoncle m.
boiler, n. chaudière f.
boisterous, adj. bruyant
bold, adj. hardi
boldface, adj. caractères, impudent
boldly, adv. hardiment
boldness, n. hardiesse f.
bolster, n. traversin m.
bolt, n. verrou m.; vb verrouiller
bomb, n. bombe f.
bombard, vb. bombarder
bombardier, n. bombardier m.
bond, n. lien m., obligation f.
bondage, n. servitude f.
bone, n. os m.
boneless, adj. sans os
bonfire, n. feu de joie m.
bonnet, n. chapeau m.
bonus, n. boni m.
bony, adj. osseux
book, n. livre m.
bookcase, n. bibliothèque f.
bookkeeper, n. teneur de livres m.
bookkeeping, n. comptabilité f.
booklet, n. opuscule m.
bookseller, n. libraire m.,
 bougquiniste m.
boon, n. bienfait m.
boor, n. rustre m.
boorish, adj. rustre
boost, vb. pousser
boot, n. bottine f.
bootblack, n. cireur m.
booth, n. baraque f., cabine f.
booty, n. butin m.
border, n. bord m., frontière f.
border-line, adj. touchant
bore, vb. forer, ennuyer
boredom, n. ennui m.
boring, adj. ennuyeux
born, adj. né; vb. naître
borrower, n. emprunteur m.
bosom, n. sein m.
boss, n. patron m.; vb. diriger

bossy, adj. autoritaire
botanical, adj. botanique
botany, n. botanique f.
botch, n. pustule f.; vb. ravauder
both, adj. and pron. tous les deux
bother, n. ennui m.
bothersome, adj. importun
bottle, n. bouteille f.
bottom, n. fond m.
bottomless, adj. sans fond
boulder, n. grosse pierre f.
boulevard, n. boulevard m.
bounce, vb. rebondir
bound, n. borne f., bound m.; vb.
 borner, bondir
boundary, n. frontière f.
boundless, adj. sans bornes,
 illimité
bound, n. largesse, prim f.
bouquet, n. bouquet m.
bow, n. arc m., archet m., révérence f., avant m.
bowels, n., pl. entrailles f., pl.
bowl, n. bol m.; vb. jouer aux
 boules
box, n. boîte f.
boxer, n. boxeur m.
boxing, n. la boxe f.
boy, n. garçon m.
boycott, vb. boycotter
boyhood, n. enfance, adolescence
 f.
brace, vb. fortifier; n. vile-
 brequin m., paire f., couple m.
bracelet, n. bracelet m.
bracket, n. console f., crochet m.
brag, vb. se vanter
braid, n. tresse f.; galon m.; vb.
 tresser, natter
brain, n. cerveau m.; cervelle f.
brake, n. frein m.
bran, n. son m.
branch, n. branche f.
brand, n. marque f.
brandy, n. eau-de-vie f.
brass, n. cuivre jaune
brassiere, n. soutien-gorge m.
brat, n. marmot m.
bravado, n. bravade f.
brave, adj. courageux
bravery, adv. courageusement
brawl, n. rixe f.
bray, vb. braire
brazen, adj. effronté
Brazil, n. le Brésil m.
breach, n. infraction f.; (mil.)
 brèche f.
bread, n. pain m.
breadth, n. largeur f.
break, n. rupture f., interruption f.;

vb. rompre, briser, casser
breakable, adj. fragile
breakage, n. cassure, rupture f.
breakfast, n. petit déjeuner m.
breast, n. poitrine f., sein m.
breath, n. haleine f., souffle m.
breathe, vb. respirer
breathless, adj. essouflé
breathlessly, adv. en haletant
breed, vb. élever
breeder, n. éleveur m.
breeding, n. éducation f., élevage
m.
breeze, n. brise (de houille) f.
breezy, adj. venteux, dégagé
brevity, n. brièveté f.
brew, vb. brasser, faire de la bière
brewery, n. brasserie f.
brick, n. brique f.
bridal, adj. nuptial
bride, n. nouvelle mariée f.
bridegroom, n. nouveau marié m.
bridesmaid, n. demoiselle
d'honneur f.
bridge, n. pont m., passerelle f.,
bridge m.
bridle, n. bride f.
brief, adj. bref m.
brief case, n. serviette f.
briefly, adv. brièvement
briefness, n. brièveté f.
brigade, n. brigade f.
bright, adj. brillant
brighten, vb. faire briller
brightness, n. éclat m.
brilliance, n. brillant, éclat m
brilliant, adj. brillant
brim, n. bord m.
bring, vb. apporter, amener, porter
brink, n. bord m.
brisk, adj. vif
brisket, n. poitrine
briskly, adv. vivement
briskness, n. vivacité f.
bristle, n. soie f.
British, adj. britannique
brittle, adj. fragile
broad, adj. large
broadcast, adj. radiodiffusé
broadcaster, n. speaker m.
broadly, adv. largement
brocaded, adj. de brocart
broil, vb. griller
broiler, n. gril m.
broker, n. courtier m.
brokerage, n. courtage m.
bronchitis, n. bronchite f.
bronze, n. bronze m.
brooch, n. broche f.
brood, n. couvée f.; vb. couver

brook, n. ruisseau m.
broom, n. balai m.
broth, n. bouillon m.
brother, n. frère m.
brotherhood, n. fraternité f.
brotherly, adj. fraternel
brown, adj. brun
browse, vb. brouter; feuilleter
bruise, n. meurtrissure f.; vb.
meurtrir
brunette, adj. and n. brune f.
brunt, n. choc m.
brush, n. brosse f.
brushwood, n. broussailles f.,pl.
brutality, n. brutalité f.
brutalize, vb. abrutir
brute, n. brute f.
bubble, n. bulle f.; vb. bouillonner
buck, n. daim, mâle m.
bucket, n. seau m.
buckle, n. boucle f.
bud, n. bourgeon m.; vb.
bourgeonner
budge, vb. bouger
budget, n. budget m.
buffalo, n. buffle m.
buffet, n. buffet m.
buffoon, n. bouffon m.
bug, n. insecte m.
bugle, n. clairon m.
build, vb. bâtir
builder, n. entrepreneur m.,
constructeur m.
building, n. bâtiment m.
bulb, n. ampoule f., bulbe m.
bulge, n. bosse f.
bulkhead, n. cloison étanche f.
bulky, adj. encombrant
bull, n. taureau m.
bulldog, n. bouledogue m.
bulldozer, n. machine à refouler f.
bullet, n. balle f.
bulletin, n. bulletin m.
bully, n. matamore m.
bulwark, n. rempart m.
bum, n. fainéant m.
bump, n. coup m., bosse f.; vb.
cogner
bumper, n. pare-chocs m.
bun, n. petit pain rond (au lait) m.
bunch, n. botte f.
bundle, n. paquet m.
bungle, vb. bousiller
bunion, n. oignon m.
bunk, n. couchette f.
bunny, n. lapin m.
bunting, n. drapeaux m., pl.
buoy, n. bouée f.
buoyant, adj. léger, flottant
burden, n. fardeau m.

burdensome, adj. onéreux
bureau, n. bureau m., commode f.
burglar, n. cambrioleur m.
burglarize, vb. cambrioler
burglary, n. vol avec effraction m.,
  cambriolage m.
burial, n. enterrement m.
burly, adj. de forte carrure
burn, vb. brûler
burner, n. bec m., brûleur m.
burning, adj. brûlant
burrow, n. terrier m.
burst, vb. éclater
bury, vb. enterrer
bus, n. autobus m.
bush, n. buisson m.
bushel, n. boisseau m.
bushy, adj. buissonneux
busily, adv. activement
business, n. affaire f.; affaires f., pl.
businesslike, adj. pratique
busy, adj. occupé
but, conj. mais, sauf (except)
butcher, n. boucher m.
butler, n. maître d'hôtel m.
butt, n. bout m.
butter, n. beurre m.
buttercup, n. bouton d'or m.
butterfly, n. papillon m.
buttock, n. fesse f.
button, n. bouton m.
buttonhole, n. boutonnière f.
buttress, n. contrefort m.
buy, vb. acheter
buyer, n. acheteur m.
buzz, n. bourdonnement m.
buzzard, n. buse f.
by, prep. par, près de (near to)
bylaw, n. règlement local m.
by-pass, n. route d'évitement f.
by-product, n. sous-produit m.
bystander, n. spectateur, assistant
  m.

C

cab, n. taxi, fiacre m.
cabaret, n. cabaret m.
cabbage, n. chou m.
cabin, n. cabane, cabine f.
cable, n. câble m.; vb. câbler
cactus, n. cactus m.
cad, n. goujat m.
café, n. café m.
caffeine, n. caféine f.
cage, n. cage f.
cake, n. gâteau m.
calamity, n. calamité f.
calcium, n. calcium m.

calculable, adj. calculable
calculate, vb. calculer
calculus, n. calcul m.
calendar, n. calendrier m.
calf, n. veau m.
caliber, n. calibre m.
calico, n. calicot m.
call, n. appel m., visite f.; vb.
  appeler, faire visite à
calligraphy, n. calligraphie f.
calling, n. vocation, profession f.
callousness, n. insensibilité f.
callow, adj. blanc-bec
callus, n. callosité f.
calm, adj. calme; vb. calmer
calmly, adv. avec calme
calmness, n. tranquillité f.
caloric, adj. calorique
calore, n. calorie f.
calumniate, vb. calomnier
Calvary, n. Calvaire m.
calve, vb. vêler
calyx, n. calice m.
camel, n. chameau m.
camellia, n. camélia m.
cameo, n. camée m.
camera, n. appareil m.
camouflage, vb. camoufler
camp, n. camp, camping m.; vb.
  camper
campaign, n. campagne f.
camper, n. campeur m.
campus, n. terrains d'un collège or
  d'une université m., pl.
can, n. boîte f., bidon m.; vb.
  pouvoir
Canada, n. le Canada m.
canal, n. canal m.
canapé, n. canapé m.
canary, n. serin m.
cancel, vb. annuler, biffer
cancellation, n. annulation f.
cancer, n. cancer m.
candelabrum, n. candélabre m.
candid, adj. sincère
candidate, n. candidat m.
candidly, adv. franchement
candidness, n. candeur f.
candied, adj. candi
candle, n. bougie f.
candlestick, n. chandelier m.
candour, n. sincérité f
candy, n. bonbon m.
cane, n. canne f.
canine, adj. canin
canister, n. boîte à thé f.
canker, n. chancre m.
canned, adj. conservé en boîtes
cannery, n. conserverie f.
cannibal, n. cannibale m.f.

cannon, n. canon, m.

cannonade, n. canonnade f.

canny, adv. avisé, rusé

canoe, n. canot m.

canon, n. chanoine m., canon (rule) m.

canonical, adj. canonique

canonize, vb. canoniser

canopy, n. dais m.

can't, vb. ne pas pouvoir

cantaloup, n. melon m., cantaloup m.

canteen, n. cantine f., bidon m

canter, n. petit galop f.; vb. aller au petit galop

canvas, n. toile f.

canvass, n. sollicitation f.; vb. solliciter

canyon, n. gorge f., défilé m.

cap, n. bonnet m., casquette f.

capability, n. capacité f.

capable, adj. capable

capably, adv. habilement

capacity, n. capacité f.

cape, n. bond m., câpre f.; vb. bondir

capital, n. capital m., capitale f.

capitalism, n. capitalisme m.

capitalization, n. capitalisation f.

capitalize, vb. capitaliser

capon, n. capon m.

capsule, n. capsule f.

captain, n. capitaine m.

captivate, vb. captiver

captive, adj. and n. captif m.

captivity, n. captivité f.

capture, n. capture f.; vb. capturer

car, n. voiture f., wagon m.

carafe, n. carafe f.

caramel, n. caramel m.

carat, n. carat m.

caravan, n. caravane f.

caraway, n. carvi, cumin m.

carbohydrate, n. carbohydrate m.

carbon, n. carbone m.

carbon dioxide, n. acide carbonique m.

carbon monoxide, n. oxyde de carbone m.

carbon paper, n. papier carbone m.

carburetor, n. carburateur m.

card, n. carte f.

cardboard, n. carton m.

cardiac, adj. cardiaque

cardigan, n. gilet de tricot m.

cardinal, n. cardinal m.

care, n. souci m.; attention f.; prendre soin de.; vb soucier de

career, n. carrière f.

carefree, adj. insouciant

careful, adj. soigneux

carefully, adv. soigneusement

carefulness, n. soin m., attention f.

careless, adj. insouciant

caress, n. caresse f.; vb. caresser

cargo, n. cargaison

caries, n. carie f.

carillon, n. carillon m.

carload, n. voiturée f.

carnal, adj. charnel

carnation, n. incarnat m.

carol, n. noël m.

carpenter, n. charpentier m.

carpet, n. tapis m.

carpeting, n. pose de tapis f.

carriage, n. voiture f., maintien m., transport m.

carrier, n. porteur m., messager m.

carrot, n. carotte m.

carrousel, n. carrousel m.

carry, vb. porter, continuer, exécuter cart, n. charrette f.

cartel, n. cartel m.

carter, n. charretier m.

cartilage, n. cartilage m.

carton, n. carton m.

cartoon, n. dessin satirique m.

carve, vb. sculpter; découper

carver, n. découpeur m., sculpteur m.

carving, n. découpage m., sculpture f.

cascade, n. cascade f.

case, n. cas m., cause f., caisse f., eui m., en tout cas (in any case)

cash, n. espèces f., pl.; (C.O.D.) livraison contre remboursement f.

cashier, n. caissier m.

cashmere, n. cachemire m.

casino, n. casino m.

cask, n. tonneau m.

casket, n. cassette f.

casserole, n. casserole f.

cassette, n. cassette f.

cast, n. coup m., trempe f., distribution f., moulage m.

castaway, n. naufragé m., rejeté m.

caste, n. caste f.

caster, n. fondeur m.

castle, n. château m.

castoff, adj. abandonné

casual, adj. casuel, insouciant

casualness, n. nonchalance f.

casualties, n. pertes f., pl.

cat, n. chat m., chatte f.

cataclysm, n. cataclysme m.

catacomb, n. catacombe f.

catalogue, n. catalogue m.

cataract, n. cataracte f.

catastrophe, n. catastrophe f.
catch, vb. attraper, saisir
catcher, n. qui attrape
catchy, adj. facile à retenir
categorical, adj. catégorique
category, n. catégorie f.
cater, vb. pourvoir (à)
caterpillar, n. chenille f.
catgut, n. corde à boyau f.
cathedral, n. cathédrale f.
Catholicism, n. catholicisme m.
catsup, n. sauce piquante f.
cattle, n. bétail m., bestiaux m., pl.
cattleman, n. éleveur de bétail m.
cauliflower, n. chou-fleur m.
cause, n. cause f.
causeway, n. chaussée f.
caution, n. prudence f.
cautious, adj. prudent
cavalier, adj. and n. cavalier m.
cavalry, n. cavalerie f.
cave, n. caverne f.
cavern, n. caverne f.
caviar, n. caviar m.
cavity, n. cavité f.
cease, vb. cesser (de)
cedar, n. cèdre m
ceiling, n. plafond m.
celebrant, n. célébrant
celebrate, vb. célébrer
celebration, n. célébration f.
celebrity, n. célébrité f.
celery, n. céleri m.
celestial, adj. céleste
celibacy, n. célibat m.
cell, n. cellule f.
cellar, n. cave f.
cellophane, n. cellophane f.
cellular, adj. cellulaire
cellulose, n. cellulose f.
cement, n. ciment m.; vb. cimenter
cemetery, n. cimetière m.
censor, n. censeur m.; vb. censurer
censorship, n. censure f.
censure, n. censure f.
census, n. recensement m.
cent, n. cent
center, n. centre m.
centerfold, n. pages centrales f., pl.
centerpiece, n. pièce de milieu f.
centigrade, adj. centigrade
centigrade thermometer, n. thermomètre centigrade m.
central, adj. central
centralize, vb. centraliser
century, n. siècle m.
ceramic, adj. céramique
ceramics, n. céramique f.
cereal, adj. and n. céréale f.

cerebral, adj. cérébral
ceremonial, adj. and n. cérémonial m.
ceremony, n. cérémonie f.
certain, adj. certain
certainly, adv. certainement
certainty, n. certitude f.
certificate, n. certificat m.; acte de naissance
certification, n. certification f.
certified, adj. certifié, diplômé, breveté
certifier, n. qui certifie
certify, vb. certifier
certitude, n. certitude f.
cervical, adj. cervical
cervix, n. utérus m
cessation, n. cessation, suspension f.
cession, n. cession f.
cesspool, n. fosse d'aisances f.
chafing dish, n. réchaud m.
chagrin, n. chagrin m.
chain, n. chaîne f.
chair, n. chaise f., fauteuil m.
chairman, n. président m.
chairperson, n. président m., présidente f.
chairwoman, n. présidente f.
chalice, n. calice m.
chalk, n. craie f.
challenge, vb. défier, contester
challenger, n. qui fait un défi, prétendant m.
chamber, n. chambre f.
chamberlain, n. chambellan m.
champ, vb. ronger, mâcher
champion, n. champion m.
championship, n. championnat m.
chance, n. chance f., par hasard m.
chancel, n. sanctuaire, choeur m.
chancellor, n. chancelier m.
chandelier, n. lustre m.
change, n. changement m.
changeable, adj. changeant
changer, n. changeur m.
channel, n. canal m.
chant, n. chant m.; vb. chanter
chaos, n. chaos m.
chap, n. gerçure f., gars m.
chapel, n. chapelle f.
chaperon, n. duègne f.; chaperon m.
chaplain, n. aumônier m.
chapter, n. chapitre m.
character, n. caractère, personnage, rôle m.
characterize, vb. caractériser
charcoal, n. charbon (m.) de bois
charge, n. charge f. prix, soin m.;

vb. charger, charger de; demander

charger, n. grand plat, cheval de bataille m.

charitable, adj. charitable

charitably, adv. charitablement

charity, n. charité f.

charm, n. charme m. vb. charmer

charmer, n. charmeur, enchanteur m.

charming, adj. charmant

charred, adj. carbonisé

chart, n. carte f.; graphique m.

chase, n. chasse f.; vb. chasser

chaser, n. chasseur m., ciseleur m.

chasm, n. abîme m.

chassis, n. chassis m.

chaste, adj. chaste

chastise, vb. châtier

chastity, n. chasteté f.

chat, n. causette f.; vb. causer

chateau, n. château m.

chattel, n. bien, meuble m.

chatter, n. bavarde m.; vb. bavarder

chatterbox, n. bavard m.

chauffeur, n. chauffeur m.

cheap, adj. bon marché, de peu de valeur

cheapen, vb. déprécier

cheapness, n. bon marché m., bas prix m., basse qualité f.

cheat, vb. tromper, tricher

cheater, n. tricheur, trompeur m.

check, n. frein m., vérification f., ticket m., addition f., chèque m.

checker, n. enregistreur m., contrôleur m.

cheek, n. joue f.

cheerfully, adv. gaiement, de bon coeur

cheerfulness, n. gaieté f., bonne humeur f.

cheerless, adj. triste, morne, sombre

cheery, adj. gai, joyeux

cheese, n. fromage m.

cheesecloth, n. gaze f.

chemical, adj. chimique

chemically, adv. chimiquement

chemist, n. chimiste m.f.

chemistry, n. chimie f.

chemotherapy, n. chimiothérapie f.

chenille, n. chenille f.

cherish, vb. chérir

cherry, n. cerise f.

chess, n. échecs m., pl.

chessman, n. pièce f.

chest, n. coffre m., poitrine f.

chestnut, n. châtaigne f.

chevron, n. chevron m.

chew, vb. mâcher

chic, adj. chic

chick, n. poussin m.

chicken, n. poulet m.

chicken-pox, n. varicelle f.

chicle, n. chicle m.

chief, n. chef m.; adj. principal

chiefly, adv. surtout, principalement

chieftain, n. chef de clan m.

chiffon, n. chiffon m.

chilblain, n. engelure f.

child, n. enfant m.f.

childbirth, n. enfantement m.

childhood, n. enfance f.

childish, adj. enfantin

childlessness, n. puérilité f., enfantillage m.

childlike, adj. comme un enfant, en enfant

Chile, n. le Chili m.

chili, n. piment m.

chill, n. froid m., frisson m. vb. refroidir

chilly, adj. un peu froid

chime, n. carillon m.; vb. carillonner

chimney, n. cheminée f.

chimpanzee, n. chimpanzé m.

chin, n. menton m.

China, n. la Chine f.

china, n. porcelaine f.

chinchilla, n. chinchilla m.

chintz, n. perse f.

chip, n. éclat m., frites f., pl.

chipmunk, n. tamia m.

chiropractor, n. chiropracteur m.

chirp, vb. pépier, gazouiller

chisel, vb. ciseler; n. ciseau m.

chivalry, n. chevalerie f.

chive, n. ciboulette f.

chlorine, n. chlore m.

chocolate, n. chocolat m.

choice, n. choix m.

choir, n. choeur m.

choke, vb. étouffer

choker, n. foulard m.

choose, vb. choisir

chop, n. côtelette f.; vb. couper

chopper, n. couperet m.

chopstick, n. baguette f., bâtonnet m.

choral, adj. choral

chord, n. accord m.

chorus, n. choeur m.

christen, vb. baptiser

christening, n. baptême m.

Christian, adj. and n. chrétien m.

Christianity, n. christianisme m.

Christmas, n. Noël m.

chronic, adj. chronique

chronicle, n. chronique f.

chronological, adj. chronologique

chrysalis, n. chrysalide f.
chrysanthemum, n. chrysanthème m.
chubby, adj. joufflu
chuckle, vb. rire tout bas
chum, n. camarade, copain m.
chummy, adj. familier, intime
chunk, n. gros morceau m.
chunky, adj. en gros morceaux
church, n. église f.
churchman, n. homme d'église m., ecclésiastique m.
churchyard, n. cimetière m.
churn, vb. baratter
chute, n. glissière f.
chutney, n. chutney m.
cicada, n. cigale f.
cider, n. cidre m.
cigar, n. cigare m.
cigarette, n. cigarette f.
cilia, n. cils m., pl.
ciliary, adj. ciliaire
cinch, n. c'est facile
cinchona, n. quinquina m.
cinder, n. cendre f.
cinema, n. cinéma m.
cinematic, adj. cinématographique
cinnamon, n. cannelle f.
cipher, n. chiffre m., zéro m.
circle, n. cercle m.; vb. entourer (de)
circuit, n. circuit m.
circular, adj. circulaire
circulation, n. circulation f.
circulator, n. circulateur m.
circumcise, vb. circoncire
circumcision, n. circoncision f.
circumference, n. circonférence f.
circumscribe, vb. circonscrire
circumstance, n. circonstance f., moyens m., pl.
circus, n. cirque m.
citation, n. citation f.
cite, vb. citer
citizen, n. citoyen m.
citizenry, n. tous les citoyens m., pl.
citizenship, n. droit de cité
citric acid, n. acide citrique m.
city, n. ville f., cité f.
civic, adj. civique
civil, adj. civil, poli, (civil servant) fonctionnaire m.
civilization, n. civilisation f.
civilize, vb. civiliser
clad, adj. habillé, vêtu
claim, n. demande f., droit m.; vb. demander
clairvoyance, n. clairvoyance f.
clairvoyant, n. voyant m.

clam, n. palourde f., mollusque m.
clamber, vb. grimper
clammy, adj. visqueux, moite
clamor, n. clameur f.
clamorous, adj. bruyant
clan, n. clan m., clique f.
clap, vb. (applaud) applaudir
clapboard, n. bardeau m.
clapper, n. claquer m., battant (of a bell) m.
claque, n. claque f.
claret, n. vin rouge de Bordeaux m.
clarify, vb. (lit.) clarifier; (fig.) éclaircir
clarinet, n. clarinette f.
clarion, n. clairon m.
clarity, n. clarté f.
clash, vb. choquer, s' entrechoquer; n. choc m.
clasp, n. agrafe, étreinte f.; vb. agrafer, étreindre
class, n. classe f.
classification, n. classification f.
classify, vb. classifier, classer
classroom, n. salle de classe f.
clatter, n. bruit m.
clause, n. clause f.
claw, n. griffe f.
claw-hammer, n. marteau à dent m.
clay, n. argile, glaise f.
clean, adj. propre; vb. nettoyer
clean-cut, adj. net, fin
cleanse, vb. nettoyer, curer
cleanser, n. chose qui nettoie f., détersif, nettoyeur m.
clear, adj. clair, net, lucide
clearing, n. éclaircissement m.
clearly, adv. clairement, nettement
clearness, n. clarté f., netteté f.
cleat, n. fer m., (naut.) taquet m.
cleavage, n. fendage m., scission f.
cleaver, n. fendeur m., fendoir m., couperet m.
cleft, n. fente f.
clemency, n. clémence f.
clench, vb. serrer
clergy, n. clergé m.
clergyman, n. ecclésiastique m.
clerical, adj. clérical, de bureau
clerk, n. employé m., commis m.
clever, adj. habile
cleverness, n. adresse f.
clew, n. fil m.
cliché, n. cliché m.
click, n. cliquetis m., déclic m.; vb. cliqueter
client, n. client m.
cliff, n. falaise f.
climax, n. comble m.

climb, n. montée f.; vb. monter, grimper

climber, n. grimpeur m., ascensionniste m.

clinch, vb. river; conclure

cling, vb. s'accrocher

clinic, n. clinique f.

clip, vb. couper; n. pince f.

clipping, n. coupure f.

clique, n. clique f.

clock, n. (large) horloge f., (small) pendule f.

clockwise, adv. dans le sens des aiguilles d'une montre

clockwork, n. mouvement d'horlogerie m.

clod, n. motte de terre f.

clog, b. entraver

clone, n. reproduction exacte f.

close, adj. clos, bien fermé

closely, adv. de près, étroitement

closeness, n. proximité, exactitude f.

closet, n. cabinet, boudoir m.

clot, n. caillot m.

cloth, n. étoffe f.

clothe, vb. vêtir, habiller

clothes, n. habits m., pl.

clothespin, n. pince f.

clothier, n. drapier m. tailleur m.

clothing, n. vêtements m., pl.

cloud, n. nuage m.

cloudburst, n. rafale de pluie f.

cloudless, adj. sans nuage

cloudy, adj. nuageux, couvert

clout, n. morceau m., pièce f.

clove, n. clou de girofle m.

clover, n. trèfle m.

clown, n. bouffon m.

cloy, vb. rassasier

club, n. massues f., cercle m.

clubfoot, n. pied bot m.

clue, n. fil m.

clumsy, adj. gauche

cluster, n. groupe m., grappe f., bouquet m.; vb. se grouper

clutch, n. griffe f., embrayage m.

clutter, vb. encombrer

coach, n. carrosse m., voiture f.

coal, n. charbon m., houille f.

coalition, n. coalition f.

coarse, adj. grossier

coarseness, n. gorssièreté f.

coast, n. côte f.

coastal, adj. de la côte, littoral

coaster, n. caboteur m., dessous de verre m.

coast guard, n. garde-côtes m.

coat, n. habit; m. couche f.

coating, n. couche f., enduit m., étoffe pour habits f.

coax, vb. cajoler

cobalt, n. cobalt m.

cobblestone, n. pierre du pavé f.

cobra, n. cobra m.

cobweb, n. toile d'araignée f.

cocaine, n. cocaïne f.

cockroach, n. blatte f.

cocky, adj. suffisant

cocoa, n. cacao m.

cocoon, n. cocon m.

cod, n. morue f.

coddle, vb. dorloter

code, n. code m.

codeine, n. codéine f.

codfish, n. morue f.

coerce, vb. contraindre

coffee, n. café m.

coffin, n. cercueil m.

cog, n. dent f.

coherent, adj. cohérent

coiffure, n. coiffure f.

coil, n. enrouler m.

coin, n. pièce de monnaie

coincide, vb. coïncider

coincidence, n. coïncidence f.

coincident, adj. coïncident

colander, n. passoire f.

cold, n. froid m., rhume m.

cold-blooded, adj. de sang froid

coldness, n. froideur f.

collaborate, vb. collaborer

collapse, vb. s'effondrer, s'affaisser

collar, n. col m.; (dog) collier m.

collarbone, n. clavicule f.

collate, vb. collationner, comparer

collation, n. collation f., comparaison f., repas froid m.

colleague, n. collègue m., f.

collect, vb. rassembler

collection, n. collection, collecte f.

collective, adj. collectif

collectively, adv. collectivement

collector, n. collectionneur m., contrôleur m.

college, n. collège m., université f.

collegiate, adj. de collège, collégial

collide, vb. se heurter

collision, n. collision f.

collusion, n. collusion f., connivence f.

colon, n. deux points m., pl.

colonel, n. colonel m.

colonial, adj. colonial

colonist, n. colon m.

colonization, n. colonisation f.

colonize, vb. coloniser

colony, n. colonie f.

color, n. couleur f.
colored, adj. coloré, de
couleur, colorie
colorful, adj. coloré, pittoresque
coloring, n. ccloris m., couleur f.
colossal, adj. colossal
colt, n. poulain m.
colter, n. coutre m.
column, n. colonne f.
coma, n. coma m.
comb, n. peigne m.
combat, n. combat m.
combination, n. combinaison f.
combustible, adj. and n. combustible m.
combustion, n. combustion f.
come, vb. venir; arriver;
partir; revenir; descendre; entrer
comedian, n. comédien m.
comedy, n. comédie f.
comely, adj. avenant
comet, n. comète f.
comfort, n. consolation f., confort
m.
comfortable, adj. commode,
confortable
comforter, n. consolateur m.
comfortless, adj. sans consolation, inconsolable, désolé
coming, n. venue, arrivée,
approche f.
comma, n. virgule f.
command, n. commandement m.
commandeer, vb. réquisitionner
commemorate, vb. commémorer
commemorative, adj.
commémoratif
commence, vb. commencer
commencement, n.
commencement, début
commend, vb. recommander, louer
commendable, adj. louable, recommandable
comment, n. commentaire m.
commerce, n. commerce m.
commercial, adj. commercial
commission, n. commission;
perpétration f.
commissioner, n. commissaire m.
commit, vb. commettre
commitment, n. engagement m.
committee, n. comité m.
commodity, n. produit m.,
commodité f., denrée f.
common, adj. commun, vulgaire
commonly, adv. communément,
ordinairement
commonplace, n. lieu commun m.
commonwealth, n. état m.
communicate, vb. communiquer

communication, n. communication
f.
communion, n. communion f.
community, n. communauté f.
commuter, n. voyageur de banlieue
m.
compact, adj., serré, compact
compactness, n. compacité f.
companion, n compagnon m.,
compagne f.
companionship, n. camaraderie f.
company, n. compagnie f.
comparable (with,) adj.
comparable (à)
comparatively, adv.
comparativement, relativement
compare, vb. comparer
comparison, n. comparaison f.
compartment, n. compartiment m.
compass, n. (naut.) boussole f.;
(geom.) compas m.
compassion, n. compassion f.
compassionate, adj. compatissant
compatible, adj. compatible
compel, vb. forcer
compensate, vb. compenser
compensation, n. compensation f.
compete, vb. rivaliser
competence, n. compétence f.
competent, adj. capable
competently, adv.
convenablement, avec compétence
competition, n. concurrence f.
competitor, n. concurrent m.
compile, vb. compiler
complacency, n. contentement m.
complacent, adj. content de soi-
même
complacently, adv. avec un air
(un ton) suffisant
complain, vb. se plaindre
complainer, n. plaignant m.,
réclameur m.
complainingly, adv. d'une manière
plaignante
complaint, n. plainte f.
complement, n. complément m.
complete, adj. complet
completely, adv. complètement,
tout à fait
completeness, n. état complet m.,
perfection f.
completion, n. achèvement m.
complex, adj. and n. complexe m.
complexion, n. teint m.
complexity, n. complexité f.
compliance, n. acquiescement m.
compliant, adj. complaisant,
accommodant
complicate, vb. compliquer

complicity, n. complicité f.

compliment, n. compliment m.

complimentary, adj. flatteur, de félicitations

component, adj. and n. composant m.

comport, vb. s'accorder (avec)

compose, vb. composer

composer, n. compositeur m.

composite, adj. composé

composition, n. composition f.

compost, n. compost m., terreau m.

composure, n. calme f., tranquillité f., sang-froid m.

compound, n. composé m., composition f.

comprehend, vb. comprendre

comprehensible, adj. compréhensible, intelligible

comprehension, n. compréhension f.

comprehensive, adj. compréhensif

compress, n. compresse f.

compressed, adj. comprimé

compression, n. compression f.

compressor, n. compresseur m

comprise, vb. comprendre

compromiser, n. compromettre m.

compulsion, n. contrainte f.

compulsive, adj. coercitif, obligatoire

compulsory, adj. obligatoire

compunction, n. componction f.

computation, n. supputation f.

compute, vb. supputer

computer, n. ordinateur m.

computerize, vb. informatiser

computer science, n. informatique f.

comrade, n. camarade m.f.

concave, adj. concave

conceal, vb. cacher

concede, vb. concéder

conceivably, adv. d'une manière concevable

conceive, vb. concevoir

concentrate, vb. concentrer

concept, n. concept m.

conception, n. conception f.

concern, n. intérêt, soin, souci m.

concerning, prep. concernant

concert, n. concert m.

concession, vb. concession f.

concise, adj. concis

concisely, adv. avec concision, succinctement

conciseness, n. concision f.

conclave, n. conclave m.

conclude, vb. conclure

conclusion, n. conclusion f.

conclusive, adj. concluant

concord, n. concorde f.

concordat, n. concordat m.

concourse, n. concours m., affluence f.

concrete, n. béton m.

concur, vb. concourir, être d'accord

concurrence, m. assentiment m.

concurrent, adj. concourant

condemn, vb. condamner

condemnable, adj. condamnable

condensation, n. condensation f.

condense, vb. condenser

condenser, n. condenseur m.

condiment, n. condiment m., assaisonnement m.

condition, n. condition f.

conditional, adj. and n. conditionnel m.

conditionally, adv. conditionnellement

condolence, n. condoléances f.

condominium, n. condominium m.

conducive, adj. favorable

conduct, n. conduite f.

conductivity, n. conductivité f.

conductor, n. conducteur, receveur (d'orchestre) m.

conduit, n. conduit, tuyau m.

cone, n. cône m.

confection, n. confection f.; (sweet) bonbon m.

confectioner, n. confiseur m.

confectionery, n. confiserie f.

confederate, adj. and n. confédéré m.

confer, vb. conférer

conference, n. entretien m.

confess, vb. avouer

confession, n. confession f.

confessional, n. confessionnal m.

confessor, n. confesseur m.

confetti, n. confetti m.

confidant, n. confident m.

confidence, n. confiance f.

confident, adj. confiant

confidently, adv. avec confiance

confine, vb. confiner; limiter

confirm, vb. confirmer

confirmation, n. confirmation f.

confirmed, adj. invétéré, incorrigible

confiscate, vb. confisquer

conflagration, n. conflagration f., incendie m.

conflict, n. conflit m.

conform, vb. conformer

conformation, n. conformation, conformité f.

conformer, n. conformiste m.
conformist, n. conformiste m.
conformity, n. conformité f.
confront, vb. confronter
confuse, vb. confondre
confusion, n. confusion f.
congenial, adj. sympathique, convenable
congenital, adj. congénital
congestion, n. (med.) congestion f.; (traffic) encombrement m.
congratulate, vb. féliciter de
congratulation, n. félicitation f.
congregate, vb. rassembler
congregation, n. assemblée f.
congress, n. congrès m.
conjecture, n. conjecture f.
conjunction, n. conjonction f.
conjunctive, adj. conjonctif
connect, vb. joindre
connection, n. connexion f.
conquer, vb. conquérir
conqueror, n. conquérant m.
conquest, n. conquête f.
conscience, n. conscience f.
conscious, adj. conscient
consciously, adv. sciemment, en parfaite connaissance
consciousness, n. conscience f.
conscript, adj. and n. conscrit m.
conscription, n. conscription f.
consecrate, vb. consacrer
consecration, n. consécration f.
consecutive, adj. consécutif
consecutively, adv. consécutivement, de suite
consensus, n. consensus m., assentiment général m.
consent, n. consentement m.
consequence, n. conséquence f.
consequent, adj. conséquent
consequential, adj. conséquent, logique
consequently, adv. par conséquent
conservation, n. conservation f.
conservatism, n. conservatisme m.
conservative, adj. conservateur
conservatively, adv. d'une manière conservatrice
conservatory, n. conservatoire m.
conserve, vb. conserver
consider, vb. considérer
considerable, adj. considérable
considerably, adv. considérablement
considerate, adj. plein d'égards
considerately, adv. avec égards, avec indulgence
consideration, n. considération f.

considering, prep. vu que, attendu que
consign, vb. consigner
consignment, n. expédition, consignation f.
consistency, n. consistance f.
consistent, adj. consistant
consolation, n. consolation f.
console, vb. consoler
consolidate, vb. consolider
consonant, n. consonne f.
conspicuous, adj. en évidence
conspiracy, n. conspiration f.
conspirator, n. conspirateur m.
conspire, vb. conspirer
constant, adj. constant
constipation, n. constipation f.
constituent, adj. constituant
constitute, vb. constituer
constitution, n. constitution f.
constrain, vb. contraindre
constraint, n. contrainte f.
constrict, vb. resserrer
construct, vb. construire
construction, n. construction f.
constructive, adj. constructif
constructor, n. constructeur m.
consul, n. consul m.
consult, vb. consulter
consultation, n. consultation f.
consume, vb. consumer
consumer, n. consommateur m.
consummate, adj. consommé
consumption, n. consommation; (med.) phtisie f.
consumptive, adj. poitrinaire, tuberculeux
contact, n. contact m.
contagious, adj. contagieux
contain, vb. contenir
container, n. récipient m.
contaminated, adj. contaminé
contemplation, n. contemplation f.
contemplative, adj. contemplatif
contemporary, adj. contemporain
contempt, n. mépris m.
contemptuous, adj. méprisant
contend, vb. lutter, soutenir
contender, n. compétiteur m., concurrent m.
content, n. contentement m.
contention, n. contention, lutte f.
contentment, n. contentement m.
contest, n. lutte f., concours m.
contestant, n. concurrent m.
context, n. contexte m.
contiguous, adj. contigu
continent, adj. and n. continent m.
continental, adj. continental
contingency, n. contingence f.

contingent, adj. contingent
continuation, n. continuation f.
continue, vb. continuer
continuous, adj. continu
continuously, adv.
 continuellement, sans interruption
contort, vb. tordre, défigurer
contour, n. contour m.
contraband, n. contrebande f.
contraception, n. procédés
 anticonceptionnels m., pl.
contract, n. contrat m.
contracted, adj. contracté, res-
 serré
contraction, n. contraction f.
contractor, n. entrepreneur m.
contradict, vb. contredire
contradictable, adj. qui peut
 être contredit
contradiction, n. contradiction f.,
 démenti m.
contraption, n. machin m.
contrast, n. contraste m.
contribute, vb. contribuer
contribution, n. contribution f.
contributor, n. contribuant m.
contributory, adj. contribuant
contrite, adj. contrit, pénitent
contrition, n. contrition f.
contrive, vb. inventer, imaginer,
 arranger
control, n. autorité f.
controllable, adj. vérifiable,
 gouvernable
controller, n. contrôleur m.
controversy, n. controverse f.
contusion, n. contusion f.
convalescence, n. convalescence
 f.
convalescent, adj. convalescent
convenience, n. convenance f.,
 commodité f.
convenient, adj. commode
convent, n. couvent m.
conventional, adj. conventionnel
converge, vb. converger
convergent, adj. convergent
conversation, n. conversation f.
converse, vb. converser
convert, vb. convertir
converter, n. convertisseur m.
convertible, adj. convertible,
 aménageable
convex, adj. convexe
convey, vb. transporter, transmettre
conveyance, n. transport m.
convict, n. forçat m.; vb.
 condamner
conviction, n. conviction,
 persuasion f.

convince, vb. convaincre
convincing, adj. convaincant
convincingly, adv. d'une manière
 convaincante
convivial, adj. jovial, joyeux
convocation, n. convocation f.
convoy, n. convoi m.
convulsion, n. convulsion f.
convulsive, adj. convulsif
cook n. cuisinier m.; vb. cuire, intr.
 faire cuire
cookbook, n. livre de cuisine m.
cookie, n. gâteau sec m.
cool, adj. frais m., fraîche f.
cooler, n. rafraîchissoir m.
coolness, n. fraîcheur f.
co-operate, vb. coopérer
co-operation, n. coopération f.
co-operative, n. coopérative f. adj.
 coopératif
co-ordinate, vb. coordonner
co-ordination, n. coordination f.
cop, n. flic m.; vb. attraper, pincer
copier, n. machine à copier f.
copious, adj. copieux
copper, n. cuivre m.
copy, n. copie f.; vb. copier
copyright, n. droit d'auteur m., pl.
coquette, n. coquette f.
coral, n. corail m., pl. coraux
cord, n. corde f.
cordial, adj. and n. cordial m.
cordiality, n. cordialité f.
cordially, adv. cordialement
cordon, n. cordon m.
corduroy, n. velours côtelé m.
core, n. coeur m.
cork, n. liège, bouchon m.
corkscrew, n. tire-bouchon m.
corn, n. maïs m.
cornea, n. cornée f.
corner, n. coin m.
cornerstone, n. pierre angulaire f.
cornet, n. cornet m.
cornice, n. corniche f.
coronary, adj. coronaire
coronation, n. couronnement f.
coroner, n. coroner m.
coronet, n. (petite) couronne f.
corporal, n. (mil.) caporal m.
corporate, adj. de corporation
corporation, n. corporation f.
corps, n. corps m.
corpse, n. cadavre m.
corpulent, adj. corpulent, gros
corpuscle, n. corpuscule m.
corral, n. corral m.
correct, adj. correct; vb. corriger
correction, n. correction f.

corrective, adj. de correction, correctif

correctly, adv. correctement, justement

correctness, n. correction f.

correlate, vb. être en corrélation; intr. mettre en corrélation

correspond, vb. correspondre

correspondence, n correspondance f.

correspondent, n. correspondant m.

corridor, n. couloir m.

corrode, vb. corroder

corrosion, n. corrosion f.

corrugate, vb. rider, plisser

corrupt, adj. corrompu; vb. corrompre

corruptible, adj. corruptible

corruption, n. corruption f.

corruptive, adj. corruptif

corsage, n. corsage m.

corset, n. corset m.

corvette, n. corvette f.

cosmetic, adj. and n. cosmétique m.

cosmic, adj. cosmique

cosmopolitan, adj. and n. cosmopolite m.f.

cosmos, n. cosmos m.

cost, n. coût; vb. coûter

costly, adj. coûteux

costume, n. costume m.

costumer, n. costumier m.

cost, n. prix, frais m.

cottage, n chaumière f.

cotton, n. coton m.

cottonseed, n. graine de coton f.

couch, n. divan m.

cough, n. toux f.; vb. tousser

could, vb. pouvait, pourrait

council, n. conseil m.

councilman, n. conseiller m.

counsel, n. conseil m.; vb. conseiller

counselor, n. conseiller m.

count, n. compte, comte m.; vb. compter

counter, n. comptoir m.; adv. à l'encontre de

counteract, vb. neutraliser

counteraction, n. action contraire f.

counterfeit, adj. faux m., fausse f.; vb. contrefaire

counterpart, n. contrepartie f.

countess, n. comtesse f.

countless, adj. innombrable

country, n. pays m., campagne, patrie f.

county, n. comté m.

coupé, n. coupé m.

couple, n. couple f.; vb. coupler

coupon, n. coupon m.

courage, n. courage m.

courageous, adj. courageux

courier, n. courrier m.

course, n. cours m., bien entendu route f., service m.

court, n. cour f.; vb. faire la cour à

courteous, adj. courtois

courtesy, n. courtoisie f.

courthouse, n. palais de justice m.

courtier, n. courtisan m.

courtroom, n. salle d'audience f.

courtship, n. cour f.

cousin, n. cousin m., cousine f.

covenant, n. pacte m.

cover, vb. couvrir, voiler, déguisé; cacher

coverage, n couverture f.

covering, n. couverture f., enveloppe f.

covet, vb. convoiter

cow, n vache f.

coward, n. lâche m.

cower, vb. se blottir

cowhide, n. peau de vache f.

coy, adj. timide

cozy, adj. confortable

crab, n. crabe m.

crab apple, n. pomme sauvage f.

crack, vb. fendre, fêler, casser; n. fente, fissure f.

cracked, adj. fendu, fêlé

cracker, n. biscuit m.

cracking, n. craquement, claquement m.

crackup, n. s'effondrer m.

cradle, n. berceau m.

craft, n. habileté f., métier m., embarcation f.

craftsman, n. artisan m.

craftsmanship, n. habileté, technique f.

crafty, adj. rusé, astucieux

cram, vb. remplir, farcir

cramp, n. crampe f., crampon m.

cranberry, n. canneberge, airelle f.

crane, n. grue f.

cranium, n. crâne m.

crank, n. manivelle f.

cranky, adj. d'humeur difficile

crash, n. faire un grand fracas

crate, n. caisse f.

crater, n. cratère m.

craven, adj. lâche, poltron

craving, n. désir ardent, besoin impérieux m.

crawl, vb. ramper, se traîner

crayon, n. pastel m.
crazed, adj. fou, dément
crazy, adj. fou m. folle f.
cream, n. crème f.
creamy, adj. crémeux, de crème
crease, n. pli m.; vb. froisser
create, vb. créer
creation, n. création f.
creative, adj. créateur m., créatrice f.
creator, n. créateur m., créatrice f.
creature, n. créature f.
credible, adj. croyable
credit, n. crédit; honneur m.
creditable, adj. estimable
creditably, adv. honorablement
creditor, n. créancier m.
creed, n. croyance f.; credo m.
creek, n. ruisseau m.
creep, vb. ramper; se glisser
cremate, vb. incinérer
crematory, n. crématorium m.
crepe, n. crêpe m.
crescent, n. croissant m.
crest, n. crête, f.
crew, n. équipage m., équipe f.
crib, n. lit d'enfant m., mangeoire f.
cricket, n. (insect) grillon m.
crier, n. crieur, huissier m.
crime, n. crime m.
criminal, adj. criminel
criminology, n. criminologie f.
crimson, adj. and n. cramoisi m.
cringe, vb. faire des courbettes,
  se lapir, s'humilier
crinkle, n. pli m., sinuosité f.
cripple, n. estropié m.; vb. estropier
crisis, n. crise f.
crisp, adj. cassant, croquant,
  croustillant
crispness, n. frisure f.
crisscross, adj. and adv. entre-
  croisé
critic, n. critique m.
critical, adj. critique
criticism, n. critique f.
criticize, vb. critiquer
critique, n. critique f.
croak, vb. coasser, croasser
crochet, vb. broder au crochet;
  crochet n.
crock, n. pot de terre m.
crockery, n. faïence f.
crocodile, n. crocodile m.
crone, n. vieille femme f.
crony, n. vieux camarade,
  compère m.
crook, n. escroc, voleur m.
crooked, adj. tordu
croon, vb. chantonner, fredonner

crop, n. récolte f.
croquette, n. croquette f.
cross, n. croix f.; adj. maussade;
  vb. croiser, se signer, rayer
crossbreed, n. race croisée f.
cross-examine, vb. contre-
  interrogatoire
cross-eye, adj. louche
cross-fertilization, n. croisement
  m.
cross-purpose, n. opposition,
  contradiction f.; malentendu m.
cross section, n. coupe en travers
  f.
crossword puzzle, n. mots croisés
  m., pl.
crotch, n. fourche f., fourchet m.
crouch, vb. s'accroupir
croup, n. croupe f.; (med.) croup m.
croupier, n. croupier m.
crouton, n. croûton m.
crow, n. corneille f.; chant du coq
  m.
crowd, n. foule f.
crowded, adj. encombré
crown, n. couronne, calotte f.,
  sommet m.; vb. couronner
crucial, adj. crucial
crucifix, n. crucifix m.
crucifixion, n. crucifixion f.;
  crucifiement m.
crucify, vb. crucifier
crude, adj. grossier, imparfait,
  fruste
cruel, adj. cruel
cruise, n. croisière f.
cruiser, n. croiseur m.
crumbs, n. miette, mie f.
crumble, vb. émietter
crunch, vb. croquer broyer
crusade, n. croisade f.
crush, vb. écraser
crust, n. croûte f.
crutch, n. béquille f.
cry, n. cri m.; vb. crier, pleurer
crying, adj. criant
cryosurgery, n. cryochirurgie f.
crypt, n. crypte f.
crystal, n. cristal m.
crystallize, vb. cristalliser
cub, n. petit m.
Cuba, n. le Cuba m.
Cuban, n. Cubain m.; adj. cubain
cube, n. cube m.
cubic, adj. cubique
cubicle, n. compartiment m., cabine
  f.
cubic measure, n. mesures de
  volume f., pl.
cubism, n. cubisme m.

cucumber, n. concombre m.
cud, n. bol alimentaire m.; panse, chique f.
cuddle, vb. serrer
cue, n. réplique f.; mot m.
cuff, n. poignet m.
cuisine, n. cuisine f.
culinary, adj. culinaire, de cuisine
cull, vb. cueillir, recueillir
culprit, n. accusé m., accusée f.
cult, n. culte m.
cultivate, vb. cultiver; adj. cultivable
cultivated, adj. cultivé
cultivation, n. culture f.
cultivator, n. cultivateur m.
cultural, adj. cultural, agricole, culturel
culture, n. culture f.
culvert, n. ponceau, petit aqueduc
cumbersome, adj. encombrant
cunning, n. ruse, adresse, finesse f.
cup, n. tasse, coupe f.; gobelet, godet m.
cupful, n. tasse, pleine tasse f.
cupboard, n. armoire f.
cupel, n. coupelle f.
Cupid, n. Cupidon m.
curable, adj. guérissable, curable
curator, n. conservateur, administrateur m.
curb, n. gourmette f.; bord, frein m. vb. mettre la gourmette à
curd, n. lait caillé, caillé m.; vb. cailler, figer
curdle, vb. cailler
cure, n. guérison f.; remède m.; vb. guérir
curfew, n. couvre-feu m.
curio, n. curiosité f.
curiosity, n. curiosité f.;
curious, adj. curieux
curl, n. boucle f.; vb. friser
curling, n. frisure
curly, adj. frisé, bouclé
currant, n. groseille f.
currency, n. monnaie f.
current, adj. and n. courant m.
currently, adv. couramment
curriculum, n. programme d'é-tudes, plan d'études m.
curry, n. cari m.
curse, n. malédiction f.; juron m., fléau m.; vb. maudire;
cursed, adj. maudit
cursor, n. curseur m.
curt, adj. brusque, bref, sec
curtail, vb. raccourcir
curtain, n. rideau m.; courtine f.
curve, n. courbe f.; vb. courber

cushion, n. coussin m.
cuspidor, n. crachoir m.
custard, n. crème f.
custodian, n. gardien m.
custody, n. garde, détention f.
custom, n. coutume f.
customary, adj. habituel
customer, n. client m.
cute, adj. gentil m., gentille f.
cuticle, n. cuticule f.
cutlery, n. coutellerie f.
cutlet, n. côtelette f.
cutthroat, n. coupe-jarret m.
cutting, n. incision f.; adj. incisif, tranchant
cutty, adj. court
cycle, n. cycle m.; vb. faire de la bicyclette
cyclist, n. cycliste m.
cyclone, n. cyclone m.
cylinder, n. cylindre m.
cynic, n. cynique m.
cynical, adj. cynique
cypress, n. cyprès m.
cyst, n. kyste m.
Czech, adj. tchèque

D

dab, n. coup léger m.; tape f.; vb. toucher légèrement
dad, n. papa m.
daffodil, n. narcisse m.
daily, adj. quotidien, journalier
dainty, adj. délicat, friand
dairy, n. laiterie f.
daisy, n. marguerite f.
dam, n. digue f.
damage, n. dommage m.; vb. endommager
damp, adj. humide
dampen, vb. humecter
dance, n. danse f.; vb. danser
dandruff, n. pellicules f., pl.
danger, n. danger m.
dangerous, adj. dangereux
dangle, vb. intr. pendiller
Danish, adj. and n. danois m.
dare, vb. oser
dark, adj. sombre
darken vb. obscurcir
darling, adj. and n.; chéri m.
dart, n. dard m.; pince f.
dash, n. fougue f.; trait m.; vb. lancer, détruire, se précipiter
data, n. données f., pl.
data processing, n. élaboration f.
date, n. date f.; rendez-vous m.

daughter, n. fille f.

daughter-in-law, n. belle-fille f.

daunt, vb. intimider

dauntless, adj. intrépide, indomptable

dawn, n. aube f.

day, n. jour m.; journée f.

daylight, n. lumière du jour f.

daylight-saving time, n. l'heure d'été f.

daze, vb. étourdir

deacon, n. diacre m.

dead, adj. mort

dead end, n. cul de sac m.; impasse f.

deadline, n. ligne de délimitation f.

deadlock, n. impasse f.

deadly, adj. mortel

deaf, adj. sourd

deafen, vb. assourdir

deaf-mute, adj. sourd-muet

deafness, n. surdité f.

dealer, n. marchand m.

dean, n. doyen

dear, adj. and n. cher m.

dearly, adv. chèrement

death, n. mort f.

deathless, adj. impérissable

deathly, adj. mortel

debacle, n. débâcle f.

debase, vb. avilir

debatable, adj. discutable

debate, n. débat m.

debater, n. orateur parlementaire, argumentateur m.

debenture, n. obligation f.

debilitate, vb. débiliter, affaiblir

debit, ñ. débit m.

debonair, adj. courtois et jovial

debris, n. débris m., pl.

debt, n. dette f.

debtor, n. débiteur m.

debunk, vb. dégonfler

debut, n. debut m.

debutante, n. débutante f.

decade, n. période de dix ans f.

decadence, n. décadence f.

decaffeinated, adj. décaféiné

decanter, n. carafe f.

decay, n. décadence f.

deceased, adj. défunt

deceit, n. tromperie f.

deceitful, adj. trompeur

deceive, vb. tromper

deceiver, n. imposteur

December, n. décembre m.

decency, n. décence f.

decent, adj. décent

deception, n. tromperie, duperie f.

deceptive, adj. décevant, trompeur

decide, vb. décider

decided, adj. de_idé, prononcé

decimal, adj. décimal

decimate, vb. décimer

decipher, vb. déchiffrer

decision, n. décision f.

decisive, adj. décisif

deck, n. pont, paquet m.

declaim, vb. déclamer

declare, vb. déclarer

decline, vb. décliner

decompose, vb. décomposer

decor, n. décor m.

decorate, vb. décorer

decoration, n. décoration f.

decorative, adj. décoratif

decorator, n. décorateur m.

decoy n. leurre m.; vb. leurrer

decrease, n. diminution f.; vb. diminuer

dedication, n. dédicace f.

deduce, vb. déduire

deduct, vb. déduire

deduction, n. déduction f.

deed, n. action f.; (law) acte notarié m.

deep, adj. profond

deepen, vb. approfondir

deeply, adv. profondément

deer, n. cerf m.

deface, vb. défigurer

default, n. défaut m.

defeat, n. défaite f.; vb. vaincre

defect, n. défaut m.

defection, n. défection f.

defective, adj. défectueux

defend, vb. défendre

defendant, n. défendeur m.

defender, n. défenseur m.

defense, n. défense f.

defenseless, adj. sans défense

defensive, adj. défensif

defer, vb. différer, déférer

deference, n. déférence f.

defiant, adj. de défi

deficiency, n. insuffisance f.

deficient, adj. insuffisant

deficit, n. déficit m.

defile, vb. souiller

define, vb. définir

definite, adj. défini

definitely, adv. d'une manière déterminée

definition, n. définition f.

definitive, adj. définitif

deflate, vb. dégonfler

deflation, n. dégonflement m.

deflect, vb. faire dévier, détourner

deform, vb. déformer
deformity, n. difformité f.
defraud, vb. frauder
defray, vb. payer
defrost, vb. déglacer
defroster, n. déglaceur m.
deft, adj. adroit
defy, vb. défier
degenerate, vb. dégénérer
degrade, vb. dégrader
degree, n. degré m.
dehydrate, vb. déshydrater
deify, vb. déifier
deign, vb. daigner
dejected, adj. abattu
dejection, n. abattement m.
delay, n. retard m.; vb. retarder
delegate, n. délégué m.; vb. déléguer
delegation, n. délégation f.
delete, vb. rayer, supprimer
deliberate, adj. délibéré; vb. délibérer
deliberately, adv. de propos délibéré
deliberation, n. délibération f.
deliberative, adj. délibératif
delicacy, n. délicatesse f.
delicate, adj. délicate
delicious, adj. délicieux
delight, n. délices f., pl.; vb. enchanter
delightful, adj. charmant
delinquency, n. délit m.
delinquent, adj. and n. délinquant m.
delirious, adj. délirant
deliver, vb. délivrer
deliverance, n. délivrance f.
delivery, n. accouchement, débit m.; livraison, distribution f.
delude, vb. tromper
delusion, n. illusion f.
deluxe, adv. de luxe
demand, n. demande f.; vb. demander
demean, vb. comporter
demeanor, n. maintien m.
demerit, n. démérite m.
demise, n. décès m., mort f.
demobilize, vb. démobiliser
democracy, n. démocratie f.
democrat, n. démocrate m.f.
demorcratic, adj. démocratique
demolish, vb. démolir
demonstrate, vb. démontrer
demonstration, n. démonstration f.
demonstrative, adj. démonstratif
demonstrator, n. démonstrateur m.
demoralize, vb. démoraliser

demote, vb. réduire à un grade inférieur
demure, adj. posé, d'une modestie affectee
den, n. antre, repaire m.
denial, n. dénégation f.; refus m.
Denmark, n. Danemark m.
denominator, n. dénominateur m.
denote, vb. dénoter
denounce, vb. dénoncer
dense, adj. dense, bête
density, n. densité f.
dent, n. bosselure f.
dental, adj. dentaire, dental
dentist, n. dentiste m.
denture, n. dentier, râtelier m.
denude, vb. dénuder
deny, vb. nier
deodorant, n. désodorisant m.
deodorize, vb. désodoriser, désinfecter
depart, vb. partir, s'en aller, quitter
department, n. département, ministère, grand magasin m.
deparmental, adj. départemental
departure, n. départ m.
dependability, n. confiance que l'on inspire f.
dependable, adj. digne de confiance
dependence, n. dépendance, confiance f.
dependent, adj. dépendant
depict, vb. peindre
depiction, n. description f.
deplorable, adj. déplorable
deplore, vb. déplorer
deport, vb. déporter
deportation, n. déportation f.
depose, vb. déposer
deposit, n. dépôt m.; vb. déposer
depositor, n. déposant m.
deprecate, vb. désapprouver, s'opposer à
depreciate, vb. déprécier
depress, vb. abaisser, abattre
depression, n. dépression, crise f.; abattement m.
depth, n. profondeur f.
deputy, n. délégué, député m.
derail, vb. dérailler
derange, vb. déranger
derive, vb. dériver
dermatology, n. dermatologie f.
derrick, n. grue f.
descend, vb. descendre
descendant, n. descendant m.
descent, n. descente f.
describe, vb. décrire
description, n. description f.

desert, n. désert, mérite m.; vb. déserter

deserter, n. déserteur m.

desertion, n. abandon m.; désertion f.

deserve, vb. mériter

deserving, adj. méritoire, de mérite

design, n. dessein, projet m.; vb. dessiner

designate, vb. désigner

designation, n. désignation f.

designer, n. dessinateur m.

designing, adj. intrigant, artificieux

desirable, adj. désirable

desire, n. désir m.; vb. désirer

desist, vb. cesser

desk, n. bureau, pupitre m.

desolate, adj. désolé

despair, n. désespoir m.; vb. désespérer

desperate, adj. désespéré

despicable, adj. méprisable

despise, vb. mépriser

despite, prep. en dépit de

despondent, adj. découragé

despot, n. despote m.

dessert, n. dessert m.

destination, n. destination f.

destine, vb. destiner

destiny, n. destin m.

destitute, adj. dénué, indigent

destitution, n. destitution f.

destroy, vb. détruire

destroyer, n. destructeur, contre-torpilleur m.

destructible, adj. destructible

destruction, n. destruction f.

destructive, adj. destructif

detach, vb. détacher

detachment, n. détachement m.

detail, n. détail m.

detain, vb. retenir, détenir

detect, vb. découvrir

detection, n. découverte f.

detective, n. agent de la police secrète, roman policier m.

detention, n. détention f.

detergent, n. détersif m.

deteriorate, vb. détériorer

determine, vb. déterminer

determined, adj. déterminé

deterrent, n. and adj. préventif m.

detest, vb. détester

detour, n. détour m.

devastate, vb. dévaster

develop, vb. développer

developer, n. révélateur m.

development, n. développement m.

device, n. expédient m.

devil, n. diable m.

devise, vb. combiner, tramer

devote, vb. consacrer

devotee, n. dévot m.; dévote f.

devotion, n. dévotion f.; dévouement m.

devour, vb. dévorer

devout, adj. dévot

dew, n. rosée f.

dexterity, n. dextérité f.

dexterous, adj. adroit

diabetes, n. diabète m.

diagnose, vb. diagnostiquer

diagnosis, n. diagnose f.

diagnostic, adj. diagnostique

diagonally, adv. diagonalement

diagram, n. diagramme m.

dial, n. cadran m.; vb. composer

dialect, n. dialecte m.

dialogue, n. dialogue m.

diameter, n. diamètre m.

diamond, n. diamant m.

diaper, n. couche f.

diaphragm, n. diaphragme m.

diarrhea, n. diarrhée f.

diary, n. journal m.

dice, n. dés m., pl.

dictaphone, n. machine à dicter f.

dictate, vb. dicter

dictation, n. dictée f.

dictator, n. dictateur m.

dictorial, adj. dictatorial

dictatorship, n. dictature f.

diction, n. diction f.

dictionary, n. dictionnaire m.

die, n. dé m.; vb. mourir

diet, n. régime m.

dietary, adj. diététique

dietetics, n. diététique f.

dietitian, n. diététicien m.

difference, n. différence f.

different, adj. différent

differential, adj. différentiel

difficult, adj. difficile

difficulty, n. difficulté f.

diffuse, adj. diffus

diffusion, n. diffusion f.

dig, vb. bêcher, creuser

digest, vb. digérer

digestible, adj. digestible

digestion, n. digestion f.

digestive, adj. and n. digestif m.

digital, adj. digital

digitalis, n. digitaline f.

dignified, adj. plein de dignité

dignify, vb. honorer, élever

dignity, n. dignité f.

digress, vb. faire une digression

digression, n. digression f.

dilate, vb. dilater

dilatory, adj. dilatoire, lent,

négligent
dilemma, n. dilemme m.
dilettante, n. dilettante, amateur m.
diligence, n. diligence f.
diligent, adj. diligent
dill, n. aneth m.
dilute, vb. diluer
dim, adj. faible, terne
dime, n. un dixième de dollar m.
dimension, n. dimension f.
diminish, vb. diminuer
dimness, n. faiblesse, obscurité f.
dimple, n. fossette f.
dine, vb. dîner
dingy, adj. défraîchi; terne
dinner, n. dîner m.
dinosaur, n. dinosaurien m.
dip, vb. plonger
diptheria, n. diphtérie f.
diploma, n. diplôme m.
diplomacy, n. diplomatie f.
diplomat, n. diplomate m.
diplomatic, adj. diplomatique
dipper, n. cuiller à pot f.
dire, adj. affreux
direct, vb. diriger, adresser;
  adj. direct
direction, n. direction f.;
  instructions f., pl.
directly, adv. directement
directness, n. rectitude, franchise f.
director, n. directeur m.
directory, n. annuaire m.
dirt, n. saleté f.
dirty, adj. sale
disabiltiy, n. incapacité f.
disable, vb. mettre hors de combat
disabled, adj. invalide
disadvantage, n. désavantage m.
disagree, vb. être en désaccord
disagreeable, adj. désagréable
disagreement, n. désaccord m.
disappear, vb. disparaître
disapperance, n. disparition f.
disappoint, vb. désappointer
disappointment, n. désappointement m.
disapproval, n. désapprobation f.
disapprove, vb. désapprouver
disarmament, n. désarmement m.
disarray, n. désarroi, désordre m.
disassemble, vb. démonter,
  déassembler
disaster, n. désastre m.
disavow, vb. désavouer
disband, vb. congédier
disbelieve, vb. ne pas croire,
  refuser de croire
discern, vb. discerner
discerning, adj. judicieux, éclaire

discharge, n. décharge f.; (mil.)
  congé m.; vb. dé_harger; congédier
discipline, n. discipline f.
disclaim, vb. désavouer, nier
disclaimer, n. dénégation m.
disclose, vb. révéler
disco, adj. disco
discolor, vb. décolorer
discomfiture, n. féfaite, déroute f.
discomfort, n. malaise m.
disconnect, vb. désunir
discontent, n. mécontentement m.
discontented, adj. mécontent
discontinue, vb. discontinuer
discord, n. discorde f.
discordant, adj. discordant, en
  désaccord
discotheque, n. discothèque f.
discount, n. escompte m.; remise f.
discourage, vb. décourager
discouragement, n.
  découragement m.
discourse, n. discours m.
discourteous, adj. impoli
discourtesy, n. impolitesse f.
discover, vb. découvrir
discovery, n. découverte f.
discreditable, adj. déshonorant, peu honorable
discrepancy, n. contradiction f.
discretion, n. discrétion f.
discriminate, vb. distinguer
discrimination, n. discernement,
  jugement m.
discuss, vb. discuter
discussion, n. discussion f.
disdain, n. dédain m.
disdainful, adj. dédaigneux
disease, n. maladie f.
disembark, vb. débarquer
disenchantment, n. désenchan-
  tement m.
disengage, vb. dégager
disentangle, vb. démêler
disfavor, n. défaveur f.
disfigure, vb. defigurer, enlaidir
disgrace, n. disgrâce f.
disgraceful, adj. honteux
disgruntled, adj. mécontent, de
  mauvaise humeur
disguise, n. déguisement m.
dish, n. plat m.; vb. (to do the
  dishes) laver la vaisselle
dishonest, adj. malhonnête(té)
dishonor, n. déshonneur m.
dishonorable, adj. déhonorant
disinfect, vb. désinfecter
disinfectant, n. désinfectant m.
disinherit, vb. déshériter
disjointed, adj. désarticulé,

disloqué

disk, n. disque m.

dislike, n. aversion f.; vb. ne pas
aimer

dislocate, vb. disloquer

dislodge, vb. déloger

disloyal, adj. infidèle

dismay, n. consternation f.

dismember, vb. démembrer

dismiss, vb. congédier

dismount, vb. descendre

disobedience, n. désobéissance f.

disobey, vb. désobéir à

disorder, n. désordre m.

disorderly, adj. désordonné

disown, vb. désavouer

disparate, adj. disparate

disparity, n. inégalité f.

dispatch, n. expédition,
promptitude, dépêche f.

dispatcher, n. expéditeur m.

dispel, vb. dissiper

dispensable, adj. dont on peut
se passer

dispense, vb. distribuer, dispenser

dispersal, n. dispersion f.

disperse, vb. disperser

displace, vb. déplacer

displacement, n. déplacement m.

display, n. exposition f.; étalage
m.; vb. étaler

displease, vb. déplaire à

disposal, n. disposition f.

dispose, vb. disposer

disposition, n. disposition, f.;
caractère m.

disproportion, n. disproportion f.

disprove, vb. réfuter

disputable, adj. contestable,
disputable

dispute, n. discussion, dispute f.

disqualify, vb. disqualifier

disregard, n. insouciance f.

disrespect, n. irrévérence f.

disrespectful, adj. irrespectueux

disrobe, vb. déshabiller, dévêtir

disrupt, vb. faire éclater, rompre

dissatisfaction, n. mécontentement
m.

dissatisfy, vb. mécontenter

dissect, vb. disséquer

disservice, n. mauvais service
rendu m.

dissimilar, adj. dissemblable

dissipate, vb. dissiper

dissipated, adj. dissipé

dissociate, vb. déassocier,
dissocier

dissolute, adj. dissolu

dissolution, n. dissolution f.

dissolve, vb. dissoudre

dissonant, adj. dissonant

distance, n. distance f.

distant, adj. distant

distaste, n. dégoût m.

distasteful, adj. désagréable

distend, vb. dilater, gonfler

distill, vb. distiller

distillery, n. distillerie f.

distinct, adj. distinct

distinction, n. distinction f.

distinctive, adj. distinctif

distinctly, adv. distinctement

distinguish, vb. distinguer

distinguished, adj. distingué

distract, vb. distraire; affoler

distracted, adj. affolé, bouleversé

distraction, n. distraction; folie f.

distraught, adj. affolé, éperdu

distress, n. détresse f.; vb. affliger

distribute, vb. distribuer

distribution, n. distribution f.

distributor, n. distributeur m.

district, m. contrée f.

distrust, n. méfiance f.

disturb, vb. déranger

disturbance, n. dérangement m.

ditch, n. fossé m.

diver, n. plongeur m.

divergence, n. divergence f.

diverse, adj. divers

diversion, n. divertissement m.

diversity, n. diversité f.

divert, vb. détourner, divertir

divide, vb. diviser

divided, adj. divisé, séparé

divine, adj. divin

divinity, n. divinité f.

divisible, adj. divisible

division, n. division f.

divorce, n. divorce m.; vb. divorcer

dizziness, n. vertige m.

dizzy, adj. pris de vertige

do, vb. faire

docile, adj. docile

dock, n. bassin m.

docket, n. registre, bordereau m.

doctor, n. docteur m.

doctrine, n. doctrine f.

document, n. document m.

documentary, adj. documentaire

dodge, vb. esquiver, éluder

doe, n. daine f.

dog, n. chien m.

doghouse, n. chenil m.

doleful, adj. lugubre

doll, n. poupée f.

dollar, n. dollar m.

dolphin, n. dauphin m.

domain, n. domaine m.

dome, n. dôme m.	**dray**, n. camion m.
domestic, adj. domestique	**drayman**, n. camionneur m.
domicile, n. domicile m.	**dread**, n. crainte f.
dominance, n. dominance,	**dreadful**, adj. affreux
prédominance f.	**dream**, n. rêve m.
dominate, vb. dominer	**dreamer**, n. rêveur m.
domination, n. domination f.	**dreamy**, adj. rêveur m., rêveuse f.
dominion, n. domination f.	**dreary**, adj. morne
donate, vb. donner	**dredge**, vb. draguer
donation, n. donation f.	**drench**, vb. tremper
done, vb. fait	**dress**, vb. habiller, vêtir, parer,
donkey, n. âne m.	orner
doom, vb. condamner	**dresser**, n. commode f.
door, n. porte f.; concierge m.f.	**dressing**, n. toilette f.; pansement
dormitory, n. dortoir m.	m.
dosage, n. dosage m.	**dressmaker**, n. couturière f.
dose, n. dose f.	**drier**, n. sécheur, dessécheur m.
dot, n. point m.	**drift**, vb. dériver
double, adj. and n. double m.	**driftwood**, n. bois flottant m.
double-breasted, adj. croisé	**drill**, n. foret, exercice m.; vb. forer
doubt, n. doute m.	**drink**, n. boisson f.; vb. boire
doubtful, adj. douteux	**drip**, vb. dégoutter
doubtless, adv. sans doute	**drive**, n. promenade en voiture f.
dough, n. pâte f.	**driver**, n. chauffeur m.
doughnut, n. pet de nonne m.	**drizzle**, n. bruine f.; vb. bruiner
dove, n. colombe f.	**droop**, vb. pencher
down, n. duvet m.	**drop**, n. goutte f.; vb. laisser tomber
downfall, n. chute f.	**dropsy**, n. hydropisie f.
downhill, n. descente f.	**drought**, n. sécheresse f.
downpour, n. averse f.	**drove**, n. troupeau m.
downright, adv. tout à fait	**drown**, vb. noyer
downstairs, adv. en bas	**drowse**, vb. s'assoupir
downtown, adv. en ville	**drowsy**, adj. somnolent
downy, adj. duveteux	**drudge**, vb. s'éreinter
doze, vb. sommeiller	**drug**, n. drogue f.
dozen, n. douzaine f.	**druggist**, n. pharmacien m.
drab, adj. gris, terne	**drum**, n. tambour, tympan m.
draft, n. dessin, courant d'air m.	**drummer**, n. tambour m.
(mil.) conscription f.	**drunk**, adj. ivre
draftsman, n. dessinateur m.	**drunkard**, n. ivrogne m.
drafty, adj. plein de courante d'air	**dry**, adj. sec m.; sèche f.
drag, vb. traîner	**dryness**, n. sécheresse f.
dragnet, n. drague, seine f.;	**dual**, adj. double
chalut m.	**duck**, n. canard m.
dragon, n. dragon m.	**duct**, n. conduit m.
drain, vb. drainer	**ductile**, adj. ductile
drainage, n. drainage m.	**duel**, n. duel m.
dram, n. drachme, goutte f.	**duellist**, n. duelliste m.
drama, n. drame m.	**duet**, n. duo m.
dramatic, adj. dramatique	**duke**, n. duc m.
dramatist, n. dramaturge m.	**dull**, adj. ennuyeux
dramatize, vb. dramatiser	**dullard**, n. lourdaud m.
drape, vb. draper	**dullness**, n. monotonie f.
drapery, n. draperie f.	**dumb**, adj. muet m., muette f.
drastic, adj. drastique	**dummy**, n. mannequin m., mort m.
draught, n. traction f.; trait m.	**dump**, n. voirie f.
draw, vb. dessiner	**dumpling**, n. boulette (de pâte) f.
drawbridge, m. pont-levis m.	**dun**, vb. importuner, talonner
drawer, n. tiroir m.	**dunce**, n. crétin m.
drawing, n. dessin m.	**dune**, n. dune f.

dungeon, n. cachot m.

duplex, adj. double

duplicate, n. double m.; vb. faire le double de

duplication, n. duplication f.

duplicity, n. duplicité f.

durable, adj. durable

durability, n. durabilité f.

duration, n. durée f.

duress, n. contrainte, coercition f.

during, prep. pendant

dusk, n. crépuscule m.

dusky, adj. sombre

dust, n. poussière f.; vb. épousseter

dusty, adj. poussiéreux

Dutch, adj. and n. hollandais m.

Dutchman, n. Hollandais m.

dutiful, adj. respectueux, fidèle

dutifully, adv. avec soummission

duty, n. devoir, droit m.; être de service

duty-free, adj. exempt de droits

dwarf, adj. and n., nain m.

dwell, vb. demeurer

dwindle, vb. diminuer

dye, n. teinture f.

dyer, n. teinturier m.

dynamic, adj. dynamique

dynamics, n. dynamique f.

dynamite, n. dynamite f.

dynamo, n. dynamo f.

dynasty, n. dynastie f.

dyslexia, n. dyslexie f.

dyspepsia, n. dyspepsie f.

dyspeptic, adj. dyspeptique

E

each, adj. chaque; pron. chacun m.

eager, ad. ardent, vif

eagerness, n. empressement m.

eagel, n. aigle m.; (mil.) aigle f.

ear, n. oreille f.

eardrum, n. tympan m.

earl, n. comte m.

early, adj. matinal, premier

earn, vb. gagner

earnest, adj. sérieux

earphone, n. casque m.

earring, n. boucle d'oreille f.

earth, n. terre f.

earthly, adj. terrestre

earthquake, n. tremblement de terre

ease, n. aise f.; avec facilité

easel, n. chevalet m.

easily, adv. largement, facilement

easiness, n. aisance, facilité f.

east, n. est m.

Easter, n. Pâques m.

eastern, adj. de l'est, oriental

eastward, adv. vers l'est

easy, adj. facile, aise

eat, vb. manger

ebb, n. reflux, déclin m.

ebony, n. ébène m.

eccentric, adj. excentrique

eccentricity, n. excentricité f.

ecclesiastic, adj. and n. ecclé- siastique m.

ecclesiastical, adj. ecclésias- tique

echelon, n. échelon m.

echo, n. écho m.

eclipse, n. éclipse f.

ecological, adj. écologique

ecology, n. écologie f.

economic, adj. économique

economical, adj. économe

economics, n. économie politique f.

economist, n. économiste m.

economize, vb. économiser

economy, n. économie f.

ecstasy, n. extase f.; transport m.

eczema, n. eczéma m.

edge, n. bord, fil m.

edging, n. pose, bordure f.

edgy, adj. d'un air agacé

edible, adj. comestible

edict, n. édit m.

edition, édition f.

editor, n. éditeur, rédacteur m.

editorial, n. article de fond m.

educate, vb. élever, instruire

education, n. éducation f.

educator, n. éducateur m.

eel, n. anguille f.

effect n. effet m.; vb. effectuer

effective, adj. efficace, effectif

effectivenss, n efficacité f.

efficacy, n. efficacité f.

efficiency, n. compétence f.; rende- ment m.

efficient, adj. capable

effort, n. effort m.

effortless, adj. sans effort

effusive, adj. démonstratif

egg, n. oeuf m.; (boiled) oeuf á la coque; (fried) oeuf sur le plat; (hard-boiled) oeuf dur

eggplant, n. aubergine f.

Egypt, n. l Égypte m.

Egyptian, n. Égyptien m.; adj. égyptien

eight, adj. and n. huit m.

eighteen, adj. and n. dix-huit m.

eighteenth, adj. and n. dix-huitième, m.f.

eight, adj. and n. huitième m.f.

eighty, adj. and n. quatre-vingt m.

either, pron. l'un ou l'autre m.; conj. ou, soit

eject, vb. rejeter, émettre

ejection, n. expulsion, éjection f.

elaborate, adv. minutieux.; vb. élaborer

elapse, vb. s'écouler

elastic, adj. and n. élastique m.

elasticity, n. élasticité f.

elate, vb. exalter, transporter

elated, adj. exalté

elbow, n. coude m.

elder, adj. and n. aîné m.

elderly, adj. d'un certain âge

elect, vb. élire

election, n. élection f.

elective, adj. électif

electorate, n. électorat m., les votants m., pl.

electric, electrical, adj. électrique

electrician, n. électricien m.

electricity, n. électricité f.

electrocute, vb. électrocuter

electron, n. électron m.

electronics, n. électronique f.

elegance, n. élégance f.

elegant, adj. élégant

elegiac, adj. élégiaque

elegy, n. élégie f.

element, n. élément m.

elementary, adj. élémentaire

elephant, n. éléphant m.

elevate, vb. élever

elevation, n. élévation f.

elevator, n. ascenseur m.

eleven, adj. and n. onze m.

eleventh, adj. and n. onzième m.f.

elf, n. elfe m.

elfin, adj. d'elfe

elicit, vb. tirer, faire jaillir

eligibility, n. éligibilité f.

eligible, adj. éligible

eliminate, vb. éliminer

elimination, n. élimination f.

elixir, n. élixir m.

elk, n. élan m.

elm, n. orme m.

elope, vb. s'enfuir

eloquence, n. éloquence f.

eloquent, adj. éloquent

eloquently, adv. d'une manière éloquente

else, adj. autre, quelqu'un d'autre.,

elsewhere, adv. ailleurs

elucidate, vb. élucider, éclaircir

elude, vb. éluder

elusive, adj. évasif, insaisissable

emaciated, adj. émacié

emancipate, vb. émanciper

emancipation, n. émancipation f.

emasculate, vb. émasculer

embalm, vb. embaumer

embankment, n. levée f.

embargo, n. embargo m.

embark, vb. embarquer

embarrass, vb. embarrasser

embarrassing, adj. embarrassant

embarrassment, n. embarras m.

embassy, n. ambassade f.

embellish, vb. embellir

embellishment, n. embellissement m.

ember, n. braise f., charbon ardent m.

embezzle, vb. détourner

embitter, vb. aigrir, envenimer

emblazon, vb. blasonner

emblem, n. emblème m.

embody, vb. incarner, incorporer

emboss, vb. graver en relief, travailler en relief

embrace, n. étreindre f.

embroider, vb. broder

embroidery, n. broderie f.

embryo, n. embryon m.

emerald, n. émeraude f.

emerge, vb. émerger

emergency, n. circonstance critique f.

emery, n. émeri m

emigrant, n. émigrant m.

emigrate, vb. émigrer

emigration, n. émigration f.

eminence, n. éminence f.

emit, vb. émettre

emolument, n. traitement m.

emotion, n. émotion f.

emotional, adj. émotif, émotionnable

emperor, n. empereur m.

emphasis, n. force f.; accent m.

emphasize, vb. mettre en relief

emphatic, adj. énergique

empire, n. empire m.

employ, vb. employer

employee, n. employé m.

employer, n. patron m.

employment, n. emploi m.

empress, n. impératrice f.

emptiness, n. vide m.

empty, adj. vide, à vide

emulate, vb. imiter

enable, vb. mettre à même (de)

enact, vb. ordonner, arrêter

enactment, n. promulgation f.; acte législatif m.

enamel, n. émail m.

encephalitis, n. encéphalite f.

enchant, vb. enchanter

enchanting, adj. ravissant

enchantment, n. enchantement m.

enclose, vb. enclore, clore

enclosure, n. action de clore, clôture

encompass, vb. entourer

encounter, vb. rencontrer f.

encourage, vb. encourager

encouragement, n. encouragement m.

encroach, vb. empiéter

encyclopedia, n. encyclopédie f.

end, n. fin, extrémité f.; bout, but, objet m.

endanger, vb. mettre en danger

endear, vb. rendre cher

endearment, n. charme, attrait m.

endeavor, n. effort m.; vb. s'efforcer, essayer

endemic, adj. endémique

ending, n. terminaison, désinence f.

endless, adj. sans fin, perpétuel

endorse, vb. endosser, appuyer

endorsement, n. endossement, approbation m.

endowment, n. dotation, fondation f.

endurance, n. résistance f.

endure, vb. supporter

enduring, adj. durable

enema, n. lavement m.

enemy, adj. and n ennemi m.

energetic, adj. énergique

energy, n. énergie f.

enfold, vb. envelopper

enforce, vb. imposer, exécuter

enforcement, n. exécution f.

enfranchise, vb. affranchir, accorder le droit de vote

engage, vb. engager, retenir, prendre, louer

engaged, adj. fiancé, occupé

engagement, n. engagement m.; fiançailles f., pl.

engaging, adj. attrayant, séduisant

engine, n. machine, locomotive f.; moteur m.

engineer, n. ingénieur, mécanicien m.; (mil.) soldat du génie m.

engineering, n. génie m.

England, n. l'Angleterre f.

English, adj. and n. anglais m.

engrave, vb. graver

engraver, n. graveur m.

engraving, n. gravure f.

enhance, vb. rehausser

enjoy, vb. jouir de, s'amuser

enjoyable, adj. agréable

enjoyment, n. jouissance f.

enlarge, vb. agrandir

enlargement, n. agrandissement m.

enlarger, n. agrandisseur, amplificateur m.

enligthen, vb. éclairer

enlightenment, n. éclaircissement m.

enlist, vb. enrôler

enmity, n. inimitié f.

enormous, adj. énorme

enough, adj. and adv. assez

enrage, vb. faire enrager

enrich, vb. enrichir

ensemble, n. ensemble m.

entail, vb. entraîner, imposer

entangle, vb. empêtrer

enter, vb. entrer dans

enterprise, n. entreprise f.

enterprising, adj. entreprenant

entertain, vb. amuser, recevoir

entertainment, n. hospitalité

enthusiasm, n. enthousiasme m.

entice, vb. attirer

entire, adj. entier

entirely, adv. entièrement

entitle, vb. donner droit à, intituler

entrails, n. entrailles f., pl.

entrance, n. entrée f.

entrap, vb. attraper, prendre au piège

entreat, vb. supplier

entry, n. entrée, inscription f.

enumerate, vb. énumérer

enunciation, n. énonciation f.

envelop, vb. envelopper

envelope, n. enveloppe f.

enviable, adj. enviable

envious, adj. envieux

environment, n. milieu m.

envoy, n. envoyé m.

envy, n. envie f.; vb. envier

epic, n. épopée f.; adj. épique

epilepsy, n. épilepsie f.

epilogue, n. épilogue m.

epoch, n. époque f.

equable, adj. uniforme, régulier

equal, adj. égal, être à la hauteur de

equality, n. égalité f.

equalize, vb. égaliser

equate, vb. égaler, mettre en équation

equation, n. équation f.

equator, n. équateur m.

equilibrium, n. équilibre m.

equip, vb. équiper

equipment, n. équipement m.

equitable, adj. équitable, juste
equity, n. équité f.
equivalent, adj. and n. équivalent m.
era, n. ère f.
eradicate, vb. supprimer
erase, vb. effacer
eraser, n. gomme f.
erect, adj. droit
erection, n. érection, construction f.
erectness, n. attitude droite f.
erode, vb. éroder, ronger
erosion, n. érosion f.
erosive, adj. érosif
erotic, adj. érotique
err, vb. errer
errand, n. course f.
errant, adj. errant
erratic, adj. irrégulier, excentrique
erring, adj. égaré
erroneous, adj. erroné
error, n. erreur f.
erudite, adj. érudit
erudition, n. érudition f.
erupt, vb. entrer en éruption
eruption, n. éruption f.
escalate, vb. escalader
escalator, n. escalier roulant m.
escape, n. fuite f.; vb. échapper
escort, n. (mil.) escorte f.; cavalier m.
esculent, adj. comestible
esoteric, adj. ésotérique
especial, adj. spécial
espionage, n. espionnage m.
espouse, vb. épouser, embrasser
Eskimo, n. Esquimau m.
esquire, n. écuyer m.
essay, n. essai m.; épreuve f.
essence, n. essence f.
essential, adj. essentiel
essentially, adv. essentiellement
establish, vb. établir
establishment, n. établissement m.
estate, n. état, rang m.; propriété f.
esteem, n. estime f.; vb. estimer
estimate, n. estimation, évaluation f.
estimation, n. jugement m.
estrange, vb. aliéner
etching, n. gravure à l'eau-forte f.
eternal, adj. éternel
eternity, n. éternité f.
ether, n. éther m.
ethical, adj. moral
ethics, n. éthique f.
Ethiopia, n. l'Éthiopie f.
ethnic, adj. ethnique
etiquette, n. étiquette f.
eucalyptus, n. eucalyptus m.

eugenic, adj. eugénique
eugenics, n. eugénisme m.; eugénique f.
Europe, n. l'Europe f.
European, adj. Européen m.
euthanasia, n. euthanasie f.
evacuate, vb. évacuer
evade, vb. éluder
evaluate, vb. évaluer
evaluation, n. évaluation f.
evangelist, n. évangéliste m.
evaporate, vb. évaporer
evaporation, n. évaporation f.
evasion, n. subterfuge f.
eve, n. veille f.
even, adj. égal, régulier
evening, n. soir m.; soirée f.
event, n. événement, cas m.
eventful, adj. plein d'événements
ever, adv. toujours; jamais
evergreen, adj. toujours vert
everlasting, adj. éternel, perétuel
every, adj. chaque, tous les m.; toutes les f.
everybody, everyone, pron. tout le monde
everyday, adj. de tous le jours, journalier
everything, n. tout m.
everywhere, adv. partout
evict, vb. évincer, expulser
eviction, n. éviction, expulsion f.
evidence, n. évidence, preuve f.
evident, adj. évident
evidently, adv. évidemment
evil, n. mal m.
evoke, vb. évoquer
evolution, n. évolution f.
evolve, vb. évoluer, développer
ewe, n. agnelle f.
exact, adj. exact
exacting, adj. exigeant
exactly, adv. exactement
exaggerated, adj. exagéré
exaggeration, n. exagération f.
exalt, vb. exalter, élever
exaltation, n. exaltation f.
examination, n. examen m.
examine, vb. examiner
example, n. exemple m.
exasperate, vb. exaspérer
exasperation, n. exaspération f.
exceed, vb. excéder
exceedingly, adv. extrêmement
excel, vb. exceller
excellence, n. excellence f.
excellent, adj. excellent
except, vb. excepter, exclure; prep. excepté, sauf
exception, n. exception f.

exceptional, adj. exceptionnel

excerpt, n. extrait m.

excess, n. excès, excédent, surpoids m.

excessive, adj. excessif

exchange, n. échange, troc m.

exchangeable, adj. échangeable

excise, n. contribution indirecte, régie f.

excitable, adj. émotionnable, excitable

excite, vb. exciter

excitement, n. agitation f.

exclaim, vb. s'écrier

exclamation, n. exclamation f.

exclude, vb. exclure(de)

exclusion, n. exclusion f.

exclusive, adj. exclusif, sélect

excommunicate, vb. excommunier

excortate, vb. excorier, écorcher

excruciating, adj. atroce, affreux

exculpate, vb. disculper, exonérer

excursion, n. excursion f.

excusable, adj. excusable

excuse, n. excuse f.

execute, vb. exécuter

execution, n. exécution f.

executive, adj. and n. exécutif m.

executor, n. exécuteur m.

exemplify, vb. expliquer par des exemples

exempt, adj. exempt; vb exempter

exercise, n. exercice m.; vb. exercer

exert, vb. employer, s'efforcer de

exertion, n. effort m.

exhale, vb. exhaler

exhaust, n. échappement m.; vb. épuiser

exhaustion, n. épuisement m.

exhaustive, adj. complet, approfondi

exhibit, vb. exposer, montrer

exhibition, n. exposition f.

exhilarate, vb. égayer

exhort, vb. exhorter

exhortation, n. exhortion f.

exhume, vb. exhumer

exile, n. exil, exilé m.; vb. exiler

exist, vb. exister

existence, n. existence f.

existent, adj. existant

exit, n. sortie f.

exodus, n. exode m.

exorcise, vb. exorciser

exotic, adj. exotique

expand, vb. étendre, déployer

expanse, n. étendue f.

expansion, n. expansion f.

expansive, adj. expansif

expatriate, vb. expatrier

expect, vb. s'attendre à, attendre

expectancy, n. attente f.

expectation, n. attente, espérance f.

expediency, n. convenance f.

expedient, n. expédient m.

expedite, vb. activer, accélérer

expedition, n. expédition f.

expel, vb. expulser

expend, vb. dépenser, épuiser

expenditure, n. dépense f.

expense, n. dépense f.; frais m., pl.

expensive, adj. coûteux, cher

experienced, adj. expérimenté

experiment, n. expérience f.

experimental, adj. expérimental

expert, adj. and n. expert m.

expiate, vb. expier

expiration, n. expiration f.

expire, vb. expirer

explain, vb. expliquer

explanation, n. explication f.

explanatory, adj. explicatif

explicit, adj. explicite

explode, vb. éclater

exploitation, n. exploitation f.

exploration, n. exploration f.

exploratory, adj. exploratif

explore, vb. explorer

explorer, n. explorateur m.

explosion, n. explosion f.

explosive, adj. and n. explosif m.

exponent, n. interprète m.

export, n. exportation f.; vb. exporter

expose, vb. exposer

exposition, n. exposition

exposure, n. exposition f.

expound, vb. exposer

express, adj. exprès; vb. exprimer

expression, n. expression f.

expressive, adj. expressif

expressly, adv. expressément

expressman, n. agent de messageries m.

expropriate, vb. exproprier

expulsion, n. expulsion f.

expunge, vb. effacer, rayer

exquisite, ajd. exquis

extant, adj. existant

extend, vb. étendre, prolonger

extension, n. extension f.

extensive, adj. étendu

extensively, adv. d'une manière étendue

extent, n. étendue f.

extenuate, vb. exténuer, atténuer

exterior, adj. and n. extérieur m.

exterminate, vb. exterminer
extermination, n. extermination f.
external, adj. externe
extinct, adj. éteint
extinction, n. extinction f.
extinguish, vb. éteindre
extirpate, vb. extirper
extol, vb. vanter
extort, vb. extorquer
extortion, n. extorsion f.
extra, adj. supplémentaire, en sus, extraordinaire
extract, n. extraire
extraction, n. extraction, origine f.
extraordinary, adj. extraordinaire
extravagance, n. extravagance, prodigalité f.
extravagant, adj. extravagant, prodigue
extravaganza, m. oeuvre fantaisiste f.
extreme, adj. and n. extrême m.
extremity, n. extrémité f.
exuberant, adj. exubérant
exude, vb. exsuder
exult, vb. exulter
exultant, adj. exultant, joyeux
eye, n. oiel m.; yeux m., pl.
eyeball, n. bulbe de l'oeil m.
eyebrow, n. sourcil m.
eyeglass, n. lorgnon m.
eyeglasses, n. lunettes f., pl.
eyelash, n. cil n.
eyelid, n. paupière f.
eyesight, n. vue f.
eyewitness, n. témoin oculaire m.

F

fable, n. fable f.
fabric, n. construction f.
fabricate, vb. fabriquer
fabulous, adj. fabuleux
face, n. figure f.; vb. faire face à
facet, n. facette f.
facial, adj. facial
facing, n. revêtement, revers m.
facsimile, n. fac-similé m.
fact, n. fait m.; en effet (in fact)
faction, n. faction f.
factual, adj. effectif, positif
fad, n. marotte f.
fade, vb. se faner, se décolorer, s'évanouir
fail, vb. manquer, faillir
faint, adj. faible, défaillant
fair, n. foire m.; adj. beau m., belle

f.;
blond, juste; passable
fairly, adj. honnêtement, impartialement
fairness, n. honnêteté f.
faith, n. foi f.
faithful, adj. fidèle
fake, vb. truquer
faker, n. truqueur m.
falcon, n. faucon m.
fall, n. chute f.; (month) automne m.
fallen, adj. tombé déchu
fallout, n. pluie radioactive f.
fallow, adj. en jachère
false, adj. faux m.; fausse f.
falsehood, n. mensonge m.
fame, n. renommée f.
familiar, adj. familier
familiarity, n. familiarité f.
familiarize, vb. familiariser
family, n. famille f.
famished, adj. affamé
famous, adj. célèbre
fan, n. éventail, ventilateur m.
fancy, n. fantaisie f.; vb. se figurer
fanfare, n. fanfare f.
fantastic, adj. fantastique
fantasy, n. fantaisie f.
far, adv. loin, jusqu'ici, autant que, beaucoup, de beaucoup
faraway, adj. lointain
fare, n. prix m.; chère f.; vb. aller
farewell, interj. and n. adieu m.
far-fetched, adj. forcé
farm, n. ferme f.
farmer, n. fermier m.
farmhouse, n. maison de ferme f.
farming, n. culture f.
far-sighted, adj. clairvoyant
farther, adj. plus éloigné; adv. plus loin
fascinate, vb. fasciner
fashion, n. mode, manière f.
fast, n. jeûne m.,; adj. rapide, en avance, en avance; vb. jeûner; adv. vite, ferme
fasten, vb. attacher
fastening, n. attache f.
fat, adj. gras m.; grasse f.
fatal, adj. fatal, mortel
fatality, n. fatalité f.
fatally, adv. fatalement, mortellement
fate, n. destin m.
father, n. père m.
fatherhood, n. paternité f.
father-in-law, n. beau-père m.
fatherless, adj. sans père
fatherly, adj. paternel
fatigue, n. fatigue f.

fatten, vb. engraisser
fatty, adj. graisseux
faucet, n. robinet m.
fault, n. faute f.; défaut m.
faultless, adj. sans défaut
faulty, adj. défectueux
favor, n. faveur f.; vb. favoriser
favorable, adj. favorable
favored, adj. favorisé
favorite, adj. and n. favori, m.; favorite f.
fawn, n. faon m.
fear n. crainte, peur f.; vb. craindre, avoir peur de
fearful, adj. craintif; effrayant
fearless, adj. intrépide
feasible, adj. faisable
feast, n. fête f.; festin m.
feather, n. plume f.
feathered, adj. emplumé
feature, n. trait m.
February, n. février m.
federal, adj. fédéral
federation, n. fédération f.
fedor, n. chapeau mou m.
fee, n. honoraires m.pl.; frais m., pl.
feeble, adj. faible
feed, n. nourriture f.; vb. nourrir
feel, vb. sentir, tâter
feeling, n. sentiment m.
feline, adj. félin
fell, adj. funeste
fellow, n. homme, garçon; compagnon m.
fellowship, n. camaraderie, bourse universitaire f.
felon, n. criminel m.
felony, n. crime m.
felt, n. feutre m.
female, n. femme, femelle f.; adj. féminin, femelle
feminine, adj. féminin
femininity, n. féminité f.
fence, n. clôture f.; vb. enclore, fair de l'escrime
fencing, n. escrime f.
fender, n. garde-boue; garde-feu m.
fern, n. fougère f.
ferry, n. passage en bac; bac m.
fertile, adj. fertile
fertility, n. fertilité f.
fertilization, n. fertilisation f.
fertilize, vb. fertiliser
fervent, adj. fervent
festival, n. fête f.
festive, adj. de fête
festoon, n. feston m.; vb. festonner
fetal, adj. foetal
fetch, vb. aller chercher, apporter
fetching, adj. attrayant

fete, vb. fêter
fetter, n. lien m.; chaîne f.; vb. enchaîner
fetus, n. foetus m.
feud, n. inimitié f.; fief m.
feudalism, n. régime féodal m.
fever, n. fièvre f.
feverish, adj. fiévreux, fébrile
feverishly, adv. fébrilement, fiévreusement
few, adj. peu de, quelques
fiancé, n. fiancé m.
fiasco, n. fiasco m.
fiat, n. décret m.
fib, n. petit mensonge m.
fiber, n. fibre f.
fickle, adj. volage
fiction, n. fiction f.; romans m., pl.
fictional, adj. de romans
fictitious, adj. fictif, imaginaire
fiddle, n. violon m.; vb. jouer du violon
fidelity, n fidélité f.
field, n. champ m.
fiendish, adj. diabolique, infernal
fierce, adj. féroce
fiery, adj. ardent
fiesta, n. fête f.
fife, n. fifre m.
fifteen, adj. and n. quinze m.
fifteenth, adj. and n. quinzième m.
fifth, adj. and n. cinquième m.
fifty, adj. and n. cinquante m.
fig, n. figue f.
fight, n. combat m.; lutte, dispute f.; vb. combattre, se disputer
fighter, n. combattant m.
figment, n. invention f.
figurative, adj. figuré
figuratvely, adj. au figuré
figure, n. figure, tournure f.; chiffre m. vb. figurer, calculer
figured, adj. à dessin
figurehead, n. homme de paille m.
filament, n. filament m.
filch, vb. escamoter
file, n. lime, file, liasse f.; archives f., pl.; classeur m.
fill, vb. remplir
filling, n. remplissage m.
film, n. film m.; pellicule f.
filter, n. filtre m.; vb. filtrer
fin, n. nageoire f.
final, adj. final
finale, n. finale m.
finally, adv. finalement, enfin
finance, n. finance f.; vb. financer
financial, adj. financier
find, vb. trouver
fine, n. amende, belle f.; fin.; vb.

mettre à l'amende; adj. beau m.

finery, n. parure f.

finesse, n. finesse f.; vb. finasser

finger, n. doigt m.

fingernail, n. ongle m.

fingerprint, n. empreinte digitale f.

finish, vb. finir

finite, adj. fini

Finland, n. la Finlande f.

Finn, n. Finlandais, Finnois m.

fire, n. feu, incendie m.

fire alarm, n. avertisseur d'incendie m.

firearm, n. arme à feu f.

fire escape, n. échelle de sauvetage f.

fire extinguisher, n. extincteur m.

fireman, n. pompier m.

fireplace, n. cheminée f.

fireproof, adj. à l'épreuve du feu

firewood, n. bois de chauffage m.

fireworks, n. feu d'artifice m.

firm, n. maison de commerce f.

firmness, n. fermeté f.

first, adj. premier; adv. d'abord

first aid, n. premiers secours m., pl

first-class, adj. de premier ordre

first-hand, adj. de première main

fiscal, adj. fiscal

fish, n. poisson m.; vb. pêcher

fisherman, n. pêcheur m.

fishing, n. pêche f.

fist, n. poing m.

fit, n. accès m.; adj. convenable, capable, propre à

fitful, adj. agité, irrégulier

fitness, n. convenance, santé physique f.; à-propos m.

fitting, n. convenable, à propos, juste

five, adj. and n. cinq m.

fix, vb. fixer, attacher, établir, arrêter

fixed, adj. fixe

fixture, n. meuble à demeure

flabby, adj. flasque

flag, n. drapeau m.; dalle f.

flagon, n. flacon m.

flagpole, n. mât de drapeau m.

flagrant, adj. flagrant

flagrantly, adv. d'une manière flagrante

flair, n. flair m.

flamboyant, adj. flamboyant

flame, n. flamme f.; vb. flamboyer

flaming, adj. flamboyant

flamingo, n. flamant m.

flank, n. flanc m.

flannel, n. flanelle f.

flap, n. coup, battant m.; patte f.;

vb. battre

flare, vb. flamboyer

flash, n. éclair m.

flashlight, n. flash m.

flashy, adj. voyant

flask, n. gourde f.

flat, n. appartement m.; adj. plat m.

flatness, n. égalité f.; aplatissement m.

flatten, vb. aplatir

flatter, vb. flatter

flattery, n. flatterie f.

flaunt, vb. parader, étaler

flavor, n. saveur f.; goût m.

flavoring, n. assaisonnement m.

flavorless, adj. fade

flaw, n. défaut m.

flawless, adj. sans défaut, parfait

flawlessly, adv. d'une manière impeccable

flax, n. lin m.

flea, n. puce f.

flee, vb. s'enfuir

fleece, n. toison f.

fleecy, adj. laineux, moutonneux

fleet, n. flotte f.

fleeting, adj. fugitif

flesh, n. chair f.

flexibility, n. flexibilité f.

flexible, adj. flexible

flicker, vb. trembloter, vaciller

flier, n. aviateur m.

flight, n. vol m.; fuite f.

flinch, vb. reculer, broncher

fling, vb. jeter

flint, n. pierre à briquet; silex m.

flirt, vb. flirter

flirtation, n. flirt m.

float, vb. flotter

flock, n. troupeau m.; vb. accourir

flog, vb. fouetter

flood, n. inondation f.

floodlight, n. lumière à grand flots f.

floor, n. plancher, parquet, carreau m.

flooring, n. plancher, parquet m.

flop, n. coup mat m.

floral, adj. floral

florist, n. fleuriste m.f.

flounder, n. flet m.

flour, n. farine f.

flourish, vb. prospérer

flow, vb. couler

flower, n. fleur f.

flowerpot, n. pot à fleurs m.

flue, n. tuyau de cheminée m.

fluency, n. facilité f.

fluent, adj. courant

fluid, adj. and n. fluide m.

flunk, vb. coller, recaler
flourescent lamp, n. lampe fluorescente f.
flurry, n. agitation f.
flush, n. rougeur, chasse f.
flute, n. flûte f.
flutter, n. voltigement m. palpiter
fly, n. mouche f.
foam, n. écume f.
focal, adj. focal
focus, n. foyer m.
foe, n. ennemi m.
fog, n. brouillard m.
foggy, adj. brumeux
foil, n. feuille f.
foist, vb. fourrer
fold, n. pli m.
folder, n. prospectus m.
foliage, n. feuillage m.
folio, n. in-folio m.
folk, n. gens m.f., pl.
folklore, n. folklore m.
follow, vb. suivre
follower, n. disciple m.
folly, n. folie f.
fond, adj. tendre; vb. aimer
fondant, n. fondant m.
fondle, vb. caresser
fondly, adv. tendrement
fondness, n. tendresse f.
food, n. nourriture f.
fool, n. sot, bête m.; sotte f.
foot, n. pied m.
footage, n. métrage m.
football, n. football, ballon m.
footing, n. pied, point d'appui m.
footnote, n. note f.
footprint, n. empreinte de pas f.
footstep, n. pas m.
footstool, n. tabouret m.
footwork, n. jeu de pieds m.
for, prep. pour; conj. car
forage, n. fourrage m.; vb. fourrager
forbear, vb. s'abstenir de, montrer de la patience
forbearance, n. patience f.
forbid, vb. défendre (à)
forbidding, adj. rébarbatif
force, n. force f.
forced, adj. forcé
forceful, adj. énergique
forcefulness, n. énergie, vigueur f.
forceps, n. forceps m.
forcible, adj. forcé
ford n. gué m.; vb. traverser à gué
forearm, n. avant-bras m.
forebears, n. ancêtres m., pl.
forecast, n. prévision f.; vb. prévoir
forecastle, n. gaillard m.
foreclose, vb. exclure, forclore

forefather, n. ancêtre m.
forefinger, n. index m.
foregone, adj. décidé d'avance
foreground, n. premier plan m.
forehead, n. front m.
foreign, adj. étranger
foreigner, n. étranger m.
foreleg, n. jambe antérieure f.
foremost, adj. premier
forensic, adj. judiciaire
foresee, vb. prévoir
foresight, n. prévoyance f.
forest, n. forêt f.
forestall, vb. anticiper, devancer
forester, n. forestier m.
foretell, vb. prédire
forever, adv. pour toujours
forevermore, adv. à jamais
forfeit, vb. forfaire
forfeiture, n. perte par confiscation, forfaiture f.
forge, n. forge f.; vb. forger, contrefaire
forger, n. faussaire, falsificateur m.
forgery, n. faux m.
forget, vb. oublier
forgetful, adj. oublieux
forgive, vb. pardonner (à)
forgiveness, n. pardon m.
forgo, vb. renoncer à
fork, n. fourchette, fourche f.
forlorn, adj. désespéré; abandonné
formal, adj. formel
formally, adv. formellement
format, n. format m.
formation, n. formation f.
formative, adj. formant, formateur
former, adj. précédent; pron. le premier
formerly, adv. autrefois, jadis, auparavant
formula, n. formule f.
forsake, vb. abandonner
fort, n. fort m.
forth, adv. en avant
forthcoming, adv. à venir
forthwith, adv. sur-le-champ
fortitude, n. courage m.
fortress, n. forteresse f.
fortunate, adj. heureux
fortune, n. fortune f.
forty, adj. and n. quarante m.
forward, adj. en avant, avancé, hardi
forwardness, n. empressement m.; effronterie f.
fossil, n. fossile m.
foster, vb. nourrir
foul, adj. sale, malpropre, dégoûtant

found, vb. fonder

foundation, n. fondation f.; fondement m.

founder, n. fondateur m.

fountain, n. fontaine f.

four, adj. and n. quatre m.

four-in-hand, n attelage à quatre m.

fourscore, adj. quatre-vingts

foursome, n. à quatre

fourteen, adj. and n. quatorze m.

fourth, adj. and n. quatrième m.

fowl, n. volaille f.

fox, n. renard m.

foxglove, n. digitale f.

foxhole, n. renardière f.

foxy, adj. rusé

foyer, n. foyer m.

fraction, n. fraction m.

fracture, n. fracture f.

fragile, adj. fragile

fragment, n. fragment m.

fragmentary, adj. fragmentaire

fragrance, n. parfum m.

fragrant, adj. parfumé

frail, adj. frêle

frailty, n. faiblesse f.

frame, n. cadre m.; structure f.

frame-up, n. coup monté m.

framework, n. charpente f.

France, n. la France f.

franchise, n. droit de vote m.

frank, adj. franc m.; franche f.

frankincense, n. encens m.

frankly, adv. franchement

frankness, n. franchise f.

frantic, adj. frénétique

fraternal, adj. fraternel

fraternally, adv. fraternellement

fraternity, n. fraternité f.

fraud, n. fraude f.; imposteur m.

fraudulent, adj. frauduleux

fraudulently, adv. frauduleusement

fraught, adj. chargé(de), plein, gros

fray, n. bagarre f.

freak, n. caprice, phénomène m.

freckle, n. tache de rousseur f.

freckled, adj. taché de rousseur

free, adj. libre; gratuit; vb. libérer, affranchir

freedom, n. liberté f.

freeze, vb. geler

freezer, n. glacière f.; congélateur m.

freight, n. fret m.

French, adj. and n. français m.

frenzy, n. frénésie f.

frequency, n. fréquence f.

frequent, adj. fréquent, fréquenter

frequently, adv. fréquemment

fresco, n. fresque f.

fresh, adj. frais, récent, nouveau m.

freshen, vb. refraîchir

freshman, n. étudiant de première année m.

freshness, n. fraîcheur f.

fret, n. fermentation

fretful, adj. chagrin

fretfulness, n. irritabilité f.

friction, n. friction f.

Friday, n. vendredi m.

friend, n. ami m.; amie f.

friendless, adj. sans amis

friendliness, n. disposition amicale f.

friendly, adj. amical

friendship, n. amitié f.

frighten, vb effrayer

frigid, adj. glacial

frill, n. volant m.

frilly, adj. froncé, ruché

frisky, adj. folâtre

frivolous, adj. frivole

frog, n. grenouille f.

frolic, vb. folâtrer

from, prep. de, depuis

front, n. front, devant m.

frontage, n. étendue de devant f.

fronteir, n. frontière f.

frost, n. gelée f.

frosting, n. glaçage m.

frosty, adj. gelé, glacé

frown, vb. froncer les sourcils

frowzy, adj. mal tenu, peu soigné

frozen, adj. gelé

frugal, adj. frugal

frugality, n. frugalité f.

fruit, n. fruit m.

fruitful, adj. fructueux fructification f.

fruitless, adj. infructueux

frustrate, vb. faire échouer

frustration, n. frustration f.

fry, vb. frire, faire frire

fryer, n. casserole f.

fuchsia, n. fuchsia m.

fudge, n. travail bâclé m.

fuel, n. combustible m.

fugitive, adj. fugitif

fugue, n. fugue f.

fulfill, vb. accomplir

fulfillment, n. accomplissement m.

full, adj. plein

fullback, n. arrière m.

fully, adv. pleinement

fumble, vb. tâtonner

fume, n. fumée f.

fumigate, vb. désinfecter

fumigator, n. fumigateur m.

fun, n. amusement m.; plaisanterie

drôlerie f.

function, n. fonction f.

fund, n. fonds m.

fundamental, adj. fondamental

funeral, n. funérailles f., pl.

fungus, n. fongus m.

funnel, n. entonnoir m.; cheminée f.

funny, adj. drôle

fur, n. fourrure f.

furious, adj. furieux

furlong, n. furlong m.

furnace, n. fourneau m.

furnish, vb. fournir, meubler

furniture, n. meubles m., pl.

furred, adj. fourré

furrier, n. fourreur m.

furrow, n. sillon m.

furry, adj. qui ressemble à la fourrure

further, adv. plus éloigné

furthermore, adv. en outre

fury, n. furie f.

fuse, vb. fondre

fuselage, n. fuselage

fusion, n. fusion f.

fuss, n. faire des histoires

fussy, adj. difficile

futile, adj. futile, vain, frivole

future, n. avenir m.

fuzz, n. duvet, flou m.

G

gab, vb. jaser

gabardine, n. gabardine f.

gable, n. pignon m.

gadget, n. truc m.

gag, n. blague, bobard f., bâillon m.; vb. bâillonner

gain, n. gain m.; vb. gagner

gait, n. allure f.

gala, n. fête de gala f.

galaxy, n. galaxie, assemblée brillante f.

gale, n. grand vent m.

gall, n. fiel m.; écorchure f.

gallant, adj. vaillant, galant

gallon, n. gallon m.

galore, adv. à foison, à profusion

galosh, n. galoche f.

galvanize, vb. galvaniser

gamble, n. jeu de hasard m.

gambol, n. gambade f.; vb. gambader

game, n. jeu, gibier m.

gander, n. jars m.

gangrene, n. gangrène f.

gangway, n. passage, passav-

ant m.

gap, n. ouverture f.

garage, n. garage m.

garb, n. vêtement, costume m.; vb. vêtir, habiller

garbage, n. ordures f., pl.

garble, vb. tronquer, altérer

garden, n. jardin m.

gardener, n. jardinier m.

gardenia, n. gardénia m.

gargle, n. gargarisme m; vb. se gargariser

garish, adj. voyant

garland, n. guirlande f.

garlic, n. ail m.

garment, n. vêtement m.

garner, vb. mettre en grenier

garnet, n. grenat m.

garnish, vb. garnir

garret, n. mansarde f.

garrison, n. garnison f.

garter, n. jarretière f.

gas, n. gaz m.

gash, n. coupure, entaille f.; vb. couper, entailler

gasket, n. garcette f.

gasoline, n. essence f.

gasp, vb. sursauter, haleter

gate, n. porte, barrière, grille f.

gather, vb. rassembler, recueillir

gathering, n. rassemblement m.

gaudy, adj. voyant

gaunt, adj. décharné

gauntlet, m. gantelet m.

gauze, n. gaze f.

gavel, n. marteau m.

gaze, vb. regarder fixement

gazette, n. gazette f.

gelatin, n. gélatine f.

gelding, n. animal châtré m.

gem, n. pierre précieuse f.

gender, n. genre m.

general, adj. and n. général m.

generation, n. génération f.

generic, adj. générique

genetic, adj. génétique

genius, n. génie m.

genteel, adj. de bon ton

gentleman, n. monsieur m.

genuine, adj. véritable

genus, n. genre m.

geography, n. géographie f.

geometry, n. géomètrie f.

germ, n. germe m.

germicide, n. microbicide m.

gestate, vb. enfanter

gesture, n. geste m.

get, vb. obtenir, recevoir, prendre, devenir, arriver, entrer, descendre

geyser, n. geyser m.

giant, n. géant m.

gibbon, n. gibbon m.

gibe, n. raillerie f.; vb. railler

giblet, n. abatis m.

gift, n. don, cadeau m.

gifted, adj. doué

gigantic, adj. géant, gigantesque

gild, vb. dorer

gill, n. ouïes f.,pl.

gimlet, n. vrille f.

ginger, n. gingembre m.

gingersnap, n. biscuit au gingembre m.

gingham, n. guingan m.

giraffe, n. girafe f.

gird, vb. ceindre

girder, n. support m.

girdle, n. gaine f.

girl, n. fille, jeune fille f.

gist, n. fond m.; essence f.

give, vb. donner, rendre, céder,
distribuer, renoncer à

given, adj. donné

giver, n. donneur m

glacial, adj. glaciaire

glacier, n. glacier m.

glad, adj. heureux

glade, n. clarière, éclaircie f.

glamour, n. éclat m.

glance, n. coup d'oeil m.

gland, n. glande f.

glare, n. clarté f.; regard enflammé m.; vb. briller, jeter
des regards

glass, n. verre m.

glasses, n. lunettes f., pl.

glassware, n. verrerie f.

glaucoma, n. glaucome m.

glaze, n. lustre m.; vb. vitrer

gleam, n. lueur f.; vb. luire

glee, n. allégresse f.

glen, n. vallon, ravin m.

glimpse, vb. entrevoir

globe, n. globe m.

globule, n. globule m.

gloom, n. ténèbres f., pl.; tristesse f.

glorify, vb. glorifier

glorious, adj. glorieux, radieux

glory, n. gloire f.

glove, n. gant m.

glow, n. lumière, chaleur f.

glucose, n. glucose m.

glue, n. colle forte f.; vb.
coller

glum, adj. maussade

glycerin, n. glycérine f.

gnarl, n. loupe f.; noeud m.

gnash, vb. grincer

gnat, n. moucheron m.

gnaw, vb. ronger

go, vb. aller

goal, n. but m.

goat, n. chèvre f.

gobble, n. avaleur, dindon m.;
vb. gober, avaler

goblet, n. gobelet m.

God, n. Dieu m.

goiter, n. goitre m.

gold, n. or m.

golden, adj. d'or

goldenrod, n. solidage m.

golf, n. golf m.

gondola, n. gondole f.

gone, adj. disparu, parti

good, n. bien m.; adj. bon m.,
bonne f.

goodness, n. bonté f.

good will, n. bonne volonté f.

goose, n. oie f.

gorge, n. gorge f.

gorgeous, adj. splendide

gorilla, n. gorille m.

gossip, n. bavardage m.; vb.
bavarder

gouge, n. gouge f.; vb. gouger

gourmet, n. gourmet m.

govern, vb. gouverner

governor, n. gouvernant m.

gown, n. robe f.

grab, vb. saisir

grace, n. grâce f.

graceful, adj. gracieux

gracious, adj. gracieux

grackle, n. mainate m.

grade, n. grade m.; qualité f.;
vb. classer

gradually, adv. graduellement

graduate, vb. graduer, prendre
ses grades

grail, n. Graal m.

grain, n. grain m.

gram, n. gramme m.

grammar, n. grammaire f.

grammar school, n. école primaire f.

grand, adj. grandiose

grandeur, n. grandeur f.

granite, n. granit m.

gran, n. concession f, subvention f.; vb. accorder; admettre

granule, m. granule m.

grape, n. raisin m.

grapefruit, n. pamplemousse f.

grapevine, n. treille f.

graph, n. courbe f.

graphic, adj. graphique, pittoresque

graphite, n. graphite m.

grasp, n. prise f.; vb. saisir

grass, n. herbe f.

grate, n. grille f.

grateful, adj. reconnaissant

grating, n. grille f.; vb. grincant, discordant

gratitude, n. gratitude f.

gravel, n. gravier m.

gravitate, vb. graviter

gravure, n gravure f.

gravy, n. jus m.

gray, adj. gris

graze, vb. paître

great, adj. grand

green, adj. vert

greenhouse, n. serre f.

greet, vb. saluer

greeting, n. salutation f.; accueil m.

gregarious, adj. grégaire

grid, n. gril m.

griddle, n. gril m.

gridiron, n. gril m.

grief, n. chagrin m.

grill, n. gril m.; vb. griller

grim, adj. sinistre

grime, n. saleté, noirceur f.

grin, n. large sourire m.

grind, vb. moudre, aiguiser

grip, n. prise f.

grit, n. grès, sable m.

groan, n. gémissement m.; vb. gémir

grocer, n. épicier m.

grocery, n. épicerie f.

groom, n. palefrenier, nouveau marié m.

groove, n. rainure f.

grope, vb. tâtonner

gross, adj. gros m.; grosse f.

grouch, n. maussaderie f.

ground, n. terre f.

grouse, n. tétras m.; vb. grogner

grove, n. bocage, bosquet m.

grovel, vb. ramper, se vautrer

grow, vb. croître, grandir, devenir, cultiver

growl, vb. grogner

grown, adj. fait, grand

growth, n. croissance f.

growl, vb. grogner

grown, adj. fait

growth, n. croissance f.

grub, n. larve f.; ver blanc m.

gruel, n. gruau m.

grumbling, n. murmure m.

grunt, n. grognement m.

guarantee, n. garantie f.; vb.

garantir

guaranty, n. garantie f.

guard, n. garde f.; vb. garder

guarded, adj. prudent, circonspect, réserve

guardian, n. gardien m.

guava, n. goyave f.

guerrilla, n. guérila f.

guess, n. conjecture f.

guest, n. invité m.

guidance, n. direction f.

guide, n. guide m.

guidebook, n. guide m.

guitar, n. guitare f.

gulch, n. ravin m.

gulf, n. golfe m.

gull, n. mouette f.

gulp, n. goulée f.

gum, n. gomme f.

gush, n. jailllissement m.

gusto, n. goût m., délectation, verve f.

guzzle, vb. ingurgiter, boire avidement

gym, n. gymnase m.

gymnasium, n. gymnase m.

gynecology, n. gynécologie f.

gypsy, n. gitane m.f.

H

habeas corpus, n. habeas corpus m

haberdasher, n. chemisier m., mercier m

haberdasbery, n. chemiserie f., mercerie f

habiliment, n. habilement m., abrêt m

habit, n. habitude f

habitable, adj. habitable

habitat, n. habitat m

habitation, n. habitation f

habitual, adj. habituel

habituate, vb. habituer, accoutumer

habitué, n. habitué m

hack 1. n. (tool) pioche f.; (horse) cheval (m.) de louage (vehicle) voiture (f.) de louage .2. vb. (h. up) hacher; (notch) entailler

hackneyed, adj. banal, rebattu

hacksaw, n. scie à métaux f

haddock, n. aigle fin m

haft, n. manche m., poignée f

hag, n. vieille sorcière f

haggard, adj. hagard

haggle, vb. marchander

hagridden, adj. tourmenté par le cauchemar

hail, 1. n. grêle f. 2. vb.(weather) grêler; (salute) saluer; (come from) venir de. 3.interj. salut

Hail Mary, n. Ave Maria m

hailstone, n. grêlon m

hailstorm, n. tempête de grêle f

hair, n. cheveux m.pl; (single on head) cheveu m.; (on body, animals) poil m

haircut, n. coupe (f.) de cheveux

hairdo, n. coiffure f

hairdresser, n. coiffeur m

hairline, n. délié m

hairpin, n. épingle (f.) à cheveux

hair-raising, adj. horripilant, horrifique

hair's-breadth, n. l'épaisseur d'un cheveu

hairspray, n. laque f

hair, adj. velu, poilu

halcyon, 1. n. alcyon m. 2. adj. calme

hale, adj sain

half, 1. n. moitié f. 2. adj demi. 3. adv à moitié

half and half, n. moitié de l'un, moitié de l'autre f

halfback, n. demi-arrière m

half-baked, adj. à moitié cuit, inexpérimenté, incomplet

half-breed, n. métis m

half brother, n. frère de père m, frère de mère m

half dollar, n. demi-dollar m

half-hearted, adj. sans enthousiasme

half-mast, adv. à mi-mât

halfpenny, n. petit sou m

halfway, adv. à mi-chemin

half-wit, n. niais m., sot m

halibut, n. flétan m

hall, n. (large room) salle f.; (entrance) vestibule m

hallmark, n. contrôle m

hallow, vb. sanctifier

halloween, n. la veille de la Toussaint f

hallucination, n. hallucination

halfway, n. corridor m., vestibule m

halo, n. auréole f

halt, 1. n. halte f. 2. vb. arrêter, tr.

halter, n. licou m., longe f., corde f

halve, vb. diviser en deux, partager en deux

halyard, n. drisse f

ham, n. jambon m

hamlet, n. hameau m

hammer, 1. n. marteau m. 2. vb. marteler

hammock, n. hamac m

hamper, 1. n. panier m. 2. vb. embrasser, gêner

hamstring, vb. couper le jarret à, couper les moyens à

hand, n. main f

handball, n. balle f

handbook, n. manuel m

handcuff, 1. n. menotte f. 2. vb. mettre les menottes à

handful, n. poignée f

handicap, n. handicap m., désavantage m

handicraft, n. métier m

handiwork, n. main-d'oeuvre f

handkerchief, n. mouchoir m

handle, 1. n. manche m. 2. vb. manier

handle bar, n. guidon m

handmade, adj. fait à la main, fabriqué à la main

handmaid, n. servante f

hand organ, n. orgue portatif m., orgue de Barbarie m

handout, n. aumône f.; compte rendu communiqué à la presse m

hand-pick, vb. trier à la main, éplucher à la main

handsome, adj. beau m., belle f

hand-to-hand, adj. corps à corps

handwriting, n. écriture f

handy, adj. (person) adroit; (thing) commode; (at hand) sous la main

handy man, n. homme à tout faire m., bricoleur m., factotum m

hang, vb. pendre

hangar, n. hangar m

hangdog, adj. avec une mine patibulaire, avec un air en dessous

hanger-on, n. dépendant m., parasite m

hang glider, n. glisseur duquel l'usager pend m

hanging, 1. n. suspension f., pendaison f. 2. adj. suspendu, pendant

hangman, n. bourreau m

hangnail, n. envie f

hangout, n. repaire m., nid m

hang-over, n. reste m. reliquat m

hangup, n. difficulté psychologique f

hank, m. écheveau m., torchette f

hanker, vb. désirer vivement, convoiter

haphazard, adv. au hasard

happen, vb. (take place) arriver; (chance to be) se trouver

happening, n. événement m

happily, adv. heureusement

happiness, n. bonheur m

happy, adj. heureux

happy-go-lucky, adj. sans souci, insouciant

harakiri, n. hara-kiri m

harangue 1. n. harangue f. 2. vb. haranguer

harass, vb. harceler, tracasser

harbinger, n. avant-coureur m., précurseur m

harbor, n. (refuge) asile m.; (port) port m

hard, 1. adj. dur; (difficult) difficile. 2. adv. fort

hard-bitten, adj. tenace dur à cuire

hard-boiled, adj. dur, tenace, boucané

hard coal, n. anthracite m

harden, vb. durcir

hard-headed, adj. pratique, positif

hard-hearted, adj. insensible, impitoyable au coeur dur

hardiness, n. robustesse f., vigueur f

hardly, adv. (in a hard manner) durement; (scarcely) à peine; (h. ever) presque jamais

hardness, n. dureté f.; (difficulty) difficulté f

hardship, n. privation f.

hardtack, n. galette f., biscuit de mer m

hardware, n. quincaillerie f

hardwood, n. bois dur m

hardy, adj. robuste

hare, n. lièvre m

harebrained, adj. écervelé, étourdi

harelip, n. bec-de-lièvre m

harem, n. harem m

hark, 1. vb. prêter l'oreille à. 2. interj. écoutez!

Harlequin, n. Arlequin m

harlot, n. prostituée f., fille de joie f

harm, 1. n. mal m. 2. vb. nuire à

harmful, adj. nuisible

harmless, adj. inoffensif

hamronic, adj. harmonique

harmonica, n. harmonica m

harmonious, adj. harmonieux

harmonize, vb. harmoniser

harmony, n. harmonie f

harness, 1. n. harpon m. 2. vb. harponner

harridan, n. vieille sorcière f., vieille mégère f

harrow, vb. herser; (fig.) tourmenter

harry, vb. harceler

harsh, adj. rude

harshness, n. rudesse f

harvest, 1. n. moisson f. 2. vb. moissonner

hash, 1. n. hachis m., émincé m. 2. vb. hacher (de la viande)

hashish, n. hachisch m

hasn't, vb. n'a pas

hassle, 1. vb. harceler. 2. n. harcèlement m

hassock, n. agenouilloir m

haste, n. hâte f

hasten, vb. hâter, tr

hastily, adv. à la hâte

hasty, adj. précipité

hat, n. chapeau m

hatch, vb. (hen) couver; (egg) éclore

hatchery, n. établissement de pisciculture m

hatchet, n. hachette f

hate, vb. haïr

hateful, adj. odieux

hatred, n. haine f

haughtiness, n. arrogance f., hauteur f

haughty, adj. hautain

haul, vb. traîner

haunch, n. hanche f., cuissot m

haunt, vb. hanter

have, vb. avoir; (h. to, necessity) devoir

haven, n. havre m.; (refuge) asile m

haven't, n. n'ont pas

havoc, n. ravage m

hawk, n. faucon m

hawker, n. colporteur m., marchand ambulant m

haswser, n. haussière f., amarre f

hawthorn, n. aubépine f

hay, n. foin m

hay fever, n. fièvre des foins f

hayfield, n. champs de foin m

hayloft, n fenil m., grenier m

haystack, n. meule de foin f

hazard, 1. n. hasard m. 2. vb. hasarder, risquer

hazardous, adj. hasardeux

haze, n. brume (f.) légère

hazel, n. noisetier m.; couleur de noisette f

hazy, adj. brumeux, nébuleux

he, pron il; (alonge, stressed, with another subject) lui

head, n. tête f

headache, n. mal (m.) de tête

headband, n. bandeau m

headfirst, adv. la tête la première

headgear, n. garniture de tête f., coiffure f

head-hunting, n. chasse aux têtes f

heading, n. rubrique f

headlight, n. phare m., projecteur m

headlong, adv. la tête la première

headman, n. chef m

headmaster, n. directeur m., principal m

head-on, adj. and adv. de front

headquarters, n. (mil.) quartier m.) général; (comm.) bureau (m.) principal

headstone, n. pierre angulaire f

headstrong, adj. volontiare, têtu, entêté

headwaters, n. cours supérieur (d'une rivière) m.,eau d'amont f

headway, n. progrès m

headwork, n. travail de tête m., travail intellectuel m

heady, adj. impétueux, capiteux

heal, vb. guérir

health, n. santé f

healthful, adj. salubre

healthy, adj. sain

heap, 1. n. tas m. 2. vb. entasser

hear, vb. entendre

hearing, n. audition f.; ouïe f

hearsay, n. ouï-dire m

hearse, n. catafalque m., corbillard m

heart, n. coeur m

heartache, n. chagrin m., peine de coeur f

heartbreak, n. déchirement de coeur m

heartbrokem adj. avec le coeur brisé, navré

heartburn, n. brûlures d'estomac f.pl., aigreur f

heartfelt, adj. sincère, qui va au coeur

hearth, n. foyer m., âtre m

heartless, adj. sans coeur, insensible, sans pitié

heart-rending, adj. à fendre le coeur, navrant, déchirant

heartsick, adj. écoeuré

heart-stricken, adj. frappé au coeur, navré

heart-to-heart, adj. à coeur ouvert, intime

hearty, adj. cordial

heat, 1. n. chaleur f. 2. vb. chauffer

heated, adj. chaud, chauffé, anime

heath, n. bruyère f., lande f

heathen, adj. and n. païen m., païenne f

heather, n. bruyère f., brande f

heatstroke, n. coup de chaleur m

heat wave, n. vague de chaleur f., onde calorifique f

heave, vb. (lift) lever; (utter) pousser; (rise) se soulever, intr.

heaven, n. ciel m., pl. cieux

heavenly, adj. céleste

heavy, adj. lourd

heavyweight, n. poids lourd m

Hebrew, 1. n. (language) hébreu m. 2. adj. hébreu

heckle, vb. poser des questions embarrassantes

hectare, n. hectare m

hectic, adj. (restless) agité

hectograph, 1. n. hectographe m. autocopiste m. 2. vb. hectographier, autocopier

hedge, n. haie f

hedgehog, n. hérisson m

hedgehop, vb. voler à ras de terre

hedgerow, n. bordure de haies f

hedonism, n. hédonisme m

heed, 1. n. attention f. 2. vb. faire attention à

heedless, adj. étourdi, imprudent, insouciant

heel, n. talon m

hefty, adj. fort, solide, costaud

hegemony, n. hégémonie f

heifer, n. génisse f

height, n. hauteur f

heighten, vb. rehausser, augmenter

heinous, adj. odieux, atroce, abominable

heir, n. héritier m

heir apparent, n. héritier présomptif m

heirloom, n. meuble m. (or bijou m.) de famille

heir presumptive, n. héritier présomptif m

helicopter, n. hélicoptère m

heliocentric, adj. héliocentrique

heliograph, n. héliographe m

heliotrope, n. héliotrope m

helium, n. hélium m

hell, n. enfer m

Hellenism, n. hellénisme m

hellish, adj. infernal, diabolique

hello, interj. (telephone) allô

helm, n. barre (f.) du gouvernail

helmet, n. casque m

helmsman, n. homme de barre m. timonier m

help, 1. n. aide f. 2. vb. aider; (at table) servir. 3. interj. au secours!

helper, n. aide m.f.

helpful, adj. (person) serviable; (thing) utile

helpfulness, n. serviabilité f., utilité f

helping, 1. n. portion f. 2. adj. secourable

helpless, adj. (forlorn) délaisse; (powerless) impuissant

helter-skelter, adv. pêle-mêle, en désordre

hem, 1. n. ourlet m. 2. vb. ourler

hematite, n. hématite f

hemisphere, n. hémisphère m

hemlock, n. ciguë f

hemoglobin, n. hémoglobine f

hemophilia, n. hémophilie f

hemmorrhage, n. hémorragie f

hemorrhold, n. hémmorroïde f

hemp, n. chanvre m

hemstitch, 1. n. ourlet m. 2. vb. ourler

hen, n. poule f.

hence, adv. (time, place) d'ici; (therefore) de là

henceforth, adv. désormais

henchman, n. homme de confiance m., acolyte m., satellite m

henequen, n. henequen m

henna, 1. n. hennè m. 2. vb. teindre au henné

henpeck, vb. mener par le bout du nez

hepatic, adj. hépatique

hepatica, n. hépatique f

her, 1. adj. son m., sa f., ses pl 2. pron. (direct) la; (indirect) lui; (alone, stressed, with prep.) elle

herald, n. héraut m

heraldic, adj. héraldique

heraldry, n. l'héraldique f

herb, n. herbe f

herbaceous, adj. herbacé

herbarium, n. herbier m

herculean, adj. herculéen

herd, n. troupeau m

here, adv. ici; (h. is) voici

hereabout, adv. par ici, près d'ici

hereafter, adv. dorénavant

hereby, adv. par ceci, par ce moyen, par là

hereditary, adj. héréditaire

herein, adv. (h. enclosed) ci-inclus

heresy, n. hérésie f

heretic, n. hérétique m.f

heretical, adj. hérétique

hereto, adv. ci-joint

heretofore, adv. jusqu'ici

herewith, adv. avec ceci, ci-joint

heritage, n. héritage m., patrimoine m

hermetic, adj. hermétique

hermit, n. ermite m

hermitage, n. ermitage m

hernia, n. hernie f

hero, n. héros m

heroic, adj. héroïque

heroically, adv. héroïquement

heroin, n. héroïne f

heroism, n. héroïsme m

heron, n. héron m

herpes, n. herpès m

herring, n. hareng m

herringbone, n. arête de hareng f

hers, pron. le sien m., la sienne f

herself, pron. le sien m., la sienne f

hertz, n. hertz m

hesitancy, n. hésitation f., incertitude f

hesitant, adj. hésitant, irrésolu

hesitate, vb. hésiter

hesitation, n. hésitation f

heterodox, adj. hétérodoxe

heterodoxy, adj. hétérodoxie f

heterogeneous, adj. hétérogène

heterosexual, adj. hétérosexuel

hew, vb. couper, tailler

hexagon, n. hexagone m

heyday, n. apogée m., beaux jours m.pl

hiatus, n. lacune f

hibernate, vb. hiberner, hiverner

hibernation, n. hibernation f

hibiscus, n. hibiscus m

hiccup, 1. n. hoquet m. 2. vb. hoqueter

hickory, n. noyer (blanc) d'Amérique m

hide, vb. cacher

hide, n. peau f

hideous, adj. hideux

hide-out, n. cachette f., lieu de retraite m

hiearchical, adj. hiérarchique

hiearchy, n. hiéarchie f

hieroglyphic, adj. hiérogly-phique

high, adj. haut

highbrow, n. intellectuel m

high fidelity, n. haute fidélité f

high-handed, adj. arbitraire, tyrannique

high-hat, vb. traiter de haut en bas

highland, n. haute terre f

highlight, 1. n. clou m. 2. vb. mettre en relief

highly, adv. extrêmement

high-minded, adj. à l'esprit élevé, généreux

Highness, n. (title) Altesse f

high school, n. lycée m

high seas, n haute mer f

high-strung, adj. nerveux, im-pressionable

high tide, n. marée haute f

highway, n. grande route f

hijacker, n. pirate de l'air m

hike, n. excursion (f.) à pied

hilarious, adj. hilare

hilariousness, n. hilarité f

hilarity, n. hilarité f

hill, n. colline f

hilt, n. poignée f., garde f

him, pron. (direct) le; (in-direct) lui; (along, stressed, with prep.) lui

himself, pron. lui-même, (re-flexive) se

hinder, vb. (impede) gêner; (prevent) empêcher

hindmost, adj. dernier

hindquarter, n. arrière-main m., arrière-train m

hindrance, n. empêchement m., obstacle m., entrave f

Hindu, 1. n. Hindou m. 2. adj. hindou

hinge, n. gond m

hint, 1. n. allusion f. 2. vb. insi-nuer

hinterland, n. hinterland m., arrière-pays m

hip, n. hanche f

hippodrome, n. hippodrome m

hippopotamus, n. hippopotame m

hire, vb. louer; (servant) engager

hireling, n. mercenaire m., stipendié m

hirsute, adj. hirsute, velu

his, 1. adj. son m. sa f., ses pl 2. pron. le sien m. la sienne f

Hispanic, adj. hispanique

hiss, vb. siffler

historian, n. historien m

historic, adj. historique

historical, adj. historique

history, n. histoire f

histrionic, adj. histrionique, théâtral

histrionics, n. parade d'émo-tions f., démonstration peu sincère f

hit, 1. n. coup m.; (success) succès m. 2. vb. frapper

hitch, 1. n. (obstacle) ani-croche f. 2. vb. (fasten) accrocher, tr

hither, 1. adv. ici. 2. adj. le plus rapproché

hitherto, adj. jusqu'ici

hive, n. ruche f

hives, n. éruption f., varicelle pustuleuse f., urticaire f

hoard, 1. n. amas m. 2. vb. amasser; (money) thésauriser

hoarse, adj. enroué

hoax, n. mystification f

hobble, vb. boitiller, clopiner, entraver

hobbyhorse, n. dada m. cheval de bois m

hobogoblin, n. lutin m., esprit follet m

hobnail, 1. n. caboche f., clou à ferrer m. 2. vb. ferrer

hobnob, vb. boire avec, fré-quenter

hobo, n. vagabond m., clochard m., ouvrier ambulant m

hock, n. jarret m

hockey, n. hockey m

hocuspocus, n. passe-passe m

hod, n. auge f

hodgepodge, n. mélange confus m

hoe, 1. n. houe f. 2. vb. houer

hog, n. proc m

hogshead, n. tonneau m., bar-rique f

hog-tie, vb. lier les quatre pattes

hoist, 1. n. treuil m., grue f. 2. vb. hisser

hold, 1. n. prise f.; (ship) cale f. 2. vb. tenir; (contain) con-tenir; (h. back) retenir; (h. up) arrêter, détenir, entraver

holdup, n. arrêt m., suspension f.; coup à main armée m

hole, n. trou m

holiday, n. jour (m., de fête; fête f.; (h.s.) vacances f.pl

holiness, n. sainteté f

Holland, n. les Pays-Bas m.pl., Hollande f

hollow, adj. and n. creux m

holly, n. houx m

hollyhock, n. passe-rose f., rose-trémière f

holocaust, n. holcauste m

hologram, n. hologramme m

holography, n. holographie f

holster, n. étui m

holy, adj. saint

Holy See, n. Saint-Siège m

Holy Spirit, n. Saint-Esprit m

Holy Week, n. semaine sainte f

homage, n. hommage m

home, n. maison f.; (hearth) foyer (m.) domestique; (at h.) à la maison chez soi

homeland, n. patrie f

homeless, adj. sans foyer, sans asile, sans abri

homelike, adj. qui resemble au foyer domestique

homely, adj. laid

homemade, adj. fait à la maison

home rule, n. autonomie f

homesick, adj. nostalgique

homespoun, adj. (étoffe) de fabrication domestique, fait à la maison, simple

homestead, n. ferme f., bien de famille m

homeward, adj. de retour

homework, n. travail fait à la maison m., devoirs m.pl

homicide, n. homicide m

homily, n. homélie f

homing pigeon, n. piegeon messager m

hominy, n. bouillie de farine de maïs f. semoule de maïs f

homogeneous, adj. homogène

homonym, n. homonyme m

homosexual, n. and adj. homosexuel m

Honduras, n. Honduras m

hone, vb aiguiser, affiler

honest, adj. honnête

honestly, adv. honnêtement, de bonne foi

honesty, n. honnêteté f

honey, n. miel m

honeybee, n. abeille domestique f

honeycomb, 1. n. rayon de miel m. 2. vb. cribler, affouiller

honeydew melon, n. melon m

honeymoon, n. lune (f.) de miel

honeysuckle, n. chèvrefeuille m

honor, 1. n. honneur m. 2. vb. honorer

honorable, adj. honorable

honorary, adj. honoraire

hood, n. capuchon m.; (vehicle) capote f

hoodlum, n. voyou m

hoodwink, vb. tromper, bander les yeux à

hoof, n. sabot m

hook, 1. n. croc m.; (fishing) hameçon m. 2. vb. accrocher

hooked, adj. crochu, recourbé

hooked rug, n. tapis à points noués simples m

hookworm, n. ankylostome m

hoop, n. cercle m

hoop skirt, n. jupe à paniers f., vertugadin m

hoot, 1. n. ululation f., hululement m., huée f. 2. vb. hululer, huer

hop, 1. n. (plant) houblon m. 2. vb. sautiller

hope, 1. n. expérance f., espoir 2. vb. espérer

hopeful, adj.. plein d'espoir

hopeless, adj. désespéré

hoplessness, n. désespoir m., état désespéré m

hopscotch, n. marelle f

horde, n. horde f

horizon, n. horizon m

horizontal, adj. horizontal

hormone, n. hormone f

horn, n. corne f.; (music) cor m

hornet, n. frelon m., guêpe-frelon f

horny, adj. corné, calleux

horoscope, n. horoscope m

horrendous, adj. horrible, horripilant

horrible, adj. horrible

horrid, adj. affreux

horrify, vb. horrifier

horror, n. horreur f

horse, n. cheval m

horseback, n. on. b) à cheval

horsefly, n. taon m

horsehair, n. crin m

horseman, n. cavalier m

horsemanship, n. équitation f., manège m

horseplay, n. jeu de mains m., badinerie grossière f

horsepower, n. puissance en chevaux f

horseradish, n. raifort m

horseshoe, n. fer à cheval m

horsewhip, 1. n. cravache f. 2. vb. cravacher, sangler

hortatory, adj. exhortatif

horticulture, n. horticulture f

hose, n. (pipe) tuyau m.;
(stockings) bas m.pl

hosiery, n. bonneterie f

hospitable, adj. hospitalier

hospital, n. hôpital m

hospitality, n. hospitalité f

hospitalization, n. hospitalisation f

hospitalize, vb. hospitaliser

host, n. hôte m

hostage, n. otage m

hostel, n. hôtellerie f., auberge f

hostelry, n. hôtellerie f., auberge f

hostess, n. hôtesse f

hostile, adj. hostile

hostility, n. hostilité f

hot, adj. chaud

hotbed, n. couche f., foyer ardent m

hot dog, n. saucisse chaude

hotel, n. hôtel m

hot-headed, adj. impétueux, exalté, emporté

hothouse, n. serre f

hound, 1. n. chien (m.) de chasse. 2. vb. poursuivre, pourchasser

hour, n. heure f

hourglass, n. sablier m

hourly, adv. à chaque heure, à l'heure

house, n. maison f.; (legislature) chambre f

housefly, n. mouche domestique f

household, n. (family) famille f. (servants) domestiques m.pl

housekeeper, n. gouvernante f

housekeeping, n. ménage m., économie domestique f

housemaid, n. fille de service f., bonne f., femme de chambre f

housewife, n. ménagère f

housework, n. ménage m

hovel, n. taudis m., bicoque f

hover, vb. planer

hovercraft, n. aéroglisseur m

how, adv. comment: (h. much) combien (de); (in exclamation) comme

however, adv. (in whatever way) de quelque manière que; (with adj.) si...que; (nevertheless) cependant

howitzer, n. obusier m

howl, vb. hurler

hub, n. moyeu m., centre m

hubbub, n. vacarme m., tinta-

marre m

huckleberry, n. airelle f

huddle, 1. n. tas confus m., fouillis m. 2. vb. entasser

hue, n. couleur f

huff, 1. n. emportement m., accès de colère m. 2. vb. gonfler, enfler

hug, 1. n. étreinte f. 2. vb. serrer dans ses bras

huge, adj. énorme

hulk, n. carcasse., ponton m

hull, n. coque f., corps m

hullabaloo, n. vacarme m

hum, vb. (insect) bourdonner; (sing) fredonner

human, humane, adj. humain

humanism, n. humanisme m

humanitarian, adj. humanitaire

humanities, n. humanités f.pl

humanity, adv. humainement

humble, adj. humble

humbug, n. blague f., tromperie f., fumisterie f

humdrum, adj. monotone, assommant

humid, adj. humide

humidify, vb. humidifier

humidor, n. boîte à cigares f

humiliate, adj. himilier

humiliation, n. humiliation f

humility, v. humilité f

humor, n. (wit) humour m.; (medical, mood) humeur f

humorous, adj. (witty) humoristique; (funny) drôle

hump, n. bosse f

humpback, n. bossu m

humus, n. humus m., terreau m

hunch, 1. n. bossef.; pressentiment m. 2. vb. arrondir, voûter

hunchback, n. bossu m

hundred, adj. and n. cent m

hundredth, n. and adj. centième m

Hungarian, 1. n. (person) Hongrois m.; (language) hongrois m. 2. adj. hongrois

Hungary, n. Hongrie f

hunger, n. faim f

hungry, adj. affamé; (be h.) avoir faim

hunk, n. gros morceau m

hunt, vb. chasser

hunter, n. chasseur m

hunting, n. chasse f

huntress, n. chasseuse f., chasseresse f

hurdle, n. claie f

hurl, vb. lancer

hurricane, n. ouragan m

hurry, 1. n. hâte f.; (in a h.) à la hâte. **2.** vb. presser, tr.; se presser, intr

hurt, vb. faire mal (à)

hurtful, adj. nuisible, pernicieux prudiciable

hurtle, vb. se choquer, se heurter

husband, n. mari m

husbandry, n. agriculture f., economie f

hush, 1. interj. chut! paix! **2.** vb. taire, imposer silence à

hus, 1. n. cosse f., gousse f. **2.** vb. écosser, éplucher

husky, adj. cossu; rauque, enroué

hustle, vb. bousculer, se presser

hut, n. cabane f

hutch, n. huche f., clapier m

hyacinth, n. jacinthe f

hybrid, n. hybride m

hydranges, n, hortensia m

hydrant, n. prise d'eau f., bouche d'incendie f

hydraulic, adj. hydraulique

hydrochloric acid, n. acide chlorhydrique m

hydroelectric, adj. hydrolélectrique

hydrogen, n. hydrogène m

hydrophobia, n. hydrophobie f

hydroplane, n. hydroplane m

hydrotherapy, n. hydrothérapie f

hyena, n. hyène f

hygiene, n. hygiène f

hygenic, adj. hygiénique

hymn, n. (song, anthem) hymne m.; (church) hymne f

hymnal, n. hymnaire m. receuil d'hymnes m

hyperacidity, n. hyperacidité f

hyperbole, n. hyperbole f

hypercritical, adj. hypercritique

hypersensitive, adj. hypersensible

hypetension, n. hypertension f

hypen, n. trait d'union m

hyphenate, vb. mettre un trait d'union à

hypnosis, n. hypnose f

hypnotic, adj. hypnotique

hypnotism, n. hypnotisme m

hynotoize, vb. hynotiser

hypochondria, n. hypocondrie f

hypochondriac, n. and adj. hypocondriaque m

hypocrisy, n. hypocrisie f

hypocrite, n. hypocrite m.f

hypocritical, adj. hypocrite

hypodermic, adj. hypodermique

hypotenuse, n. hypoténuse f

hypotehses, n. hypothèse f

hypothetical, adj. hypothétique

hysterectomy, n. hystérectomie f

hysteria, n. hystérie f

hysterical, adj. hystérique

I

I, pron. je, moi

Iambe, adj. ïambique

Iberia, n. l' Ibérie f.

Ice, n. glace f.

Ice cream, n. glace f.

Icing, n. glacé m.

Icon, icône f.

Idea, n. idée f.

Ideal, adj. and n. idéal m.

Identical, adj. identique, même

Identification, n. identification f.

Ideology, n. idéologie f.

Idiocy, n. idiotie f.

Idiom, n. idiome, idiotisme m.

Idiot, adj. and n. idiot m.; imbécile m.f.

Idle, adj. désoeuvré, paresseux

Idleness, n. oisiveté f.

Idol, n. idole f.

Idyl, idylle f.

Idylic, adj. idyllique

If, conj. si

Ignorance, n. ignorance f.

Ignorant, adj. ignorant

Ignore, vb. feindre d'ignorer

Ill, n. mal; adj. malade

Illegal, adj. illégal

Illegitimate, adj. illégitime

Illicit, adj. illicite

Illiteracy, n. analphabétisme m.

Illiterate, adj. illettré

Illness, n. maladie f.

Illogical, adj. illogique

Illuminate, vb. illuminer

Illumination, n. illumination, enluminure f.

Illusion n. illusion f.

Illusive, adj. illusoire

Illustrative, adj. explicatif, qui éclaircit

Illustrious, adj. illustre

Ill will, adj. mauvais vouloir m.; malveillance f.

Image, n. image f.

Imagery, n. images f., pl.; langage figuré m.

Imaginative, adj. imaginatif

Imagine, vb. imaginer

Imam, n. imam m.

Imbecile, n. imbécile m.

Imitate, vb. imiter

Imitation, n. imitation f.

Immanent, adj. immanent

Immature, adj. pas mûr, prématuré

Immediate, adj. immédiate

Immense, adj. immense

Immerse, vb. immerger, plonger

Immigrant, n. immigrant, immigré m.

Immigrate, vb. immigrer

Imminent, adj. imminent

Immobile, adj. fixe, immobile

Immoral, adj. immoral

Immortal, adj. and n. immortel m.

Immunity, n. exemption, immunité f.

Immunize, vb. immuniser

Impact, n. choc, impact m.

Impale, vb. empaler

Impart, vb. donner, communiquer, transmettre

Impartial, adj. impartial

Impatience, n. impatience f.

Impatient, adj. impatient

Impede, vb. entraver, empêcher

Impediment, n. entrave, empêchement f. obstacle m.

Impel, vb. pousser, forcer

Impenetrable, adj. impénétrable

Impenitent, adj. impénitent

Imperative, n. impératif m.; adj. urgent, impérieux

Imperceptible, adj. imperceptible

Imperfect, adj. and n. imparfait m.

Imperial, adj. impérial

Impersonate, vb. personnifier, représenter

Impertinence, n. impertinence f.

Impervious, adj. impénétrable

Impetuous, adj. impétueux

Impetus, n. élan m.; vitesse, acquise f.

Implacable, adj. implacable

Implant, vb. inculquer, implanter

Implement, n. outil m.

Implicate, vb. impliquer, entremêler

Implication, n. implication f.

Implicit, adj. implicite

Implied, adj. implicite, tacite

Implore, vb. implorer

Imply, vb. impliquer

Impolite, adj. impoli

Imponderable, adj. impondérable

Import, n. portée, signification f.

Importance, n. importance f.

Important, adj. important

Importation, n. importation f.

Importune, vb. importuner

Impose, vb. imposer

Imposition, n. imposition f.

Impossible, adj. impossible

Impotence, n. impuissance f.

Impotent, adj. impuissant

Impoverish, vb. appauvrir

Impregnate, vb. imprégner, féconder

Impressrio, n. imprésario m.

Impress, vb. imprimer(à)

Impression, n. impression f.

Impressive, adj. impressionnant

Imprison, emprisonner

Improbable, adj. improbable

Impromptu, adv. adj. and n. impromptu m

Improper, adj. inconvenant

Improve, vb améliorer

Improvement, n. amélioration f.

Improvise, vb. improviser

Impugn, vb. attaquer, contester

Impulse, n. impulsion f.

Impulsion, n. impulsion f.

Impunity, n. impunité f.

Impure, adj. impur

Impurity, n. impureté f.

Impute, vb. imputer

In, prép. en, dans, à, par, pour

Inadvertent, adj. inattentif, négligent

Inalienable, adj. inaliénable

Inaugural, adj. inaugural

Incandescence, n. incandescence f.

Incandescent, adj. incandescent

Incapacitate, vb. rendre incapable

Incarcerate, vb. incarcérer

Incarnate, vb. incarner

Incendiary, n. incendiaire m.

Incense, n. encens m.

Incentive, n. stimulant, aiguillon m.

Inception, n. commencement m.

Incest, n. inceste m.

Inch, n. pouce m.

Incident, n. incident m.

Incinerator, n. incinérateur m.

Incipient, adj. naissant

Incision, n. incision, entaille f.

Incisive, adj. incisif, tranchant

Incisor, n. incisive f.

Incite, vb. inciter, instiguer

Incline, vb. incliner

Include, vb. renfermer

Inclusive, adj. inclusif

Incognito, adj. and adv. incognito

Income, n. revenu m.

Incomparable, adj. incomparable

Inconvenience, n. inconvénient m.

Incorporate, vb. incorporer

Incorrigible, adj. incorrigible

Increase, n. augmentation f.
Incredible, adj. incroyable
Incredulous, adj. incrédule
Incriminate, vb. incriminer
Incumbent, n. titulaire, bénéficiaire m.
Incur, vb. encourir
Incurable, adj. incurable
Indeed, adv. en effet
Indefatigable, adj. infatigable, inlassable
Indefinite, adj. indéfini
Indefinitely, adv. indéfiniment
Indelible, adj. indélébile, ineffaçable
Indemnity, n. garantie, indemnité, f.; dédommagment m.
Indent, vb. denteler, découper, entailler
Independence, n. indépendance f.
Independent, adj. indépendant
In-depth, adj. profond
Index, n. index m.
India, n. l'Inde f.
Indicate, vb. indiquer
Indication, n. indication f.
Indicative, adj. and n. indicatif m.
Indicator, n. indicateur m.
Indict, vb. accuser, inculper
Indifference, adj. indifférent
Indigenous, adj. indigène
Indigent, adj. indigent, pauvre
Indigestion, n. dyspepsie, indigestion f.
Indignant, adj. indigné
Indignity, n. indignité f.; affront m.
Indirect, adj. indirect
Indiscreet, adj. indiscret
Indiscretion, n. imprudence f.
Indispensable, adj. indispensable
Indisposed, adj. souffrant
Individual, n. individuel, isolé
Indoctrinate, vb. endoctriner
Indolent, adj. indolent, paresseux
Indorse, vb. endosser, sanctionner
Induce, vb. persuader, produire
Induct, vb. installer, conduire
Inductive, adj. inductif
Indulge, vb. contenter, favoriser
Indulgent, adj. indulgent
Industry, n. industrie, assiduité f.
Ineligible, adj. inéligible
Inept, adj. inepte, mal à propos
Inert, adj. inerte, apathique
Inertia, n. inertie f.
Inevitable, adj. inévitable
Inexplicable, adj. inexplicable
Infallible, adj. infaillible
Infamous, adj. infâme

Infamy, n. infamie f.
Infance, n. enfance f.
Infant, n. enfant m.f.; bébé m.
Infantile, adj. enfantin, enfantile
Infantryman, n. soldat d'infanterie m.
Infatuated, adj. infatué, entiché
Infect, vb. infecter
Infection, n. infection f.
Infectious, adj. infectieux
Infer, vb. déduire
Inference, m. inférence f.
Inferior, adj. and n. inférieur m.
Infernal, adj. infernal
Inferno, n. enfer m.
Infest, vb. infester
Infidelity, n. infidélité f.
Infiltrate, vb. infiltrer
Infinite, adj. and n. infini m.
Infinity, n. infinité f.
Infirm, adj. infirme, faible, maladif
Inflame, vb. enflammer
Inflate, vb. gonfler
Inflict, vb. infliger
Infliction, n. infliction; peine f.
Influence, n. influence f.
Influential, adj. influent
Influenze, n. grippe, influenza f.
Inform, vb. informer
Information, n. renseignements m., pl.
Infringe, vb. enfreindre, violer
Infuriate, vb. rendre furieux
Ingenious, adj. ingénieux
Ingredient, n. ingrédient m.
Inhabit, vb. habiter
Inhale, vb. inhaler, aspirer
Inherent, adj. inhérent
Inherit, vb. hériter
Inhibit, vb. arrêter, empêcher
Inhuman, adj. inhumain, barbare
Inimical, adj. ennemi, hostile, défavorable
Inimitable, adj. inimitable
Iniquity, n. iniquité f.
Initial, n. initiale f.
Initiate, vb. commencer, initier
Initiation, n. commencement, début m.; initiation f.
Initiative, n. initiative f.
Inject, vb. injecter
Injection, n. injection f.
Injure vb. nuire blesser, abîmer
Injurious, adj. nuisible, injurieux
Injury, n. personne préjudice m.; blessure f.
Injustice, n. injustice f.
Ink, n. encre f.
Inland, adj. and n. intérieur m.
Inmate, n. habitant, pensionnaire m.

Inn, n. auberge f.
Innocence, n. innocence f.
Innocent, adj. innocent
Innocuous, adj. inoffensif
Innovation, n. innovation f.
Innumerable, adj. innombrable
Inoculate, vb. inoculer
Inquest, n. enquête f.
Inquire, vb. se renseigner
Insane, adj. fou m.; folle f.
Insanity, n. folie, démence f.
Inscribe, vb. inscrire, graver
Inscription, n. inscription f.
Insect, n. insecte m.
Inseparable, adj. inséparable
Insert, vb. insérer
Inside, n. dedans m.
Insidious, adj. insidieux
Insight, n. perspicacité, pénétration f.
Insignia, n. insignes m., pl.
Insignificant, adj. insignifiant
Insinuate, vb. insinuer
Insinuation, n. insinuation f.
Insipid, adj. insipide, fade
Insist, vb. insister
Insistence, n. insistance f.
Insistent, adj. qui insiste, importun
Insolence, n. insolence f.
Insolent, adj. insolent
Insomnia, n. insomnie f.
Inspect, vb. examiner, inspecter
Inspection, n. inspection f.
Inspector, n. inspecteur m.
Inspiration, n. inspiration f.
Inspire, vb. inspirer
Install, vb. installer
Instance, n. exemple m.
Instant, n. instant m.
Instantaneous, adj. instantané
Instantly, adv. à l'instant
Instead, adv. au lieu de cela
Instigate, vb. instiguer
Instill, vb. instiller, faire pénétrer, inculquer
Instinct, n. instinct m.
Instinctive, adj. instinctif
Institute, vb. instituer
Instruct, vb. instruire
Instruction, n. instruction f.
Instructor, n. (mil.) instructeur, m.; chargé de cours m.
Instrument, n. instrument m.
Insufficient, adj. insuffisant
Insular, adj. insulaire
Insulate, vb. isoler
Insulation, n. isolement m.
Insulin, n. insuline f.
Insult, vb. insulter
Insuperable, adj. insurmontable

Insurance, n. assurance f.
Insure, vb. assurer
Insurgent, adj. and n. insurgé m.
Intact, adj. intact
Integral, adj. intégrant
Integrate, vb. intégrer, compléter, rendre entier
Integrity, n. intégrité f.
Intellect, n. esprit; intellect m.
Intellectual, adj. and n. intellectuel m.
Intelligent, adj. intelligent
Intelligible, adj. intelligible
Intend, vb. avoir l'intention de
Intense, adj. intense
Intensive, adj. intensif
Intention, n. intention f.
Intercede, vb. intervenir, intercéder
Intercept, vb. intercepter, capter
Interdict, vb. interdire, prohiber
Interest, n. intérêt m.
Interesting, adj. intéressant
Interface, n. entreface f.
Interfere, vb. intervenir
Interim, adv. entre temps, en attendant
Interject, vb. lancer, émettre
Interjection, n. interjection f.
Interlude, n. intermède, interlude m.
Intermarry, vb. se marier
Interment, n. enterrement m.
Intermittent, adj. intermittent
Intern, vb. interne m.
Internal, adj. interne
International, adj. international
Interne, n. interno m.
Interpret, vb. interpréter
Interpretation, n. interprétation f.
Interpreter, n. interprète m.f.
Interrogate, vb. interroger, questionner
Interrogation, n. interrogation f.
Interrupt, vb. interrompre
Intersect, vb. entrecouper, intersecter
Intersection, n. intersection f.
Intersperse, vb. entremêler, parsemer
Interval, n. intervalle m.
Intervene, vb. intervenir
Intervention, n. intervention f.
Interview, n. entrevue f.
Intestine, n. intestin m.
Intimacy, n. intimité f.
Intimate, adj. intime
Intimidate, vb. intimider
Into, prep. en, à, dans
Intonation, n. intonation f.
Intone, vb. entonner, psalmodier

Intoxicate, vb. enivrer
Intravenous, adj. intraveineux
Intrepid, adj. intrépide, brave, courageux
Intricate, adj. compliqué
Intrigue, n. intrigue f.
Intrinsic, adj. intrinsèque
Introduce, vb. introduire
Introspection, n. introspection f; recueillement m.
Introver, n. introverti m.
Intrude (on), vb. importuner
Intruder, n. intrus m.
Intuition, n. intuition f.
Inundate, vb. inonder
Invade, vb. envahir
Invader, n. envahisseur m.
Invalid, adj. and n. infirme m.f.
Invariable, adj. invariable
Invasion, n. invasion f.
Invective, n. invective f.
Invent, vb. inventer
Invention, n. invention f.
Inventor, n. inventeur m.
Invest, vb. investir, placer
Investigation, n. investigation f.
Investment, n. placement m.
Invidious, adj. odieux, haïssable, ingrat
Invigorate, vb. fortifier, vivifier
Invincible, adj. invincible
Invisible, adj. invisible
Invitation, n. invitation f.
Invite, vb. inviter
Invocation, n. invocation f.
Invoice, n. facture f.
Invoke, vb. invoquer
Involuntary, adj. involontaire
Involve, vb. impliquer, entraîner
Iodine, n. iode m.
Iraq, n. l'Irak m.
Irate, adj. en colère, furieux
Ireland, n. l'Irlande f.
Iris, n. iris m.
Irish, adj. irlandais
Irk, vb. ennuyer
Iron, n. fer m.
Irony, n. ironie f.
Irrational, adj. irrationnel, absurde
Irrefutable, adj. irréfutable, irrécusable
Irregular, adj. irrégulier
Irrelevant, adj. non pertient, hors de propos
Irresistible, adj. irrésistible
Irresponsible, adj. irresponsable
Irreverent, adj. irrévérent, irrévérencieux
Irrevocable, adj. irrévocable
Irrigate, vb. irriguer, arroser

Irrigation, n. irrigation f.
Irritability, n. irritabilité f.
Irritant, n. irritant m.
Irritate, vb. irriter
Islam, n. Islam m.
Island, n. île f.
Isolate, vb. isoler
Isolation, n. isolement m.
Isosceles, adj. isoscèle
Israel, n. l'Israël m.
Issuance, n. délivrance f.
Issue, n. issue, question, émission f.; résultat m.
It, pron. il m.; elle f.; le m., la f., lui
Italy, n. l'Italie f.
Itch, n. démangeaison f.
Item, n. article; détail m.
Itinerant, adj. ambulant
Its, adj. son m.; sa f.; ses pl.; pron. le sien m.; la sienne f.
Itself, pron. lui-même m.; elle-même f.
Ivory, n. ivoire m.
Ivy, n. lierre m.

J

Jab, n. coup de pointe, coup sec m.
Jackal, n. chacal m.
Jackass, n. âne, idiot m.
Jacket, n. veston m.; jaquette f.
Jacknife, n. couteau de poche m.
Jade, n. rosse, haridelle f.
Jaded, adj. surmené, éreinté
Jaged, adj. déchiqueté, entaillé
Jaguar, n. jaguar m.
Jail, n. prison f.
Jailer, n. gardien, geôlier m.
Jam, n. foule, presse, confiture f.
Jamb, n. jambage, chambranle m.
Janitor, n. concierge, portier m.
January, n. janvier m.
Japan, n. le Japon m.
Japanese, n. Japonais
Jar, n. pot, son discordant m.
Jargon, n. jargon m.
Jasmine, n. jasmin m.
Jaundice, n. jaunisse f.
Jaunt, n. petite excursion, balade f.
Javelin, n. javelot m.; javeline f.
Jaw, n. mâchoire f.
Jay, n. geai m.
Jazz, n. jazz m.
Jealous, adj. jaloux
Jealousy, n. jalousie f.
Jeans, n. jeans m., pl.

jeer, n. raillerie, moquerie, huée f.

jelly, n. gelée f.

jellyfish, n. méduse f.

jeopardize, vb. exposer au danger, mettre en danger, hasarder

jeopardy, n. danger m., péril m.

jerk, n. saccade f.

jerky, adj. saccadé, coupé

jersey, n. jersey, tricot de laine m.

Jerusalem, n. Jérusalem m.

jester, n. railleur, farceur, bouffon m.

Jesus, n. Jésus m.

jet, n. jet, jet d'eau m.

jettison, n. jet à la mer m.

jetty, n. jetée f.; môle m.

Jew, n. Juif m.; Juive f.

jewel, n. bijou m.

jeweler, n, bijoutier, joaillier m.

jewelry, n. bijouterie f.

Jewish, adj. juif m.; juive f.

jib, n. foc m.

jiffy, n. instant, clin d'oeil m.

jig, n. gigue f.; calibre, gabarit m.

jilt, vb. délaisser

jingle, n. tintement m., oliquctis m.

jinx, n. porte-malheur m.

jittery, adj. très nerveux

job, n. travail; emploi m.

jobber, n. intermédiaire, marchandeur m.

jockey, n. jockey m.

jocular, adj. facétieux, jovial

jocund, adj. enjoué

jodhpurs, n. pantalon d'équitation m.

jog, n. coup, cahot m.; secousse f.

joggle, n. petite secousse f.

join, vb. joindre, se joindre à

joiner, n. menuisier m.

joint, n. joint m.; adj. commun

jointly, adv. ensemble, conjointement

joist, n. solive, poutre f.

joke, n. plaisanterie f.; vb. plaisanter

joker, n. farceur, blagueur, joker m.

jolly, adj. joyeux

jolt, n. cahot, choc m.; secousse f.; vb. cahoter, secouer, ballotter

jonquil, n. jonquille f.

jostle, vb. coudoyer

journal, n. journal m.

journalism, n. journalisme m.

journalist, n. journaliste m.

journey, n. voyage m.; vb. voyager

journeyman, n. compagnon m.

jovial, adj. jovial, gai

jowl, n. mâchoire f.

joy, n. joie f.

joyful, adj. joyeux

jubilant, adj. réjoui, jubilant, exultant

jubilee, n. jubilé m.

Judaism, n. judaïsme m.

judge, n. juge m.

judgement, n. jugement m.

judicial, adj. judiciaire

judiciary, adj. judiciaire

judicious, adj. judicieux, sensé

jug, n. cruche f.

juggle, vb. jongler

jugular, adj. jugulaire

juice, n. jus m.

juicy, adj. juteux

July, n. juillet m.

jumble, n. brouillamini, fouillis m.

jump, n. saut m.; vb. sauter

junction, n. jonction f.; embranchement m.

juncture, n. jointure, jonction, conjoncture f.

June, n. juin m.

jungle, n. jungle, brousse f.

junior, adj. and n. cadet, subalterne m.

juniper, n. genévrier, genièvre m.

junk, n. rebut m.

junket, n. jonchée f.; festin m.

jurisdiction, n. juridiction f.

jurist, n. juriste, légiste m.

juror, n. juré, membre du jury m.

jury, n. jury m.

just, adj. juste

justice, n. justice f.

justifiable, adj. justifiable, justifié

justification, n. justification f.

justify, vb. justifier

jut, vb. faire saillie

jute, n. jute m.

juvenile, adj. juvénile

K

kale, n. chou m.

kaleidoscope, n. kaléidoscope m.

kangaroo, n. kangourou m.

karat, n. carat m.

karate, n. karaté m.

keen, adj. aiguisé, aigu, pénétrant

keep, vb. tenir, garder, continuer à

keeper, n. gardien m.

keepsake, n. souvenir m.

keg, n. caque f.; barillet m.

kennel, n. chenil m.

kerchief, n. fichu, mouchoir m.

kernel, n. grain m.; amande f.

kerosene, n. pétrole m.

ketchup, n. sauce piquante à

kettle, n. bouilloire f.
key, n. clef, clé f.
keyhole, n. entrée de clef f.
khaki, n. kaki m.
kick, n. coup de pied m.
kid, n. gosse m.f., chevreau m.
kidnap, vb. enlever de vive force
kidnaper, n. auteur de l'enlèvement m.
kidney, n. rein, rognon m.
kidney bean, n. haricot nain m.
kill, vb. tuer
killer, n. tueur, meurtrier m.
kiln, n. four, séchoir m.
kilocycle, n. kilocycle m.
kilowatt, n. kilowatt m.
kilt, n. kilt m.
kimono, n. kimono m.
kin, n. parent m.
kind, n. genre m.
kindergarden, n. jardin d'enfants m.
kindle, vb. allumer
kindling, n. allumage m.
kindness, n. bonté f.
kindred, n. parenté f.
kinetic, adj. cinétique
king, n. roi m.
kiss, n. baiser m.; vb. baiser, embrasser
kitchen, n. cuisine f.
kite, n. cerf-volant m.
kitten, n. petit chat m.
knack, n. tour de main m.
knapsack, n. havresac m.
knead, vb. pétrir, malaxer
knee, n. genou m.
kneecap, n. genouillère f.
knife, n. couteau m.
knock, n. coup m.
knot, noeud m.
know, vb. savoir, connaître
knowing, adj. intelligent, instruit
knowledge, n. connaissance f.
knuckle, n. articulation du doigt, jointure
kodak, n. kodak m.
Korea, n. la Corée f.
kosher, adj. cacher

L

label, n. étiquette m.
labor, n. travail m.; ouvriers m., pl.
laboratory, n. laboratoire m.
laborer, n. travailleur m.
laborious, adj. laborieux
labor union, n. syndicat m.

laburnum, n. cytise m.
labyrinth, n. labyrinthe m.
lac, n. gomme-laque
lace, n. dentelle f.; cordon, point, lacet m.
lacerate, vb. lacérer, déchirer
laceration, n. lacération f.
lack, n. manque, besoin, défault m.; vb. manquer de
lackadaisical, adj. affecté, minaudier, apathique
lacking, adj. manquant (de)
laconic, adj. laconique
lacquer, n. laque m.
lacrosse, n. crosse canadienne f.
lactic, adj. lactique
lactose, n. lactose f.
lacy, adj. de dentelle
lad, n. garçon, jeune homme
ladder, n. échelle f.
lade, vb. charger (de), jeter
lady, n. dame f.
lading, n. chargement m.
ladle, n. cuiller à pot
lady, n. dame f.
ladybug, n. coccinelle f.
lag, repris de justice
lagoon, n. lagune f.
laid, adj. vergé
laid-back, adj. décontracté
lair, n. tanière f.; repaire m.
laissez faire, n. laissez faire m.
laity, n. les laïques m., pl.
lake, n. lac m.
lamb, n. agneau m.
lamb's wool, n. laine d'agneau
lambent, adj. qui effleure, qui rayonne doucement
lame, adj. boiteux
lament, vb. se lamenter, pleurer
lamentable, adj. lamentable, déplorable
lamentation, n. lamentation f.
laminate, vb. laminer
lamp, n. lampe f.
lamplighter, n. allumeur m.
lamp post, n. lampadaire m.
lampoon, n. pasquinade f.
lance, n. lance f.
lancer, n. lancier m.
land, n. terre f.
landholder, n. propriétaire, foncier m.
landing, n. débarquement, mise à terre m.
landlord, n. propriétaire m.f.
landmark, n. borne f.
landscape, n. paysage m.
landslide, n. éboulement m.
landward, adv. vers la terre

lane, n. sentier m.; ruelle f.
language, n. langue f.; langage m.
languid, adj. languissant
languish, vb. languir
languor, n. langueur f.
lank, adj. grand et maigre
lanolin, n. lanoline f.
lantern, n. lanterne f.
lap, n. genoux m., pl.
lapel, n. revers m.
lapin, n. lapin m.
lapse, n. laps m.; faute f.
larceny, n. larcin, vol m.
lard, n. saindoux m.
large, adj. grand
largely, adv. en grande partie
largo, n. largo m.
lariat, n. lasso m.
lark, n. alouette f.
larkspur, n. pied d'alouette,
 delphinium m.
larva, n. larve f.
laryngitis, n. laryngite f.
larynx, n. larynx m.
lascivious, adj. lascif
laser, n. laser m.
lash, n. lanière f.; coup de fouet m.
lass, n. jeune fille f.
lassitude, n. lassitude f.
lasso, n. lasso m.
last, adj. dernier, enfin
lasting, adj. durable
latch, n. loquet m.
latchet, n. cordon de soulier m.
late, adj. and adv. tard, en retard,
 feu, dernier
lately, adv. dernièrement
latecomer, n. retardataire
latent, adj. latent, caché
lateral, adj. latéral
lath, n. latte f.
lathe, n. tour m.
lather, n. mousse, écume f.
Latin, n. Latin, latin m.
latitude, n. latitude f.
latrine, n. latrines f.
latten, n. fer-blanc, laiton
latter, adj. and pron. dernier
lattice, n. treillis m.
laud, vb. louer
laudable, adj. louable
laudanum, n. laudanum m.
laudatory, adj. élogieux
laugh, n. rire m.
laughable, adj. risible
laugher, n. rieur m.
laughing, adj. rieur, enjoué
laughter, n. rire m.
launch, vb. lancer, mettre à la mer
launder, vb. blanchir

laundry, n. buanderie f.
laundryman, n. blanchisseur m.
laureate, adj. and n. lauréat m.f.
laurel, n. laurier m.
lava, n. lave f.
lavatory, n. lavabo m.
lave, vb. laver, baigner
lavender, n. lavande f.
lavish, adj. prodigue, somptueux
lavishly, adv. à profusion
lavishness, n. prodigalité f.
law, n. loi f.; droit m.
lawful, adj. légal
lawless, adj. sans loi
lawn, n. pelouse f.
lawsuit, n. procès m.
lawyer, n. avocat, avoué,
 jurisconsulte m.
lax, adj. lâche, mou, relâche
laxative, n. laxatif m.
laxity, n. relâchement m.
lay, vb. poser
layer, n. couche f.
layman, n. laïque m.
lazy, adj. paresseux
lead, n. plomb m.; mine f.
leaden, adj. de plomb
leader, n. chef m.
leaf, n. feuille f.
leaflet, n. feuillet m.
leafy, adj. feuillu
league, n. ligue, lieue f.
leak, n. fuite f., voie d'eau f.
leakage, n. fuite d'eau f.
leaky, adj. qui coule, qui fait eau
lean, vb. s'appuyer, s'incliner,
 pencher, incliner; adj maigre
leap, vb. sauter
leap year, n. année bissextile f.
learn, vb. apprendre
learned, adj. savant, docte
learning, n. science, instruction f.
lease, n. bail m.
leash, n. laisse, attache f.
least, n. permission f.
leaven, n. levain m.; vb. faire lever
lecherous, adj. lascif, libertin
lecture, n. conférence f
lecturer, n. conférencier m
ledge, n. bord m.
ledger, n. grand livre m.
leech, n. sangsue f.
leek, n. poireau m
leeward, adj. and adv. sous le
 vent
left, adj. and n. gauche f.; à gauche
leftist, n. gaucher m.
leg, n. jambe, patte f.
legacy, n. legs m.
legal, adj. légal

legality, n. légalité f.
legalization, n. légalisation
legalize, vb. rendre égal
legally, adv. légalement
legate, vb. léguer
legation, n. légation
legend, n. légende f.
legendary, adj. légendaire
legible, adj. lisible
legion, n. légion f.
legionary, adj. de légion
legislate, vb. faire les lois
legislation, n. législation f.
legislator, n. législateur m.
legislature, n. législature f.
legitimate, adj. légitime
legume, n. légume m.
leisure, n. loisir m.
leisurely, adv. à loisir
lemon, n. citron m.
lemonade, n. limonade f.
lend, vb. prêter
lenght, n. longueur, durée f.
lengthen, vb. allonger
lengthwise, adv. en long
lengthy, adj. assez long
lenient, adj. indulgent
lens, n. lentille f.; objectif m.
Lent, n. carême m.
Lenten, adj. le carême
lentil, n. lentille f.
lento, adv. lento
leopard, n. léopard m.
leper, n. lépreux m.
leprosy, n. lèpre f.
lesbian, n. lesbienne f.
lesion, n. lésion f.
less, adj. moindre; moins de
lesser, adj. moindre
lesson, n. leçon f.
lest, conj. de peur que
let, vb. laisser, louer
letdown, n. déception f.
lethal, adj. mortel
lethargic, adj. léthargique
lethargy, n. léthargie f.
letter, n. lettre f.
letterhead, n. en-tête de lettre m.
lettuce, n. laitue f.
levee, n. lever m.
level, adj. égal
lever, n. levier m.
levity, n. légèreté f.
levy, n. levée f.
lewd, adj. impudique
lexicon, n. lexique m.
liability, n. responsabilité f.
liable, adj. responsable de sujet à
liar, n. menteur m.
libation, n. libation f.

libel, n. diffamation f.
libelous, adj. diffamatoire
liberal, adj. libéral, généreux
liberalism, n. libéralisme m.
liberality, n. libéralité f.
liberate, vb. libérer
libertine, n. libre-penseur m.
liberty, n. liberté f.
libidinous, adj. libidineux
libido, n. libido m.
librarian, n. bibliothécaire m.
library, n. bibliothèque f.
libretto, n. livret m.
licnese, n. permis m.; patente f.
licentious, adj. licencieux
lick, vb. lécher
licorice, n. réglisse f.
lid, n. couvercle m.
lie, n. mensonge m.; vb. mentir
lien, n. privilège m.
lieutenant, n. lieutenant m.
life, n. vie f.
lifeguard, n. garde du corps m.
life insurance, n. assurance sur la vie f.
lifeless, adj. sans vie
life preserver, n. appareil de sauvetage m.
lifetime, n. vie f.; vivant m.
lift, vb. lever
ligament, n. ligament m.
ligature, n. ligature f.
light, n. lumière f.; adj. léger, clair
lighten, vb. alléger, éclairer
lighthouse, n. phare m.
lightly, adv. légèrement
lightness, n. légèreté f.
lightning, n. éclair m.
lignite, n. lignite m.
likable, adj. agréable
like, adj. pareil; même, égal; vb. aimer bien, trouver bon
likelihood, n. probabilité f.
likely, adj. probable
liken, vb. comparer
likeness, n. ressemblance f.
likewise, adv. de même
lilac, n. lilas m.
lily, n. lis, muguet m.
limb, n. membre m.; grosse branche f.
limber, adj. souple, flexible
limbo, n. limbes m., pl.
lime, n. chaux, lime f.
limelight, n. lumière oxhydrique f.
limestone, n. pierre à chaux f.; calcaire m.
limit, n. limite f.
limitation, n. limitation f.
limitless, adj. sans limite

limousine, n. limousine f.
limp, adj. flasque
limpid, adj. limpide
linden, n. tilleul m.
line, n. ligne f.
lineage, n. lignée, race f.
lineal, adj. linéaire
linen, n. toile f.; linge m.
linger, vb. s'attarder
lingerie, n. lingerie f
liniment, n. liniment m.
lining, n. doublure f.
link, n. chaînon, anneau m.
linoleum, n. linoléum m.
linseed, n. graine de lin f.
lint, n. charpie f.
lion, n. lion m.
lip, n. lèvre f.
liquefy, vb. liquéfier
liqueur, n. liqueur f.
liquid, adj. and n. liquide m.
liquidate, vb. liquider
liquidation, n. liquidation f.;
 acquittement m.
liquor, n. boisson alcoolique f.
lisle, n. fil d'Écosse m.
lisp, vb. zézayer; n. zézaiement m.
list, n. liste f.
listen, vb. ecouter
listless, adj. inattentif
litany, n. litanie f.
literacy, n. degré d'aptitude
 à lire et à écrire m.
literal, adj. littéral
literary, adj. littéraire
literate, adj. lettré
literature, n. littérature f.
lithe, adj. flexible, pliant
lithograph, vb. lithographier
lithography, n. lithographie f.
litigant, n. plaideur m.
litigation, n. litige m.
litmus, n tournesol m.
litter, n. litière f.; fouillis m.
little, n. and adv. peu m.; adj. petit
liturgical, adj. liturgique
liturgy, n. liturgie f.
live, vb. vivre
lively, adj. vif m.; vive f.
liven, vb. animer, activer
liver, n. foie m.
livery, n. livrée f.
livestock, n. bétail m.
livid, adj. livide, blême
lizard, n. lézard m.
llama, n. lama m.
lo, interj. voilà
load, n. charge f.; fardeau m.
loaf, n. pain m.
loafer, n. fainéant m.

loam, n. terre grasse f.
loan, n. prêt, emprunt m.
loath, adj. fâché, peiné; vb. détester
loathing, n. dégoût m.
loathsome, adj. dégoûtant
lobby, n. vestibule m.
lobe, n. lobe m.
lobster, n. homard m.
local, adj. local
locale, n. localité, scène f.
locality, n. localité f.
localize, vb. localiser
location, n. placement m.
locker, n. armoire f.
locket, n. médaillon m.
lockjaw, n. tétanos m.
locksmith, n. serrurie m.
locomotive, n. locomotive f.
lode, n. filon m.
lodge, vb. loger
lodger, n. locataire m.
lodging, n. logement m.
loft, n. grenier m.
lofty, adj. élevé, hautain
log, n. bûche f.; loch m.
loge, n. loge f.
logic, n. logique f.
logical, adj. logique
loins, n. reins m., pl.
loiter, vb. fiâner
lollipop, n. sucre d'orge m.
London, n. Londres m.
lone, adj. solitaire, délaissé
lonely, adj. isolé
loneliness, n. solitude f.
long, adj. long m.; longue f.
longevity, n. longévité f.
loom, n. métier m.
loop, n. boucle f.
loophole, n. meurtrière f.
loose, adj. lâche
loosen, vb. desserrer
loot, n. butin m.
lop, vb. élaguer, ébrancher
loquacious, adj. loquace
lord, n. seigneur, lord m.
lordship, n. seigneurie f.
lose, vb. perdre
loss, n. perte f.
lot, n. sort, terrain m.
lotion, n. lotion f.
lottery, n. loterie f.
lotus, n. lotus, lotos m.
loud, adj. fort, bruyant
lounge, n. sofa, hall m.
louse, n. pou m.
lout, n. rustre m.
louver, n. auvent m.
lovable, adj. aimable

love,n. amour m.
lovely, adj. beau m.; belle f.
lover, n. amoureux m.
low, adj. bas m.; basse f.
lower, vb. baisser
lowly, adj. humble
loyal, adj. loyal
loyalist, n. loyaliste m.
loyalty, n. loyauté f.
lozenge, n. pastille f.
lubricant, n. lubrifiant m.
lubricate, vb. lubrifier
lucid, adj. lucide
luck, n. chance f.
lucky, adj. heureux
lucrative, adj. lucratif
ludicrous, adj. risible
lug, vb. traîner, tirer
luggage, n. bagages m., pl.
lukewarm, adj. tiède
lull, n. moment de calme m.
lullaby, n. berceuse f.
lumbago, n. lumbago m.
lumber, n. bois de charpente m.
luminous, adj. lumineux
lump, n. masse f.
lumpy, adj. grumeleux
lunacy, n. folie f.
lunar, adj. lunaire
lunatic, n. aliéné m.
lunch, n. déjeuner m.
luncheon, n. déjeuner m.
lung, n. poumon m.
lunge, n. embardée f.
lure, vb. leurrer; attirer
lurid, adj. blafard, sombre
lurk, vb. se cacher
luscious, adj. délicieux
lush, adj. luxuriant
lust, n. luxure f.
luster, n. lustre m.
lustful, adj. lascif, sensuel
lustrous, adj. brillant, lustré
lusty, adj. vigoureux
lute, n. luth m.
Lutheran, adj. luthérien
luxuriant, adj. exubérant
luxurious, adj. luxueux
luxury, n. luxe m.
lying, n. mensonge m.
lymph, n. lymphe f.
lynch, vb. lyncher
lyre, n. lyre f.
lyric, adj. lyrique
lyricism, n. lyrisme m.

M

macaroni, n. macaroni m.

machine, n. machine f.
machinery, n. machiniste m.
machismo, n. phallocratie f.
macho, adj. phallocrate
mackerel, n. maquereau m.
mad, adj. fou m.; folle f.
madam, n. madame f.
made, adj. fait, fabriqué
mafia, n. mafia f.
magazine, n. revue f.
magic, n. magie f.
magistrate, n. magistrat m.
magnanimous, adj. magnanime
magnate, n. magnat m.
magnesium, n. magnésium m.
magnet, n. aimant m.
magnificance, n. magnificence f.
magnificent, adj. magnifique
magnify, vb. grossir
magnitue, n grandeur f.
mahogany, n. acajou m.
maid, n. bonne f.
maiden, adj. de jeune fille
mail, n. courrier m.
mailman, n. facteur m.
maim, vb. estropier, mutiler
main, adj. principal
mainland, n. continent m.
maintain, vb. maintenir, soutenir
maintenance, n. entretien m.
maize, n. maïs m.
majestic, adj. majestueux
majesty, n. majesté f.
major, n. commandant m.
majority, n. majorité f.
make, n. fabrication f. vb. faire,
  fabriquer
maker, n. fabricant m.
malady, n. maladie f.
malaria, n. malaria f.
male, adj. and n. mâle m.
malevolent, adj. malveillant
malice, n. méchanceté f.
malicious, adj. méchant
malign, vb. calomnier
malignant, adj. malin m.;
  maligne f.
malleable, adj. malléable
malnutirition, n. sous-alimentation
  f.
malpractice, n. méfait m.
malt, n. malt m.
mammal, n. mammifère m.
man, n. homme m.
manage, vb. diriger, mener,
  conduire
management, n. direction f.
manager, n. directeur, ménager m.
mandate, n. mandat m.
mandatory, adj. obligatoire

mandolin, n. mandoline f.
mane, n. crinière f.
maneuver, n. manoeuvre f.
manganese, n. manganèse m.
manger, n. mangeoire f.
mangle, vb. mutiler
manhood, n. virilité f.
mania, n. manie, folie f.
maniac, adj. and n. fou m.;
  folle f.
manicure, n. manucure m.f; soin
  des ongles m.
manifest, adj. manifeste
manifesto, n. manifeste m.
manifold, adj. divers, multiple
manipulate, vb. manipuler
mankind, n. genre humain m.
manly, adj. viril
manner, n. manière f.; moeurs f., pl.
mannerism, n. maniérisme, m.;
  affectation f.
mansion, n. château, hôtel m.
mantel, n. manteau m.; tablette f.
manual, adj. and n. manuel m.
manufacture, n. manufacture f.;
  produit m.
manufacturer, n. fabricant m.
manure, n. fumier m.
manuscript, adj. and n. manus-
  crit m.
many, adj. beaucoup de, bien
map, n. carte géographique f.
maple, n. érable m.
mar, vb. gâter
marble, n. marbre m.
march, n. march f.; vb. marcher
March, n. mars m.
mare, n. jument f.
margarine, n. marge f.
marine, n. marine f.; fusilier
  marin m.; adj. marin, de mer
mariner, n. marin m.
marionette, n. marionnette f.
marital, adj. matrimonial
maritime, adj. maritime
market, n. marché m.
market place, n. place due
  marché f.
marmalade, n. confiture f.
marquee, n. marquise f.
marquis, n. marquis m.
marriage, n. mariage m.
married, adj. marié
marrow, n. moelle f.
marry, vb. épouser, se marier
marsh, n. marais m.
marshal, n. maréchal m.
martial, adj. martial
martyr, n. martyr m.
marvel, n. merveille f.; vb.

s'étonner de.
marvelous, adj. merveilleux
mascara, n. mascara m.
mascot, n. mascotte f.
masculine, adj. masculin
mash, n. purée f.
mask,, n. masque m.; vb. masquer
mason, n. maçon m.
masquerade, n. mascarade f., bal
  masqué m.
mass, n. masse f.
massacre, n. massacre m.; vb.
  massacrer
massage, n. massage m.
masseur, n. masseur m.
massive, adj. massif
mass meeting, n. réunion f.
mast, n. mât m.
master, n. maître m.; vb. maîtriser
masterpiece, n. chef-d'oeuvre m.
mastery, n. maîtrise f.
masticate, vb. mâcher
mat, n. paillasson m.
match, n. allumette f.; égal, mariage
  m.; vb. assortir
material, n. matière; étoffe f.; adj.
  matériel
maternal, adj. maternel
maternity, n. maternité f.
mathematical, adj. mathématique
mathematics, n. mathématiques f.,
  pl.
matinee, n. matinée f.
matriarch, n. femme qui porte
  les chausses f.
matrimony, n. mariage m.
matron, n. matrone f.
matter, n. matière, affaire f.; sujet
  m.; vb. importer
mattress, n. matelas m.
mature, adj. mûr.; vb. mûrir
maturity, n. maturité, échéance f.
maudlin, adj. larmoyant
mausoleum, n. mausolée m.
maxim, n. maxime f.
maximum, n. maximum m.
may, vb. pouvoir
May, n. mai m.
maybe, adv. peut-être
mayhem, n. mutilation f.
mayonnaise, n. mayonnaise f.
mayor, n. maire m.
maze, n. labyrinthe m.
me, pron. me, moi
meadow, n. pré m.; prairie f.
meager, adj. maigre
meal, n. repas m.; farine f.
mean, n. moyenne f.; moyens
  m.,pl.; moyen m.; adj. humble,
  avare;

vb. vouloir dire, se proposer
meaning, n. sens m.
meantime adv. sur ces entrefaites
measles, n. rougeole f.
measure, n. mesure f.; vb. mesurer
measurement, n. mesurage m.
meat, n. viande f.
mechanic, n. mécanicien m.
mechanical, adj. mécanique
mechanism, n. mécanisme m.
mechanize, vb mécaniser
medal, n. médaille f.
meddle, vb. se mêler
media, n. organes de communication m., pl.
median, n. médian
mediate, vb. agir en médiateur
medical, adj. médical
medicate, vb. médicamenter
medicine, n. médecine m.
medieval, adj. médiéval
mediocre, adj. médiocre
mediocrity, n. médiocrité f.
meditate, vb. méditer
meditation, n. méditation f.
medium, n. milieu, intermédiaire,
 médium m.
medley, n. mélange m.
meek, adj. doux m.; douce f.
meekness, n. douceur f.
meet, vb. rencontrer, faire
 la connaissance de; faire face à
meeting, n. réunion f.
megahertz, n. mégahertz m.
megaphone, n. mégaphone m.
melancholy, n. mélancolie f.
mellow, adj. moelleux
melodous, adj. mélodieux
melodrama, n. mélodrame m.
melody, n. mélodie f.
melon, n. melon m.
melt, vb. fondre
meltdown, n. fusion f.
member, n. membre m.
membrane, n. membrane f.
memnto, n. mémento m.
memoir, n. mémoire m.
memorable, adj. mémorable
memorandum, n. mémorandum m.
memorial, n. souvenir, monument
 m.; adj. commémoratif
memorize, vb. apprendre par
 coeur
memory, n. mémoire f.
menace, n. menace; vb. menacer
menagerie, n. ménagerie f.
mend, vb. raccommoder, corriger
mendacious, adj. menteur
mendicant, n. and adj. mendiant m.
menial, adj. servile

menstruation, n. menstruation f.
menswear, n. habillements
 masculins m., pl.
mental, adj. mental
mentality, n. mentalité f.
menthol, n. menthol m.
mention, n. mention f.; vb.
 mentionner, il n'y a pas de quoi
menu, n. menu m.
mercantile, adj. mercantile
merchandise, n. marchandise f.
merchant, n. négociant m.; adj.
 marchand
merciful, adj. miséricordieux
merciless, adj. impitoyable
mercury, n. mercure m.
mercy, n. miséricorde f.; à la merci
 de
mere, adj. simple
merely, adv. simplement
merge, vb. fusionner
merger, n. fusion f.
merit, n. mérite m.; vb. mériter
meritorious, adj. méritant, méritoire
mermaid, n. sirène f.
merriment, n. gaieté f.
merry, adj. gai
mesh, n. maille f.
mesmerize, vb. magnétiser
mess, n. fouillis, gâchis m.; (mil.)
 popote f.; vb. gâcher
message, n. message m.
messenger, n. messager m.
messy, adj. malpropre
metabolism, n. métabolisme m.
metal, n. métal m.
metallic, adj. métallique
metamorphosis, n. métamorphose
 f.
metaphysics, n. métaphysique f.
meteor, n. météore m.
meter, n. mètre, compteur m.
method, n. méthode f.
meticulous, adj. méticuleux
metric, n. métrique
metropolis, n. métropole f.
metropiltan, adj. métropolitain
mettle, n. ardeur f.
mezzanine, n. mezzanine f.
microbe, n. microbe m.
microfiche, n. microfiche f.
microfilm, n. microfilm m.
microform, n. microforme f.
microphone, n. microphone m.
microscope, n. microscope m.
microscopic, adj. microscopique
mid, adj. du milieu, moyen
middle, n. milieu m.
midget, n. nain m.
midnight, n. minuit m.

midriff, n. diaphragme m.
midwife, n. sage-femme f.
mien, n. mine f ; air m.
might, n. puissance f.
mighty, adj. puissant
migrate, vb. émigrer
migration, n. migration f.
mild, adj. doux m.; douce f.
mildew, n. rouille f.
mile, n. mille m.
mileage, n. kilométrage m.
military, adj. militaire
milk, n. lait m.
milkman, n. laitier m.
mill, n. moulin m.; filature,
usine f.; vb. moudre, fourmiller
miller, n. meunier m.
millimeter, n. millimètre m.
milliner, n. modiste f.
million, n. million m.
mince, vb. hacher
mind, n. esprit, avis m.; envie f.; vb.
faire attention à, écouter, s'occuper
de, prendre garde, garder,
n'importe
mindful, adj. attentif
mine, n. mine f.; pron. le mien m.; la
mienne f.
miner, n. mineur m.
mineral, adj. and n. minéral m.
mingle, vb. mêler
minature, n. miniature f.
miniaturize, vb. miniaturiser
minimize, vb. réduire au minimum
minimum, n. minimum m.
mining, n. exploitation minière,
pose de mines f.
minister, n. ministre m.
ministry, n. ministère m.
mink, n. vison m.
minnow, n vairon m.
minor, adj. and n. mineur m.
minority, n. minorité f.
minstrel, n. ménestrel m.
mint, n. la monnaie f.; vb. frapper
minute, n. minute f.; adj.
minuscule; minutieux
miracle, n. miracle m.
miraculous, adj. miraculeux
mirage, n. mirage m.
mire, n. boue f.; bourbier m.
mirror, n. miroir m.
mirth, n. gaieté f.
misappropriate, vb. détourner,
dépréder
misbehave, vb. se mal conduire
miscellaneous, adj. divers
mischief, n. mal m.; malice f.
misconstrue, vb. mal interpréter,
tourner en mal

misdemeanor, n. délit m.
miser, n. avare m.f.
miserable, adj. malheureux, misérable
misery, n. misère f.
misfortune, n. malheur m.
misgiving, n. doute m.
mishap, n. mésaventure f.
mislead, vb. romper, égarer
misplace, vb. mal placer
mispronounce, vb. mal prononcer, estropier
miss, vb manquer, vous me
manquez
Miss, n. mademoiselle f.
missile, n. projectile, m.
mission, n. mission f.
missionary, adj. and n. mis-
sionnaire m.f.
mist, n. brume f.
mistake, n. erreur f.; vb. comprendre mal, se tromper
mister, n. monsieur m.
mistletoe, n. gui m.
mistreat, vb. maltraiter
mistress, n. maîtresse f.
misty, adj. brumeux
misunderstand, vb. mal
comprendre
misuse, vb. faire
mauvais usage; maltraiter
mite, n. denier m.; obole f.
mitigate, vb. adoucir
mitten, n. moufle f.
mix, vb. mêler
mixture, n. mélange m.
mix-up, n. embrouillement m.
moan, n. gémissement m.
moat, n. fossé m.
mob, n. foule, populace f.
mobile, adj. mobile
mobilization, n. mobilisation f.
mobilize, vb. mobiliser
mock, vb. se moquer de, singer
mockery, n. moquerie f.
mod, adj. à la mode
mode, n. mode m.
model, n. modèle m.
moderate, adj. modéré; vb.
modérer
modern, adj. moderne
modest, adj. modeste
modesty, n. modestie f.
modify, vb. modifier
modish, adj. à la mode
modulate, vb. moduler
moist, adj. moite
moisten, vb. humecter
moisture, n. humidité f.
molar, n. and adj. molaire f.

molasses, n. mélasse f.
mold, n. moule m.; moisissure f.; vb. mouler
moldy, adj. moisi
mole, n. taupe f.; grain de beauté m.
molecule, n. molécule f.
molest, vb. molester
mollify, vb. adoucir, apaiser
molten, adj. fondu, coulé
moment, n. moment m.
momentary, adj. momentané
momentous, adj. important
monastery, n. monastère m.
Monday, n. lundi m.
monetary, adj. monétaire
money, n. argent m.; monnaie f.
mongrel. n. métis m.
monitor, n. moniteur m.
monk, n. moine m.
monkey, n. singe m.
monologue, n. monologue m.
monopoly, n. monopole m.
monotone, n. monotone m.
monotonous, adj. monotone
monotony, n. monotonie f.
monsoon, n. mousson f.
monster, n. monstre m.
monstrosity, n. monstruosité f.
monstrous, adj. monstrueux
month, n. mois m.
monument, n. monument m.
monumnetal, adj. monumental
mood, n. humeur f.; mode m.
moon, n. lune f.
moonlight, n. clair de lune m.
moor, n. lande f.
mooring, n. amarrage m.
moot, adj. discutable
mop, n. balai à laver m.
moped, n. cyclomoteur m
moral, n. morale f., moralité f.
morale, n. moral m.
moralist, n. moraliste m.f.
morality, n. moralité, morale f.
morally, adv. moralement
morbid, adj. morbide
more, adj. and adv. plus, plus de
moreover, adv. de plus
mores, n. moeurs f., pl.
morgue, n. morgue f.
morning, n. matin m.; matinée f.
moron, n. idiiot
morose, adj. morose
morsel, n. morceau m.
mortal, adj. and n. mortel m.
mortar, n. mortier m.
mortgage, n. hypothèque f.
mortify, vb. mortifier
mortuary, adj. mortuaire

Moslem, adj. and n. musulman m.
mosquito, n. moustique m.
moss, n. mousse f.
most, n. le plus.; adj. le plus, la plupart.
moth, n. mite f.
mother, n. mère f.
mother-in-law, n. belle-mère f.
motif, n. motif m.
motion, n. mouvement, signe m.
motionless, adj. immobile
motivate, vb. motiver
motive, n. motif m.
motor, n. moteur m.
motorist, n. automobiliste m.
motto, n. devise f.
mound, n. tertre m.
mount, n. mont m.; monture f. vb. monter
mountain, n. montagne f.
mountaineer, n. montagnard m.
mountainous, adj. montagneux
mourn, vb. pleurer
mournful, adj. triste
mourning, n. deuil m.
mouse, n. souris f.
mouth, n. bouche f.
movable, adj. mobile
move, vb. mouvoir, remuer, bouger, émouvoir
movement, n. mouvement m.
mow, vb. faucher, tondre
much, adj. pron. and adv.beaucoup; (too much) trop, (so much) tant
mucilage, n. mucilage m.
muck, n. fumier n.
mucous, adj. muqueux
mud, n. boue f.
mud-bank, n. de vase m.
muddle, vb. brouiller, troubler
muddler, n. brouillon m.
muddy, adj boueux
muff, n. manchon m.
muffin, n. petit pan m.
muffle, vb. emmitoufler
mug, n. gobelet, pot m.
mulberry, n. mûre f.
mulch, n. paillis m.
mule, n. mulet m.
mull, n. cap promontoire m.
muller, n. molette
multiple, adj. multiple m.
multiply, vb. multiplier
multitude, n. multitude f.
mum, n. maman f.; adj. muet
mumble, vb. marmotter
mummer, n. mime
mummy, n. momie, maman f.
mumps, n. oreillons m., pl.
munch, vb. mâcher

mundane, adj. mondain	nameless, adj. sans nom, anonyme
mungoose, n. mangouste f.	
municipal, adj. municipal	name-plate, n. plaque f.
munificent, adj. munificent	namesake, n. homonyme m.
munition, n. munition f.	nanny, n. bonne d'enfant
mural, n. peinture murale f.	nap, n. petit somme m.
murder, n. meurtre m.	nape, n. nuque f.
murderer, n. meurtrier m.	napkin, n. serviette f.
murmur, n. murmure m.; vb. murmurer	napkin ring, rond de serviette m.
muscle, n. muscle m.	narcissus, n. narcisse m.
muse, n. muse f.; vb. méditer	narcotic, adj. and n. narcotique m.
museum, n. musée m.	narrate, vb. raconter
mush, n. brouillage m.	narration, n. narration f.
mushroom, n. champignon m.	narrative, n. récit, narré m.
music, n. musique f.	narrator, n. narrateur m.
musical, adj. musical, musicien	narrow, adj. étroit
musician, n. musicien m.	narrow minded, adj. à l'esprit étroit
Muslim, adj. and n. musulman m.	
muslin, n. mousseline f.	nasal, adj. nasal, du nez
must, vb. devoir, falloir	nasty, adj. désagréable
mustache, n. moustache f.	natal, adj. natal
muster, vb. rassembler	nation, n. nation f.
musty, adj. moisi, suranné	national, national m.
mutation, n. mutation f.	nationalism, n. nationalisme m.
mute, adj. muet	nationalist, n. nationaliste m.
mutilate, vb. mutiler	nationalize, vb. nationaliser
mutiny, vb. mutinerie f.	native, n. natif m ; indigène m.f.
mutter, vb. grommeler	nativity, n. naissance f.
mutton, n. mouton m.	natural, adj. naturel
mutual, adj. mutuel	naturalism, n. naturalisme m.
muzzle, n. muselière f.	naturalist, n. naturaliste m.
my, adj. mon m.; ma f.; mes pl.	naturalize, vb. naturaliser
myopia, n. myopie f.	naturalness, n. naturel m.
myuriad, n. myriade f.	nature, n. nature f.
myrtle, n. myrte m.	naught, n. néant, rien
myself, pron. moi-même, moi	naughty, adj. méchant
mystagogue, n. mystagogue m.	nausea, n. nausée f.
mystery, n. mystère m.	nauseous, adj. nauséeux
mystic, adj. mystique, initié, magicien	nauseousness, n. nature nauséabonde f.
mystical, adj. mystique	nautical, adj. marin, nautique
mystify, vb. mystifier	naval, adj. naval
myth, n. mythe m.	nave, n. nef f.
mythical, adj. mythique	navel, n. nombril m.
mythology, n. mythologie f.	navigable, adj. navigable
	navigate, vb. naviguer
	navigation, n. navigation f.
	navigator, n. navigateur m.
N	navy, n. marine f.
	nay, adv. non, bien plus
	near, adj. proche.; adv. prés.
nab, vb. happer, pincer, saisir	nearly, adv. de près, presque
nag, vb. gronder	nearness, n. proximité
nail, n. ongle, clou m.	near-sighted, adj. myope
nail-brush, n. brosse à ongles f.	neat, adj. propre, soigné
nail-file, n. lime à ongles f.	neatness, n. propreté f.
naïve, adj. naïf; m. naïve f.	nebula, n. nébuleuse f.
naked, adj. nu, à nu	nebulous, adj. nébuleux
name, n. nom m.	necessary, adj. nécessaire
named, adj. nommé, désigné	necessitate, vb. nécessiter

necessity, n. nécessité f.
neck, n. cou, goulot m.
necklace, n. collier m.
nectar, n. nectar m.
need, n. besoin m.
needful, adj. nécessaire
needfully, adv. nécessairement
needle, n. aiguille f.
needle point, n. pointe d'aiguille f.
needless, adj. inutile
needlessness, n. inutilité f.
needs, adv. nécessairement
needy, adj. nécessiteux
nefarious, adj. infame
negative, adj. négatif
neglect, n. négligence f.
negligee, n. négligée f.
negligent, adj. négligent
negligible, adj. négligeable
negotiate, vb. négocier
negotiation, n. négociation f.
neigh, vb. hennir
neighbor, n. voisin, prochain m.
neighborhood, n. voisinage m.
neither, adj. and pron. ni l'un ni l'autre
neon, n. néon m.
neophyte, n. néophyte m.
neoplasm, n. néoplasme m.
nephew, n. neveu m.
nepotism, n. népotisme m.
Neptune, n. Neptune m.
nerve, n. nerf m.; audace f.
nerve cell, n. cellule nerveuse f.
nerve racking, adj. horripilant
nervous, adj. nerveux
nest, n. nid m.
nest egg, n. nichet m.
nesting, adj. nicher
nestle, vb. se nicher
net, n. filtre m.; adj. net m.; nette f.
Netherlands, (the) n. les Pays Bas m., pl. Hollande f.
network, n. réseau m.
neuralgia, n. névralgie f.
neurology, n. neurologie f.
neurotic, adj. and n. nevrosé m.
neuter, adj. neutre
neutral, adj. and n. neutre m.
neutralize, vb. neutraliser
neutron, n. neutron m.
never, adv. jamais
nevertheless, adv. néanmoins
new, adj. nouveau m.; nouvelle f.; neuf m.; neuve f.
newel, adj. tout flambant neuf
news, n. nouvelle f.; nouvelles f., pl.
newsboy, n. vendeur de journaux m.

newscast, n. journal parlé m.; informations f., pl.
newspaper, n. journal m.
newsreel, n. film d'actualité m.
New Testament, n. le Nouveau Testament m.
new year, n. nouvel an m.
next, adj. prochain; adv. ensuite
nexus, n. connexion f.
nib, n. bec m.; pointe f.
nibble, vb. grignoter
nice, adj. bon, agréable
niceness, n. goût agréable m.
nick, n. entaille f.
nickel, n. nickel m.
nickname, n. surnom m.
nicotine, n. nicotine f.
niece, n. nièce f.
nifty, adj. pimpant
night, n. nuit f.; soir m.
night cap, n. bonnet de nuit m.
night club, n. boite de nuit f.; établissement de nuit m.
nightgown, n. chemise de nuit f.
nightingale, n. rossignol m.
nightly, adv. tous les soirs, toutes le nuits
nightmare, n. cauchemar m.
nimble, adj. agile
nine, adj. and n. neuf m.
nineteen, adj. and n. dix-neuf m.
ninety, adj. and n. quatre-vingt-dix m.
ninth, adj. and n. neuvième m.
nip, n. pincement m.; pince f.
nipple, n. mamelon m.
nitrogen, n. nitrogène m.
no, adj. and adv. non, pas, ne...pas de
nob, n. caboche f.
nobility, n. noblesse f.
noble, adj. noble
nobleman, n. gentilhomme m.
nobleness, n. noblesse f.
nobly, adv. noblement
nobody, pron. personne
nocturnal, adj. nocturne
nocturnally, adv. nocturnement
nod, n. signe de la tête m.
node, n. noeud m.
nohow, adv. en aucune façon
noise, n. bruit m.
noiseless, adj. silencieux
noisome, n. puant, fétide
noisy, adj. bruyant
nomad, n. nomade m.f.
nominal, adj. nominal
nominate, vb. nommer, désigner
nomination, n. nomination, présentation f.

nominee, n. personne nommée f.; candidat choisi m.

nonability, n. inhabilité

non acceptance, n. non acceptation f.

nonaligned, adj. non-aligné

nonchalant, adj. nonchalant

noncombatant, adj. and n. non-combattant m.

noncommissioned, adj. sans brevet

noncommittal, adj. qui n'engage à rien

nondescript, adj. indéfinissable

none, pron. aucun

nonentity, n. nullité f.

non-proliferation, n. non-prolifération m.

non-resident, n. and adj. non-résident m.

nonsense, n. absurdité f.

non-stop, adj. sans arrêt

noodles, n. nouilles f., pl.

nook, n. coin m.; recoin m.

noon, n. midi m.

noonday, n. midi m.

noose, n. noeud coulant m.

nor, conj. ni; ni...ne

norm, n. norme f.

normal, adj. normal

normality, n. normalité f.

normalize, vb. normaliser

normally, adv. normalement

north, n. nord m.

northeast, n. nord-est m.

northern, adj. du nord

North Pole, n. pôle Nord m.

northwest, n. nord-ouest m.

Norway, n. la Norvège f.

Norwegian, n. Norvégien m.

nose, n. nez m.

nosebleed, n. saignement de nez m.

nose dive, n. vol piqué m.

nosalgia, n. nostalgie f.

nostalgic, adj. nostalgique

nostril, n. narine f.; naseau m.

nostrum, n. panacée f.; remède de charlatan m.

nosy, adj. fouinard

not, adv. pas, non pas, ne...pas, non

notability, n. notabilité f.

notable, adj. and n. notable m.

notary, n. notaire m.

notation, n. notation

notch, n. coche, encoche

note, n. note f.; billet m.

notebook, n. carnet m.

noted, adj. célèbre

notepaper, n. papier à notes m.

noteworthy, adj. remarquable, mémorable

nothing, pron. rien

notice, n. avis, préavis m.; attention f.; vb. remarquer

noticeable, adj. remarquable, apparent

notification, n. notification f.

notify, vb. avertir

notion, n. idée f.

notoriety, n. notoriété f.

notorious, adj. notoire

notwithstanding, adv. tout de même

noun, n. substantif, nom m.

nourish, vb. nourrir

nourishment, n. nourriture f.

novel, n. roman m.

novelist, n. romancier m.

novelty, n. nouveauté f.

November, n. novembre m.

novice, n. novice m.f.

now, adv. maintenant, à présent

nowhere, adv. nulle part

nozzle, n. ajutage m.

nuance, n. nuance f.

nuclear, adj. nucléaire

nude, adj. nu; n. le nu m.

nugget, n. pépite f.

nuisance, n. ennui m.; peste f.

null, adj. nul

number, n. nombre, chiffre m.

numerical, adj. numérique

numerous, adj. nombreux

nun, n. religieuse f.

nuncho, n. nonce m.

nuptial, adj. nuptial

nurse, n. garde-malade m.f.

nursery, n. chambre des enfants, pépinière f.

nurture, n. nourriture f.; vb. nourrir

nut, n. noix f.; écrou m.

nutcracker, n. casse-noix m.

nutrition, n. nutrition f.

nutritious, adj. nutritif

nutshell, n. coquille de noix f.

nylon, n. nylon m.

nymph, n. nymphe f.

O

oak, n. chêne m.

oar, n. rame f.

oasis, n. oasis f.

oath, n. serment, juron m.

oatmeal, n. farine d'avoine f.

oats, n. avoine f.

obodurate, adj. obstiné
obedience, n. obéissance f.
obedient, adj. obéissant
obeisance, n. salut m.
obelisk, n. obélisque m.
obey, vb. obéir à
obituary, n. nécrologe m.
object, n. objet m.
objection, n. objection f.
objectionable, adj. répréhensible
objective, adj. and n. objectif m.
obligation, n. obligation f.
obligatory, adj. obligatoire
oblige, vb. obliger
oblivion, n. oubli m.
obnoxious, adj. odieux
obscene, adj. obscène
obscure, adj. obscur
obsequious, adj. obséquieux
observance, n. observance f.
observation, n. observation f.
observe, vb. observer
observer, n. observateur m.
obsession, n. obsession f.
obsolete, adj. désuet
obstacle, n. obstacle m.
obstetrician, n. accoucheur m.
obstinate, adj. obstiné
obstroperous, adj. tapageur
obstruct, vb. obstruer
obstruction, n. obstruction f.
obtain. vb. obtenir
obtrude, vb. mettre en avant
obviate, vb. prévenir, éviter
obvious, adj. évident
occasion, n. occasion f.
occasional, adj. de temps en temps
occult, adj. occulte
occupant, n. occupant m.
occupation, n. occupation f.;
métier m.
occupy, vb. occuper
occur. vb. avoir lieu, se présenter à l'esprit
occurrence, n. occurrence f.
ocean, n. océan m.
octagon, n. octogone m.
octave, n. octave f.
October, n. octobre m.
octopus, n. poulpe m.
ocular, adj. oculaire
oculist, n. oculiste f.
odd, adj. impair, dépareillé,
bizarre
oddity, n. singularité f.
odds, n. inégalité, cote f.
odious, adj. odieux
odor, n. odeur f.
of, prep. de
off, adv. à...de distance, rompu;

prep. de
offend, vb. offenser, enfreindre la
loi
offender, n. offenseur, délinquant
m.
offense, n. offense f.; délit m.
offensive, n. offensive f.; adj.
offensif, offensant
offer n. offre f.; vb. offrir
offering, n. offre, offrande f.
office, n. office, bureau m.;
fonctions f., pl.
officer, n. (mil) officier, fonctionnaire m.
official, adj. officiel
officiate, vb. officier
officious, adj. officieux
offshore, adv. au large
offspring, n. descendant m.
often, adv. souvent
oil, n. huile f.
oilcloth, n. toile cirée f.
oily, adj. huileux
ointment, n. onguent m.
okay, interj. très bien
old, adj. vieux m.
old-fashioned, adj. démodé
Old Testament, n. l'Ancien
Testament m.
olfactory, adj. olfactif
oligarchy, n. oligarchie f.
olive, n. olivier m.; olive f.
omelet, n. omelette f.
omen, n. présage m.
ominous, adj. de mauvais augure
omission, n. omission f.
omit, vb. omettre
omnibus, n. omnibus m.
omnipotent, adj. omnipotent,
tout-puissant
on, prep. sur
once, adv. une fois, autrefois
one, adj. un, seul m.
one-sided, adj. unilatéral
onion, n. oignon m.
only, adj. seul; adv. seulement
onslaught, n. assaut m.
onward, adj. and adv. en avant
opal, n. opale f.
opaque, adj. opaque
open, adj. ouvert; vb. ouvrir
opening, n. ouverture f.
opera, n. opéra m.
opera glasses, n. jumelles f., pl.
operate, vb. opérer; actionner
operatic, adj. d'opéra
operation, n. opération f.;
fonctionnement m.
operator, n. opérateur m.
operetta, n. opérette f.

opinion, n. opinion f.
opponent, n. adversaire m.f.
opportunism, n. opportunisme m.
opportunity, n. occasion f.
oppose, vb. (put in opposition)
  opposer; (resist) s'opposer à
opposite, adj. opposé, adv.
  vis-à-vis; prep. en face de
opposition, n. opposition f.
oppress, vb. opprimer
oppression, n. oppression f.
oppressive, adj. oppressif;
  (heat, etc.) accablant
optic, adj. optique
optician, n. opticien m
optimism, n. optimisme m
optimistic, adj. optimiste
option, n. option f.
optional, adj. facultatif
optometry, n. optométrie f.
opulent, adj. opulent, riche
or, conj. ou, (negative) ni
oracle, n. oracle m.
oral, adj. oral
orange, n. orange f.
orangeade, n. orangeade f.
oration, n. discours m.
orator, n. orateur m.
oratory, n. art oratoire m.
orbit, n. orbite f.
orchard, n. verger m.
orchestra, n. orchestre m.
orchid, n. orchidée f.
ordain, vb. ordonner
ordeal, n. épreuve f.
order, n. ordre m.; commande f.;
  vb. ordonner, commander
orderly, adj. ordonné
ordinance, n. ordonnance f.
ordinary, adj. and n. ordinaire m.
ordination, n. ordination f.
ore, n. minerai m.
organ, n. orgue m.; organe m.
organdy, n. organdi m.
organic, adj. organique
organism, n. organisme m.
organist, n. organiste m.f.
organization, n. organisation f.
organize, vb. organiser
orgy, n. orgie f.
orient, vb. orienter
Orient, n. Orient m.
Oriental, n. Oriental m.; adj. oriental
orientation, n. orientation f.
origin, n. origine f.
original, adj. original, originel
originality, n. originalité f.
ornament, n. ornement m.
ornamental, adj. ornemental
ornate, adj. orné

ornithology, n. ornithologie f.
orphan, n. orphelin m.
orphanage, n. orphelinat m.
orthodox, adj. orthodoxe
orthopedics, n. orthopédie f.
osmosis, n. osmose f.
ostensible, adj. prétendu
ostentation, adj. plein d'ostentation
ostracize, vb. ostraciser
ostrich, n. autruche f.
other, adj. and pron. autre
otherwise, adv. autrement
ought, vb. devoir
ounce, n. once f.
our, adj. notre (possessive)
ours, pron. le nôtre m.
ourself, pron. nous-même, nous
oust, vb. évincer
ouster n. éviction f.
out, adv. dehors
outbreak, n. commencement m.
outburst, n. éruption f.
outcast, n. paria m.
outcome, n. résultat m.
outdoors, adv. dehors
outer, adj. extérieur
outfit, n. équipement m.
outgrowth, n. conséquence f.
outing, n. promenade f.
outlandish, adj. bizarre
outlaw, vb. proscrire
outlet, n. issue f.
outline n. contour m.
out-of-date, adj. suranné
output, n. rendement m.
outrage, n. outrage m.
outrageous, adj. outrageant
outrank, vb. occuper un rang
  supérieur
outright, adv. complètement
outrun, vb. dépasser
outside, adv. dehors; prep. en
  dehors de
outskirts, n. extrémité m.; bords f.,
  pl.
outspread, vb. étendre, déployer
outstanding, adj. non payé
outstay, vb. rester plus longtemps
  que
outstretched, adj. étendue, tendu
outwalk, vb. marcher plus vite que
outward, adj. extérieur, du dehors
outwardly, adv. extérieurement
outwardness, objectivité f.
outwear, durer plus longtemps que
oval, adj. and n. ovale m.
ovation, n. ovation f.
oven, n. four m.
over, prep. sur, au-dessus de, au

delà de; plus de; adv. partout
overbearing, adj. arrogant
overcoat, n. pardessus m.
overcome, vb. vaincre, succomber à
overdue, adj. arriéré, échu
overflow, vb. déborder
overhaul, vb. examiner en détail, remettre au point
overhead, adj. général; adv. en haut
overkill, n. exagération rhétorique f.
overlook, vb. avoir vue sur, négliger
overnight, adv. pendant la nuit
overpower, vb. subjuguer, accabler
overrule, vb. décider contre
overrun, vb. envahir
oversee, vb. surveiller
oversight, n. inadvertance f.
overstuffed, adj. rembourré
overt, adj. manifeste
overtake, vb. rattraper, arriver à
overtax, vb. surtaxer, surcharger pressurer
overthrow, vb. renverser
overtime, n. heures supplémentaires f., pl.
overtone, n. harmoniques m., pl.
overtop, vb. s'élever au-dessus de
overture, n. ouverture f.
overturn, vb. renverser
overview, n. vue d'ensemble f.
overweight, n. excédent m.
overwhelm, vb. accabler (de)
owe, vb. devoir
owing, adj. dû
owl, n. hibou m.
own, adj. propre; vb. posséder
owner, n. propriétaire m.f.
ox, n. boeuf m.
oxide, oxyde m.
oxygen, n. oxygène m.
oxygen mask, n. masque d'oxygène m.
oyster, n. huître f.
ozone, n. ozone m.

P

pace, n. pas m.; allure f.; vb. arpenter
pacific, adj. pacifique
pacify, vb pacifier
pack, n. paquet m.; bande f.; vb. emballer, entasser
package, n. paquet m.
pact, n. pacte, contrat m.

paddle, n. pagaie f.
pagan, adj. and n. païen m.
page, n. (of a book) d'un livre
pageant, n. spectacle m.
pall, n. seau m.
pain, n. douleur, peine f.
pair, n. paire f.
pajamas, n. pyjama m.
palace, n. palais m.
palate, n. palais m.
pale, adj. pâle
pallid, adj. pâle, blême
paltry, adj. mesquin
pamper, vb. choyer
pamphlet, n. brochure f.
pan, n. casserole f.
panacea, n. panacée f.
pane, n. vitre f.
panel, n. panneau m.
pang, n. angoisse f.
panic, n. panique f.
pant, vb. haleter
pantomime, n. pantomime m.
pantry, n. office f.
pants, n. pantalon m.
paper, n. papier m.
par, n. pair m.; égalité f.
parable, n. parabole f.
parade, n. parade f.
paradox, n. paradoxe f.
paraffin, n. paraffine f.
paragraph, n. alinéa m.
paralyze, vb. paralyser
paramedic, n. assistant médical m.
parameter, n. paramètre m.
paramount, adj. souverain
paraphrase, vb. paraphraser
parasite, n. parasite m.
parcel, n. paquet; colis postal m.
parch, vb. dessécher
parchment, n. parchemin m.
pardon, n. pardon m.
pare, vb. peler (fruit)
parent, n. père m.; mère f.; parents (parents) m., pl.
parentage, n. naissance f.
parenthesis, n. parenthèse f.
park, n. parc m.; vb. stationner
parley, n. conférence f.; pourparler m.
parliament, n. parlement m.
parlor, n. petit salon m.
parochial, adj. paroissial, de clocher
parody, n. parodie f.
parole, n. parole f.
parrot, n. perroquet m.
parsley, n. persil m.
parson, n. pasteur m.
part, n. partie, part f.; vb. diviser,

partager, se séparer
partial, adj. partiel, partial
participate, vb. participer
particle, n. particule f.
partition, n. partage m.; cloison f.
partner, n. associé m.
party, n. parti, groupe m.;
réception f.
pass, vb. passer, passer par
passage, n. passage m.
passenger, n. voyageur, air
passager m.
passion, n. passion f.
passive, adj. and passif m.
passport, n. passeport m.
pastime, n. passe-temps m.
pastor, n pasteur m.
pastry, n. pâtisserie f.
pasture, n. pâturage m.
pasty, adj. en pâte, pâteux
pat, vb. taper
patch, n. pièce f.; vb. rapiécer
patent, n. brevet d'invention m.
paternal, adj. paternel
paternity, n. paternité f
path, n. sentier m.
pathetic, adj pathetique
pathology, n. pathologie f.
pathos, n. pathétique m.
patience, n. patience f.
patient, n. malade m.f.; adj. patient
patio, n. patio m.
patriarch, n. patriarche m.
patriot, n. patriote m.f.
patrol, n. patrouille f.
patrolman, n. agent, patrouilleur m.
patron, n. protecteur, client m.
pattern, n. modèle, dessin m
pause, n. pause f.
paver, vb. paver
pavement, n. pavé, trottoir m.
pavillion, n. pavillon m.
pay, n. salaire m.; vb. payer
payment, n. payement m.
pea, n. pois m.
peace, n. paix f.
peach, n. pêche f.
peak, n. sommet, m.
peal, n. retentissement m.; vb.
sonner, retentir
peanut, n. arachide f.
pear, n. poire f.
pearl, n. perle f.
peasant, n. paysan m.
peck, vb. becqueter
peculiar, adj. particulier, singulier
pecuniary, adj. pécuniaire
pedagogue, n. pedagogue m.
pedagogy, n. pédagogie f.
pedal, n. pédale f.

pedant, n. pédant m.
peddle, vb. colporter
pedestal, n. piédestal m.
pedestrian, n. piéton m.
pediatrician, n. pédiatre m.
pedigree, n. généalogie f.
peel, n. pelure f.; vb. peler
pen, n. plume f.
penalty, n. peine f.
penance, n. pénitence f.
pencil, n. crayon m.
pending, prep. pendant
penetrate, vb. pénétrer
penetration, n. pénétration f.
peninsula, n. peninsule f.
penitent, adj. pénitent, contrit
penny, n. sou m.
pension, n. pension f.
pensive, adj. pensif
people, n. gens m.f, pl; peuple m.
pepper, n. poivre m.
perambulator, n. voiture d'enfant f.
perceive, vb. apercevoir
percent, pour cent
percentage, n. pourcentage m.
perceptible, adj. perceptible
perception, n. perception f.
perch, n. perchoir m.; perche f.
perdition, n. perte f.
peremptory, adj. péremptoire
perennial, adj. perpétuel, vivace
perfect, adj. parfait
perfection, n. perfection f.
perform, vb. accomplir, jouer
perfume, n. parfum m.
perhaps, adv. peut-être
peril, n. péril m.
perilous, adj. périlleux
perimeter, n. perimètre m.
period, n. période f.; point m.
periphery, n. périphérie f.
perish, vb. périr
perishable, adj. périssable
perjury, n. parjure m.
permanent, adj. permanent
permeate, vb. filtrer
permission, n. permission f.
permit, n. permis m.; vb. permettre
pernicious, adj. pernicieux
perpetrate, vb. perpétrer
perpetual, adj. perpétuel
perplex, vb. mettre dans la
perplexité
persecute, vb. persécuter
persecution, n. persécution f.
perseverance, n. persévérance f.
persevere, vb. persévérer
persist, vb. persister
person, n. personne f.
personage, n. personnage m.

personality, n. personnalité f.
personnel, n. personnel m.
perspective, n. perspective f.
perspiration, n. transpiration f.
perspire, vb. transpirer
persuade, vb. persuader
pertain, vb. appartenir
pertinent, adj. pertinent
perturb, vb. troubler
pervade, vb. pénétrer
perverse, adj. entêté
pessimism, n. pessimisme m.
pestilence, n. pestilence f.
pet, n. animal familier m.
petal, n. pétale m.
petition, n. pétition f.
petroleum, n. pétrole m.
phantom, n. fantôme m.
pharmacy, n. pharmacie f.
phase, n. phase f.
phenomenal, adj. phénoménal
philosopher, n. philosophe m.
philosophy, n. philosophie f.
phobia, n. phobie f.
phonograph, n. phonographe m.
photocopy, n. photocopie f.
phrase, n. phrase f.
physical, adj. physique
physician, n. médecin m.
piano, n. piano m.
picnic, n. pique-nique m.
picture, n. tableau m., film m.
pie, n. tarte f.
piece, n. morceau m.
pier, n. jetée f.; quai m.
pierce, vb. percer
piety, n. piété f.
pigeon, n. pigeon m.
pile, n. pieu, tas m.; vb. entasser
pilgrim, n. pèlerin m.
pill, n. pilule f.
pillar, n. pilier m.
pillow, n. oreiller m.
pilot, n. pilote m.
pin, n. épingle f.; vb. épingler
pinch, vb. pincer
pine, n. pin m.; vb. languir
pineapple, n. ananas m.
pink, adj. and n. rose m.
pinnacle, n. pinacle m.
pint, n. pinte f.
pious, adj. pieux
pipe, n. tuyau m.; pipe f.
piquant, adj. piquant
pirate, n. pirate m.
pistol, n, pistolet m.
piston, n. piston m.
pit, n. fosse f.
pitcher, n. cruche f.; lanceur m.
pitiful, adj. pitoyable

pity, n. pitié f; dommage m.; vb. plaindre
pivot, n. pivot, axe m.
pizza, n. pizza f.
place, n. endroit, lieu m.; vb. mettre
placid, adj. placide
plague, n. peste f.; fléau m.
plaid, n. plaid, tartan m.
plain, n. plaine f.; adj. clair, simple, quelconque
plaintiff, n. demandeur m.
plan, n. plan m.; vb. faire le plan de
plane, n. plan
planet, n. planète f.
plant, n. plante f.; vb. planter
plantation, n. plantation f.
planter, n. planteur m.
plasma, n. plasma m.
plaster, n. plâtre m.
plastic, adj. plastique
plate, n. plaque, assiette f.
plateau, n. plateau m.
platform, n. plate-forme f.; quai m.
platter, n. plat m.
plausible, adj. plausible
play, n. jeu m.; pièce de théâtre f.; vb. jouer, jouer à, jouer de
playmate, n. camarade de jeu m.f.
playwright, n. dramaturge m.
plea, n. défense, excuse f.
plead, vb. plaider, alléguer
pleasant, adj. agréable
please, vb. plaire à, contenter, s'il vous plaît
pleasure, n. plaisir m.
pleat, n. pli m.
pledge, n. gage, engagement m.
plenty, n. abondance f.
pliable, adj. pliable
pliers, n. pinces f., pl.
plight, n. état m.
plot, n. intrigue f.; complot m.
plow, n. charrue f.; vb. labourer
pluck, n. courage m.
plum, n. prune f.
plume, n. panache m.
plump, adj. grassouillet
plunge, n. plongeon m.; vb. plonger
plural, adj. and. pluriel m.
plus, n. plus m.
pneumonia, n. pneumonie f.
poach, vb. pocher
pocket, n. poche f.
poem, n. poésie, poème f.
poet, n. poète m.
poetry, n. poésie f.
poignant, adj. poignant
point, n. point m.
poise, n. équilibre m.
poison, n. poison m.; vb.

empoisonner
Poland, n. la Pologne f.
polar, adj. polaire
pole, n. pôle m.; perche f.
police, n. police f.
policeman, n. agent de police m.
polish, vb. polir, cirer
polite, adj. poli
politics, n. politique f.
poll, n. scrutin m.
pollute, vb. polluer
pomp, n. pompe f.
pond, n. étang m.
ponder, n. réfléchir
pony, n. poney m.
pool, n. mare, piscine f.
poor, adj. pauvre
popular, adj. populaire
population, n. population f.
poroh, n. véranda f.
pore, n. pore m.; vb. absorber dans
pork, n. porc m.
pornography, n. pornographie f.
porous, adj. preux
port, n. port, bâbord, porto m.
portable, adj. portatif
portfolio, n. portefeuille m.
portion, n. portion f.
portrait, n. portrait m.
portray, vb. peindre, dépeindre
Portugal, n. le Portugal m.
pose, n. pose f.
position, n. position f.
positive, adj. positif m.
possess, vb. posséder
possession, n. possession f.
possibility, n. possibilité f.
possible, adj. possible
possibly, adv. il est possible
post, n. poste f.; poteau, poste m.
postage, n. affranchissement m.
postal, adj. postal
post card, n. carte postale f.
posterior, adj. postérieur
posterity, n. postérité f.
post office, n. bureau de poste m.
postpone, vb. remettre
posture, n. posture f.
pot, n. pot m.; marmite f.
potato, n. pomme de terre f.
potent, adj. puissant
potential, adj. and n. potentiel m.
pottery, n. poterie f.
pouch, n. sac m.
poultry, n. volaille f.
pound, n. livre f.
pour, vb. verser, tomber à verse
poverty, n. pauvreté f.
powder, n. poudre f.
practical, adj. pratique

practiccally, ad. pratiquement
practice, n. exercice m.; habitude,
 pratique f.; vb. pratiquer
practiced, adj. expérimenté
prairie, n. savane f.
praise, n. éloge m.; vb. louer
prank, n. fredaine f.
pray, vb. prier
prayer, n. prière f.
preach, n. prêcher
preacher, n. prédicateur m.
precaution, n. précaution f.
precede, vb. précéder
precept, n. précepte m.
precious, adj. précieux
precipice, n. précipice m.
precise, adj. précis
precision, n. précision f.
preclude, vb. empêcher
precocious, adj. précoce
predict, vb. prédire
predispose, vb. prédisposer
preface, n. préface f.
prefer, vb. préférer
preferable, adj. préférable
preference, n. préférence f.
prefix, n. préfixe m.
pregnant, adj. enceinte
prejudice, n. préjugé m.
preliminary, adj. préliminaire
prelude, n. prélude m.
premature, adj. prématuré
premeditate, vb. préméditer
premier, n. premier ministre m.
première, n. première f.
premise, n. lieux m., pl.; prémisse f.
premium, n. prix m.
preparation, n. préparation f.;
 preparatifs m., pl.
prepare, vb. préparer
preponderant, adj. prépondérant
preposition, n. préposition f.
preposterous, adj. absurde
prerequisite, n. nécessité préalable
 f.
prescribe, vb. prescrire
prescription, n. prescription,
 ordonnance f.
presence, n. présence f.
presently, adv. tout à l'heure
preserve, n. confiture f.; vb.
 préserver
preside, vb présider
president, n. président m.
press, n. presse f.; vb. presser
pressure, n. pression f.
prestige, n. prestige m.
presume, vb. présumer
presumptuous, adj. présomptueux
pretend, vb. prétendre, simuler

pretense, n. faux semblant m.
prentionious, adj. préntentieux
pretext, n. prétexte m.
pretty, adj. joli
prevail, vb. prévaloir
prevalent, adj. répandu
prevent, vb. empêcher, prévenir
prevention, n. empêchement m.
preventive, adj. préventif
previous, adj. antérieur
prey, n. proie f.
price, n. prix m.
priceless, adj. inestimable
prick, n. piqûre f.
pride, n. orgueil m.
priest, n. prêtre m.
prim, adj. affecté
primary, adj. premier, primaire
prime, n. combine m.; adj. premier, de première qualité
primitive, adj. primitif
prince, n. prince m.
principal, adj. principal
principle, n. principe m.
print, n. empreinte, impression, épreuve f.; vb. imprimer
priority, n. priorité f.
prism, n. prisme m.
prison, n. prison f.
privacy, n. retraite f.
private, adj. particulier privé
privation, n. privation f.
prize, n. prix m.
probability, n. probabilité f.
probable, adj. probable
probe, vb. sonder
problem, n. problème m.
procedure, n. procédé m.
proceed, vb. procéder, avancer
process, n. procédé m.
proclaim, vb. proclamer
procure, vb. procurer
prodigal, adj. and n. prodigue m.
prodigy, n. prodige m.
produce, vb. produire
product, n. produit m.
production, n. production f.
productive, adj. productif
profane, adj. profane
profess, vb. professer
professional, adj. professionnel
professor, n. professeur m.
proficient, adj. capable
profile, n. profil m.
profit, n. profit m.
profound, adj. profond
profuse, adj. profus, prodigue
program n. programme m.
progress, n. progrès m.; marche f.
prohibit, vb. défendre

prohibition, n. défense f.
prohibitive, adj. prohibitif
project, n. projet m.; vb. projeter, faire saillie
proliferation, n. prolifération f.
prolong, vb. prolonger
prominent, adj. saillant
promiscuous, adj. sans distinction
promise, n. promesse f.
promote, vb. promouvoir, encourager
prompt, adj. prompt
pronounce, vb. prononcer
pronunciation, n. prononciation f.
proof, n. preuve, épreuve f.
prop, n. appui
propagate, vb. propager
proper, adj. propre, convenable
property, n. propriété f.
prophecy, n. prophétie f.
prophesy, vb. prophétiser
prophet, n. prophète m.
proportion, n. proportion f.
proportionate, adj. proportionné
proposal, n. proposition, demande en mariage f.
propose, vb. proposer
proposition, n. proposition, affaire f.
proprietor, n. propriétaire m.f.
proscribe, vb. proscrire
prose, n. prose f.
prosecute, vb. poursuivre
prospect, n. perspective f.
prospective, adj. en perspective
prosper, vb. prospérer
prosperity, n. prospérité f.
prosperous, adj. prospère
prostrate, adj. prosterné
protect, vb. protéger
protégé n. protégé m.
protein, n. protéine f.
protest, n. protestation f.; protêt m.; vb. protester
protocol, n. protocole m.
protrude, vb. saillir
prove, vb. prouver, éprouver
proverb, n. proverbe m.
provide, vb. pourvoir, fournir
province, n. province f.
provision, n. provision f.
provocation, n. provocation f.
provoke, vb. provoquer, irriter
prowl, vb. rôder
proximity, n. proximité f.
prudence, n. prudence f.
prudent, adj. prudent
prune, n. pruneau m.
psalm, n. psaume m.
psychiatry, n. psychiatrie f.

psychology, n. psychologie f.	**quandary**, n. embarras m.
public, n. public m.; adj. public m.; publique f.	**quantitative**, adj. quantitatif
publicaton, n. publication f.	**quantity**, n. quantité f.
publish, vb. publier	**quarnatine**, n. quarantaine f.
pudding, n. pouding m.	**quarrel**, n. querelle f.
puddle, n. flaque f.	**quarreler**, n. querelleur m.
pull, vb. tirer	**quarrelling**, n. querelle f.
pulp, n. pulpe f.	**quarry**, n. carrière f.
pulpit, n. chaire f.	**quart**, n. quart de gallon m.
pulsate, vb. battre	**quartan**, n. fièvre quarte f.
pulse, n. pouls m.	**quarter**, n. quart, quartier m.
pump, n. pompe f.; vb. pomper	**quarterly**, adj. trimestriel
pumpkin, n. potiron m.	**quartern**, n. quart de pinte m.
punctual, adj. ponctuel	**quartet**, n. quatuor m.
punctuate, vb. ponctuer	**quartz**, n. quartz m.
puncture, n. piqûre f.	**quasar**, n. quasar m.
punish, vb. punir	**quaver**, vb. chevroter
punishment, n. punition f.	**quavering**, n. trille, trémolo m.; cadence f.
pupil, n. elève m.f.; pupille f.	**quay**, n. quai m.; vb. garnir de quais
puppet, n. marionnette f.	**queasiness**, n. nausées f., pl.
purchase, n. achat m.; vb. acheter	**queasy**, adj. sujet à des nausees
pure, adj. pur	**queen**, n. reine f.
puree, n. purée f.	**queen bee**, n. reine-abeille f.
purge, vb. purger	**queer**, adj. bizarre, étrange, drôle
purpose, n. but m.	**quell**, vb. réprimer
purse, n. bourse f	**queller**, n. personne qui réprime f.
pursue, vb. poursuivre	**quench**, vb. éteindre, étancher
pursuit, n. poursuite, occupation f.	**quenchable**, adj. extingible
push, n. poussée f.; vb. pousser	**quencher**, n. personne f.
put, vb. mettre	**querulous**, adj. plaintiff, maussade
puzzle, n. problème m.; vb. embarrasser	**querulously**, adv. d'un ton dolent en se plaignant
pyramid, n. pyramide f.	**query**, n. question f.
python, n. pythonisse f.	**quest**, n. recherche f.
	question, n. question f.; vb. interroger, mettre en doute
Q	**questionable**, adj. douteux
	questioning, n. questions f.
	question mark, n. point d'interrogation m.
quack, n, charlatan, empirique	**questionnaire**, n. questionnaire m.
quackery, n. charlatanisme m.	**quibble**, n. argutie, chicane f.
quackish, adj. de charlatan	**quick**, adj. rapide, vif; adv. vite
quad, cadrat m.	**quicken**, vb. accélérer
quaestor, n. questeur m.	**quickening**, adj. vivifiant, qui ranime
quag, n. fondrière f.	**quiet**, n. tranquillité f.; adj. tranquille
quail, n. caille f.	**quietness**, n. tranquillement
quaint, adj. étrange	**quill**, n. (for writing) plume d'oie f.
quake, vb. trembler	**quilling**, n. tuyautage m.
Quaker, n. Quakeresse f.; Quakeress n.	**quilt**, n. courtepointe f.
quaking, n. tremblement m.	**quilting**, adj. quinaire
quakingly, adv. en tremblant	**quinaine**, n. quinine f.
qualifiable, adj. qualifiable	**quint**, n. quinte f.
qualification, n. réserve; compétence, qualification f.	**quintain**, n. quintaine f.
qualify, vb. qualifier, modifier	**quinte**, n. quinte f.
qualifying, adj. qualificatif	**quip**, n. mot piquant m.
quality, n. qualité f.	**quirk**, n. sarcasme m.
qualm, n. scrupule m.	

quit, vb. quitter, abandonner
quite, adv. tout à fait
quitter, n. personne qui quitte f.
quiver, vb. trembler
quivering, n. tremblement m.
quiz, n. petit examen m.; vb. examiner
quizzing, n. raillerie f.
quoin, n. coin m.
quoit, n. palet
quorum, n. quorum m.
quota, n. quote-part f.; contingent m.
quotation, n. citation, cote f.
quote, vb. citer

R

rabbi, n. rabbin m.
rabbit, n. lapin
rabble, n. tourbe f.
rabid, adj. enragé
rabies, n. rage, hydrophobie f.
race, n. (people) race f.; vb. lutter à la course
race-track, n. piste f.
rack, n. râtelier, (torture) chevalet de torture m.
racket, n. (tennis) raquette f.; (noise) tintamarre m.
racoon, n. raton laveur m.
racy, adj. qui a un goût de terroir
radar, n. radar m.
raddle, n. ocre rouge f.
radiance, n. _lat m.
radiant, adj. radieux
radiate, vb. irradier
radiation, n. rayonnement m.
radical, adj. and n. radical m.
radicular, adj. radiculaire
radio, n. télégraphie sans fil f.
radioactive, adj. radio-actif
radish, n. radis m.
radium, n. radium m.
radius, n. rayon m.
raffle, n. loterie, tombola f.
rag, n. chiffon m.
ragamuffin, n. gueux, polisson
rage, n. rage, fureur f.
ragged, adj. en haillons
ragweed, n. ambroisie f.
raid, n. (police) descente f.
rail, n. barre f.
railroad, n. chemin de fer m.
railway, n. chemin de fer m.
raiment, n. vêtement m.
rain, n. pluie f.; vb. pleu-voir

raincoat, n. imperméable m.
rainfall, n. chute de pluie f.
rainy, adj. pluvieux
raise, vb. (bring up,) élever; (lift) lever; cultiver
raisin, n. raisin sec m.
rake, n. râteau m.; vb. râteler
raking, n. ratissage m.
rally, n. ralliement, rassemblement m.
ram, n. bélier m.
ramification, n. ramification f.
rammer, n. pilon m.
ramp, n. rampe f.
rampart, n. rempart m.
ramrod, n. baguette f.
ramshackle, adj. qui tombe en ruines
ranch, n. ranch m.
rancid, adj. rance
random, n. hasard m.
range, n. étendue, portée f.
rank, n. rang m.; vb. ranger
ransack, vb. fouiller; (pillage) saccager
ransom, n. rançon f.
rant, n. déclamation extravagante f.
rap, n. coup m.; vb. frapper
rapid, adj. and n. rapide m.
rapper, n. frappeur, râfleur d'antiquités m.
rapture, n. ravissement m.
rare, adj. rare
rarely, adv. rarement
rascal, n. coquin m.
rask, n. éruption f.; adj. téméraire
raspberry, n. framboise f.
rat, n. rat m.
rate, n. taux m.; vitesse f.
rather, adv. plutôt
ratify, vb. ratifier
ration, n. ration f.
rational, adj. raisonnable
rattle, n. (toy) hochet, (noise) fracas m.; vb. faire claquer
rave, vb. délirer; (rave about) s'extasier sur
raven, n. corbeau m.
raw, adj. cru
ray, n. rayon m.
rayon, n. rayonne f.
razor, n. rasoir m.
reach, n. portée f.; vb. atteindre; étendre, arriver à
react, vb. réagir
reaction, n. reaction f.
reactionary, adj. réactionnaire
read, vb. lire
reader, n. (person) lecteur m.
readily, adv. promptement

ready, adj. prêt
real, adj. réel
realist, n. réaliste m.f.
reality, n. réalité f.
realization, n. réalisation f.
realize, vb. s'apercevoir de, réaliser
really, adv. vraiment
realm, n. royaume m.
reap, vb. moissonner
rear, n. queue f.; adj. situé à l'arrière
reason, n. raison,; vb. raisonner
reasonable, adj. raisonnable
reassure, vb. rassurer
rebate, n. rabais m.
rebel, adj. and n. rebelle m.f
rebellion, n. rébellion f.
rebellious, adj. rebelle
rebirth, n. renaissance f.
rebound, vb. rebond m.
rebuke, n. réprimande f.; vb. réprimander
rebuttal, n. réfutation f.
recall, vb. (remember) se rappeler
recede, vb. s'éloigner
receipt, n. quittance f.
receive, vb. recevoir
receiver, n. (phone) récepteur m.
recent, adj. récent
receptacle, n. réceptacle m.
reception, n. réception f.; accueil m.
receptive, adj. réceptif
recess, n. recoin m.; vacances f., pl.; récréation f.
recipe, n. recette f.
reciprocate, vb. payer de retour
recite, vb. réciter
reckless, adj. téméraire
reckon, vb. compter
reclaim, vb. défricher
recline, vb. reposer
recognition, n. reconnaissance f.
recognize, vb. reconnaître
recoil, vb. reculer
recollect, vb. se rappeler
recommend, vb. recommander
recommendation, n. recommandation f.
recompense, n. récompense f.
reconcile, vb. réconcilier
record, n. registre, antécédents m.; mention f.; vb. enregistrer
recount, vb. raconter
recover, vb. recouvrer, se rétablir
recovery, n. recouvrement, rétablissement m.
recruit, n. recrue f.; vb. recruter
rectangle, n. rectangle m.
rectify, vb. rectifier

recuperate, vb. recouvrer se rétablir
recur, vb. revenir
recycle, vb. recycler
red, adj. and n. rouge m.
redeem, vb. racheter
redemption, n. rachat m.
redress, n. justice f.; vb. redresser, réparer, faire justice à
reduce, vb. réduire
reed, n. roseau m.; (music) anche f.
reef, n. récif m.
reel, n. bobine f.
refer, vb. référer
referee, n. arbitre m.
reference, n. référence f.
refill, vb. remplir
refine, vb. raffiner
reflect, vb. réfléchir
reflection, n. réflexion f.
reform, n. réforme f.; vb. réformer
reformation, n. réforme f.
refractory, adj. réfractaire
refrain from, vb. se retenir de
refresh, vb. rafraîchir
refreshment, n. rafraîchissement m.
refrigerator, n. réfrigérateur m.
refuge, n refuge m.
refugee, n. réfugié m.
refund, n. remboursement m. vb. rembourser
refusal, n. refus m.
refuse, n. rebut m.; vb. refuser
refute, vb. réfuter
regain, vb. regagner
regal, adj. royal
regard, n. égard m.; amitiés f., pl.; vb. regarder
regent, adj. and n. régent m.
regime, n. régime m.
regiment, n. régiment m.
region, n. région f.
register, n. registre m.; vb. enregistrer, recommander
regret, n. regret m.; vb. regretter
regular, adj. régulier
regularity, n. régularité f.
regulate, vb. régler
regulation, n. règlement m.
regulator, n. régulateur m.
rehabilitate, vb. réhabiliter
rehearse, vb. répéter
reign, n. règne m.; vb. régner
rein, n. rêne f.
reindeer, n. renne m.
reinforce, vb. renforcer
reinforcement, n. renfort m.
reject, vb. rejeter
rejoice, vb. réjouir
rejoin, vb. rejoindre; (reply)

répliquer

relapse, n. rechute f.

relate, vb. raconter, se rapporter (à) (relate to); entrer en rapport avec

relation, n. relation f.; (relative) parent m.

relative, n. parent m.; adj. relatif

relax, vb. relâcher

relay, n. relais m.; vb. relayer

release, n. délivrance f.; vb. libérer

relent, vb. se laisser attendrir

relevant, adj. pertinent

reliabiltiy, n. sûreté f.

reliable, adj. digne de confiance

reliant, adj. confiant

relic, n. relique f.

relief, n. (ease) soulagement, (help) secours, (projection) relief m.

relieve, vb. (ease) soulager, secourir

religion, n. religion f.

religious, adj. religieux

relish, n. goût m.; vb. goûter

reluctant, adj. peu disposé (à)

rely (upon), vb. compter (sur)

remain, vb. rester

remainder, n. reste m.

remark, n. remarque f.; vb. remarquer

remarkable, adj. remarquable

remedy, n. remède m.; vb. rémédier à

remember, vb. se souvenir de

reminisce, vb. raconter ses souvenirs

remit, vb. remettre

remnant, n. reste, vestige, coupon m.

remorse, n. remords m.

remote, adj. éloigné, vague

removal, n. enlèvement m.

remove, vb. enlever

rend, vb. déchirer

render, vb. rendre

renew, vb. renouveler

renewal, n. renouvellement m.

renounce, vb. renoncer à, répudier

renovate, vb. renouveler

renown, n. renommée f.

rent, n. réparation f.; vb. réparer

repay, vb. rendre, (refund) rembourser

repeat, vb. répéter

repel, vb. repousser

repent, vb. se repentir

repertoire, n. répertoire m.

repetition, n. répétition f.

replace, vb. replacer; (take the place of) remplacer

reply, n. réponse f.; vb. répondre

report, n. rapport m.; vb. rapporter

repose, n. repos m.

represent, vb. représenter

representation, n. représentation f.

repress, vb. réprimer

reprimand, n. réprimande f.

reproduce, vb. reproduire

reproduction, n. reproduction f.

reproof, n. réprimande f.

reprove, vb. réprimander

reptile, n. reptile m.

republic, n. république f.

republican, adj. and n. républicain m.

repulsive, adj. répulsif

reputation, n. réputation f.

repute, n. renom m.; vb. réputer

request, n. requête f.; vb. demander

require, vb. exiger

requirement, n. exigence f.

requisite, adj. nécessaire

requisition, n. réquisition f.

rescue, n. délivrance f.; vb. délivrer

research, n. recherche f.

resemble, vb. ressembler à

resent, vb. être froissé de

reservation, n. réserve

reserve, n. réserve f.; vb. réserver

reservoir, n. réservoir m.

reside, vb. résider

residence, n. résidence f.

resident, n. habitant m.; adj. résidant

resign, vb. résigner; se démettre (de)

resignation, n. résignation, démission f.

resist, vb. résister (à)

resistance, n. résistance f.

resolute, adj. résolu

resolution, n. résolution f.

resolve, vb. résoudre

resonant, adj. résonnant

resound, vb. résonner

resource, n. ressource f.

respect, n. respect, (reference) rapport m.; vb. respecter

respectable, adj. respectable

respectful, adj. respectueux

respective, adj. respectif

respiration, n. respiration f.

respite, n. répit m.

respond, vb. répondre

response, n. réponse f.

responsibility, n. responsabilité f.

responsible, adj. responsable

rest, n. repos, (remainder) reste m.; les autres m.f., pl.; vb. se reposer

restaurant, n. restaurant m.

restful, adj. qui repose
restrain, vb. contenir
restraint, n. contrainte f.
restrict, vb. restreindre
result, n. résultat m.; vb. résulter
resume, vb. reprendre
résumé, n. résumé m.
resurrect, vb. ressusciter
retail, n. détail m.
retain, vb. retenir
retaliate, vb. user de représailles
retard, vb. retarder
reticent, adj. réservé
retire, vb. se retirer
retort, n riposte f.
retreat, n. retraite f.; vb. se retirer
retrieve, vb. recouvrer
reunion, n. réunion f.
reveal, vb. révéler
revel, vb. s'ébattre
revelation, n. révélation f.
revenue, n. revenu m.
revere, vb. révérer
reverend, adj. révérend
reverent, adj. respectueux
reverie, n. rêverie f.
revert, vb. revenir
review, n. revue f.
revise, vb. réviser
revoke, vb. révoquer
revolt, n. révolte f.; vb. se révolter
revolution, n. révolution f.
revolutionary, adj. révolutionnaire
revolve, vb. tourner
revolver, n. revolver m.
reward, n. récompense f.;
 vb. récompenser
rheumatism, n, rhumatisme m.
rhinoceros, n rhinocéros m.
rhubarb, n. rhubarbe f.
rhyme, n. rime f.; vb. rimer
rhythm, n. rythme m.
rhythmical, adj. rythmique
rib, n. côte f.
ribbon, n. ruban m.
rice, n. riz m.
rich, adj. riche
rid, vb. débarrasser
riddle, n. énigme f.
ride, n. promenade f.; vb. (horse)
 aller à cheval; (vehicle) aller en
 voiture
rider, n. cavalier m.
ridge, n. crête f.
ridiculous, adj. ridicule
rifle, n. fusil m.
right, n. droit m.; adj. (correct,
 proper) juste; avoir raison bien
righteous, adj. juste
rigid, adj. rigide

rigor, n. rigueur f.
rigorous, adj. rigoureux
rim, n. bord m.; (wheel) jante f.
ring, n. anneau m.; (ornament)
 bague f.; (circle) cercle
rip, n. fente f.; vb. fendre
ripe, adj. mûr
ripple, n. ride f.; vb. rider
rise, n. (increase) augmentation f.;
 (rank) avancement m.; vb. se lever
risk, n. risque m.; vb. risquer
rite, n. rite m.
ritual, adj. rituel
river, n. fleuve m.
rivet, n. rivet m.
road, n. route f.
roam, vb. errer
roast, n. rôti m.; vb. rôtir
rob, vb. voler
robber, n. vol m.
robe, n. robe f.
robin, n. rouge-gorge m.
robot, n. automate m.
robust, adj. robuste
rock, n. rocher m.; vb. balancer; (child) bercer
rocket, n. fusée f.
rocky, adj. rochoux
rod, n. verge f.
rodent, adj. and n. rongeur m.
rogue, n. coquin m.
roguish, adj. coquin
role, n. rôle m.
Roman, n. Romain m.; adj. romain
romance, n. roman de chevalerie
 m.
romantic, adj. romanesque;
 romantique
romp, n. tapage m.; vb. batifoler
roof, n. toit m.
room, n. place, chambre, salle f.
root, n. racine, (source) source f.;
 vb. enraciner
rope, n. corde f.
rosary, n. rosaire m.
rose, n. rose f.
rosin, n. colophane f.
rosy, adj. de rose
rot, n. pourriture f.; vb. pourrir
rotary, adj. rotatoire
rotate, vb. tourner
rotation, n. rotation f.
rouge, n. rouge m.
rough, adj. rude; (sea weather)
 gros m.; grosse f.
round adj. round, l'aller et le retour
 m.; n. rond m.; (circuit) tournée f.
rouse, vb. (wake) réveiller, secouer
rout, n. (mil.) déroute f.
route, n. route f.

routine, n. routine f.
rove, vb. errer (par)
rover, n. rôdeur m.
row, n. rang m.; dispute f.; vb. ramer
rowdy, adj. tapageur
royal, adj. royal
rub, vb. frotter
rubber, n. caoutchouc m.
ruby, n. rubis m.
ruddy, adj. rouge
rudiment, n. rudiment m.
rue, vb. regretter
ruffian, n. bandit m.
ruffle, n. fraise f.; vb. froncer
rug, n. tapis m.
ruler, n. souverain m.; règle f.
rum, n. rhum m.
Rumania, n. la Roumanie f.
rumba, n. rumba f.
rumble, vb. gronder
rumor, n. rumeur f.
run, vb. courir, marcher, déteindre, couler, s'enfuir
rung, n. échelon m.
rupture, n. rupture f.
rural, adj. rural
rush, n. (haste) hâte, ruée f.; coup, jonc m.; vb. se précipiter
Russia, n. la Russie f.
rust, n. rouille f.; vb. rouiller
rustle, n. (leaves) bruissement m.
rusty, adj. rouillé
rut, n. ornière f.
ruthless, adj. impitoyable
rye, n. seigle m.

S

Sabbath, n. sabbat m.
saber, n. sabre m.
sable, n. zibeline f.
sabotage. n. sabotage m.; vb. saboter
saboteur, n. saboteur m.
saccharin, n. saccharine f.
sachet, n. sachet m.
sack, n. sac m.; vb. saccager
sacrament, n. sacrement m.
sacred, adj. sacré
sacrifice, n. sacrifice m.; vb. sacrifier
sacrilege, n. sacrilège m.
sad, adj. triste
sadden, vb. attrister
saddle, n. selle f.; vb. seller
sail, n. voile f.; vb. faire voile
sailor, n. marin m.

saint, adj. and n. saint m.
salad, n. salade f.
salary, n. appointements m., pl.
sale, n. vente f.
saliva, n. salive f.
salmon, n. saumon m.
salt, n. sel m.; vb. saler
salute, n. salut m.; vb. saluer
salvage, n. sauvetage m.
salvation, n. salut m.
salve, n. onguent m.
sample, n. échantillon m.
sanatorium, n. sanatorium m.
sanctify, vb. sanctifier
sanction, n. sanction f.
sanctuary, n. sanctuaire m.
sand, n. sable m.
sandal, n. sandale f.
sandwich, n. sandwich m.
sane, adj. sain d'esprit
sanity, n. santé d'esprit f.
sap, n. sève f.
sapphire, n. saphir m.
sarcasm, n. sarcasme m.
sardine, n. sardine f.
satellite, n. satellite m.
satin, n. satin m.
satire, n. satire f.
satisfaction, n. satisfaction f.
satisfactory, adj. satisfaisant
saturate, vb. saturer
Saturday, n. samedi m.
sauce, n. sauce f.
saucer, n. soucoupe f.
sausage, n. saucisse f.
savage, adj. and n. sauvage m.f.
savior, n. sauveur m.
savor, n. saveur f.
saw, n. scie f.; vb. scier
say, vb. dire
scab, n. croûte, gale f.
scald, vb. échauder
scalp, n. cuir chevelu m.; vb. scalper
scan, vb. (examine) scruter
scandal, n. scandale m.
scar, n. cicatrice f.
scarce, adj. rare
scare, vb. effrayer; n. panique f.
scarf, n. écharpe f.
scathing, adj. cinglant
scatter, vb. éparpiller
scenario, n. scénario m.
scene, n. scène f.
scenery, n. (landscape) paysage m.
scent, n. parfum m.; odeur f.; vb. flairer, sentir
schedule, n. plan m.
scheme, n. plan m.
scholar, n. savant m.

scholarship, n. (school) bourse f.

school, n. école f.

sciatica, n. sciatique f.

science, n. science f.

scientist, n. homme de science m.

scissors, n. ciseaux m., pl.

scoff at, vb. se moquer de

scold, vb. gronder

scoop out, vb. évider

scorch, vb. roussir

Scotland, n. l'Écosse f.

scour, vb. nettoyer

scourge, n. fléau m.

scout, n. éclaireur, boy-scout m.

scowl, vb. se renfrogner

scramble, vb. avancer péniblement

scream, n. cri m.; vb. crier

screen, n. écran m.; (folding
  screen) paravent m.

screw, n. vis f.; vb. visser

scribble, vb. griffonner

scroll, n. rouleau m.

scrub, vb. frotter

scruple, n. scrupule m.

scrupulous, adj. scrupuleux

scrutinize, vb. scruter

sculptor, n. sculpteur m.

sculpture, n. sculpture f.

scythe, n. faux f.

sea, n. mer f.

seam, n. couture f.

seaport, n. port de mer m.

search, n. recherche f.; vb.
  chercher

season, n. saison f.; vb.
  assaisonner

seat, n. siège m.; vb. asseoir

secondary, adj. secondaire

secret, adj. and n. secret m.

secretary, adj. secrétaire m.f.

sect, n. secte f.

section, n. section f.

sedative, adj. and n. sédatif m.

seduce, vb. séduire

see, vb. voir

seek, vb. chercher

seem, vb. sembler

segment, n. segment m.

segregate, vb. séparer

seize, vb. saisir

seldom, adv. rarement

select, vb. choisir

self, n. moi m.; personne f.

selfish, adj. égoïste(me)

sell, vb. vendre

semantics, n. sémantique f.

semester, n. semestre m.

semicircle, n. demi-cercle m.

seminary, n. séminaire m.

senate, n. sénat m.

senator, n. sénateur m.

senile, adj. sénile

sensation, n. sensation f.

sense, n. sens m.

sensitive, adj. sensible

sentiment, n. sentiment m.

September, n. septembre m.

serenade, n. sérénade f.

serene, adj. serein

sergeant, n. sergent m.

serious, adj. sérieux

sermon, n. sermon m.

serpent, n. serpent m.

serum, n. sérum m.

serve, vb. servir

srvice, n. service, (church) office m.

session, n. session f.

seven, adj. and n. sept m.

seventeen, adj. and n. dix-sept m.

seventh, adj. and n. septième m.

sever, vb. séparer, couper

several, adj. and pron. plusieurs

sever, adj. sévère

sew, vb. coudre

sex, n. sexe m.

sexton, n. sacristain m.

shadow, n. ombre f.

shaggy, adj. poilu, hirsute

shallow, adj. peu profond

shame, n. honte f.

shameful, adj. honteux

shampoo, n. shampooing m.

shape, n. forme f.; vb. former

share, n. part, (finance) action f.;
  vb. partager

shark, n. requin m.

sharp, adj. (cutting) tranchant;
  (clever) fin; (piercing) perçant;
  (music) dièse

shatter, vb. briser

shave, vb. raser

shawl, n. châle m.

she, pron. elle

sheaf, n. (grain) gerbe f.

sheath, n. étui m.

shed, n. hangar m.; vb. verser

sheep, n. mouton m.

sheet, n. (bed) drap m.; (paper,
  metal) feuille f.

shelf, n. rayon m.

shelter, n. abri m.; vb. abriter

shepherd, n. berger m.

sherbet, n. sorbet m.

sherry, n. xérès m.

shield, n. bouclier m.

shine, vb. briller, intr. (shoes) cirer

ship, n. navire, vaisseau m.

shipment, n. envoi m.

shirk, vb. esquiver

shirt, n. chemise f.

shiver, n. frisson m.; vb. frissonner
shock, n. choc m.; vb. choquer
shoe, n. soulier m.
shore, n. rivage m.
short, adj. court
shot, n. coup m.
should, vb. devoir (in conditional)
shoulder, n. épaule f.
shout, n. cri m.; vb. crier
shove, vb. pousser
shovel, n. pelle f.
shower, n. averse f.
shrewd, adj. sagace
shriek, n. cri perçant m.
shrill, adj. aigu
shrimp, n. crevette f.
shrine, n. châsse f.
shrink, vb. rétrécir
shroud, n. linceul m.
shudder, n. frisson m.; vb.
 frissonner
shun, vb. fuir
shut, vb. fermer
shy, adj. timide
sick, adj. malade
side, n. côte f.
siege, n. siège m.
sieve, n. tamis m.
sift, vb. cribler
sigh, n. soupir m.; vb. soupirer
signature, n. signature f.
significant, adj. significatif
signify, vb. signifier
silence, n. silence m.
silent, adj. silencieux
silk, n. soie f.
silken, adj. de soie
silver, n. argent m.; adj. d'argent
similar, adj. semblable
simple, adj. simple
simply adv. simplement
simultaneous, adj. simultané
sin, n. péché m.; vb. pécher
since, adv. prep. depuis; conj.
 (time) depuis que; (cause) puisque
sincere, adj. sincère
sincerity, n. sincérité f.
singer, n. chanteur m.
single, adj. (one) seul; (particular)
 particulier; (not married) célibataire
singular, adj. and n. singulier m.
sinner, n. pécheur m.; pécheresse
 f.
sinus, n. sinus m.
sip, vb. siroter
sir, n. monsieur m.
sirloin, n. aloyau m.
sister, n. soeur f.
sister-in-law, n. belle-soeur f.
sit, vb. (sit down) s'asseoir; (be

seated) être assis
site, n. emplacement m.
situate, vb. situer
situation, n. situation f.
six, adj. and n. six m.
sixteen, adj. and n. seize m.
sixth, adj. and n. sixième m.
size, n. grandeur, (person)
 taille, (shoes, gloves) pointure f.
skate, n. patin m.
skeleton, n. squelette m.
sketch, n. croquis m.; vb. esquisser
ski, n. ski m.; vb. faire du ski
skill, n. adresse f.
skim, vb. (milk) écrémer; (book)
 feuilleter; (surface) effleurer
skin, n. peau f.; vb. écorcher
skip, vb. sauter
skirt, n. jupe f.
sky, n. ciel m.
slab, adj. lâche; n. dalle, plaque f.
slacken, vb. (slow up) ralentir;
 (loosen) relâcher
slacks, n. pantalon m.
slander, n. calomnie f.; vb.
 calomnier
slang, n. argot m.
slant, n. inclinaison, pente f.
slap, n. claque f.
slate, n. ardoise f.
slave, n. esclave m.f.
slay, vb. tuer
sled, n. traîneau m.
sleet, n. neige à moitié fondue f.
sleeve, n. manche f.
sleigh, n. traîneau m.
slender, adj. mince, svelte
slice, n. tranche f.
slight, adj. léger, mince
slim, adj. svelte
slit, n. fente f.; vb. fendre
slope, n. pente f.; vb. incliner
slot, n. fente f.
slow, adj. lent, tardif
slowness, n. lenteur f.
sluggish,m adj. paresseux
slumber, vb. sommeiller
sly, adj. (crafty) fusé
small, adj. petit
smart, adj. (clever) habile, (stylish)
 élégant; vb. cuire
smash, vb. briser
smear, n. tache f.; vb. salir
smell, n. odeur f.; vb. sentir
smelt, n. éperlan, m; vb. fondre
smile, n. vb. sourire m.
smite, vb. frapper
smoke, n. fumée f.; vb. fumer
smolder, vb. couver
smooth, adj. lisse; vb. lisser

smother, vb. étouffer

snack, n. casse-croûte m.

snag, n. obstacle caché m.

snail, n. escargot m.

snake, n. serpent m.

snare, n. piège m.

snarl, vb. grogner

snatch, vb. saisir

sneak, vb. se glisser furtivement

sneer, vb. ricaner; n. rire

snob, n. snob m.

snow, n. neige f.; vb. neiger

snug, adj. confortable

so, adv. si; tellement; (thus) ainsi

soak, vb. tremper

soap, n. savon m.

soar, vb. prendre son essor

sociable, adj. sociable

social, adj. social

sock, n. chaussette f.

socket, n. douille f.

sod, n. motte f.

sofa, n. canapé m.

soft, adj. doux m., douce f. (yielding) mou m., molle f.

soil, n. terrier m.; vb. souiller

sojourn, n. séjour m.; vb. séjourner

solace, n. consolation f

solar, adj. solaire

soldier, n. soldat m.

sole, n. (shoe) semelle, (fish) sole f.

solicit, vb. solliciter

solid, adj. and n. solide n.

solitary, adj. solitaire

solitude, n. solitude f.

solution, n. solution f.

solve, vb. résoudre

somber, adj. sombre

some, adj. quelque m. or f.

somebody, someone, pron. quelqu'un

something, pron. quelque chose m.

somewhat, adv. quelque peu

somewhere, adv. quelque part

son, n. fils m.

song, n. chant m.; chanson f.

son-in-law, n. gendre m.

soon, adv. bientôt, tôt

soot, n. suie f.

soothe, vb. calmer

sophisticated, adj. blasé

soprano, n. soprano m.

sordid, adj. sordide

sore, adj. douloureux, endolori, susceptible

sorrow, n. douleur f.

sorrowful, adj. affligé, triste

sorry, adj. fâché, désolé

sort, n. sorte f.; vb. trier

soul, n. âme f.

sound, adj. en bon état, bon; vb. sonner, retentir

soup, n. potage n.

sour, adj. aigre

source, n. source f.

south, n. sud m.

southeast, n. sud-est m.

southern, adj. du sud

souvenir, n. souvenir m.

sow, vb. semer

space, n. espace m.

spacious, adj. spacieux

spade, n. bêche f.; (cards) pique m.

Spain, n. l'Espagne f.

span, n. empan m.; (bridge) travée f.

spank, vb. fesser

spanking, n. fessée f.

spark, n. étincelle f.

sparkle, vb. étinceler

spasm, n. spasme m.

speak, vb. parler

speaker, n. (public) orateur m.

special, adj. spécial

species, n. espèce f.

specify, vb. spécifier

speciment, n. spécimen m.

spectacle, n. spectacle m.

spectator, n. spectateur m.

speculate, vb. spéculer

speed, n. vitesse f.

spend, vb. (money) dépenser; (time) passer

sphere, n. sphère f.

spice, n. épice f.

spider, n. araignée f.

spill, vb. répandre

spin, vb. (thread) filer; tourner

spinach, n. épinards m., pl.

spine, n. épine dorsale f.

spirit, n. esprit m.

spiritual, adj. spirituel

spit, n. crachat m., salive f.

spite, n. dépit m.

splash, vb. éclabousser

splendid, adj. splendide

splendor, n. splendeur f.

split, vb. fendre

spoil, n. butin m.; vb. gâter

sponge, n. éponge f.

sponsor, n. (law) garant m.

spontaneous, adj. spontané

spool, n. bobine f.

spoon, n. cuiller f.

sporadic, adj. sporadique

sport, n. sport, (fun) jeu m.

spouse, n. époux m.; épouse f.

spout, n. bec m.; vb. jaillir

sprain, n. entorse f.

sprawl, vb. s'étaler
spead, n. étendue f.; vb. étendre
sprightly, adj. éveillé
sprinkle, vb. asperger
spry, adj. alerte
spur, n. éperon m.; vb. éperonner
spurious, adj. faux m.
spurn, vb. repousser
spurt, n. jet m.; vb. jaillir
squad, n. escouade f.
squadron, n. escadron m.
squalid, adj. misérable
squall, n. rafale f.
squander, vb. gaspiller
square, n. (geom.) carré m.; adj.
 carré
squat, vb. s'accroupir
squeak, vb. crier
squeeze, vb. serrer, presser
squirrel, n. écureuil m.
squirt, vb. seringuer
stab, vb. poignarder
stability, n. stabilité f.
stable, n. écurie f.; adj. stalle
staff, n. bâton, (personnel)
 personnel m.
stage, n. estrade, scène, phase f.
stagflation, n. stagflation f.
stagger, vb. (totter) chanceler
stagnant, adj. stagnant
stain, n. tache f.; vb. (spot)
 tacher; (color) teinter
stairs, n. escalier m.
stale, adj. (bread) rassis
stalk, n. tige f.
stall, n. (stable, church) stalle f.
stamina, n. vigueur f.
stammer, vb. bégayer
stampede, n. sauve-qui-peut n.
star, n. étoile, (movie) vedette f.
starch, n. amidon m.
stare, vb. regarder fixement
stark, adj. pur
starvation, n. faim f.
starve, vb. intr. mourir de faim
state, n. état m.; vb. déclarer
statement, n. déclaraton f.
statesman, n. homme d'état m.
static, adj. statique
stationary, adj. stationnaire
stationery, n. papeterie f.
statistics, n. statistique f.
statue, n. statue f.
stay, vb. rester
steady, adj. ferme, soutenu
steak, n. bifteck m.
steal, vb. voler
steam, n. vapeur f.
steep, adj. raide
steeple, n. clocher m.

stem, n. (plant) tige f.
stenographer, n. sténographe m.f.
stenography, n, sténographie f.
sterile, adj. stérile
stern, adj. sévère
stethoscope, n. stéthoscope m.
stew, n. ragoût m.
stick, n. bâton m.; vb.
 (paste) coller
stiff, adj. raide
stifle, vb. étouffer
stimulant, n. stimulant m.
stimulate, vb. stimuler
stimulus, n. stimulant m.
stingy, adj. mesquin
stitch, n. (sewing) point m.;
 (knitting) maille f.; vb. coudre
stole, n. étole f.
stomach, n. estomac m.
stone, n. pierre f.
stool, n. escabeau m.
stoop, vb. se pencher
stop, n. arrêt m.; vb. arrêter,
 (prevent) empêcher (de); (cease)
 cesser
storm, n. orage m.; tempête f.
stormy, adj. orageux
story, n. histoire f.; (floor) étage m.
stouts, adj. gros m. grosse f.
stove, n. fourneau m.
straight, adj. and adv. droit
straighten, vb. redresser
strait, n. (geographical) détroit m.
strand, n. plage f.
strange, adj. étrange
stranger, n. étranger m.
strangle, vb. étrangler
strap, n. courroie f.
strategic, adj. stratégique
strategy, n. stratégie f.
straw, n. paille f.
strawberry, n. fraise f.
stray, adj. égaré
streak, n. raie f.; vb. rayer
street, n. rue f.
strength, n. force f.
strengthen, vb. fortifier
strenuous, adj. énergique
stress, n. force, tension f.; (gramm.)
 accent m.; vb. accentuer
stretch, vb. étendre
stretcher, n. brancard m.
strict, adj. strict
stride, n. enjambée f.
strife, n. lutte f.
string, n. ficelle, (music) corde f.
strip, n. bande f.; vb. dépouiller
stripe, n. bande f.; (mil.) galon m.
strive, vb. s'efforcer (de)
stroke, n. coup m.; vb. caresser

stroll, n. tour m.	**summer**, n. été m.
strong, adj. fort	**sumn**, n. soleil m.
structure, n structure f.	**sunburn**, n. hâle m.
struggle, n. lutte f.; vb. lutter	**Sunday**, n. dimanche m.
stub, n. souche f.	**sunny**, adj. ensoleillé
stubborn, adj. opiniâtre, obstiné, têtu	**sunshine**, n. soleil m.
student, n. étudiant m.	**superb**, adj. superbe
studio, n. atelier m.	**superfluous**, adj. superflu
study, n. étude f.; (room) cabine de travail m.; vb. étudier	**superintendent**, n. surveillant m.
stumble, vb. trébucher	**superior**, adj. and n. supérieur m.
stump, n. (tree) souche f.	**supersede**, vb. remplacer
stun, vb. étourdir	**superstition**, n. superstition f.
stunt, n. tour de force m.	**superstitious**, adj. superstitieux
stupid, adj. stupide	**supervise**, vb. surveiller
stupidity, n stupidité f.	**supper**, n. souper m.
sturdy, adj. vigoureux	**supplement**, n. supplément m.
stutter, vb. bégayer	**suppose**, vb. supposer
style, n. style m.	**suppress**, vb. supprimer
stylish, adj. élógant	**suppression**, n. suppression f.
subconscious, adj. subconscient	**supreme**, adj. suprême
subdue, vb. subjuguer	**sure** adj. sûr
sublimate, vb. sublimer	**surface**, n. surface f.
sublime, adj. sublime	**surge**, n. houle f.
submerge, vb. submerger	**surgeon**, n. chirurgien m.
submission, n. soumission f.	**surgery**, chirurgie f.
submit, vb. soumettre	**surpass**, vb. surpasser
subsequent, adj. subséquent	**surplus**, n. surplus m.
subsidy, n. subvention f.	**surprise**, n. surprise f.; vb. surprendre
substance, n. substance f.	**surround**, vb. entourer
substitute, n remplaçant m.; vb. substituer	**survive**, vb. survivre
subtle, adj. subtil	**suspect**, vb. soupçonner
subract, vb. soustraire	**suspend**, vb. suspendre
suburb, n. faubourg m.	**suspense**, n. incertitude f.
subversive, adj. subversif	**suspension**, n. suspension f.
subway, n. métro (politain) m.	**suspicion**, n. soupçon m.
success, n. succès m.	**sustain**, vb. soutenir
succession, n. succession	**swamp**, n. marais m.
successive, adj. successif	**swan**, n. cygne m.
successor, n. successeur m.	**swarm**, n. essaim m.
succumb, vb. succomber	**sway**, n. (rule) domination, (motion) oscillation f. ; vb. gouverner
such, adj. tel, pareil	**swear**, n. jurer
suck, vb. sucer	**sweat**, n. sueur f.; vb. suer
suction, n. succion f.	**Sweden**, n. la Suède f.
sudden, adj. soudain	**sweet**, adj. doux m., douce f.; sucré
sue, vb. poursuivre	**swell**, vb. gonfler, enfler
suffer, vb. souffrir	**swollen**, vb. enfler, s'enfler
suffice, vb. suffire	**swerve**, vb. s'écarter, se détourner
sufficient, adj. suffisant	**swift**, adj. rapide
sugar, n. sucre m.	**swiss**, vb. nager
suggest, vb. suggérer	**swine**, n. cochon m.
suggestion, n. suggestion f.	**swing**, vb. balancer
suit, n. (law) procès, (clothes) complet m.; (cards) couleur f.; vb. convenir (à)	**Switzerland**, n. la Suisse f.
suitable, adj. convenable	**sword**, n. épée f.
suitcase, n. valise f.	**syllable**, n. syllabe f.
sum, n. somme f.	**symbol**, n. symbole m.
	sympathetic, adj. compatissant
	sympathy, n. compassion f.
	symphony, n. symphonie f.

symptom, n. symptôme m.
syndicate, n. syndicat m.
syndrome, n. syndrome m.
synonym, n. synonyme m.
synthetic, adj. synthétique
syrup, n. sirop m.
system, n. système m.
systemtaic, adj. systématique

T

tabernacle, n. tabernacle m.
table, n. table f.
tablecloth, n. nappe f.
tablespoon, n. cuiller à bouche f.
tablet, n. tablette f.
tabular, adj. arrangé en tableaux
tack, n. (nail) brouqette f.; vb. clouer
tacking, n. cloutage m.
tackle, n. attirail m.
tackler, n. plaqueur m.
tacky, adj. collant, visqueux
tact, n. tact m.
tactful, adj. plein de tact
tactless, adj. sans tact
tadpole, n. têtard m.
taffeta, n. taffetas m.
tag, n. étiquette f.
tail, n. queue f.
tailor, n. tailleur m.
take, vb. prendre; (lead) conduire
tale, n. conte m.
talent, n. talent m.
talk, n. conversation f.; vb. parler
talkative, adj. bavard
tall, adj. grand
tame, adj. (animal) apprivoisé
tamper, vb. toucher à
tan, n. (leather) tan m.; (skin) hâle m.
tangible, adj. tangible
tangle, n. embrouillement m.
tank, n. réservoir, (mil.) char (d'assaut) m.
tap, n. (water) robinet m.; (knock) petit coup m.; vb. frapper légèrement
tape, n. ruban m.
tapestry, n. tapisserie f.
tar, n. goudron m.
target, n. cible f.
tariff, n. tarif m.
tarnish, vb. ternir
task, n. tâche f.
taste, n. goût m.; vb. goûter
tasty, adj. savoureux
tavern, n. taverne f.
tax, n. impôt m.; vb. imposer

taxi, n. taxi m.
taxpayer, n. contribuable m.
tea, n. thé m.
teach, vb. enseigner; (to do) apprendre à
teacher, n. instituteur, (school) professeur m.
team, n. (animals) attelage m.,; (people) équipe f.
tear, n. larme, (rip) déchirure f.; vb. déchirer
tease, vb. taquiner
teaspoon, n. cuiller à thé f.
technical, adj. technique
technique n. technique f.
tedious, adj. ennuyeux
telegram, n. télégramme m.
telephone, n. téléphone m.; vb. téléphoner
telescope, n. télescope m.
television, n. télévision f.
tell, vb. dire; (story, etc.) raconter
teller, n. (bank) caissier m.
temper, n. (humor) humeur f.; (anger) colère, (metals) trempe f.
temperament, n. tempérament m.
temperence, n. tempérance f.
temperature, n. température f.
tempest, n. tempête f.
temple, n. temple m.; (forehead) tempe f.
temporary, adj. temporaire
tempt, vb. tenter
temptation, n. tentation f.
ten, adj. and n. dix m.
tenant, n. locataire m.f.
tendency, n. tendance f.
tender, adj. tendre
tendon, n. tenon m.
tennis, n. tennis m.
tenor, n. (music) ténor m.
tense, adj. tendu
tent, n. tente f.
tentative, adj. tentatif, expérimental
tenth, adj. and n. dixième m.
term, n. terme m.; (school) trimestre m.; (conditions) conditions f., pl.
terrace, n. terrasse f.
terrible, adj. terrible
terrify, vb. terrifier
territory, n. territoire m.
terror, n. terreur f.
test, n. épreuve f.; vb. mettre à l'épreuve
testament, n. testament m.
testify, vb. témoigner (de); (declare) affirmer
testimony, n. témoignage m.

text, n. texte m.
textile, adj. textile
texture, n. texture f.
than, conj. que; de (between numbers)
thank, vb. remercier, merci
that, (those, pl.) adj. ce cet m., cette f., ces, pl.; demonstrative pron. celui-là m., celle-là f., ceux-là m., pl.; conj. que; (purpose) pour que
the, art. le m., la f., les, pl.
theater, n. théâtre m.
theft, n. vol m.
their, adj. leur, leurs pl.
theirs, pron. le leur m., la leur f., les leurs pl.
them, pron. eux m., pl. elles f.; pl.; les (direct), leur (indirect)
theme, n. thème m.
themselves, pron eux-mêmes m., elles-mêmes f.; (reflexive) se
then, adv. alors; (after that) ensuite
theology, n. théologie f.
theory, n. théorie f.
therapy, n. thérapie f.
there, adv. là, y, il, en cela
therefore, adv. donc
thermometer, n. thermomètre m.
they, pron. ils m., elles f.
thick, adj. épais
thicken, vb. épaissir
thief, n. voleur m.
thigh, n. cuisse f.
thimble, n. dé m.
thin, adj. mince
thing, n. chose f.
third, n. tiers m.; adj. troisième
thirst, n. soif f.
thirsty, adj. avoir soif
thirteen, adj. and n. treize m.
thirty, adj. and n. trente m.
this, sg. (these, pl.) adj. ce, cet m., cette f., ces pl.; demonstrative pron. celui-ci m.f., ceux-ci m., pl., celles-ci f., pl.
thorough, adj. complet, entier
though, conj. quoique
thought, n. pensée f.
thoughtful, adj. pensif
thousand, adj. and n. mille m.
thread, n. fil m.
threat, n. menace f.
threaten, vb. menacer
three, adj. and n. trois m.
thrift, n. économie f.
thrill, n. tressaillement m.; vb. tressaillir, intr.; faire frémir
thrive, vb. prospérer

throat, n. gorge f.
throne, n. trône m.
through, prep and adv. à travers, avoir fini
throughout, adv. partout
throw, vb. jeter
thumb, n. pouce m.
thunder, n. tonnerre m.; vb. tonner
Thursday, n. jeudi m.
thus, adv. ainsi
tickle, vb. chatouiller
tide, n. marée f.
tie, n. lien m.; cravate f.; vb. attacher; (bind) lier; (knot) nouer
tiger, n. tigre m.
tight, adj. serré
tighten, vb. serrer
tile, n. (roof) tuile f.
till prep. jusqu'à; conj. jusqu'à ce que
timber, n. (building) bois de construction m.
time, n. temps m.; (occasion) fois f.; (clock) heure f.; (what time is it?) quelle heure est-il?
timid, adj. timide
timidity, n. timidité f.
tin, n. étain m.
tint, n. teinte f.
tiny, adj. tout petit
tip, n. (money) pourboire m.; (end) bout m.
tire, n. (car, etc.) pneu(matique) m.; vb. fatiguer
tired, adj. fatigué
tissue, n. tissu m.
title, n. titre m.
to, prep à, de
tobacco, n. tabac m.
today, adv. aujourd'hui
toe, n. orteil m.
together, adv. ensemble
toilet, n. toilette f.
token, n témoignage, (coin) jeton m.
tolerance, n. tolérance f.
tolerant, adj. tolérant
tolerate, vb. tolérer
tomato, n. tomate f.
tomb, n. tombeau m.
tomorrow, adv. demain
ton, n. tonne f.
tone, n. ton m.
tongue, n. langue f.
tonic, adj. and n. tonique m.
tonight, adv. cette nuit; (evening) ce soir
tonsil, n. amygdale f.
too, adv. trop; (also) aussi
tool, n. outil m.
tooth, n. dent m.

toothache, n. mal de dents m.

toothbrush, n. brosse á dents f.

top, n. (mountain, etc.) sommet, (table) dessus m.

topic, n. sujet m.

torment, n. tourment m.; vb. tourmenter

torture, n. torture f.; vb. torturer

toss, vb. (throw) jeter, s'agiter

total, adj. and n. total m.

touch, n. (touching) attouchement, (sense) toucher, (contact) contact m.
pointe f.; vb. toucher

tough, adj. dur

tour, n. tour m.

tourist, n. touriste m.f.

tournament, n. tournoi m.

tow, vb. remorquer

toward, prep. (place, time) vers; (feelings, etc.) envers

towel, n. serviette f.

tower, n. tour f.

town, n. ville f.

toy, n. jouet m.

trace, n. trace f.

track, n. piste f.; (railroad) voie f.

tract, n. (space) étendue f.

tractor, n. tracteur m.

trade, n. commerce, (job) métier m.; vb. commercer

trader, n. commerçant m.

tradition, n. tradition f.

traditional, adj. traditionnel

traffic, n. circulation f.

tragedy, n. tragédie f.

tragic, adj tragique

trail, n. trace f.

train, n. train m.; (dress) traîne f.; (retinue) suite f.; vb. (sports) entraîner

traitor, n. traitre m.

tramp, n. (steps) bruit de pas; (person) chemineau m.

tranquil, adj. tranquille

tranquility, n. tranquillité f.

transaction, n. opération f.

transfer, n. transport m.; (ticket) billet de correspondance m.; vb. transférer

transform, vb. transformer

transfusion, n. transfusion f.

translate, vb. traduire

translation, n. traduction f.

transmit, vb. transmettre

transparent, adj. transparent

transport, n. transport m.; vb. transporter

trap, n. piège m.; vb. prendre au piège

trash, n. (rubbish) rebut m.

travel, n. voyage m.; vb. voyager

traveler, n. voyageur m.

tray, n. plateau m.

tread, vb. marcher

treasure, n. trésor m.

treasurer, n. trésorier m.

treasury, n. trésor m.

treat, vb. traiter

treatment, n. traitement m.

treaty, n. traité m.

tree, n. arbre m.

tremble, vb. trembler

tremendous, adj. terrible

trench, n. tranchée f.

trend, n. tendance f.

trespass, vb. empiéter

trial, n. (law) procès m.; (test) épreuve f.

triangle, n. triangle m.

tribulation, n. tribulation f.

tributary, n. (river) affluent m.; adj tributaire

trick, n. ruse f.; vb. duper

tricky, adj. astucieux

trifle, n. bagatelle f.

trigger, n. détente f.

trim, adj. soigne.; vb. (put in order) arranger; (adorn) garnir; tailer

trinket, n. breloque f.

trip, n. voyage m.; vb. trébucher

triple, adj. and n. triple m.

trite, adj rebattu

triumph, n. triomphe m.

trivial, adj. trivial

trophy, n. trophée m.

tropic, adj. tropique m.

trot, n. trot m.; vb. intr. trotter

trouble, n. (misfortune) malheur m.; (difficulty) difficulté f.; dérangement m.; vb. (worry) inquiéter, déranger

troublesome, adj. gênant

trousers, n. pantalon m.

trousseau, n. trousseau m.

trout, n. truite f.

truce, n. trève f.

truck, n. camion m.

true, adj vrai

truly, adv. vraiment

trumpet, n. trompette f.

trunk, n. (clothes) malle f.; (body, tree) tronc m.

trust, n. confiance f.; (business) trust m.; vb. se confier à; (entrust) confier

trustworthy, adj. digne de confiance

truth, n. vérité f.

truthful, adj. sincère

try, vb. essayer; (law) mettre en

jugement

tub, n. baignoire f.

tube, n. tube m.

tuberculosis, n. tuberculose f.

tuck, n. (fold) pli m.; vb. plisser, serrer

Tuesday, n. mardi m.

tug, n. (boat) remorqueur m.; vb. (pull) tirer

tuition, n. (prix de l') enseignement m.

tumble, vb (fall) tomber

tumor, n. tumeur f.

tuna, n. thon m.

tune, n. air m.; (concord harmony) accord m.; vb. accorder

tunnel, n. tunnel m.

turf, n. gazon m.

Turk, n. Turc m., Turque f.

turkey, n. dindon m.

Turkey, n. la Turquie f.

turmoil, n. tumulte m.

turn, n. tour m.; (road) détour m.; vb. tourner

turnip, n. navet m.

turret, n. tourelle f.

turtle, n. tortue f.

tutor, n. précepteur m.

twelfth, adj. and n. douzième m.

twelve, adj. and n. douze m.

twenty, adj. and n. vingt m.

twice, adv. deux fois

twig, n. brindille f.

twilight, n. crépuscule m.

twin, adj. and n. jumeau m., jumelle f.; jumeaux m., pl., jummelles f., pl.

twine, n. ficelle f.

twinkle, vb. scintiller

twist, vb. tordre

two, adj. and n. deux m.

type, n. type m.; (printing) caractère m.; vb. taper à la machine

typical, adj. typique

typist, n. dactylo(graphe) m.f.

tyranny, n. tyrannie f.

tyrant, n. tyran m.

U

udder, n. mamelle f.

ugliness, n. laideur f.

ugly, adj. laid

ulcer, n. ulcère m.

ulterior, adj. ultérieur

ultimate, adj. dernier

umbrella, n. parapluie m.

umpire, n. arbitre m.f.

unable, adj. incapable; (u.to) dans l'impossibilité de

unanimous, adj. unanime

uncertain, adj. incertain

uncle, n. oncle m.

unconscious, n. inconscient m. ; adj. (aware) inconscient; (faint) sans connaissance

uncover, vb. découvrir

under, prep. sous.; adv. au-dessous,

underestimate, vb. sous-estimer

undergo, vb. subir

underground, adj. souterrain

underline, vb. souligner

underneath, adv. en dessous

undershirt, n. gilet de dessous m.

understand, vb. comprendre

undertake, vb. entreprendre

undertaker, n. entrepreneur de pompes funèbres m.

underwear, n. vêtements de dessous m., pl.

undo, vb. défaire

undress, vb. déshabiller

uneasy, adj. gêné

uneven, adj. inégal

unexpected, adj. inattendu

unfair, adj. injuste

unfit, adj. peu propre (à)

unfold, vb. déplier

unforgettable, adj. inoubliable

unfortunate, adj. malheureux

unhappy, adj. malheureux

unicorn, n. licorne f.

unidentified, adj. peu idiomatique

uniform, adj. and n. uniforme m.

uniformity, n. uniformité f.

uniformly, adv. uniformément

unify, vb. unifier

union, n. union f.

unique, adj. unique

unisex, adj. unisexuel

unit, n. unité f.

unite, vb. unir

United Nations, n. Nations Unies f., pl.

United States, n. les États-Unis m., pl.

unity, n. unité f.

universal, adj. universel

universe, n. univers m.

university, n. université f.

unleaded, adj. sans plomb

unless, conj. à moins que...ne

unlike, adj. dissemblable

unload, vb. décharger

unlock, vb. ouvrir

untie, vb. dénouer

until, conj. jusqu'à ce que

unusual, adj. insolite
up, prep. vers le haut de, au haut
uphold, vb. soutenir
upholster, vb. tapisser
upon, prep. sur
upper, adj. supérieur
upright, adj. droit
uproar, n. vacarme m.
upset, vb. renverser
upstairs, adv. en haut
uptight, adj. tendu
upward, adj. dirigé en haut; adv. en montant
urge, vb. (beg) prier
urgency, n. urgence f.
urgent, adj. urgent
us, pron. nous
use, n. usage m.; vb. employer, se servir de
useful, adj. utile
useless, adj. inutile
usher, n. huissier m.
usual, adj. usuel
utensil, n. ustensile m.
utilize, vb. utiliser, se servir de
utmost, n. le plus, tout son possible; adj. (greatest) le plus grand
utter, adj. absolu; vb. prononcer; (cry) pousser
utterance, n. emmission f.
uvula, n. luette, uvule f.

V

vacancy, n. vide m., vacance f.
vacant, adj. vide
vacate, vb. quitter, évacuer
vacation, n. vacances f.,pl.
vaccinate, vb. vacciner
vaccine, n. vaccin m.
vacuum, n. vide m.; (vacuum cleaner) aspirateur m.
vagrant, adj. vagabond
vague, adj. vague
vain, adj. vain
valiant, adj. vaillant
valid, adj. valide
valley, n. vallée f.
valuable, adj. de valeur
value, n. valeur f.; vb. évaluer
valve, n. soupape f.
vanilla, n. vanille f.
vanish, vb. s'évanouir
vanity, n. vanité f.
vanquish, vb. vaincre
vapor, n. vapeur f.
varied, adj. varié

variety, n. variété f.
various, adj. divers
varnish, n. vernis m.; vb. vernir
vary, vb. varier
vasectomy, n. vasectomie f.
vast, adj. vaste
vault, n. voûte f.
vegetable, n. légume m.
vehicle, n. véhicule m.
veil, n. voile m.
vein, n. veine f.
velvet, n. velours m.
vengeance, n. vengeance f.
vent, n. ouverture f.
venture, n. aventure f.; vb. hasarder
verb, n. verbe m.
verdict, n. verdict m.
verify, vb. vérifier
verse, n. vers m., pl.
version, n. version f.
vertical, adj. vertical
very, adv. très
vessel, n. vaisseau m.
vest, n. gilet m.
veteran, n. vétéran m.
veto, n. véto m.
vibrate, vb. vibrer
vibration, n. vibration f.
vice, n. vice m.
vicinity, n. voisinage m.
vicious, adj. méchant
victim, n. victime f.
victor, n. vainqueur m.
victory, n. victoire f.
view, n. vue f.
vigil, n. veille f.
village, n. village m.
villain, n. scélérat m.
vine, n. vigne f.
vinegar, n. vinaigre m.
vintage, n. vendange, (year of wine) année f.
violence, n. violence f.
violent, adj. violent
violet, n. violette f.; adj. violet
violin, n. violon m.
virgin, n. vierge f.
virtual, adj. virtuel, de fait
virtue, n. vertu f.
virus, n. virus m.
visible, adj. visible
vision, n. vision f.
visit, n. visite f.; vb. visiter
visitor, n. visiteur m.
visual, adj. visuel
vital, adj. vital
vitamin, n. vitamine f.
vivid, adj. vif m.; vive f.
vocabulary, n. vocabulaire m.
vocal, adj. vocal

voice, n. voix f.

void, adj. (law) nul

volcano, n. volcan m.

volume, n. volume m.

volunteer, n. volontaire m.; vb. s'engager

vomit, vb. vomir

vote, n. vote m.; vb. voter

vow, n. voeu m.

vowel, n. voyelle f.

voyage, n. voyage m.

vulgar, adj. vulgaire

vulnerable, adj. vulnérable

W

wade, vb. traverser à gué

waffle, n. gaufre (américaine) f.

wag, vb. agiter

wage, vb. (war) faire la guerre

wages, n. salaire m.

wagon, n. chariot m.

wail, vb. gémir

waist, n. taille f.

wait (for), vb. attendre

waiter, n. garçon m.

wake, vb. éveiller, réveiller

walk, n. promenade f.; vb. marcher; (take a walk) se promener

wall, n. mur m.

wallcovering, n. tenture f.

wallet, n. portefeuille m.

wallpaper, n. papier peint m.; papier à tapisser m.

walnut, n. noix f.

walrus, n. morse m.

waltz, n. valse f.

wander, vb. errer

want, n. besoin m.; vb. vouloir

war, n. guerre f.

ward, n. (hospital) salle f.; (charge) pupille m.f.

ware, n. marchandises f., pl.

warlike, adj. guerrier

warm, adj. chaud, avoir chaud; vb. chauffer

warmth, n. chaleur f.

warn, vb. avertir

warning, n. avertissement m.

warp, vb. détourner

warrant, n. mandat m.; vb. garantir

warrior, n. guerrier m.

wash, vb. laver

washing machine, n. machine à laver f.

washroom, n. salle de bain f.

wasp, n. guêpe f.

waste, n. perte f. gaspillage m., prodigalité f.

watchful, adj. vigilant

watchmaker, n. horloger m.

watchman, n. gardien m.

water, n. eau f.

waterbed, n. aqualit m.

water color, n. aquarelle f.

waterfall, n. chute d'eau f.

waterproof, adj. imperméable

wave, n. vague f.; (sound) onde f.; permanente; vb. agiter; (hair) onduler

waver, vb. vaciller

wavy, adj. ondoyant, onduleux

wax, n. cire f.

way, n. (road) chemin m.; (distance) distance, manière f.; côté m.

we, pron. nous

weak, adj. faible

weaken, vb. affaiblir

weakness, n. faiblesse f.

wealth, n. richesse f.

wealthy, adj. riche

weapon, n. arme f.

wear, vb. porter

weary, adj. las fatigué

weasel, n. belette f.

weather, n. temps m.

weave, vb. tisser

weaver, n. tisserand m.

web, n. (fabric) tissu m.; (spider) toile f.

wedding, n. noces f., pl.; adj. de noces, de mariage

wedge, n. coin m.

Wednesday, n. mercredi m.

weed, n. mauvaise herbe f.

week, n. semaine f.

weekday, n. jour de semaine m.

week-end, n. week-end m., fin de semaine f.

weekly, adj. hebdomadaire

weep, vb. pleurer

weigh, vb. peser

weight, n. poids m.

weird, adj. mystérieux

welcome, adj. bienvenu

welfare, n. bien-être m.

well, n. (water) puits m.; adv. bien

well-known, adj. bien connu

west, n. ouest m.

western, adj. de l'ouest

wet, adj. mouillé; (weather) pluvieux; vb. mouiller

whale, n. baleine f.

what, adj. quel m.; pron. ce qui (subject), ce que (object), qu'est-ce qui, quoi, qu'est-ce que

whatever, adj. quel que soit...qui,

quelque...que ce soit; adv. quoi que
ce soit; pron. tout ce qui, tout ce
que, quoi que ce soit

wheat, n. blé m.

wheel, n. roue f.

when, conj quand

whenever, conj. toutes les
fois que

where, con. où

wherever, conj. partout où

whether, conj. soit que; (if) si

which, adj. quel; pron. (relative)
qui; lequel; (interrogative) lequel

whichever, pron. n'importe lequel

while, conj. pendant que; (whereas)
tandis que

whim, n. caprice m.; lubie f.

whip, n. fouet m.; vb. fouetter,
battre

whirl, vb. faire tourner, tourner

whirlpool, n. tourbillon d'eau m.

whirlwind, n. tourbillon de vent m.

whisker, n. (man) favori m.;
(animals) moustache f.

whiskey, n. whisky m.

whisper, vb. chuchoter

whistle, n. sifflet m.; vb. siffler

white, adj. blanc m., blanche f.

who, pron. qui, qu'est-ce qui

whoever, pron. qui que cr soit,
quiconque

whole, adj. entier

wholesale, adj. and adv. en gros

wholesome, adj. sain

wholly, adv. entièrement

whom, pron. que; lequel; qui est-ce
que

whose, pron. dont; de qui; duquel
m., de laquelle f., desquels m., pl.

why, adv. pourquoi

wicked, adj. méchant f.

wickedness, n. méchanceté f.

wide, adj. large

widen, vb. élargir

widespread, adj. répandu

widow, n. veuve f.

widower, n. veuf m.

width, n. largeur f.

wield, vb. manier

wife, n. femme f.

wig, n. perruque f.

wild, adj. sauvage

wilderness, n. désert m.

wildlife, n. faune f.

will, n. volonté f.; testament m.; vb.
vouloir; (bequeath) léguer

willful, adj. obstiné

willing, adj. bien disposé

wilt, vb. flétrir

win, vb. gagner

wind, n. vent m.

window, n. fenêtre, (shop)
débanture f.

windy, adj. venteux

wine, n. vin m.

wing, n. aile f.

wink, n. clin d'oeil m.; vb. clignoter

winner, n. gagnant m.

winter, n. hiver m.

wipe vb. essuyer

wire, n. fil de fer m.

wireless, adj. sans fil

wisdom, n. sagesse f.

wise, adj. sage

wish, n. désir m.; vb. désirer

wit, n. esprit m.

witch, n. sorcière f.

with, prep. avec

withdraw, vb. retirer

wither, vb. flétrir

withhold, vb. refuser

within, adv. dedans

without, prep. sans

witness, n. témoin m.

witty, adj. spirituel

wizard, n. sorcier m.

woe, n. malheur m.

wolf, n. loup m.

woman, n. femme f.

womb, n. matrice f.

wonder, vb. se demander; (be
surprised) être étonné

wonderful, adj. merveilleux

woo, vb. faire la cour à

wood, n. bois m.

wooden, adj. de bois

wool, n. laine f.

woolen, adj. de laine

word, n. mot m.

work, n. travail m.; vb. travailler

worker, n. travailleur m.

workman, n. ouvrier m.

world, n. monde m.

wordly, adj. mondial

worm, n. ver m.

worn, adj. usé

worry, n. souci m.; vb. tracasser,
préoccuper

worse, adj. pire; adv. pis

worship, n. culte m.; vb. adorer

worst, adj. le pire; adv. le pis

worth, n. valeur f.; vb. valoir; adj.
valant, qui mérite

worthless, adj. indigne; (without value) sans valeur

worthy, adj. digne

would, vb. vouloir

wound, n. blessure f.; vb. blesser

wrap, vb. envelopper

wrapping, n. couverture f.

wrath, n. courroux m.
wreath, n. couronne f.
wreck, n. (ship) naufrage m.;
  (remains) débris m., pl.
wrench, vb. tordre
wrestle, vb. lutter
wretched, adj. misérable
wring, vb. tordre
wringer, n. essoreuse (à linge) f.
wrinkle, n. ride f.; vb. rider, plisser
wrist, n. poignet m.
wrist watch, n. montre-bracelet f.
write, vb. écrire
write-off, n. annulation, non-valeur
  f.
writer, n. écrivain m.
writhe, vb. se tordre
written, adj. écrit, par écrit
wrong, adj. faux m., fausse f.;
wrongdoer, n. injuste, méchant m.

X

x-rays, n. rayons X m., pl.
xylophone, n. xylophone m.

Y

yacht, n. yacht m.
yam, n. igname f.
yard, n. (house) cour f.; (lumber)
  chantier, (measure) yard m.
yarn, n. fil m.
yawn, n. bâille(ment) m.; vb. bâiler
year, n. and m.; (duration) année f.
yearly, adj. annuel
yearn (for), vb. soupirer (après)
yell, vb. hurler
yellow, adj. and n. jaune m.
yes, adv. oui
yesterday, adv. hier
yet, adv. encore; conj. néanmoins
yield, vb. (resign) céder; produire
yoke, n. joug m.
yolk, n. jaune m.
you, pron. vous
young, adj. jeune
your, adj. votre, vos pl.;
  ton m., ta f., tes pl.
yours, pron. le vôtre; le tien m.,
  la tienne f.
yourself, pron. vous-même; toi-
  même;(reflexive) vous, te
youth, n. jeunesse f.
youthful, adj. (young) jeune;
  (of youth) de jeunesse

Z

zap, vb. frapper d'une façon
  soudaine et inattendue
zeal, n. zèle m.
zealous, adj. zélé
zebra, n. zèbre m.
zero, n. zéro m.
zest, n. entrain m.; (taste)
  saveur f.
zip code, n. code postal m.
zone, n. zone f.
zoo, n. jardin zoologique